Marina Spiazzi
Marina Tavella Margaret Layton

Performer B2

Seconda edizione di Performer First Tutor

Student's Book

PER IL COMPUTER E PER IL TABLET

L'eBook multimediale

1 REGÌSTRATI

Vai su **my.zanichelli.it** e regìstrati come studente

2 ATTIVA IL TUO LIBRO

Una volta entrato in **myZanichelli**, inserisci la **chiave di attivazione** che trovi sul bollino argentato in questa pagina

3 CLICCA SULLA COPERTINA

Puoi:
- **scaricare l'eBook offline** sul tuo computer o sul tuo tablet
- **sfogliare un'anteprima** dell'eBook online

LINGUE ZANICHELLI

Realizzazione editoriale:
- Coordinamento redazionale: Federica Gusmeroli (Studio Zebra, Bergamo)
- Redazione: Manuela Zaini
- Progetto grafico e impaginazione: Dario Zannier (Studio Indaco, Milano)
- Ricerca iconografica: Marta Fortini

Contributi:
- Rilettura linguistica: Simon Tanner (Verba Volant, Torino)
- *Grammar reference*: Michela Evelina Porro
- *Writing reference*: Consortium Linguae (Ilaria Beretta, Alessandra Casati, Silvia Sar)

Realizzazione eBook:
- Coordinamento redazionale: Federica Gusmeroli (Studio Zebra, Bergamo)
- Sviluppo software Booktab: duDAT srl, Bologna
- Interattivizzazione degli esercizi: Preparé Italia, Battipaglia
- Realizzazione e revisione dell'eBook: Studio Zebra, Bergamo

***Guarda!*:**
- Progettazione esecutiva e sviluppo software: Yoomee Technologies, Bologna / Ravenna

Copertina:
- Progetto grafico: Miguel Sal & C., Bologna
- Ideazione: Studio 8vo, Bologna
- Realizzazione: Francesca Ponti e Roberto Marchetti
- Immagine di copertina: 1000 Words/Shutterstock. SFIO CRACHO/Shutterstock. Artwork Studio 8vo, Bologna

Prima edizione: 2014
Seconda edizione: marzo 2018

Ristampa:

5 4 3 2 2018 2019 2020 2021 2022

Zanichelli garantisce che le risorse digitali di questo volume sotto il suo controllo saranno accessibili, a partire dall'acquisto dell'esemplare nuovo, per tutta la durata della normale utilizzazione didattica dell'opera. Passato questo periodo, alcune o tutte le risorse potrebbero non essere più accessibili o disponibili: per maggiori informazioni, leggi my.zanichelli.it/fuoricatalogo

---

File per sintesi vocale
L'editore mette a disposizione degli studenti non vedenti, ipovedenti, disabili motori o con disturbi specifici di apprendimento i file pdf in cui sono memorizzate le pagine di questo libro. Il formato del file permette l'ingrandimento dei caratteri del testo e la lettura mediante software screen reader. Le informazioni su come ottenere i file sono sul sito http://www.zanichelli.it/scuola/bisogni-educativi-speciali

---

Grazie a chi ci segnala gli errori
Segnalate gli errori e le proposte di correzione su **www.zanichelli.it/correzioni**.
Controlleremo e inseriremo le eventuali correzioni nelle ristampe del libro.
Nello stesso sito troverete anche l'errata corrige, con l'elenco degli errori e delle correzioni.

Zanichelli editore S.p.A. opera con sistema qualità
certificato CertiCarGraf n. 477
secondo la norma UNI EN ISO 9001:2015

Questo libro è stampato su carta che rispetta le foreste.
www.zanichelli.it/chi-siamo/sostenibilita

Fotocomposizione: Fratelli Sala

Stampa: Rotopress International s.r.l.
Via E. Mattei 106, 40138 Bologna
per conto di Zanichelli editore S.p.A.
Via Irnerio 34, 40126 Bologna

Menu delle competenze

Asse dei linguaggi	Indicazioni nazionali	Nel libro
Padroneggiare la lingua straniera per interagire in diversi ambiti e contesti e per comprendere gli aspetti significativi del mondo in cui viviamo in prospettiva interculturale.	Leggere e comprendere le idee fondamentali di testi complessi tratti da riviste, quotidiani, internet, riguardanti argomenti di diversa natura.	**ATTIVITÀ DI COMPRENSIONE SCRITTA:** nelle sezioni **Towards INVALSI**, per esempio *Friends can shape your life* p. 18; nelle sezioni **Reading**, per esempio Reading and Use of English Part 5, p. 22; nelle sezioni **Use of English**, per esempio Reading and Use of English Part 1 e Part 2, p. 21.
	• Comprendere espressioni e frasi relative a particolari aree semantiche. • Comprendere le idee fondamentali di testi orali complessi su argomenti sia concreti che astratti.	**ATTIVITÀ DI COMPRENSIONE ORALE:** • nelle sezioni **Vocabulary Activator**, per esempio es. 2 e 3 p. 29; • nelle sezioni **Towards INVALSI**, per esempio es. 4 p. 31; nelle sezioni **Listening**, per esempio Listening Part 3, p. 52.
	• Esprimere un'opinione su argomenti di attualità, esponendo i pro e i contro delle diverse opinioni nell'ambito di una discussione di gruppo. • Produrre testi orali riguardanti temi di interesse personale, quotidiano, sociale o professionale.	**ATTIVITÀ DI INTERAZIONE ORALE:** • nelle attività di **Warm-Up**, per esempio es. 2 p. 43, es. 1 p. 44, es. 1 e 2 p. 103; nelle attività di **Discuss**, per esempio es. 7 p. 113; • nelle sezioni **Speaking**, per esempio Speaking Part 2, p. 63.
	Produrre testi scritti riguardanti un'ampia gamma di argomenti e saper riferire a se stessi idee presentate in un testo.	**ATTIVITÀ DI PRODUZIONE SCRITTA:** nelle sezioni **Writing**, per esempio Writing Part 2, p. 66; nelle attività di **Writing**, per esempio es. 8 p. 113.
	• Osservare espressioni comunicative e verbi fraseologici in contesti d'uso. • Utilizzare in modo adeguato le strutture grammaticali e rilevare le eventuali variazioni di significato e le differenze con la L1.	**RIFLESSIONE SULLA LINGUA:** • nelle sezioni **Focus on Vocabulary**, per esempio es. 3 e 4 p. 95; nelle sezioni **Collocations**, per esempio es. 5 e 6 p. 97; nelle sezioni **Word Formation**, per esempio es. 5 e 6 p. 113; • nelle sezioni **Grammar 1**, **Grammar 2** e nella **Grammar Reference**; nelle sezioni **Use of English**, per esempio Reading and Use of English Part 1 e Part 4, p. 111.
	Utilizzare le risorse digitali per: • utilizzare il metodo della "flipped classroom"; • esercitarsi a comprendere i prodotti della comunicazione audiovisiva (brani di ascolto e filmati).	• nelle sezioni **Vocabulary Activator**, video di lessico all'inizio di ogni unità, per esempio p. 107; • nelle sezioni **21st-century skills**, video e attività di comprensione di un breve filmato, per esempio es. 2-4 p. 117, nelle sezioni **Towards INVALSI** e **Reading**, ascolto di testi.

Le competenze del 21° secolo	Nel libro
LEARNING AND INNOVATION SKILLS (Competenze di apprendimento e innovazione)	- **21st-century skills**: ***Problem solving***, p. 39 - **Learn by doing**: ***Decision making***, p. 27 - **Dossier 2**: ***Communication and collaboration***, p. 155
INFORMATION, MEDIA AND TECHNOLOGY SKILLS (Competenze informatiche, dei media e tecnologiche)	- **21st-century skills**: ***Analysing media***, p. 105 - **Learn by doing**: ***Thinking creatively***, p. 91 - **Dossier 1**: ***Access information***, p. 151
LIFE AND CAREER SKILLS (Competenze sociali e professionali)	- **21st-century skills**: ***Being flexible***, p. 53 - **Learn by doing**: ***Guiding and leading others***, p. 143 - **Dossier 4**: ***Initiative and self-direction***, p. 163

Contents

Unit	Vocabulary	Towards INVALSI	Grammar	Use of English
7 A techno world	VIDEO *Technology* p. 95 Collocations and expressions for technology p. 97 Word formation: prefixes p. 101	Reading: *How to regulate artificial intelligence* p. 96 Listening: Different views on technology p. 97	Passives p. 98 **FM** *Be supposed to / be expected to...* p. 98 *Have/Get something done* p. 102 Expressing emphasis with *so* and *such* p. 102	*The Circle* (FIRST Part 2) p. 99 *Drones* (FIRST Part 3) p. 99
8 A sporting life	VIDEO *Sport* p. 107 Collocations and expressions for sport p. 109 Word formation: word families (1) p. 113	Reading: *A sporting brain* p. 108 Listening: Danger in sports p. 109	Gerunds and infinitives p. 110 **FM** Verbs + both *-ing* and infinitive p. 110 Relative clauses p. 114	*Zorbing: a new sport* (FIRST Part 1) p. 111 Key word transformations (FIRST Part 4) p. 111
Review Units 7-8 p. 119				
9 Saving our planet	VIDEO *The environment* p. 121 Phrasal verbs and expressions for the environment p. 123 Word formation: word families (2) p. 127	Reading: *91% of plastic isn't recycled* p. 122 Listening: Microplastic contamination p. 123	Reported speech p. 124 **FM** *Say* and *tell* p. 124 Reporting verbs p. 128 Reported questions p. 128	*He said we must save the bees!* (FIRST Part 2) p. 125 Key word transformations (FIRST Part 4) p. 125
10 Money and business	VIDEO *Money and business* p. 133 Phrasal verbs and collocations for business p. 135 Word formation: suffixes to form verbs p. 139	Reading: *Startups* p. 134 Listening: Successful teenage millionaires p. 135	Causative verbs p. 136 **FM** Uses of *get* p. 136 Linkers of reason and result p. 140	*Shop till you drop* (FIRST Part 1) p. 137 *Smart money* (FIRST Part 3) p. 137
Review Units 9-10 p. 145				

Dossier 1 **Global awareness**	Global ambassadors p. 148	Zero hunger challenge p. 149
Dossier 2 **Civic literacy**	Youth's rights and responsibilities p. 152	Young people, social media and civic literacy p. 153
Dossier 3 **Health literacy**	How to plan a healthy diet p. 156	Emotional eating p. 157
Dossier 4 **Environmental literacy**	The increase of greenhouse gases p. 160	Breathe less... or ban cars p. 161
Dossier 5 **Economic literacy**	Why study economics? p. 164	A beginner's guide to economics p. 165

Com'è fatto il libro

GUARDA! NEW!

L'icona da inquadrare con lo smartphone per vedere i **video** e ascoltare gli **audio** di tutta la Unit.

NEW!

BUILD UP TO B2

Sezione introduttiva di ripasso dei principali **tempi verbali** anche attraverso **mappe**.

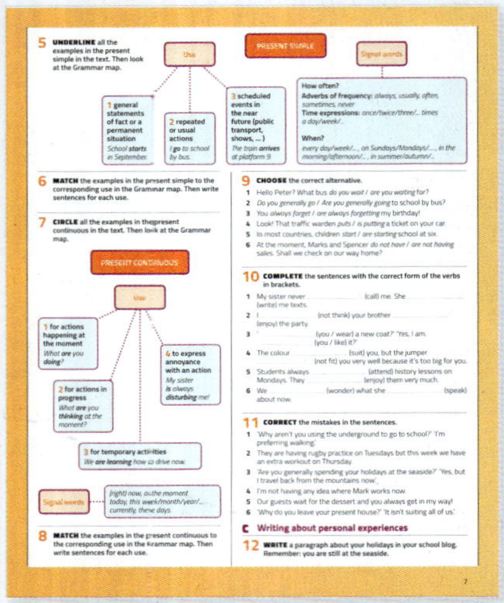

NEW!

VOCABULARY ACTIVATOR

Introduce il **lessico** della Unit.

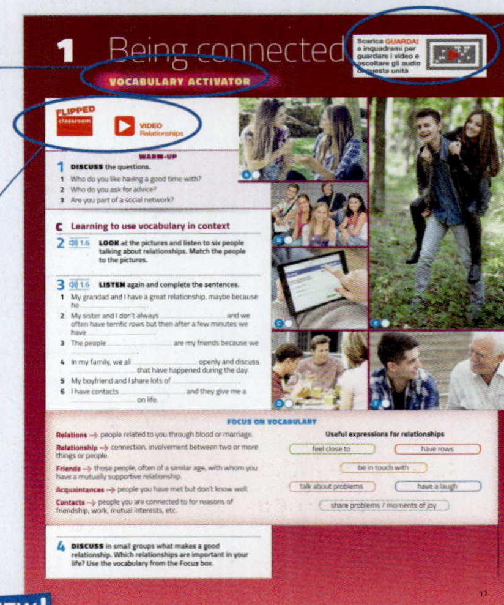

NEW!

FLIPPED CLASSROOM + VIDEO

Video per introdurre il lessico, che possono essere usati con la **flipped classroom**.

TOWARDS INVALSI NEW!

Il primo *Reading* della Unit è dedicato alla preparazione dell'**INVALSI,** in abbinamento a un'attività di *Listening*. Sono presenti anche approfondimenti lessicali su **phrasal verbs**, **collocations** e **expressions**.

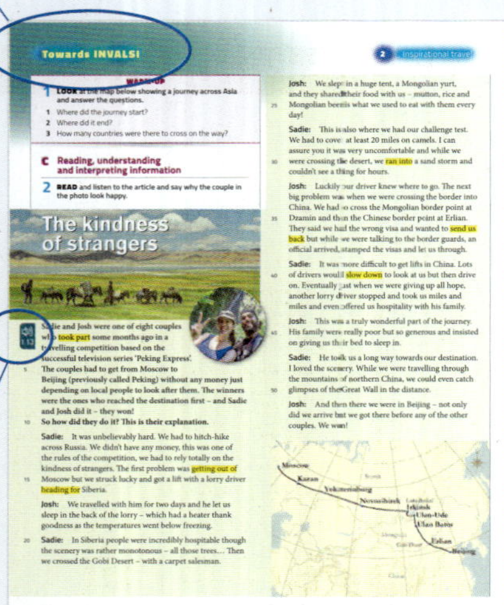

AUDIO NEW!

Tutti i brani di *Reading*.

1.13

READING

Il secondo *Reading* della Unit prepara alla **certificazione FIRST**. Sono presenti anche approfondimenti lessicali su **word formation.**

LISTENING

Attività per la preparazione della **certificazione FIRST**.

NEW!

21ST-CENTURY SKILLS

Competenze trasversali per vivere e lavorare nel mondo di oggi, per esempio *Decision making*.

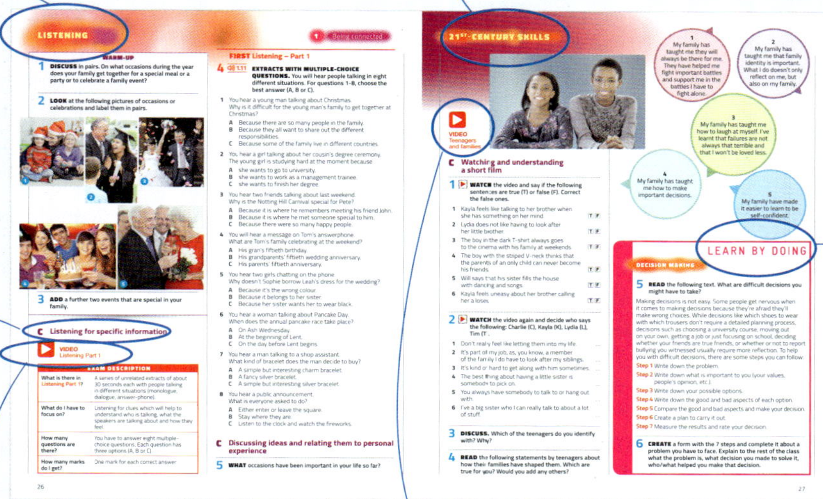

NEW!

LEARN BY DOING

Compito di realtà per la valutazione delle competenze. La griglia per la valutazione è nella **Teacher's Guide**.

C NEW!

Icona che indica le **competenze disciplinari**, per esempio *Listening for specific information.*

VIDEO

Spiegazione delle singole parti della **certificazione FIRST**, per esempio *Listening Part 1.*

VIDEO NEW!

Testimonianze e **interviste** su temi di attualità, per esempio *Teenagers and families.*

NEW!

DOSSIER

I **5 Dossier** sono dedicati alle 21st-century skills, per esempio *Health literacy.*

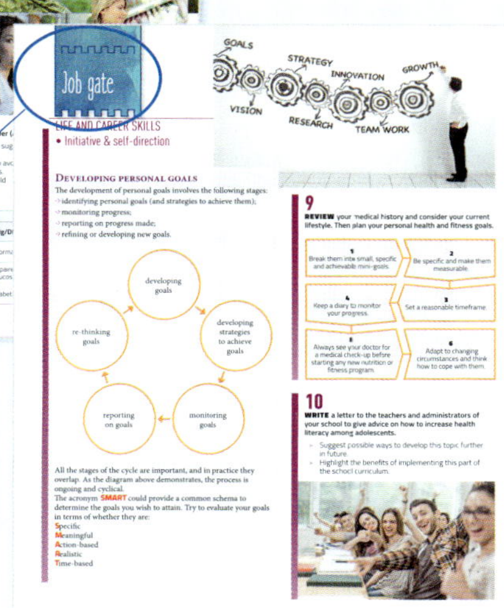

JOB GATE NEW!

È una "finestra sul lavoro" che sviluppa competenze da sfruttare in ambito lavorativo, per esempio *Developing personal goals*. Da usare anche per l'Alternanza Scuola-Lavoro.

NEW!

PHRASAL VERBS E LINKERS

Sezione di approfondimento sui principali **phrasal verbs** e **linkers** con **mappe.**

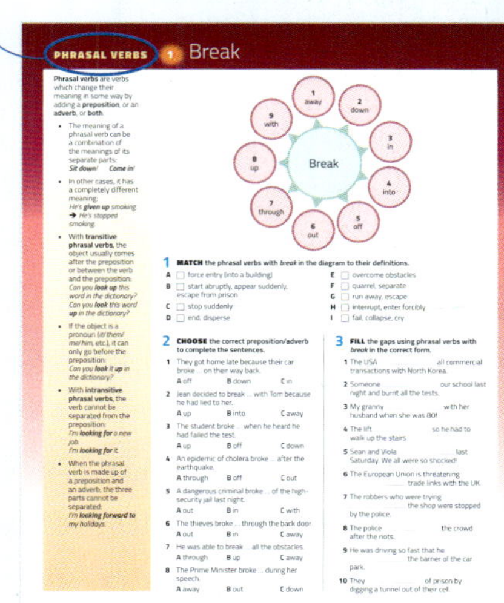

A general introduction to FIRST

The Cambridge English: First (FCE) is an internationally recognised qualification at the B2 level of the Common European Framework of Reference for Languages. It is divided into 4 papers testing different areas of language competence. These are:

Paper 1 Reading and Use of English

Paper 2 Writing

Paper 3 Listening

Paper 4 Speaking

PAPER 1: READING AND USE OF ENGLISH

You have 1 hour and 15 minutes to complete this part of the exam.
The Reading and Use of English paper contains seven parts.
For Parts 1 to 3, the test contains texts with accompanying grammar and vocabulary tasks.
Part 4 consists of separate items with a grammar and vocabulary focus.
For Parts 5 to 7, the test contains a range of texts and reading comprehension tasks. The texts may be a solid piece of writing or two or more shorter related pieces. The task types are multiple choice, open cloze, word formation and key word transformations for the Use of English parts and multiple choice, gapped text and multiple matching for the Reading parts. Answers are written on a separate answer sheet.

- **Part 1: multiple-choice cloze.** In this part there are 8 questions. You are given a text from which eight words have been removed. For each numbered gap, there are four possibilities (A, B, C or D) given in a multiple-choice option and you must choose which option fits each gap.
  This task tests vocabulary and grammar usage. Each correct answer receives 1 mark.
- **Part 2: open cloze.** In this part there are 8 questions. As in Part 1, there is a text with eight numbered gaps, but this time there are no options given and you must decide which word is missing in each gap. This task tests vocabulary and grammar usage. Each correct answer receives 1 mark.
- **Part 3: word formation.** In this part there are 8 questions. You are given a text with eight gaps, each of which has a root word given in bold. This root word must be modified to fit the gap. This may require the use of a prefix or suffix, or other internal changes. This task tests vocabulary and grammar usage. Each correct answer receives 1 mark.
- **Part 4: key word transformations.** In this part there are 6 questions. You are given a lead-in sentence, a key word in bold and a gapped second sentence. You must complete the second sentence so that it has the same meaning as the first sentence. From two to five words can be used. You must use the key word, and it cannot be modified. This task tests vocabulary and grammar usage. Each correct answer receives up to 2 marks.
- **Part 5: multiple choice.** In this part there are 6 questions based on a text or related texts. Each question has a possible four answers (A, B, C or D), and you must choose the one you consider most suitable. This task tests comprehension of detail, opinion, attitude and purpose, as well as the main idea or meaning from the context. It may also focus on text organisation, like examples or comparisons. Each correct answer receives 2 marks.
- **Part 6: gapped text.** In this part there are 6 questions. Six sentences have been removed from a text, leaving numbered gaps. The sentences are placed after the text in a jumbled order with an extra sentence that is not from the text. You must choose which sentence matches which gap in the text. This task tests your ability to recognise text structure and look for links and cohesion. Each correct answer receives 2 marks.
- **Part 7: multiple matching.** In this part there are 10 questions, followed by a text or several short texts. You must relate each question to elements in the text or texts.
  This task tests comprehension of specific information, detail, opinion and attitude. Each correct answer receives 1 mark.

PAPER 2: WRITING

You have 1 hour and 20 minutes to complete this part of the exam.
The Writing paper contains two parts. The first part is an obligatory question and the second part gives you a choice between various types of writing tasks. Each part of the Writing paper has a specific purpose and specific target audience. Both parts carry equal marks.

- **Part 1: an essay.** In this part there is one compulsory task. You are given an essay title and 2 or 3 prompts in the form of notes, and you are required to respond to a specific task. The language skills tested are describing, explaining and expressing opinions. You must write 140-190 words.
- **Part 2: a choice from options that may include an email, an essay, an article, a letter, a report, a review or a short story.** In this part, one task must be selected from four. You can choose from three questions (questions 2-4) taken from the list given above, and question 5, which is based on a set text.
  In all options, the task may ask you to advise, compare, describe, explain, express or justify opinions, or make recommendations. You must write 140-190 words.

PAPER 3: LISTENING

You have around 40 minutes to complete this part of the exam. The Listening paper contains four parts, each of which contains a recorded text or texts with corresponding comprehension tasks.
Each part is heard twice. The task types are multiple choice, sentence completion, multiple matching and a second multiple choice.

- **Part 1: multiple choice.** In this part there are 8 questions. You will hear eight brief, unrelated texts of about 30 seconds each. They can be monologues or interacting speakers. For each text, there is one multiple-choice question with three options (A, B or C).
  The questions may test general understanding, purpose or attitude and opinion, or ask about place, situation or genre. Each correct answer receives 1 mark.
- **Part 2: sentence completion.** In this part there are 10 questions. You will hear a monologue which lasts about 3 minutes. You are required to complete ten gapped sentences with information from the recording. This task tests comprehension of detail, specific information, like numbers and prices, or stated opinions. Each correct answer receives 1 mark.
- **Part 3: multiple matching.** In this part there are 5 questions. You will hear five short related monologues of about 30 seconds each. You must match the correct option from a list of eight to the appropriate text. This task tests general understanding but also understanding of detail, purpose, attitude, relationship, topic, situation, genre and opinion. Each correct answer receives 1 mark.
- **Part 4: multiple choice.** In this part there are 7 questions. You will hear a text which lasts for about 3 minutes. It may be an interview or interacting speakers. There are seven multiple-choice questions, each of which has three options (A, B or C). You must choose the most suitable answers for the questions after listening to the recording. This task tests understanding of opinion, attitude and gist, as well as specific information.
  Each correct answer receives 1 mark.

PAPER 4: SPEAKING

This part of the exam lasts about 14 minutes. The Speaking paper contains four parts. The task types are an interview, an individual long turn, a collaborative task and a discussion. In the exam, there are two candidates and two examiners.
One examiner acts as interlocutor and also as assessor. This examiner manages the interaction by asking questions or by providing cues for the candidates. The other examiner acts only as assessor and does not join in the conversation. The second examiner normally sits in the background.
There are four different areas that are assessed in the speaking exam. These areas are:

1 grammar and vocabulary;

2 discourse management;

3 pronunciation;

4 interactive communication.

Each area is given a mark out of a possible 5, where 3 is adequate, below 3 is not adequate and 4 or 5 are considered an effective and competent level.

- **Part 1: interview.** This part lasts 2 minutes. It is a conversation between the interlocutor and each of the candidates based on general and social interactional language. It is designed to allow candidates to relax and give basic personal information about themselves. The questions relate to your everyday life, your interests, areas of study and future plans. You should respond to direct questions and listen to the other candidate's replies. Although you are not invited directly to do so, you may also talk to the other candidate if you so wish. The mark scheme ranges from 1 (weak) to 5 (excellent).
- **Part 2: long turn.** This part includes an individual 'long turn' for each candidate, which lasts about 1 minute, followed by a 30 second response from the other candidate. Each candidate is given two photographs and in turn is asked to describe and compare the pictures as well as express personal opinions. A prompt is also given in the form of a direct question written above the photographs. The mark scheme ranges from 1 (weak) to 5 (excellent).
- **Part 3: collaborative task.** This part lasts 4 minutes. It is a two-way conversation between the candidates. You are given spoken instructions and written stimuli to be used in a decision-making task. This part gives you an opportunity to show your ability to exchange ideas, express and justify an opinion, agree or disagree, make suggestions, evaluate and reach a decision through oral negotiation. The mark scheme ranges from 1 (weak) to 5 (excellent).
- **Part 4: discussion.** This part lasts 4 minutes. It is a discussion linked to the topics from Part 3. The interlocutor directs the interaction through questions which encourage you to discuss the topics raised in Part 3 in a broader context. This part allows you to show your ability to discuss issues at a deeper level. The mark scheme ranges from 1 (weak) to 5 (excellent).

Build up to B2

Scarica **GUARDA!** e inquadrami per ascoltare gli audio di questa unità

1. BACK TO SCHOOL

WARM-UP

1 **DISCUSS.** How do you feel at the end of the holidays? Do you want the holidays to continue or are you looking forward to going back to school and seeing your school friends?

2 **WORK** in pairs and make a list of four positive things about returning to school in September.

C Reading and understanding a text

3 **READ** and listen to the blogs. Then say if these students are happy to go back to school.

1.1

Posted 1st Sept 10.40
by Tracy

Holidays are great and it isn't cool to say you like school, but I have to say that when September comes round again and the new school year is approaching, I begin to feel excited. Excited about seeing all my mates and getting back into the rhythm and yes I'm looking forward to learning new stuff.

Posted 1st Sept 11.10
by Sharon

Hey Tracy, good for you, it's not easy to be honest about certain things and actually I agree, I too am getting excited about seeing everyone again and hearing about the summer. So much is going on in everyone's lives and it's great to get together and chat about our lives each day. But there's good and bad. Unfortunately we also have to go to lessons and do homework!

Posted 1st Sept 12.00
by Simon

My family and I are travelling back home after a wonderful holiday by the sea. Everything was really idyllic, blue sea, sunshine, fun times… but guess what, I'm already thinking about meeting up with my schoolmates and telling them about the highs and lows of the summer. During the holidays, I don't miss getting up early and all that studying, but I miss seeing everyone and the daily routine – don't ask me why, but school is part of our lives. We sometimes hate it, but when it's not there, we miss it!

4 **READ** the blogs again and do the following activities.

A **ANSWER** the following questions.

1. Who says everyone has busy exciting lives?
2. Who is travelling home after a holiday?
3. Who thinks it is unpopular to admit that you like school?
4. Who has mixed feelings about school?
5. Who is looking forward to the new school year?

B **FIND** the words in the text which mean the following:

1. fantastic (para. 1);
2. friends (para. 1);
3. unspecified things (para. 1);
4. think the same (para. 2);
5. feeling enthusiastic (para. 2);
6. perfect (para. 3);
7. feel the lack of (para 3).

C **LOOK** for these phrases in the text and discuss their meaning.

- not cool
- come round again
- look forward to
- going on
- get together
- highs and lows

5 **UNDERLINE** all the examples in the present simple in the text. Then look at the Grammar map.

PRESENT SIMPLE

Use

- **1** general statements of fact or a permanent situation
  *School **starts** in September.*
- **2** repeated or usual actions
  *I **go** to school by bus.*
- **3** scheduled events in the near future (public transport, shows, ...)
  *The train **arrives** at platform 9.*

Signal words

How often?
Adverbs of frequency: *always, usually, often, sometimes, never*
Time expressions: *once/twice/three/... times a day/week/...*

When?
every day/week/... , on Sundays/Mondays/... , in the morning/afternoon/... , in summer/autumn/...

6 **MATCH** the examples in the present simple to the corresponding use in the Grammar map. Then write sentences for each use.

7 **CIRCLE** all the examples in the present continuous in the text. Then look at the Grammar map.

PRESENT CONTINUOUS

Use

- **1** for actions happening at the moment
  *What **are** you **doing**?*
- **2** for actions in progress
  *What **are** you **thinking** at the moment?*
- **3** for temporary activities
  *We **are learning** how to drive now.*
- **4** to express annoyance with an action
  *My sister **is** always **disturbing** me!*

Signal words
(right) now, at the moment
today, this week/month/year/...
currently, these days

8 **MATCH** the examples in the present continuous to the corresponding use in the Grammar map. Then write sentences for each use.

9 **CHOOSE** the correct alternative.

1 Hello Peter? What bus *do you wait* / *are you waiting* for?
2 *Do you generally go* / *Are you generally going* to school by bus?
3 You *always forget* / *are always forgetting* my birthday!
4 Look! That traffic warden *puts* / *is putting* a ticket on your car.
5 In most countries, children *start* / *are starting* school at six.
6 At the moment, Marks and Spencer *do not have* / *are not having* sales. Shall we check on our way home?

10 **COMPLETE** the sentences with the correct form of the verbs in brackets.

1 My sister never …… (call) me. She …… (write) me texts.
2 I …… (not think) your brother …… (enjoy) the party.
3 '…… (you / wear) a new coat?' 'Yes, I am. …… (you / like) it?'
4 The colour …… (suit) you, but the jumper …… (not fit) you very well because it's too big for you.
5 Students always …… (attend) history lessons on Mondays. They …… (enjoy) them very much.
6 We …… (wonder) what she …… (speak) about now.

11 **CORRECT** the mistakes in the sentences.

1 'Why aren't you using the underground to go to school?' 'I'm preferring walking.'
2 They are having rugby practice on Tuesdays but this week we have an extra workout on Thursday.
3 'Are you generally spending your holidays at the seaside?' 'Yes, but I travel back from the mountains now.'
4 I'm not having any idea where Mark works now.
5 Our guests wait for the dessert and you always get in my way!
6 'Why do you leave your present house?' 'It isn't suiting all of us.'

C Writing about personal experiences

12 **WRITE** a paragraph about your holidays in your school blog. Remember: you are still at the seaside.

2. TEEN HOLIDAY TIMES

WARM-UP

1 DISCUSS. How well do you know Europe? Match the places in box A to the countries in box B.

A	B
Minorca ▪ Dublin ▪ Warsaw ▪ Berlin ▪ Inverness ▪ Nice ▪ Athens ▪ Barcelona ▪ Oslo ▪ Cork ▪ Munich ▪ Ibiza ▪ Fiords ▪ Edinburgh ▪ Krakow ▪ Bruges ▪ Mykonos ▪ Brussels ▪ Paris	Scotland ▪ Ireland ▪ Germany ▪ Spain ▪ Belgium ▪ Greece ▪ Poland ▪ Norway ▪ France

2 WORK in pairs and say which of these places you have visited. When did you go? How long did you stay?

C Reading and understanding a text

3 READ and listen to the text about different types of holiday and say which student went on which holiday.

A ☐ Judy went dancing on deck while her parents were chatting below.

B ☐ Dermot and his family helped out while also finding time to sightsee.

C ☐ Alistair was very active in the mountains.

D ☐ Beatrice enjoyed a beach holiday.

1.2

Holiday 1

My family and I went on this amazing holiday in Greece last summer. We stayed in a campsite on the mainland coast where there were wonderful facilities for teens – like a huge water park, a bowling alley and billiard tables. There was an open air cinema and lessons in water sports like paddle boarding or scuba diving. What's more, as well as enjoying all these activities we were also eating delicious Greek food!

Holiday 2

We went on a very unusual holiday this summer, we decided to try a family volunteering holiday. The one we chose was in Ireland, where we stayed in an animal rescue centre. The holiday meant we could do some useful work such as feeding the rescued animals and building shelters for them, but also had time to explore the area and visit places of interest like the Aran islands. While we were staying there, we helped save a lamb that fell 5 metres onto the beach below.

Holiday 3

For the first time ever, we went on an activity holiday this summer in the mountains in Poland. We climbed mountains, went canoeing, cycling and riding. While we were cycling or trekking, we were also admiring the wonderful natural scenery. My parents thought it was excellent value and although the food was very strange at times, we had a great time.

Holiday 4

Last summer we chose a Norwegian cruise for our family holiday. We all agreed that it offered something for everyone. While our parents were enjoying the beauty of the scenery and the interesting stops in picturesque ports, we could enjoy the teen club on deck 14 with its air hockey, a big-screen PlayStation or the water park with a 200-foot long inner tube ride. In the evening, while the older generation were chatting, we danced or just relaxed in the club – it was just great.

4 FIND the words in the text which mean the following:

1 available services (Holiday 1);
2 very tasty (Holiday 1);
3 buildings offering protection (Holiday 2);
4 unusual (Holiday 3);
5 scenic, charming (Holiday 4);
6 talk in a relaxed way (Holiday 4).

5 **UNDERLINE** all the examples in the past simple in the text. Then look at the Grammar map.

PAST SIMPLE

Use

1 to speak about finished states, events and actions that took place at a specific time in the past
*We **stayed** in a campsite on the coast last summer.*

2 to describe completed actions happening in sequence
*My parents **climbed** mountains, I and my sister **cycled** or **went** canoeing.*

Signal words

yesterday, ago
last week/month/year/...
in 2015, in the XX century, ...

---

6 **MATCH** the examples in the past simple to the corresponding use in the Grammar map. Then write sentences for each use.

---

7 **CIRCLE** all the examples in the past continuous in the text. Then look at the Grammar map.

PAST CONTINUOUS

Use

1 to talk about an action in progress at a particular time in the past
*Last night, at 8, I **was having** dinner.*

2 to talk about two continuous parallel actions
*I **was studying** and my sister **was watching** TV.*

3 to talk about an activity in progress interrupted by another event
*While we **were having** a picnic, it started to rain.*

4 to set the scene at the beginning of a story and to give background information
*She **was walking** along that dark road and ...*

5 to talk about a temporary situation in the past
*I **was working** in London last week.*

Signal words

while, when, meanwhile, in the meantime

---

8 **MATCH** the examples in the past continuous to the corresponding use in the Grammar map. Then write sentences for each use.

---

9 **COMPLETE** the text with the correct past tense form of the verbs in brackets.

Last summer Sean and Mary **(1)** ...DECIDED... (decide) to redecorate their sitting room. They **(2)** ...DIDN'T CHOOSE... (not choose) a dark colour but **(3)** ...PREFERED... (prefer) a cream paint for the walls and brown for the ceiling. They **(4)** ...BEGAN... (begin) painting, but they **(5)** ...FOUND... (find) the walls **(6)** ...WERE... (be) too wet. While they **(7)** ...WERE WAITING... (wait) for the walls to dry, Mary **(8)** ...REMEMBERED... (remember) that she **(9)** ...HAD... (have) a call to make. What **(10)** ...DID HE DECIDE... (Sean / decide) to do? He **(11)** ...THOUGHT... (think) he would do the ceiling. He **(12)** ...WAS CLIMBING... (climb) the ladder when the doorbell **(13)** ...RANG... (ring). It **(14)** ...WAS... (be) his aunt Amy, coming to spend the weekend with them.

---

10 **COMPLETE** the sentences with the correct past tense form of the verbs from the box.

do ▪ wake up ▪ run ▪ get ▪ study ▪ take ▪ strike ▪ be ▪ rain ▪ meet

1 When they ...WOKE UP... that morning, the sky was dark and it ...WAS RAINING... .
2 As the goalkeeper ...RAN... to seize the ball, a bottle from the crowd ...STRIKED... him.
3 When Malcolm ...MET... Jennifer at school yesterday, she ...WAS STUDYING... Maths for her test.
4 What ...WERE U DOING... (you) before you ...GOT... this job?
5 We ...TOOK... ages to reach the resort, but once there everything ...WAS... wonderful.

---

11 **CORRECT** the mistakes in the sentences.

1 ~~Did you study~~ WERE U STUDYING when I called you yesterday?
2 We were playing tennis when Rob ~~was breaking~~ BROKE his ankle.
3 While she ~~left~~ WAS LEAVING Boston, the sun was shining.
4 She heard a loud noise while she ~~talked~~ WAS TALKING to her boyfriend.
5 When Rachel ~~was~~ arrived, we were doing the gardening.

C Talking about personal experiences

12 **WORK** in pairs. Think about a memorable event that happened during your summer holidays and tell your partner.

WARM-UP

1 DISCUSS in pairs. Do you prefer reading or going to the cinema? Have you ever read a book because you enjoyed the film? Or have you ever gone to see a film of a book you particularly liked? Did you enjoy the book or the film more?

C Reading and understanding a text

2 READ and listen to the two contrasting opinions below and say which you agree with.

The film or the book?

1.3

William: The film

I have often found that a great book usually makes a great film and sometimes the film is even better. How can it be better? Well, have you ever seen a historical drama or a film of one of the classics like *Romeo and Juliet*? It is quite hard for the modern mind to imagine the setting, the clothes and the customs of another age, while a film gives us all the background effortlessly. All the advances in technology that have taken place over the last few years also mean there are super special effects that add so much to films like *The Lord of the Rings* or *Game of Thrones*.

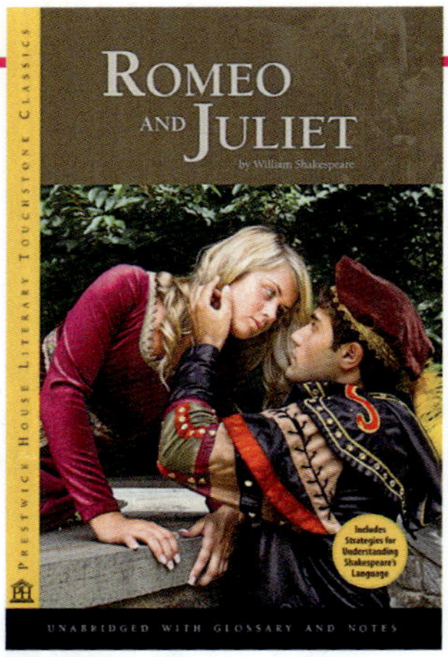

Kirsty: The book

Ever since I started reading, I have always preferred the book to the film. Even when the film version has been really well done and really close to the original, I have never found the film better. It is different, quicker to get through, of course, and it gives the atmosphere, particularly in films where the background is important. However the book stimulates our imagination and allows each of us to form our own idea of the protagonists and their world. Also, the film hasn't got the same detail or the deeper thoughts of the characters.

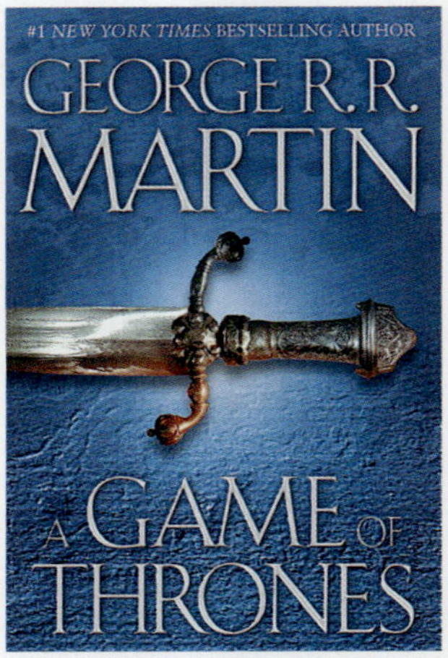

3 READ the text again and do the following activities.

A FIND the words in the text which mean the following:

1. location in time and place (para. 1);
2. habits (para. 1);
3. the scene behind the characters or objects in the foreground (para. 1);
4. finish (para. 2);
5. permits (para. 2).

B FORM questions for the answers.

1. William has often found that a great book usually makes a great film. WHAT DOES WILLIAM THINK ABOUT BOOKS AND MOVIES?
2. Because a film can give you the setting, the clothes and the customs of another age. WHY IS THE FILM BETTER?
3. These advances have meant that films like *Game of Thrones* or science fiction films can have super special effects. WHAT MAKES THE FILM BETTER?
4. Kirsty has always preferred the book to the film. WHAT DOES KIRSTY PREFER?
5. Because it is quicker and gives the atmosphere. WHAT'S A GOOD THING ABOUT FILMS
6. The book stimulates the imagination and gives more details and the deeper thoughts of the characters. AND A GOOD THING 'BOUT BOOKS

4 UNDERLINE all the examples in the present perfect in the text. Then look at the Grammar map.

PRESENT PERFECT

Use

1 to talk about life experiences (with *ever/ never/ yet* in questions and negative sentences)
Have you ever seen a historical film?
I have never found the film better.
I haven't seen that film yet.

3 to talk about recent past events (with *already/ just/ recently*)
I have already seen that film.
I have just finished reading that book.
I have recently seen the film version of Moby Dick.

2 to say something has happened several times (with *up to now/ so far*)
I have done five exercises up to now.
I have been to France twice so far this year.

5 MATCH the examples in the present perfect to the corresponding use in the Grammar map. Then write sentences for each use.

6 CHOOSE the correct past participle of the verbs from the box to complete the sentences.

speak ▪ write ▪ send ▪ prefer ▪ buy ▪ have ▪ fall ▪ see

1. Have you ever .... a book for your mother's birthday?
2. I have never .... asleep during a film.
3. They have never .... an email to the wrong person.
4. We have never .... such a good version of *Oliver Twist*.
5. Have you ever .... in front of a large audience?
6. Has Sean already .... a book about how to study Maths?
7. We have just .... a class discussion about reading the classics.
8. My sister Kate has always .... watching the video to reading the book.

7 COMPLETE the sentences with *ever, never, just, already, yet.*

1. Can you hear that noise? The train has .... arrived.
2. Hasn't she finished baking the cake .... ?
3. Have you .... seen such an amusing film?
4. She has .... taken that Maths exam three times.
5. I have .... had nightmares. I'm very lucky.
6. It is the most interesting book I have .... read.
7. Meg hasn't come back home .... Perhaps the bus is late.
8. He has .... eaten sushi because he doesn't like raw fish.

8 REORDER the prompts below and write sentences using the present perfect.

1. lose / your car keys / ever / you?
2. this year / Paris / I / so far / visit / three times
3. the bus / already / Oh no! / leave
4. just / to collect / the lesson / go / the teacher / the books / for
5. *Star Wars* / yet / the latest / see / film?
6. books / not read / about ghosts / they / or vampires / ever
7. four times / watch / it's great! / already / I / that film
8. try / a poem / to write / you / ever? // yet / try / no / I

9 COMPLETE the sentences with the present perfect of the verbs in brackets.

1. My parents .... (never / visit) New York.
2. No, he .... (not see) that film yet.
3. Don't phone John! I .... (already / do) it.
4. I .... (just / finish) my homework.
5. Yes, the match .... (already / start).
6. Their plane .... (just / land).

C Talking about personal experiences

10 MAKE a list of five books you have never read but would like to read and five films you have seen and would recommend to a friend. Compare your list with a classmate by asking and answering questions using the present perfect.

WARM-UP

1 DISCUSS in pairs. Look at the image of a vision board and discuss what it is.

2 DISCUSS as a class. What are you inspired by? What would you put on a vision board?

SPORT CHAMPIONS OR MUSICIANS OR PEOPLE IN GENERAL WHO FIGHT FOR WHAT THEY BELIEVE IN

3 READ the ideas about future plans below and say which one you identify with.

1 I have a careful plan for the future where I know what I'm going to do at each phase of my life.

2 I'm not going to plan anything for my future, I'll just accept events as they happen and go with the flow.

3 I know that I'll do the opposite of what others are going to plan for me. I'll rebel against any control over my future.

4 I'm going to take time consciously deciding what the best path will be and then organise things to make sure it will happen.

C Reading and understanding a text

4 READ and listen to the article and try to answer the question of the title.

1.4

Do we have any influence over our destiny?

What will the future be? Different people view the future differently. Some accept what will happen in the way we accept that our train leaves at a certain time tomorrow morning. Others see it as pre-destined and unchangeable, like saying 'my dad is starting a new job next week' and nothing will change that. But others say we can influence our future by being positive and having dreams.

You can learn to say 'from today I'm going to listen to my inner voice, I'm going to believe anything is possible'. You will soon see how your life changes. You will become more focused, you will look for opportunities and above all you won't fall into the trap of self-pity. Push yourself and don't settle for what is easy – expect the best from yourself and guess what – you'll get it!

5 READ the texts again and do the following activities.

A FIND the words in the texts which mean the following:

1 cautious;
2 full aware;
3 fixed, inalterable;
4 concentrated;
5 situation impossible or difficult to get out of;
6 feeling sorry for yourself.

B LOOK for these phrases in the texts and discuss their meaning in pairs.

- go with the flow
- make sure
- have dreams
- listen to your inner voice
- believe anything is possible
- not settle DON'T SAY IT'S FINE WHEN YOU CAN HAVE MORE
- expect the best

C ANSWER the questions about the article.

1 What is an example of something that happens regardless of what we plan? SOMETHING THAT HAPPENS SUDDENLY
2 What is an example of something planned and going to happen? MAKE AN APPOINTMENT
3 How can we influence our future according to the article? BY BEING POSITIVE AND HAVING DREAMS
4 How will your life change according to the writer? I'LL BE MORE FOCUSED AND I'LL LOOK FOR OPPORTUNITIES AND I WON'T FALL INTO SELF-PITY

6 UNDERLINE all the examples of verbs with a future meaning in the text. Then look at the Grammar map.

FUTURE TENSES

FUTURE SIMPLE

1 future predictions
*You **will be** better tomorrow.*

2 beliefs and opinions about the future
*Scientists think it **will** probably **be** warmer in the future.*

3 an inevitable future action/fact
*Next week I'**ll be** sixteen.*

4 promises
*I'**ll phone** you when I arrive in London.*

5 spontaneous decisions
*It's really hot in here. I'**ll turn** on the air conditioning.*

6 offers to do something
*I'**ll give** you a lift home after the film.*

PRESENT SIMPLE

1 fixed future events
*Martina's party **starts** at 9.30.*

2 programmes/timetables
*When **does** the train to London **leave**?*

PRESENT CONTINUOUS

1 planned actions
*We'**re meeeting** at 8 in front of the cinema.*

2 near future actions with time reference
*Tomorrow morning I'**m leaving** very early.*

BE GOING TO

1 predictions based on present evidence
*The sky is blue. It'**s going to be** a sunny day.*

2 intentions
*They **are going to move** to Montreal.*

7 MATCH the examples to the corresponding use in the Grammar map. Then write sentences for each use.

8 CHOOSE the correct alternative.

1 I don't think I *will* / *am going to* change my plans.
2 The kettle is boiling, I *make* / *will make* some tea.
3 Promise me you *are calling* / *will call* as soon as you arrive.
4 'Why are you putting on your coat?' '*It's going to rain* / *It will rain.*'
5 What time *is the exhibition opening* / *does the exhibition open*?
6 Josh can't come to the swimming pool with us this afternoon. He *is going to visit* / *is visiting* his grandmother.

9 WRITE questions for the answers in bold type.

1 They are getting married **on Saturday**.
2 They are going to build a new hotel **in the town centre**.
3 **No**, the flight does not take off at 9.00 but at 10.30.
4 **John** will pick you up at the station.
5 **No**, I won't be late for the lecture.
6 Blake will look for **new job opportunities**.

10 COMPLETE the sentences with the correct future form of the verbs in brackets.

1 It's already half past six. It .... (get) dark soon.
2 This pie smells delicious. I think I .... (have) a slice.
3 'What .... (you / do) about the tickets for the concert?' 'I expect they .... (be) sold out.'
4 I'm sure he .... (not rebel) against his parents.
5 What .... (happen) to our planet in twenty years' time?
6 She doesn't feel well so she .... (see) the doctor this afternoon at 3 o'clock.
7 That dress looks cool. I .... (try) it.
8 Look, you've broken the vase! I .... (help) you tidy up.

C Writing about personal experiences

11 WRITE about yourself using the future forms and the prompts.

- school
- friends
- sport
- hobbies
- family
- holidays

WARM-UP

1 DISCUSS in pairs.

1 What makes you stressed?

2 What do you do when you have problems?

- ☐ Talk to your parents.
- ☐ Talk to friends.
- ☐ Look for some form of professional advice.
- ☐ Try to sort it out by yourself without telling anyone.
- ☐ Other ....

C Reading and understanding a text

2 READ and listen to the blogs, then add the correct name to the answers below.

1.5

1 I'm writing to ask your advice about a particular friendship. Jo and I have been friends ever since starting High School but she ignores me now and looks the other way when she sees me. I think I may have offended her or she might feel I have changed. What should I do? Should I call her or wait for her to change back? **Sue**

2 I have the most fantastic boyfriend, he is everything I've ever wanted and more but… he's a smoker and it is driving me round the bend. I hate anything to do with smoking. What can I do? If he doesn't give up, I may have to end our relationship. Please help! **Maddy**

3 Some of my schoolmates are planning a camping holiday in the mountains this summer. I would love to go and they have asked me several times if I can come, but I'm finding it difficult to ask my parents. I've never been away on holiday without them and I'm frightened they might say no or they could find reasons to keep me at home. What should I do? **Tony**

A Dear ...., you won't know how your parents feel about this until you ask them. You may well be worrying unnecessarily, after all going away with friends is now so normal they shouldn't find it a problem. I think you should take the plunge and just ask.

B Dear ...., we can all try to change our own bad habits but it's much more difficult to make others change. What you could do is pass on all the information you can find about the damage that smoking can do to the smoker's health and also to those around them – hopefully that should help.

C Dear ...., I really feel for you. Friendships are hard and they can change like the tide and bring joy or pain. My advice is that you should wait. Trying to confront your friend could make the situation worse and increase the tension. It may be a phase that could pass.

3 READ the blogs again and do the following activities.

A ANSWER the questions.

Who

1 thinks they can change their boyfriend's habits?

2 thinks their parents might give the wrong answer?

3 thinks their friendship might be changing?

4 should try to persuade their boyfriend with facts about healthy living?

5 could try waiting to see if the situation changes?

6 might be surprised by their parents' reaction?

B FIND the words in the text which mean the following:

1 special (para. 1);

2 irritated (para. 1);

3 fearful (para. 3);

4 harmful effect (para. B);

5 sympathise with (para. C);

6 the regular rise and fall of the sea (para. C).

C LOOK for these phrases in the text and discuss their meaning.

- look the other way
- driving me round the bend
- take the plunge
- pass on
- change like the tide

4 **UNDERLINE** all the examples of present conditional and modal verbs in the text. Then look at the Grammar map.

CONDITIONALS AND MODAL VERBS

CONDITIONAL

- to talk about imaginary situations
  *I **would travel** around the world.*

ADVICE

- **1** to give advice
  *You **should study** harder.*
- **2** to ask for advice
  ***Should** I **buy** this T-shirt?*
- **3** to express suggestion or opinion
  *You **shouldn't be** so critical!*

POSSIBILITY/ PROBABILITY

- **1** to express probability
  *This **may/ might be** the beginning of a great career as a writer.* (*might* expresses less probability than *may*)
- **2** to express predictions about the future
  *Temperatures **may rise** in the future.*
- **3** to express possibility in the past
  *Not so long ago people **could smoke** in cinemas.*

5 **MATCH** the examples of present conditional and modal verbs to the corresponding use in the Grammar map. Then write sentences for each use.

6 **COMPLETE** the sentences with the correct form of the present conditional.

1. Barbara ....WOULD LIKE.......... (like) to visit the British Museum when she goes to London.
2. ....COULD YOU WIN.......... (you / win) easily playing tennis against George?
3. You ....WOULDN'T LIE.......... (not lie) to me, would you?
4. I ....'D STAY.......... (stay) here with you longer, but my train leaves at 5.
5. It's no use trying to convince him, he ....WOULDN'T ACCEPT.......... (not accept).
6. They ....MIGHT PREFER.......... (prefer) to move house – theirs is too small.
7. We ....WOULDN'T HAVE.......... (not have) a cat, we love dogs.
8. ....SHOULD SHE WEAR.......... (she / wear) that dress at the wedding?

7 **COMPLETE** the second sentence so that it has a similar meaning to the first sentence.

1. It is possible that he gives up smoking.
   He ....MIGHT QUIT.......... smoking.
2. There is a possibility that Bob knows the whole story.
   Bob ....MAY KNOW.......... the whole story.
3. Perhaps Tricia doesn't want to change school.
   Tricia ....MAY NOT WANT.......... to change school.
4. Your parents probably feel bad about it, but I'm not sure.
   Your parents ....MIGHT FEEL BAD.......... about it.
5. It is possible he won't call you back.
   He ....MAY NOT.......... call you back.

8 **REWRITE** the sentences using *should* or *shouldn't*.

1. What's the right place for me to park my car? (WHERE SHOULD I PARK MY CAR?)
2. It's wrong that you ignore your old school friend. (YOU SHOULDN'T IGNORE YOUR OLD SCHOOL FRIEND)
3. Why doesn't he ask for advice? (HE SHOULD ASK FOR ADVICE)
4. She isn't careful enough about what she eats. (SHE SHOULD BE MORE CAREFUL ABOUT WHAT SHE EATS)
5. I wonder whether it is better to wait and let him cool down. (WE SHOULD WAIT AND LET HIM COOL DOWN)

9 **WRITE** what you would say in the following situations.

1. Your car is broken. Ask your friend for a lift home politely. (MY CAR IS BROKEN, MAY I ASK YOU A LIFT HOME PLEASE?)
2. Your mother wants to buy your dad a birthday present. Give her some advice. (YOU SHOULD BUY DAD A NEW TIE)
3. Your friend is crying. DON'T CRY, YOU'LL GET BETTER SOON
4. You see some students smoking inside the school and you know it's not allowed. GUYS YOU SHOULDN'T BE SMOKING HERE
5. You want to buy a white shirt. Tell the assistant politely. (HI MISS, SORRY I'D LIKE TO BUY A WHITE SHIRT, DO YOU HAVE ONE?)

C Writing about personal experiences

10 **WORK** in pairs. Think of a real or imaginary problem and write a short text asking for advice. Ask your partner for a reply.

CHOOSE the correct option (A, B, C or D) to complete the sentences.

1 My father was born 45 years .... in a small town near Milan.
A last **B** before **C** since **D** ago

2 They .... at their aunt's until the decorators have finished.
A stay **B** stayed **C** are staying **D** stays

3 I'm sure I .... this woman before.
A don't see **B** haven't seen **C** didn't see **D** am not seeing

4 Yesterday about 80,000 people .... the World Cup Final at the stadium at 8 p.m.
A have watched **B** watched **C** were watching **D** watch

5 According to the schedule, our visit to the museum .... at 10 o'clock.
A starts **B** is starting **C** is going to start **D** shall start

6 I think John .... a famous singer one day.
A is becoming **B** is going to become **C** will become **D** would become

7 Wait! Don't get up, I .... the table for you.
A will clear **B** am going to clear **C** am clearing **D** clear

8 It seems to me you .... yourself tonight.
A don't enjoy **B** wouldn't enjoy **C** didn't enjoy **D** aren't enjoying

9 How many people .... there at the concert last night?
A did **B** could **C** were **D** be

10 The lecturer spoke loudly but I .... anyway.
A not understood **B** didn't understand **C** understood not **D** don't understand

11 You .... borrow your brother's bike without even asking.
A couldn't **B** shouldn't **C** might not **D** could

12 Paula .... never forget her wonderful holiday in Tuscany.
A will **B** may **C** does **D** had

13 John is very upset. I think you .... take him out tonight!
A had **B** did **C** would **D** should

14 I can't understand. What .... ?
A means the poem **B** do the poem means **C** do the poem mean **D** does the poem mean

15 He .... use his car because he didn't have his keys.
A shouldn't **B** couldn't **C** wouldn't **D** might not

16 'Can I help you?' 'Yes, please. I .... my wallet.'
A lost **B** lose **C** have lost **D** am losing

17 Last year I went to England and I .... with a host family for three weeks.
A stayed **B** have stayed **C** was staying **D** would stay

18 He's always .... his coursebook at home!
A forgotten **B** to forget **C** forgot **D** forgetting

19 I think this is the best book he .... so far.
A wrote **B** has written **C** is writing **D** was writing

20 Fiona .... be interested in the offer you made her. That's why she didn't call back.
A doesn't **B** couldn't **C** may not **D** shouldn't

SCORE: ..../20

1 Being connected

Scarica **GUARDA!** e inquadrami per guardare i video e ascoltare gli audio di questa unità

VOCABULARY ACTIVATOR

FLIPPED classroom

VIDEO Relationships

WARM-UP

1 DISCUSS the questions.

1 Who do you like having a good time with?
2 Who do you ask for advice?
3 Are you part of a social network?

C Learning to use vocabulary in context

2 1.6 **LOOK at the pictures and listen to six people talking about relationships. Match the people to the pictures.**

3 1.6 **LISTEN again and complete the sentences.**

1 My grandad and I have a great relationship, maybe because he ....
2 My sister and I don't always .... and we often have terrific rows but then after a few minutes we have ....
3 The people .... are my friends because we ....
4 In my family, we all .... openly and discuss .... that have happened during the day.
5 My boyfriend and I share lots of ....
6 I have contacts .... and they give me a .... on life.

FOCUS ON VOCABULARY

Relations ···> people related to you through blood or marriage.

Relationship ···> connection, involvement between two or more things or people.

Friends ···> those people, often of a similar age, with whom you have a mutually supportive relationship.

Acquaintances ···> people you have met but don't know well.

Contacts ···> people you are connected to for reasons of friendship, work, mutual interests, etc.

Useful expressions for relationships

- feel close to
- have rows
- be in touch with
- talk about problems
- have a laugh
- share problems / moments of joy

4 DISCUSS in small groups what makes a good relationship. Which relationships are important in your life? Use the vocabulary from the Focus box.

WARM-UP

1 **DISCUSS** in pairs. What do you look for in a friend? What is the difference between online friends and in-person friends?

C Reading, understanding and interpreting information

2 **READ** the questions below and try to give an answer. Then read and listen to the article.

1.7

Friends can shape your life

An important but little known area of psychology is that of the influence of friendship on our lives. The influence of parents and brothers or sisters on our development as people always receives a lot of attention, but what about friends? Friends have a huge influence on our lives. They can provide comfort and joy, reduce stress, prevent loneliness and isolation, and even strengthen our health. However, friendship is now changing, the network of possible contacts is growing all the time thanks to the abundance of social networks on the Internet. Is this a good thing or a bad thing? Let's see what an expert says.

Q How is friendship changing?

A The word 'friendship' now covers a vast area of contacts. A lot of people, teenagers as well as adults, usually chat with online friends, but friends on social network sites don't necessarily know each other at all. Sometimes they have never physically met, but are friends of friends. This kind of contact is not what we generally think of as friendship.

Q What is real friendship?

A I am not saying that online social contact is not real friendship, I am just saying that it is different. Friendship is a mutually supporting relationship normally based on common interests. Chatrooms where people discuss interests or let off steam about social problems can be supportive as well.

Q Are online friendships replacing traditional friendships?

A No, they are not replacing any other kind of relationship, they are adding a new form of contact. In many cases online friends are traditional friends too. Our mates, that we hang out with, go out with, have fun with and cry with – when we need comforting – are often also the people we chat to online or text, or WhatsApp. We have rows and make up with them online or face-to-face, but not in the same way.

Q What makes a good friend?

A In any form of friendship, genuine interest and care are key words. Listening is an essential quality. Are we prepared to stop what we are doing and listen to someone who needs help? Friends do not always get on with each other, but need to have time to listen to each other in moments of difficulty.

Q Are true friends, friends for life?

A We often have different friends in different phases of our lives. Early friendships in our childhood play a vital role because they are happening while important developmental changes are taking place. Teen friendships shape our romantic feelings. They are a training ground for the later long-term relationships that will evolve through adulthood.

Q Is there a downside to friendship?

A Close friends support you through thick and thin but friends can also make you miserable. Those who know you best know how to hurt you best. Being a friend is a great honour and responsibility so treasure your friends, be there when they need you, spend time doing things together. Are you devoting time and energy to developing your relationships? Remember friendships can give you important life skills. Our friends, online or in-person, help shape who we are.

3 **READ** the article again and do the following activities.

A1 According to the article, which is an important but little understood area of psychology?

A The influence of parents and siblings on our development.
B The influence of friendship on our development.

A2 Which are the four benefits of friendship given in the article?

A3 How is friendship changing according to the expert?

A4 Which of the following meanings is closest to the expression 'let off steam' as used in line 22?

A Boil water (for a hot drink).
B Create vapour.
C Release repressed energy or emotions.
D Become increasingly angry.

A5 Decide if the following sentences are true (T) or false (F).

A Online friendships are replacing traditional friendships. T F
B They are becoming a new form of contact. T F
C They are often in-person friends too. T F
D They offer less than real friends. T F

A6 Which are the key words to describe a good friendship, according to the article?

A7 Explain the different phases of friendship in your own words.

A8 Which of the meanings below is closest to the expression 'through thick and thin' in lines 55-56?

A Whether you want to or not.
B In favourable and unfavourable conditions.
C In all types of weather.
D Disagreeably excessive or exaggerated.

A9 Say which of these tips for being a better friend is NOT mentioned in the article.

A Treasure your friends.
B Spend time doing things together.
C Make yourself available when needed.
D Show that you can be trusted.
E Make the effort to develop the relationship.

A10 Which of the following best summarises the viewpoint of the article?

A New advances in technology should be reflected in new forms of friendship.
B It is sometimes hard to make friends or maintain friendships.
C Friendship is a value and the web is a useful resource to make new friends.
D The relationships we make influence our lives and who we are.

C Listening and understanding information

4 1.8 **LISTEN** to five different people talking about relationships. Listen again and decide for each speaker if the following views on friendships and relationships are true (T) or false (F).

Speaker 1
Relationships within the family are an important base for later relationships. T F

Speaker 2
Sometimes the strongest friendships are within the family. T F

Speaker 3
A family occasion like a wedding anniversary is a moment for forming new friendships. T F

Speaker 4
Our time at school is an opportunity to learn about getting on with others. T F

Speaker 5
There are different kinds of friendship, those that last a long time and those that last as long as you are doing the same thing. T F

Phrasal verbs for relationships

Phrasal verbs are made of a **verb** + an **adverb**, or a **preposition** or **both** (See p. 204).

5 **MATCH** the highlighted phrasal verbs (1-5) in the article to their definitions (A-E).

1 [ ] hang out with
2 [ ] go out with
3 [ ] have fun with
4 [ ] make up (with)
5 [ ] get on (with)

A date
B enjoy being together
C become friends again after a quarrel
D spend time with
E have a good relationship with

6 **COMPLETE** the sentences with the correct form of the phrasal verbs from exercise 5.

1 My brother is .... with my best friend at the moment.
2 Are you studying this afternoon or are you .... with your friends in the park?
3 Although my step-mother is much older than me, she has a wonderful sense of humour and we always .... when we're together.
4 I often have rows with my mum about homework but we usually .... after a while.
5 My father and his boss don't .... , they spend the whole time arguing.

Present simple and present continuous

1 **UNDERLINE** examples of present simple and of present continuous in the article on page 18. Then explain the function of the two tenses.

2 **MATCH** sentences 1-8 to their uses A-H.

1 ☐ Friends **do not** always **get on** with each other all the time.
2 ☐ A lot of people usually **chat** with online friends.
3 ☐ We **hang out** with our mates every day.
4 ☐ The sun **rises** in the East.
5 ☐ He **is visiting** his relatives in London this week.
6 ☐ How **is** friendship **changing**?
7 ☐ More and more teenagers **are using** social networks.
8 ☐ You **are** always **chatting** during the lesson.

A show current trends
B permanent situations
C express a complaint or show irritation
D state general truths
E temporary situations
F actions taking place or in progress
G habitual actions
H emphasise frequency

Grammar reference 1.1, 1.2

3 **COMPLETE** the sentences with the correct form of the verbs in brackets.

1 No friendship .... (develop) easily.
2 'What .... (you / do) in the kitchen?' 'I .... (prepare) coffee for my dad.'
3 They .... (not post) on Facebook as much as I do.
4 I'm sure your brother and sister .... (not / always / get along) because they .... (often / have) terrific rows.
5 At the moment, Sean .... (study) Maths with a friend of his.
6 You .... (always / listen) to loud music!
7 We .... (take) five courses this semester.
8 Social networks .... (change) relationships.
9 What's all that noise? What .... (happen)?
10 Hi Nick. How .... (your new job /go)?

4 **WRITE** sentences with the present simple and the present continuous using the prompts below.

1 I / rarely / travel / by / plane.
2 They / become / more and more / interested / in / online games.
3 My / friends / often / help / me.
4 Why / you / use / always / my / computer?
5 My / friend / never / wear / earrings.
6 Look! / What / happen / over / there?

FREQUENT MISTAKES **Stative and dynamic verbs**

Stative verbs describe states rather than actions and **are not used in the continuous forms**.
Common stative verbs include: *want, like, remember, know, be, hear, seem.*

Dynamic verbs describe physical or mental activites. They **are used both in the simple and continuous forms**.

Some verbs can be both stative and dynamic verbs, depending on the meaning.
*What **do you think** about that novel?* (think = have an opinion)
*You look sad! What **are you thinking** about?* (think = reflect on)

Grammar reference 1.3

5 **CHOOSE** the correct alternative to complete the sentences.

1 I often *am hearing / hear* my neighbours arguing.
2 The court *hears / is hearing* evidence about the murder this morning.
3 We *are seeing / see* our friends this evening.
4 I often *see / am seeing* adults looking suspiciously at me.
5 Your perfume *smells / is smelling* fantastic.
6 Why *are you smelling / do you smell* those flowers?
7 How *are you feeling / do you feel* after that injection?
8 When *do you feel / are you feeling* we become adults?

6 **PUT** the verbs in brackets into the correct form of the present simple and present continuous.

1 They .... (have) a snack before the lesson.
2 What .... (you / think) about this magazine?
3 We .... (see) our friends tonight at 8.
4 My husband .... (always / taste) the food while I'm cooking!
5 She .... (think) about buying a new car.
6 Leave me alone. I .... (try) to concentrate.

USE OF ENGLISH

VIDEO
Reading and Use of English Part 1

EXAM DESCRIPTION	
What is there in Reading and Use of English Part 1?	A text where there are eight gaps (missing words or phrases). Below the text, there are four possible answers (A, B, C or D) for each gap. You have to choose the correct answer.
What do I have to focus on?	Grammar and vocabulary: **1** phrasal verbs (*take over*) **2** word + preposition (*depend on*) **3** preposition + noun (*in addition*) **4** collocations (*science fiction*) **5** words that have similar meaning (*shows, portrays, depicts*)
How many questions are there?	Eight.
How many marks do I get?	One mark for each correct answer.

FIRST Reading and Use of English – Part 1

1 **MULTIPLE-CHOICE CLOZE. For questions 1-8, read the text below and decide which answer (A, B, C or D) best fits each gap. There is an example at the beginning (0).**

New friends

It's hard for my parents to understand, but friendship **(0)** IS CHANGING. I still have schoolfriends of course and guys I hang **(1)** .... in town, but I also have new friends, friends from all over the world through the social networks.

To my mum and dad, Facebook, Twitter and Snapchat **(2)** .... almost alien words – well, they do use texts and WhatsApp – but generally speaking they **(3)** .... time chatting and messaging online as negative. 'Why **(4)** .... you studying?' or 'Why don't you talk face-to-face?' are typical objections.

But I enjoy my online contacts. We **(5)** .... really well, we discuss problems, talk about lots of interesting things and often **(6)** .... a good laugh. It's fun to hear about situations and realities so different to mine. It's sometimes easier to talk about personal things to someone not directly involved or someone who can see your problems in a different light. It's a less intense **(7)** .... than that with family members. We never have rows or need to **(8)** .... after a heated discussion. If we get angry, we just log off.

0	**A** change	**B** **is changing**	**C** changed	**D** changes
1	**A** out of	**B** with	**C** on	**D** out with
2	**A** are	**B** are being	**C** is	**D** aren't
3	**A** are seeing	**B** sees	**C** see	**D** saw
4	**A** are	**B** aren't	**C** do	**D** don't
5	**A** get on	**B** get up	**C** make up	**D** take place
6	**A** has	**B** are having	**C** have	**D** not have
7	**A** relation	**B** relations	**C** friend	**D** relationship
8	**A** get on	**B** make up	**C** go out with	**D** hang out

VIDEO
Reading and Use of English Part 2

EXAM DESCRIPTION	
What is there in Reading and Use of English Part 2?	A text where there are eight gaps to fill with one word only.
What do I have to focus on?	The missing words focus on grammar or vocabulary.
How many questions are there?	Eight.
How many marks do I get?	One mark for each correct answer.

FIRST Reading and Use of English – Part 2

2 **OPEN CLOZE. For questions 1-8, read the text below and think of the word which best fits each gap. Use only one word in each gap. There is an example at the beginning (0).**

Me and my pet

My best friend **(0)** IS my dog. Don't laugh, our **(1)** .... is very deep.

First of all, Kim listens to me – yes, I really **(2)** .... problems and moments of joy with him. I tell him about having **(3)** .... with classmates, not getting **(4)** .... with my terrible brother, what **(5)** .... happening at school. I explain my misunderstandings, my disappointments and Kim licks my hand in sympathy. He greets me with joy when I **(6)** .... home and seems to know when I need a bit of comfort.

OK, we can't hang out together or **(7)** .... out to the cinema, but we have long walks in the park and relax together to watch our favourite programmes on TV or streaming. We get on so well and **(8)** .... lots of fun!

WARM-UP

1 DISCUSS in pairs.

1 Is science connected to how we live our lives?
2 Can scientists help us in developing better relationships?

C Recognising specific information within a text

2 READ and listen to the article and say how the world is getting smaller.

VIDEO
Reading and Use of English Part 5

EXAM DESCRIPTION	
What is there in Reading and Use of English Part 5?	A text with six multiple-choice questions. Each question has four options.
What do I have to focus on?	The emphasis is on detailed understanding of the text, so you need to focus on: opinion, detail, attitude, tone, purpose and the main idea of the text.
How many questions are there?	Six.
How many marks do I get?	Two marks for each correct answer.

1.9

Six degrees of separation

Have you heard of the theory that we are all connected and that even two complete strangers have, through their network of friends or acquaintances, just six degrees of separation? This theory sounds new but scientists have been trying for decades to prove that the world is made up of social networks that are in some way interconnected. According to this theory, everything and everybody in the world is just six or fewer connections away from everything and everybody else, so any two people can be connected through a 'friend of a friend' network within six steps.

The original idea came from Hungarian author Frigyes Karinthy in 1929. He wrote a short story that investigated many of the problems that have fascinated generations of mathematicians, physicists and sociologists within the field of network theory. Karinthy thought that the modern

FIRST Reading and Use of English – Part 5

3 MULTIPLE-CHOICE QUESTIONS. Read the article again. For questions 1-6, choose the answer (A, B, C or D) which you think fits best according to the text.

1 The theory is based on the idea that all the individuals in the world
A actually know each other.
B are related.
C can be linked through mutual connections.
D are physically nearer than they think.

2 The theory
A is completely new.
B has been around for centuries.
C has never been used before.
D has been fascinating scientists for many years.

3 What is meant in the text by 'two complete strangers' (line 2)?
A Two people you know through someone else.
B Two people who have never met.
C Two people who have only just met.
D Two people who know each other but not very well.

4 Karinthy believed that social distances were getting smaller in spite of
A people not knowing each other.
B people living very far apart.
C scientists' research in this field.
D time differences.

5 Other examples of how the theory has fascinated people are
A a book, a game and a film.
B a play, a film and a game.
C a play and a film.
D a card game, a musical and a film.

6 Recent experiments of the theory have shown that
A the theory is actually far from the reality of social connections.
B it requires far more than six degrees to find a connection between two people who don't know each other.
C any two people are between six or seven degrees of separation apart.
D degrees of connection are based on coincidence rather than acquaintance.

world was 'shrinking' because of this ever-increasing connectedness of human beings. His idea was that the rapid growth of networks around the world was overcoming the enormous geographical distances, making the actual social distances smaller. As a result, any two individuals could be connected through at most five acquaintances.

Karinthy hasn't been the only writer to find the idea fascinating. An American author, John Guare, used the idea in a play, followed by a 1993 film starring Will Smith. US students have also invented a game called *Six Degrees of Kevin Bacon*, based on the idea that any Hollywood actor could be connected to the actor Bacon through films they have appeared in. It started as a joke but many have been playing it ever since and the actor himself has turned the game into a possibility of social good by creating a Six Degrees site connecting people and causes. A lovely example of using a social network for social good.

In Guare's play a character says: 'I read somewhere that everybody on this planet is separated by only six other people. Six degrees of separation between us and everyone else on this planet. I find it extremely comforting that we're so close. I am bound to everyone on this planet by a trail of six people.'

The idea has attracted a lot of interest and researchers and scientists have been carrying out different experiments to test the theory. A few years ago, Microsoft examined its instant-messenger network of 30 billion electronic conversations between 180 million people. And the results? They have been showing similar findings. The researchers concluded that any two people are divided by an average of 6.6 degrees of separation. To put this in a less mathematical way, you are linked through seven or fewer contacts to the Queen of England or the President of the United States.

Have you ever thought that in just a few steps we may all be connected? Exciting, isn't it? Are you surprised? Don't be, this is the result we have all been waiting for.

4 FIND the words in the text which mean the following:

1 specific area (para. 2);
2 getting smaller (para. 2);
3 real (para. 2);
4 tied together (para. 4);
5 path, series of steps (para. 4);
6 joined, connected (para. 5).

Word formation: nouns

Nouns can be formed from adjectives, verbs or other nouns by using **suffixes**. Some of the most common are: ***-ian***, ***-ance/-ence***, ***-(i)ty***, ***-dom***, ***-ship***, ***-ment***, ***-ness***, ***-sion/-tion***, ***-y***, ***-er***, ***-ist***.

5 FIND the nouns in the text that are formed with the suffixes above and say from which words they derive.

6 FORM nouns from the words in the box.

active ▪ free ▪ excite ▪ sad ▪ divide ▪ explore ▪
jealous ▪ adolescent ▪ drive ▪ endure ▪ mature ▪
important ▪ champion ▪ discuss ▪ science

7 MAKE nouns from the words given to complete the sentences.

1 Do you believe in the .... of finding your soul mate? (POSSIBLE)
2 I'd like to become a .... when I leave school. (JOURNAL)
3 He has a lot of .... , he writes beautiful stories. (IMAGINE)
4 Our .... dates back to when we were children. (FRIEND)
5 The text speaks about the .... of childhood for the Romantic poets. (IMPORTANT)
6 .... is the enemy of love relationships. (BORE)
7 What is your .... of Emily's boyfriend? (IMPRESS)
8 The idea of being connected to everyone brings me a feeling of true .... (HAPPY)

C Discussing ideas and expressing opinions

8 DISCUSS the questions.

1 What do you think about the theory of everyone being connected? Do you find the idea appealing? Why or why not?
2 Do you agree that the world is getting smaller?

9 WRITE a brief paragraph of 6-8 lines about the six degrees of separation theory.

Present perfect simple and past simple

1 READ sentences 1-2 and answer questions A-B.

1 The original idea **came** from Hungarian author Frigyes Karinthy in 1929.
2 US students **have invented** a game.

Which sentence
A focuses on an action which happened at an unspecified time in the past?
B speaks about an action that took place at a specific time in the past?

Grammar reference 1.4, 1.5, 1.6

2 COMPLETE the text using the present perfect simple or the past simple of the verbs in brackets.

Videos of animal friendships **(1)** .... (become) so popular on social media that they **(2)** .... (attract) the interest of some scientists who **(3)** .... (recently / claim) that animal alliances could help us understand how species **(4)** .... (start) to communicate long ago. Research **(5)** .... (gradually / destroy) some boundaries between man and other animals. Other species share abilities that once **(6)** .... (be) considered exclusive to humans, including some emotions.
A few years ago, Dennis the duckling and Fred the Labrador **(7)** .... (provide) a wonderful example of animal friendship. The dog and his owner Jeremy **(8)** .... (find) and **(9)** .... (rescue) Dennis and the two animals **(10)** .... (become) friends.

Present perfect continuous and duration form

3 READ sentences 1-3 and answer questions A-C.

1 What a delicious smell! Susan **has been baking** biscuits.
2 Scientists **have been trying** to improve this theory for decades.
3 Many **have been playing** the game ever since.

Which sentence
A describes the beginning of an action which has continued ever since up to the present?
B emphasises the length of time an action has been happening?
C describes the present effect of a recent and continuous action which may or may not be completed?

Grammar reference 1.7

FREQUENT MISTAKES *For and since*

4 READ the sentences and decide if there is any difference in meaning. What information is being highlighted in each sentence?

1 I have been studying English **for** ten years now.
2 I have been studying English **since** I started school.

Grammar reference 1.8

5 COMPLETE the sentences using the present perfect simple or continuous of the verbs in the box.

browse ▪ keep ▪ stand ▪ make ▪ lead ▪ know ▪ cry ▪ not meet ▪ attend ▪ have ▪ be (X2)

1 My brother........................ (always) by me in times of trouble.
2 Kate and I went to London together last summer and we .... in touch ever since.
3 'How long .... (you) this car?' 'For a month.'
4 Your eyes are red. Obviously you .... !
5 .... (your uncle) a very solitary life since his wife died?
6 Jacob and Sarah .... the same club for months but .... yet.
7 We .... very close since we met last summer.
8 Bob Graham, my new IT teacher, ... (recently) new acquaintances in the school.
9 Most young people .... the net ever since they were children.
10 'How long .... (he) her best friend?' 'He .... her for more than 20 years.'

6 COMPLETE the second sentence using the word in capital letters so that it has a similar meaning to the first sentence.

1 Carol fell in love with Brian when she saw him for the first time. SINCE
Carol .... they met.
2 Everyone is here now so we can start the meeting. ARRIVED
Everyone .... so we can start the meeting.
3 When did they get engaged? LONG
How .... engaged?
4 The last time they had a row was two months ago. FOR
They .... two months.
5 They began to get on well when they were children. BEEN
They .... they were children.
6 They stopped hanging out together two weeks ago. NOT
They .... together for two weeks.

WARM-UP

1 **WORK** in pairs. Ask and answer questions about your family and friends.

1 What is your family like? Are there many of you?
2 Who is your favourite relative? Why?
3 Would you like to have a small or a large family when you grow older? Why or why not?
4 What is the best way to spend time with friends?

C Developing social interaction

2 **LOOK** at the photograph. Who do you think these people are and what are they doing?

3 1.10 **LISTEN** to a student doing Part 1 of the Speaking exam and tick the questions which correspond to each answer given by the speaker.

The place where you live
- [x] Where are you from?
- [ ] How long have you lived in your town?
- [ ] What do you like about your town?

Your family
- [x] Do you have a large family?
- [x] What's your father's / mother's job?
- [ ] Do you spend much time with your family?
- [ ] What do you do together?

Your home
- [x] Do you live in a house or a flat?
- [ ] What do you like about your house?
- [ ] Do you have a garden?

Study / Work
- [x] How long have you been learning English?
- [ ] Do you like studying languages?
- [x] What do you find difficult about studying English?
- [x] Do you have a favourite subject?

Hobbies / Interests
- [x] What do you do in your spare time?
- [x] What do you like doing with friends?
- [ ] Do you practise any sports?

Future plans / ambitions
- [x] Have you decided what to do when you finish school?
- [x] What job would you like to do?
- [ ] What are your personal ambitions?

4 1.10 **LISTEN** to the exam again and decide on a mark out of five to give the candidate (1 = weak; 5 = excellent). Compare your mark to your classmates' and give reasons for your grading.

VIDEO
Speaking Part 1

EXAM DESCRIPTION	
What is there in Speaking Part 1?	An interview between the examiner and two candidates. Each candidate is asked questions about his or her personal details and given the opportunity to talk about what he or she does and his/her likes and dislikes.
What do I have to focus on?	It is important to appear relaxed and give complete answers – not just 'yes' or 'no' – but not take too long as each candidate must have time to speak.
How long does it last?	Two minutes.
Mark scheme	The mark scheme ranges from 1 (weak) to 5 (excellent).

FIRST Speaking – Part 1

5 **INTERVIEW.** Roleplay in groups of three. Using some of the questions in exercise 3, take turns being the interlocutor, the assessor and the candidate.

PROCESS LANGUAGE

Speaking – Part 1

Giving personal information
Hello. / Good morning. / Good afternoon.
How do you do. / Nice to meet you.

I come from …
I've always lived …

There are (three) of us in my family. There is me, …
My father/mother is a …

What I like about my house is …

I'm in the third year of High/Secondary School …

I like doing …

I think I will … but I haven't decided yet.
My ambition is …

Speaking reference p. 194

6 **PREPARE** a brief speech presenting yourself to the class. Talk about your family, where you live, your interests and hobbies, and your aspirations for the future.

WARM-UP

1 DISCUSS in pairs. On what occasions during the year does your family get together for a special meal or a party or to celebrate a family event?

2 LOOK at the following pictures of occasions or celebrations and label them in pairs.

3 ADD a further two events that are special in your family.

C Listening for specific information

VIDEO
Listening Part 1

EXAM DESCRIPTION	
What is there in Listening Part 1?	A series of unrelated extracts of about 30 seconds each with people talking in different situations (monologue, dialogue, answer-phone).
What do I have to focus on?	Listening for clues which will help to understand who is talking, what the speakers are talking about and how they feel.
How many questions are there?	You have to answer eight multiple-choice questions. Each question has three options (A, B or C).
How many marks do I get?	One mark for each correct answer.

FIRST Listening – Part 1

4 1.11 **EXTRACTS WITH MULTIPLE-CHOICE QUESTIONS.** You will hear people talking in eight different situations. For questions 1-8, choose the best answer (A, B or C).

1 You hear a young man talking about Christmas.
Why is it difficult for the young man's family to get together at Christmas?
- A Because there are so many people in the family.
- B Because they all want to share out the different responsibilities.
- C Because some of the family live in different countries.

2 You hear a girl talking about her cousin's degree ceremony.
The young girl is studying hard at the moment because
- A she wants to go to university.
- B she wants to work as a management trainee.
- C she wants to finish her degree.

3 You hear two friends talking about last weekend.
Why is the Notting Hill Carnival special for Pete?
- A Because it is where he remembers meeting his friend John.
- B Because it is where he met someone special to him.
- C Because there were so many happy people.

4 You hear a message on Tom's answerphone.
What are Tom's family celebrating at the weekend?
- A His gran's fiftieth birthday.
- B His grandparents' fiftieth wedding anniversary.
- C His parents' fiftieth anniversary.

5 You hear two girls chatting on the phone.
Why doesn't Sophie borrow Leah's dress for the wedding?
- A Because it's the wrong colour.
- B Because it belongs to her sister.
- C Because her sister wants her to wear black.

6 You hear a woman talking about Pancake Day.
When does the annual pancake race take place?
- A On Ash Wednesday.
- B At the beginning of Lent.
- C On the day before Lent begins.

7 You hear a man talking to a shop assistant.
What kind of bracelet does the man decide to buy?
- A A simple but interesting charm bracelet.
- B A fancy silver bracelet.
- C A simple but interesting silver bracelet.

8 You hear a public announcement.
What is everyone asked to do?
- A Either enter or leave the square.
- B Stay where they are.
- C Listen to the clock and watch the fireworks.

C Discussing ideas and relating them to personal experience

5 WHAT occasions have been important in your life so far?

21ST-CENTURY SKILLS

VIDEO
Teenagers and families

C Watching and understanding a short film

1 ▶ **WATCH** the video and say if the following sentences are true (T) or false (F). Correct the false ones.

1 Kayla feels like talking to her brother when she has something on her mind. T F
2 Lydia does not like having to look after her little brother. T F
3 The boy in the dark T-shirt always goes to the cinema with his family at weekends. T F
4 The boy with the striped V-neck thinks that the parents of an only child can never become his friends. T F
5 Will says that his sister fills the house with dancing and songs. T F
6 Kayla feels uneasy about her brother calling her a loser. T F

2 ▶ **WATCH** the video again and decide who says the following: Charlie (C), Kayla (K), Lydia (L), Tim (T).

1 Don't really feel like letting them into my life. ...
2 It's part of my job, as, you know, a member of the family I do have to look after my siblings. ...
3 It's kind of hard to get along with him sometimes. ...
4 The best thing about having a little sister is somebody to pick on. ...
5 You always have somebody to talk to or hang out with. ...
6 I've a big sister who I can really talk to about a lot of stuff. ...

3 **DISCUSS.** Which of the teenagers do you identify with? Why?

4 **READ** the following statements by teenagers about how their families have shaped them. Which are true for you? Would you add any others?

1
My family has taught me they will always be there for me. They have helped me fight important battles and support me in the battles I have to fight alone.

2
My family has taught me that family identity is important. What I do doesn't only reflect on me, but also on my family.

3
My family has taught me how to laugh at myself. I've learnt that failures are not always that terrible and that I won't be loved less.

4
My family has taught me how to make important decisions.

5
My family have made it easier to learn to be self-confident.

LEARN BY DOING

DECISION MAKING

5 **READ** the following text. What are difficult decisions you might have to take?

Making decisions is not easy. Some people get nervous when it comes to making decisions because they're afraid they'll make wrong choices. While decisions like which shoes to wear with which trousers don't require a detailed planning process, decisions such as choosing a university course, moving out on your own, getting a job or just focusing on school, deciding whether your friends are true friends, or whether or not to report bullying you witnessed usually require more reflection. To help you with difficult decisions, there are some steps you can follow:

Step 1 Write down the problem.
Step 2 Write down what is important to you (your values, people's opinion, etc.).
Step 3 Write down your possible options.
Step 4 Write down the good and bad aspects of each option.
Step 5 Compare the good and bad aspects and make your decision.
Step 6 Create a plan to carry it out.
Step 7 Measure the results and rate your decision.

6 **CREATE** a form with the 7 steps and complete it about a problem you have to face. Explain to the rest of the class what the problem is, what decision you made to solve it, who/what helped you make that decision.

WARM-UP

1 **DISCUSS** in pairs. Family occasions are meant to be happy and serene, but sometimes there can be tensions and disappointments. Talk about what is positive and what can be negative about family get-togethers.

C Expressing ideas and opinions in an essay

2 **DECIDE** if the following sentences about essay writing are true (T) or false (F).

1 An essay is always written for a teacher and should have a formal style. T F
2 Grammar and spelling accuracy are less important than vocabulary. T F
3 A good essay is well organised with a clear introduction, development and conclusion. T F
4 You should not include personal opinions in an essay. T F

3 **PUT** the following parts of an opinion essay into the logical order.

A ☐ developing points on one side
B ☐ introduction – presenting the situation
C ☐ conclusion
D ☐ developing the points on the opposing or different side

4 **READ** the following essay and say which paragraphs correspond to the points in exercise 3.

Are surprise parties a good idea?

In theory, the idea of surprise parties sounds wonderful, but I think there are several points to consider before arranging one.

First of all, not all people enjoy surprises. There are some people who don't like anything unexpected. Also, you need to really think about who you are inviting and whether this person gets on with that person.

On the other hand, surprise parties are a wonderful sign of affection. Arranging one shows your friend or family member that you have spent a lot of time and have taken a lot of trouble – just for them. This is particularly true when you are organising it in a place they really like.

Therefore, I believe that although some people are embarrassed by extra attention, most people are thrilled by a surprise party and see it as proof of their friends' and family's affection.

5 **READ** the essay again and answer the questions.

1 Is the title referred to in the first paragraph?
2 How are the second and third paragraphs linked?
3 How does the essay end?
4 What is the general tone of the essay?

VIDEO
Writing Part 1

EXAM DESCRIPTION	
What is there in Writing Part 1?	There is an essay title to respond to along with accompanying notes to guide your writing.
What do I have to focus on?	You have to write an essay giving your opinion on the essay title and reasons for your opinion, or giving two sides to the argument and then your opinion. You must use the ideas given and also provide an idea of your own. You will be judged on content, organisation and language accuracy.
How many questions are there?	One compulsory question (140-190 words).
How many marks do I get?	Up to five possible marks for this section.

FIRST Writing – Part 1

6 **AN ESSAY.** In your English class you have been talking about family occasions. Now your teacher has asked you to write an essay of between 140-190 words. Write your essay using all the notes and giving reasons for your point of view.

Why are family occasions sometimes stressful?

Notes
Write about:

1 difficulties in preparing the occasion before it happens
2 family members who don't get on
3 .... (your own idea)

PROCESS LANGUAGE

Writing – Part 1

Introducing the topic
It is well known that ... / First of all ... / Some people say that ...

Introducing and developing your positive ideas
In my opinion ... / I have found that ... / On some occasions ...

Introducing and developing your contrasting ideas
However ... / On the other hand ... / I think that ...

Concluding with your final opinion on the question
So, finally I believe that ... / Therefore ... / In the end ...

Writing reference p. 196

2 Inspirational travel

VOCABULARY ACTIVATOR

Inquadrami per guardare i video e ascoltare gli audio di questa unità

FLIPPED classroom

VIDEO Travelling

WARM-UP

1 **DISCUSS** in pairs. Why do people travel? Think of as many reasons as you can. Make a list and compare it with your classmates.

C Learning to use vocabulary in context

2 1.12 **LOOK** at the pictures and listen to five people talking about travelling experiences. Match the people to the pictures.

3 1.12 **LISTEN** again and complete the sentences.

1 Martin was travelling in Guatemala on his way to ....MEXICO........ .
2 Trudy was ....VISITING........ the Niagara Falls when she ended up at the ....CANADIAN BOARDER........ .
3 Deepak and his wife Anjali had never been to Europe so they decided ....TO FLY........ to Zurich where they ....TOOK........ a train to St Moritz.
4 They were travelling on ....THE TRAIN........ when they became separated from ....THEIR LUGGAGE........ .
5 Fiona and her friend Rod had never ....TRIED KAYAKING........ before but decided ....TO RENT........ kayaks and go into the ....OCEAN........ .
6 When Han ....WALKED TOWARDS........ the small monkey, it jumped away.

4 **DISCUSS** in small groups. Have you ever found yourself in a particular situation when travelling? What were you doing? What happened? Use the vocabulary from the Focus box.

FOCUS ON VOCABULARY

Verbs associated with travel HANDBRAKE
cross, fly, get on/off, get there, spend, reach, set off, travel

go on a journey
plan a journey/holiday/trip
take a train/bus/boat/plane
take a trip

Nouns associated with travel
destination, holiday, honeymoon, landscape, luggage, scenery

cruise: a holiday on a large boat
journey: the process of getting from one place to another
outing/excursion: a brief visit or tour
tour: a journey or trip visiting different places
trip: a specific journey
voyage: a long journey by sea

Useful expressions for travelling

- ask directions
- get lost
- take photos
- get a lift
- hitch-hike (AUTOSTOP)
- head back
- make it back
- walk towards/away from

WARM-UP

1 LOOK at the map below showing a journey across Asia and answer the questions.

1 Where did the journey start?
2 Where did it end?
3 How many countries were there to cross on the way?

C Reading, understanding and interpreting information

2 READ and listen to the article and say why the couple in the photo look happy.

The kindness of strangers

1.13

Sadie and Josh were one of eight couples who took part some months ago in a travelling competition based on the successful television series 'Peking Express'. The couples had to get from Moscow to Beijing (previously called Peking) without any money just depending on local people to look after them. The winners were the ones who reached the destination first – and Sadie and Josh did it – they won! So how did they do it? This is their explanation.

Sadie: It was unbelievably hard. We had to hitch-hike across Russia. We didn't have any money, this was one of the rules of the competition, we had to rely totally on the kindness of strangers. The first problem was getting out of Moscow but we struck lucky and got a lift with a lorry driver heading for Siberia.

Josh: We travelled with him for two days and he let us sleep in the back of the lorry – which had a heater thank goodness as the temperatures went below freezing.

Sadie: In Siberia people were incredibly hospitable though the scenery was rather monotonous – all those trees… Then we crossed the Gobi Desert – with a carpet salesman.

Josh: We slept in a huge tent, a Mongolian yurt, and they shared their food with us – mutton, rice and Mongolian beer is what we used to eat with them every day!

Sadie: This is also where we had our challenge test. We had to cover at least 20 miles on camels. I can assure you it was very uncomfortable and while we were crossing the desert, we ran into a sand storm and couldn't see a thing for hours.

Josh: Luckily our driver knew where to go. The next big problem was when we were crossing the border into China. We had to cross the Mongolian border point at Dzamin and then the Chinese border point at Erlian. They said we had the wrong visa and wanted to send us back but while we were talking to the border guards, an official arrived, stamped the visas and let us through.

Sadie: It was more difficult to get lifts in China. Lots of drivers would slow down to look at us but then drive on. Eventually just when we were giving up all hope, another lorry driver stopped and took us miles and miles and even offered us hospitality with his family.

Josh: This was a truly wonderful part of the journey. His family were really poor but so generous and insisted on giving us their bed to sleep in.

Sadie: He took us a long way towards our destination. I loved the scenery. While we were travelling through the mountains of northern China, we could even catch glimpses of the Great Wall in the distance.

Josh: And then there we were in Beijing – not only did we arrive but we got there before any of the other couples. We won!

3 **READ** the article again and do the following activities.

A1 Where did the idea of the competition come from?

A A previous travelling competition.
B A television series.

A2 What did the winners have to do in order to win the competition?

A3 Why did the contestants have no money to use for the journey?

A Because they didn't have jobs.
B Because they had no bags with them.
C Because this was one of the rules of the competition.
D Because they had to earn money on the journey.

A4 Which of the following meanings is closest to the expression 'struck lucky' as used in line 15?

A Something fortunate happened.
B They felt they were lucky people.
C Good luck followed them.
D They prayed for luck to come.

A5 Say whether the following information is true (T) or false (F).

A The first difficulty to overcome was getting out of the Russian capital. T F
B Their first lift took them across Mongolia. T F
C They slept in many different places including a lorry and a huge tent. T F
D They didn't have to ride on camels. T F

A6 What was the typical daily diet the couple used to eat in Mongolia?

A7 Say which of these landscapes they did NOT see.

A The Gobi Desert
B Siberian trees
C Mongolian yurts
D Russian mountain valleys

A8 Which of the following meanings is closest to the expression 'let us through' in line 38?

A Enabled us to climb over the border.
B Gave us permission to continue our journey.
C Showed us the easiest route.
D Allowed us to wait where we were.

A9 Which emotions did Sadie and Josh feel when they arrived in Beijing?

A10 Which of the following best summarises the content of the article?

A The explanation of a reality television show and what is expected of the participants.
B An account of the way it is possible to travel with very little money and no local knowledge.
C An account of a fascinating and difficult travelling experience within the context of a competition.
D The personal experiences of a couple who want others to follow in their paths.

C Listening for specific information

4 1.14 **LISTEN** to a young woman talking about travelling for her job. Listen again and complete the sentences with one-three words.

1 Katy loves her job but finds the amount .... difficult because she doesn't like to be away from home.
2 The two most essential things Katy can't .... are her laptop and her handbag.
3 She carries money and credit cards and basic make-up with her in case she ....
4 She likes to .... messages to friends and family while travelling.
5 The next essential she always takes with her is a pair of ....
6 Her last essential is a soft toy that has always .... her adventures.

Phrasal verbs for travelling

5 **MATCH** the highlighted phrasal verbs (1-6) in the article to their definitions (A-F).

1 ☐ take part (in)
2 ☐ get out of
3 ☐ run into
4 ☐ send back
5 ☐ head for
6 ☐ slow down

A meet unexpectedly
B go in the direction of
C participate in
D decrease your speed
E cause to return
F exit from

6 **COMPLETE** the sentences with the correct form of the phrasal verbs from exercise 5.

1 Unexpectedly in the middle of the desert we .... other couples from the competition.
2 The road was very narrow and full of bends so the cars had to ....
3 It was a great relief when we finally left the town and .... the open countryside.
4 The organisers decided to .... two couples who had lost their way.
5 Eight different couples .... the competition.
6 Many situations on our journey were difficult to ....

Past simple and past continuous

1 **UNDERLINE** examples of past simple and of past continuous in the article on page 30. Then explain the function of the two tenses.

2 **MATCH** sentences 1-3 to their uses A-C.

1 ☐ We **travelled** with him for two days some months ago.
2 ☐ While we **were crossing** the desert, we **ran into** a sand storm.
3 ☐ We **were doing** some revision while our classmates **were reading** a survey about the SDGs (Sustainable Development Goals).

A emphasise things which happened simultaneously in the past
B a past action in progress which is interrupted by a single past action
C describe an action in the past at a specific time

Grammar reference 1.5, 2.1, 2.2

3 **COMPLETE** the sentences with the correct past simple or past continuous form of the verbs in the box.

run away ▪ travel ▪ know ▪ fill in ▪ play ▪ can ▪ study ▪ not listen ▪ give up ▪ talk ▪ watch ▪ arrive ▪ give ▪ start

1 She .... the application form as the secretary .... her.
2 The burglar .... when the police .... at the house.
3 Why .... (our driver) where to go?
4 When we .... all hope, another lorry driver .... us a lift.
5 He .... to his wife while she .... to him.
6 We .... football in the park when it .... to rain.
7 At 7 o'clock I .... for my English test.
8 While we .... through the mountains of northern China, we .... even catch glimpses of the Great Wall.

Used to and *would* + bare infinitive

4 **LOOK** at the example sentences 1-2 and answer the questions below. Then decide if *used to* and *would* have the same meaning or not.

1 In the past, Mongolians **used to eat** mutton and rice and Mongolian beer every day.
A Do Mongolians still eat mutton and rice?
B Did they do so in the past?

2 Lots of drivers **would slow down** to look at us but then drive on.
A Is this a present habit or a past habit?

Grammar reference 2.3

5 **COMPLETE** these sentences about yourself with *used to* and *would*.

1 When I was three, I ....
2 When I was five, my grandfather ....
3 I ...., when I was a kid.
4 My parents .... (not) when I was fourteen.
5 I ...., but I do it now.
6 I .... a lot, but I prefer to stay at home these days.

FREQUENT MISTAKES ***Be used to / Get used to***

6 **LOOK** at the example sentences 1-2 and think about the difference in meaning. Then answer questions A-B.

1 Toby **is getting used to living** in Africa.
2 Toby **is used to living** in Africa.

Which sentence
A is a gradual process?
B is an acquired state?

Grammar reference 2.4

7 **COMPLETE** the sentences with a suitable form of *be/get used to*.

1 She is very tired this morning. She .... (go) to bed late.
2 .... (you) to our climate or do you miss the Italian sunshine?
3 When I started high school, I needed a lot of help, but now I .... (do) all the homework on my own.
4 She .... (drink) coffee and that kept her awake.
5 At first, I was really nervous about driving in England, but now I .... it.
6 Our new flat is on a very busy street. I expect we .... (accept) all that noise.

VIDEO
Reading and Use of English Part 3

EXAM DESCRIPTION	
What is there in Reading and Use of English Part 3?	A text with eight gaps to fill with one word only. The stems of the missing word are given in bold beside the text and must be changed in some way to complete the sentence correctly.
What do I have to focus on?	The focus of this part of the exam is mainly lexical but you are also required to show an understanding of structure and how the meaning or the function of words can change through prefixes or suffixes, internal changes or using compounds.
How many questions are there?	Eight.
How many marks do I get?	One mark for each correct answer.

FIRST Reading and Use of English – Part 3

1 WORD FORMATION. For questions 1-8, read the text below. Use the word given in capitals at the end of some of the lines to form a word that fits in the gap in the same line. There is an example at the beginning (0).

Space travel

Many people are **(0)** FASCINATED by the idea of space travel.	**FASCINATE**
When man **(1)** .... on the Moon in far-off 1969, some people began	**LAND**
(2) .... of rising up above the Earth. Among them Richard Branson, the	**DREAM**
famous billionaire and **(3)** .... of Virgin. Branson admitted that before leaving school he had already thought about flying off into space. Now that he is one of the	**FOUND**
(4) .... men in the world he can fulfill his dreams. In fact the first space	**RICH**
(5) .... will probably be passengers aboard his Virgin Galactic. Last year the company announced that it was ready to test the first commercial passenger spaceflight designed to carry six passengers and two pilots. On its test flight it flew to an altitude of 100 kilometres. Selected guests on board felt the thrilling	**TOUR**
(6) .... of seeing the Earth from	**FREE**
above and feeling the **(7)** .... of microgravity. A flight into space costs $250,000 but amazingly 500 people had already signed	**SENSE**
up to go before the **(8)** .... of this year.	**BEGIN**

VIDEO
Reading and Use of English Part 4

EXAM DESCRIPTION	
What is there in Reading and Use of English Part 4?	Six separate items, each with a lead-in sentence, a key word in bold and a gapped second sentence of which only the beginning and end are given.
What do I have to focus on?	You have to complete the second sentence so that it has a similar meaning to the above sentence. The gap must be filled with between two and five words including the key word in bold. The key word cannot be changed. A range of grammatical structures and lexical items is being tested.
How many questions are there?	Six.
How many marks do I get?	Two marks for each correct answer.

FIRST Reading and Use of English – Part 4

2 KEY WORD TRANSFORMATIONS. For questions 1-6, complete the second sentence so that it has a similar meaning to the first sentence, using the word given. Do not change the word given. You must use between two and five words, including the word given. Here is an example (0).

0 There was a lot of traffic and it was hard to exit the town centre.
OUT
There was a lot of traffic and it was hard TO GET OUT OF the town centre.

1 My grandfather would often talk to us about the exciting journeys he went on in his youth.
USED
My grandfather often .... about the exciting journeys he went on in his youth.

2 I once met a famous explorer just by chance.
INTO
I once .... a famous explorer.

3 The lorry was going in the direction of the harbour when the driver picked up a hitch-hiker.
FOR
The lorry .... the harbour when the driver picked up a hitch-hiker.

4 The train didn't go as fast when it reached the difficult bend.
DOWN
The train .... the difficult bend.

5 There was a storm on our flight back home.
WERE
While .... home, there was a storm.

6 I used to meet my brother after school when I was little.
WOULD
I .... after school when I was little.

READING

WARM-UP

1 **DISCUSS** in pairs.

1 Do you enjoy travelling? Which means of transport do you consider the quickest, the most comfortable and the most exotic?

2 Why did people travel in the past? What do you think had fascinated or stimulated famous travellers from the past before they set off on difficult and dangerous journeys?

C Recognising links within a text

2 **READ and listen to the article and say which famous travellers are mentioned in it.**

VIDEO
Reading and Use of English Part 6

EXAM DESCRIPTION	
What is there in Reading and Use of English Part 6?	A text from which six sentences have been removed. These sentences are placed in a random order at the end of the text with a seventh sentence that doesn't fit any of the gaps. Candidates need to choose which sentence fits each gap.
What do I have to focus on?	Follow the development of ideas and events, think of the text as a whole.
How many questions are there?	Six.
How many marks do I get?	Two marks for each correct answer.

FIRST Reading and Use of English – Part 6

3 **GAPPED TEXT. Read the article again. Six sentences have been removed from the article. Choose from the sentences A-G the one which fits each gap (1-6). There is one extra sentence which you do not need to use.**

A Now we jump on a plane, relax on a train or set out on a car journey across Europe without a thought.

B On the other hand many more took on more than they had bargained for and never returned.

C Some were fascinated by the beauty of the landscape and the less expensive lifestyle.

D I don't think so.

E The same inspiration that in more recent times led the space scientists to persevere in the conquest of space.

F Probably the first tourism began with the religious pilgrimages that wound their way around Europe in the early Middle Ages.

G It took courage and determination to set out across new territory or new seas to look for what Europeans had never witnessed before.

1.15

The art of travelling

People have travelled from the earliest times. First of all for food to find new hunting grounds, then for exploration, conquest and trade. When did people begin to travel for pleasure? **1** On foot or on horseback, these early tourists travelled in groups staying in the equivalent of hotels or hostels and sharing meals and company.

Then there was a period when travelling was regarded as an elitist activity and young aristocrats or artists headed for Italy or Greece to see the classical world. **2** Others took back samples of what they had seen, statues and paintings, to adorn their houses back home.

Discovery and exploration were another two inspiring reasons to travel. **3** Imagine the extraordinary sensations of Columbus and his crew when they first saw a coastline on the other side of the Atlantic Ocean or of David Livingstone and Henry Stanley when they realised they had found the source of the River Nile.

We owe our knowledge of the Earth as a geographic wonder, and of the cultures, traditions and languages of so many and so different nations, to those intrepid seekers, to the scientists, explorers, mountaineers and discoverers whose thirst for information and love of adventure led them into unexplored or unknown

places. **4** .... Man even managed to reach the Moon that had remained unobtainable as a destination for so long and is still seen as a challenge.

We live in an age where travel has become an everyday reality and it's hard to think back to times where each journey was a voyage into the unknown. **5** .... We wouldn't be so relaxed about travelling if there was uncertainty about ever coming back. In recent years we could take a ferry, a train or a coach from one country to another without any worry because we had the reassurance of all those travellers before us who had been travelling, and exploring and experiencing new worlds so long ago. What's more, many of them had passed on their experiences, they had written all the information down for us, as Marco Polo did, opening up all the possibilities to the East.

Has all the romance gone from travelling? Has it become too easy to buy a ticket online and, depending on our economic means, journey off to the other side of the world? **6** .... There are still places that few have managed to see, still sensations and landscapes to discover that most people hadn't dreamed of seeing before the first pictures or stories emerged. We travel to see new places but we also travel for new experiences just like all those people who have travelled before us and like them, in discovering exotically different lands and peoples, we also discover ourselves.

4 FIND the words in the text which mean the following:

1. areas where you can chase and kill animals (para. 1);
2. commercial exchange for goods (para. 1);
3. specimens (para. 2);
4. make more beautiful (para. 2);
5. something difficult to accomplish (para. 4);
6. natural scenery (para. 6).

Word formation: adjectives

Adjectives can be formed from verbs or nouns by using **suffixes**. Some of the most common are: ***-al***, ***-ary***, ***-ic***, ***-en***, ***-able/-ible***, ***-ive***, ***-ous***, ***-ful***, ***-ent***,***-y/-ly***, ***-ate***, ***-ish***.

5 FIND the adjectives in the text that are formed with the suffixes above and say from which words they derive.

6 FORM adjectives from the words in the box.

invent ▪ child ▪ comic ▪ beauty ▪ luck ▪ read ▪ fruit ▪ fatal ▪ persist ▪ consider ▪ excite ▪ station

7 MAKE adjectives from the words given to complete the sentences.

1. Many journeys in the past were extremely .... (DANGER)
2. Explorers often dreamed of finding an .... land. (IDYLL)
3. Marco Polo was .... to travel to the East when he did. (FORTUNE)
4. Early tourists had to be .... to reach a .... destination. (PERSIST/DESIRE)
5. Travelling in the past was rarely .... and usually very .... (COMFORT/PREDICT)
6. .... explorers became famous and rich in the past. (SUCCESS)
7. One of the most .... journeys of all time was on a raft across the Pacific Ocean from South America to the Polynesian islands. (IMPRESS)
8. The desire to discover new lands and learn about new countries and traditions is part of mankind's .... curiosity. (NATURE)

C Discussing and interpreting events

8 DISCUSS the questions.

1. Which were the most important or most interesting journeys in the past?
2. What difficulties did they have?
3. Have you ever been to an unusual destination?

9 WRITE a brief paragraph of 10/12 lines about the most interesting or unusual place you have visited.

Past simple and past perfect simple

1 READ sentences 1-6 and answer questions A-F.

1 The first tourism **began** with the religious pilgrimages that **wound** their way around Europe in the early Middle Ages.
2 It was the first time they **had seen** a coastline on the other side of the Atlantic Ocean.
3 The plane **had** already **taken off** when the passenger **reached** the airport.
4 Travellers **had** always **wanted** to explore new lands.
5 When Columbus and his crew **saw** a coastline, they **felt** an extraordinary sensation.
6 It **took** courage and determination to set out across new territory or new seas to look for what Europeans **had** never **witnessed** before.

Which sentence

A describes completed actions which happened in sequence?
B employs an adverb of frequency?
C describes an action which happened at a specific time in the past and is finished?
D contains an adverbial clause expressing anteriority?
E talks about a past event which happened before another past event?
F talks about the first time something happened in the past?

Grammar reference 1.5, 2.5

2 COMPLETE the sentences with the past simple or the past perfect of the verbs in brackets.

1 John .... (spend) several years travelling around the world before he .... (realise) that he .... (want) to write a book about all the things he .... (see).
2 'You .... (look) excited when you .... (come) across Susan last night.' 'Yes, it .... (be) the first time we .... (meet) since 2015.'
3 When Rachael .... (return) from her journey to Spain, she .... (start) to think of her next holiday.
4 '............ (you / get) the tickets online this morning?' 'No, I .... (already / buy) them at the travel agent's yesterday.'
5 After they .... (dream) of their trip to Portugal, the air company .... (tell) them that the flight was overbooked.
6 By the time he .... (retire), he .... (visit) every European country.

Past perfect continuous

3 READ sentences 1-3 and answer questions A-B.

1 They **had been waiting** there for more than two hours when the bus finally arrived.
2 The tourists were exhausted because they **had been riding** in the desert.
3 How long **had** he **been studying** Russian before he moved to Moscow?

Which sentence

A describes an action that started in the past and continued up until another time in the past?
B describes an action before another action in the past to show cause and effect?

Grammar reference 2.6

4 COMPLETE the sentences with the past perfect simple or continuous of the verbs from the box.

be delayed ▪ do ▪ spend ▪ wait ▪ look for ▪ decorate ▪ share

1 The group of tourists got on well because they .... meals and company.
2 She came back home because she .... all her money.
3 His hands were dirty because he .... the house all day. It was something he .... (never) before.
4 I .... for half an hour when they announced that the plane ....
5 .... (he) a new job for long when they offered him that position in the London branch?

5 COMPLETE the second sentence using the word in capital letters so that it has a similar meaning to the first sentence.

1 Tom was thrilled for his first time in New York. NEVER
Tom was thriled because he .... New York before.
2 The place looked familiar to us, but in fact it was completely new. BEFORE
Even though the place looked familiar to us, we ....
3 She made sure she had her passport before she left. AFTER
She left .... she had her passport.
4 The bus driver began driving at 7 a.m., and by 2 p.m. he was exhausted. FOR
The bus driver .... seven hours.
5 I studied all day and I was too tired to go out. BEEN
I was too tired to go out because I ....
6 We got to the party quite late and most of the guests weren't there. ALREADY
We got to the party quite late and most of the guests .... home.

- CHEETAH
- SAVANA
- SULTRY
- SAFARI
- CLAWS
- FANGS
- TIRE
- OPEN TRUCK
- DRY GRASS
- SPARE TIRE
- FUR WITH SPOTS

WARM-UP

1 **LOOK** at the photographs. In pairs, make a list of useful words and phrases to describe them.

C Developing confidence and fluency

VIDEO
Speaking Part 2

EXAM DESCRIPTION	
What is there in Speaking Part 2?	An individual 'long turn' in which each candidate has the opportunity to speak for a minute about two photos and to answer a question with a brief response from the second candidate.
What do I have to focus on?	The 'long turn' should include describing, comparing and expressing opinions.
How long does it last?	One minute for each candidate plus a thirty-second response.
Mark scheme	The mark scheme ranges from 1 (weak) to 5 (excellent).

PROCESS LANGUAGE

Speaking – Part 2

Describing pictures
To begin with ... / First of all ...
In this photo I can see ...
The people in the photo are ...
They look ...

Comparing pictures
In this picture ... whereas in that one ...
A key difference is that ...
There are more ... in this one than ...

Giving your opinion
I think ...
I prefer ... because ...
The ... is better/worse because ...
I think most people would agree that ...

Speaking reference p. 194

FIRST Speaking – Part 2

2 **INDIVIDUAL LONG TURN.** Here are two photographs showing different ways of travelling. Compare them and say how the people feel about the way they are travelling. You have one minute to do this.

What sensations and feelings do these travellers have?

- DOUBLE DECKER
- STEEPLE
- CLOCK TOWER
- ARCHITECTURE
- SITS
- ROOF
- TOURISTS
- CAMERA
- DOWN TOWN
- CENTRE

OPEN TOP

C Expressing personal opinions on a given topic

3 **CLASS DISCUSSION.** Think of unusual forms of transport and choose one to talk about to your classmates.

- Choose something which is interesting but with possible dangers attached.
- Make some notes about the possible advantages and disadvantages.
- Find a picture or illustration and be prepared to talk for at least one minute.

WARM-UP

1 DISCUSS in pairs. What kind of traveller are you? Do you need home comforts when you travel or can you survive with very little? How would you cope with only bare essentials?

2 READ the sentences in exercise 3 and try to guess what word or phrase is missing.

C Listening for specific information

VIDEO
Listening Part 2

EXAM DESCRIPTION

What is there in Listening Part 2?

A monologue which lasts approximately three or four minutes.

What do I have to focus on?

You are looking for details which can be dates or numbers, specific information and stated opinion. You will hear the text twice.

How many questions are there?

There are ten sentences with gaps to be filled with words or phrases relating to the listening exercise. The sentences are in the same order as they appear in the listening exercise.

How many marks do I get?

One mark for each correct answer.

FIRST Listening – Part 2

3 1.16 **SENTENCE COMPLETION.** You will hear a lecturer talking about an incredible voyage. For questions 1-10, complete the sentences with a word or short phrase.

While he was collecting plants as specimens in the South Pacific, Thor Heyerdahl began to doubt that people from Southeast Asia **(1)** .... to populate Polynesia.

He found that the Polynesians had a lot in common with South Americans like **(2)** .... and their physical appearance.

When he returned home, he was determined to prove that the first people who populated Polynesia had come **(3)** .... and not the West.

Heyerdahl never **(4)** .... or swim but decided to build a raft and attempt the impossible journey.

He put together a **(5)** .... and they built a raft with nine logs and an open bamboo cabin.

The name of the raft came from a legendary Peruvian **(6)** ....

The raft departed from Callao in Peru with six men on board and a Spanish-speaking **(7)** ....

They had a radio which gave them daily information about the weather but **(8)** .... would have been impossible.

They survived on **(9)** .... that landed on the raft.

All the crew, except the parrot, **(10)** .... after 101 days at sea and proved that Heyerdahl's theory was possible.

(Adapted from www.history.com)

4 DECIDE in pairs what you might say to someone who wants to set off on a journey following the prompts below.

- backpacking
- cycling
- visiting a capital city

21ST-CENTURY SKILLS

VIDEO
An amazing trip

C Watching and understanding a short film

1 WATCH the first part of the video (from 00:00 to 00.35) and write the following information:

1 the places Carolyne has travelled to: ....
2 what she thinks of Peru: ....
3 how she found the people in Peru: ....
4 who she travelled with: ....

2 WATCH the whole video and tick the things you see.

1 ☐ ancient ruins
2 ☐ people dancing in costumes
3 ☐ people crossing a lake by boat
4 ☐ mist and rain
5 ☐ an avalanche
6 ☐ people on horseback
7 ☐ coca tea leaves
8 ☐ tents
9 ☐ a signpost
10 ☐ a market

3 WATCH the video again and add the missing words to the following sentences.

1 I didn't find the .... or food difficult at all.
2 I was sitting on this .... over a lake and there was all mountain ....
3 I was just watching the .... striking on top of the mountain.
4 There was no .... going in and I just hit a .... sat down and thought, 'I can't do this'.
5 And they use it to like help with ....
6 I met one person who was really really ....

4 LOOK at this picture and answer the questions.

1 Who is the man?
2 What language did he speak?
3 What languages couldn't he speak?
4 How did he make everybody feel?

5 READ the prompts and write down the difficulties the woman had to face during her trip.

- Food
- Walking uphill
- Personal hygiene

6 EXPLAIN how Carolyne faced the problems during the trip to Peru and what she learnt about herself.

7 DISCUSS in pairs. Were you impressed by Carolyne's travelling experience? Have you had any difficult or dangerous experiences when travelling? Do you know anybody who has? What are your travelling ambitions for the future?

PROBLEM SOLVING

The ability of problem solving implies finding solutions to different kinds of non-familiar problems in both conventional and innovative ways. Effective problem solving usually involves a number of steps: identifying the problem, gaining more information about it, thinking about and analysing possible solutions, and finally taking a course of action. Here is a very simple example.

Problem	Ultimate goal
I want to take a holiday in Patagonia, but I don't know how to get there and I don't have enough money.	*I want to go to Patagonia.*

Chain diagrams can be used to represent a sequence of events needed for a solution. A chain diagram illustrates the money - transport/accommodation - holiday example as follows:

How to get the money → Find transport and accommodation → Take holiday

8 WORK in groups. Imagine you have just reached your destination by plane but you have to face one of these problems:

1 You have left your bag with passport, money and vouchers on the plane.
2 Your luggage has arrived but it's open and there are some pieces missing.
3 Your luggage hasn't arrived.
4 The hotel was overbooked.
5 You get sick during the trip.

Use chain diagrams to discuss ways of solving the problems.

9 SHARE and compare the findings of the different groups and vote for the best solutions.

WARM-UP

1 DISCUSS in pairs.

1 Travelling on your own for the first time can be daunting and exhilarating. Have you had this experience yet? Talk about the contrasting feelings of wanting to be independent but being concerned about facing new situations on your own while away from home.

2 What is a 'gap year'? Have you heard this expression? What do you think it is?

C Expressing ideas and opinions in an essay

2 READ the following points for and against a gap year and put them in order of importance for you and your classmate.

FOR
- ☐ it will look good on your CV
- ☐ you could learn another language
- ☐ you could learn new skills
- ☐ you could see interesting new places
- ☐ seeing different realities would help you understand and appreciate your own
- ☐ you will meet interesting new people from all over the world

AGAINST
- ☐ expensive
- ☐ you could be homesick
- ☐ it could be risky
- ☐ you might find yourself a year behind
- ☐ it could be stressful
- ☐ it could be difficult to fit back in when you return

3 READ the following points of view about spending a year away from home and discuss which is most similar to the way you might feel.

'I spent my gap year as an assistant teacher in a village school in Africa. The reality of such a different way of life was very difficult to adjust to but I felt I gained an enormous amount as a person. I now know that I am capable of accepting and making the most of difficult situations and coping on my own.'

'I liked the idea of the voluntary work building shelters in the Brazilian jungle but when I arrived I found the heat, the insects and the very basic living conditions too hard. I couldn't fit in and couldn't really communicate and left the camp after the first month.'

TIP An essay should be well organised, with an introduction, the candidate's opinion on the ideas given, the candidate's own idea and an appropriate conclusion.

FIRST Writing – Part 1

4 AN ESSAY. In your English class you have been talking about gap years. Now your English teacher has asked you to write an essay of between 140-190 words.
Write your essay using all the notes and giving reasons for your point of view.

Is it a good idea to take a year off between finishing school and starting a university course or a job?
Notes Write about:
1 how it can be an enriching experience 2 how it could be unsettling 3 .... (your own idea)

PROCESS LANGUAGE

Writing – Part 1

Sequencing

first/firstly, second/secondly/ ...
then/next/in addition/further/also/ ...
finally/in conclusion/to summarise/all in all/ ...

Giving examples

for example/for instance ...
that is ...
such as ...

Making contrasts

however ...
nevertheless ...
although/though/but ...
despite/in spite of ...
while/whereas ...
on the other hand/on the contrary ...

Writing reference p. 196

Review Units 1-2

VOCABULARY ACTIVATOR

1 CHOOSE the correct alternative to complete the sentences.

1 My aunt has a lot of *acquaintances / relations* that she has met casually but not many real friends.
2 It is often said that we can choose our friends but not our *contacts / relations*.
3 My *contacts / relations* on social media have reached 500!
4 Which is the best part of the holiday, the *journey / travel* or the arrival at your *excursion / destination*?
5 On our holiday in the mountains the *scenery / country* was amazing!
6 We tried hitch-hiking to get back to our campsite but we got *hidden / lost* and had to ask for *directions / indications*.

2 COMPLETE the sentences using the phrases in the box. You may have to change them.

feel close to ▪ get a lift ▪ be in touch with ▪ make it back ▪ walk away from ▪ share problems

1 There are not many people I .... but those few relationships are really important to me.
2 That man is not very courageous, he is the kind that .... any possible difficulties.
3 Can I .... with you tomorrow morning? My dad's car is at the mechanic's.
4 John hurt his foot during the race and almost didn't .... to the stadium.
5 I attended an international summer school in July and now I .... students from all over the world.
6 One of the best things about having friends is having someone to .... with.

GRAMMAR

3 CHOOSE the correct alternative to complete the sentences.

1 'What *do you do / are you doing* this evening? Can you *come / coming* to the gym?' 'No, I'*m studying / study* for the geography test on Thursday and anyway I'*ve been / went* to the gym three times this week.'
2 'Is your dad in? I *want / am wanting* to ask him something.' 'No, he *works / is working* in Spain this week.'
3 '*Have you seen / Are you seeing* that great new detective film on at the Odeon?' 'No, I *used to / would* like detective films but I *don't like / am not liking* them any more.'
4 '*Have you run / Did you run* into Katy yet this morning?' 'Yes, I *have run / ran* into her at the bus stop.'
5 I *just spoke / have just spoken* to Jeff. He's on holiday by the sea and he says it's cold and it *rains / is raining*.

4 COMPLETE the text using the correct form of the verbs in brackets.

Some of the most interesting journeys begin with a simple idea. My friends and I **(1)** .... (chat) and relaxing one afternoon when one of us **(2)** .... (receive) a text message from a cousin in Mexico. The cousin, Marco, **(3)** .... (think) about a trek in the Mexican mountains and **(4)** .... (ask) my friend Jim if he **(5)** .... (want) to join him. Well, to cut a long story short, we all **(6)** .... (join) him. We **(7)** .... (set) off by plane one frosty morning in January and **(8)** .... (arrive) at our destination, Mexico City, at 4 o'clock in the afternoon. The next morning we **(9)** .... (walk) around this wonderful old Aztec city high in the central mountains when we **(10)** .... (meet) our guide. He **(11)** .... (take) us to Puebla where we **(12)** .... (explore) the ancient pyramid at Cholula and then we **(13)** .... (head) for the ruins at Oaxaca. The wonderful thing was that while we **(14)** .... (move) around we **(15)** .... (also / admire) the historic sites and the magnificent views.

USE OF ENGLISH

FIRST Reading and Use of English – Part 1

5 MULTIPLE-CHOICE CLOZE. For questions 1-8, read the text below and decide which answer (A, B, C or D) best fits each gap. There is an example at the beginning (0).

NETWORKING

Networking is a process that **(0)** FACILITATES the exchange of information and ideas among individuals or groups that share a common interest. It can be a way for friends to keep **(1)** .... or be connected for reasons to do with finding jobs or creating working possibilities. The network can be based on shared interests or shared experiences; people you **(2)** .... to school with; people you **(3)** .... with now or simply people it's fun to **(4)** .... a laugh with.
Networking **(5)** .... much easier due to social networking websites. There are networking platforms, which **(6)** .... online meeting places to join groups, post blogs, share content and create online profiles with the objective of connecting and **(7)** .... with other people that have similar interests. Although you don't physically go out with these contacts, you can learn to **(8)** .... people.

0	**A** is facilitating	**B** **facilitates**	**C** facilitated	**D** facilitate
1	**A** in touch	**B** on touch	**C** touching	**D** by touch
2	**A** been	**B** goes	**C** have went	**D** went
3	**A** worked	**B** have worked	**C** are working	**D** works
4	**A** be	**B** have	**C** had	**D** need
5	**A** has become	**B** have become	**C** became	**D** becoming
6	**A** is providing	**B** provided	**C** provide	**D** provides
7	**A** hang out	**B** hanging out	**C** hanging on	**D** hanging into
8	**A** be with	**B** share	**C** make up	**D** get on with

FIRST Reading and Use of English – Part 2

6 **OPEN CLOZE. For questions 1-8, read the text below and think of the word which best fits each gap. Use only one word in each gap. There is an example at the beginning (0).**

A JOURNEY TO A DIFFERENT WORLD

Five kilometres, or 3.1 miles, is not a great distance on land but five kilometres vertically in the ocean separates different worlds. This year I **(0)** ......HAD...... the opportunity to make that short journey to another world on the first manned mission to the deepest known hydrothermal vents, five thousand metres down on the ocean floor.

The goal of the expedition **(1)** .... to study the limits of life at deep-sea vents in the Cayman Trough which scientists have **(2)** .... studying for years. I **(3)** .... already led a British expedition the year before investigating the same vents with a remotely operated vehicle, so I was delighted to join the team in one of the few machines that can carry people beyond five kilometres deep.

This is a water world without walls, inhabited by creatures of ethereal beauty. From the vantage point of my 10-centimetre porthole, I was watching and **(4)** .... photos of life forms with outlines like blown glass, while small crustaceans **(5)** .... hovering around like flies, keeping pace with our descent.

At five kilometres deep, our time on the sea floor was limited to three-and-a-half hours and all too soon, the visit to the vents was over, and we began to head **(6)** .... to the world above. Here there is no one to ask for **(7)** .... if you get lost, but the deep ocean had one more gift to give. With the lights switched off during ascent, I pressed my face against the porthole like I **(8)** .... to do as a child waiting at the window, and saw the bioluminescent displays of deep-sea animals: brilliant flashes of light in the darkness – an unforgettable spectacle.

FIRST Reading and Use of English – Part 3

7 **WORD FORMATION. For questions 1-8, read the text below. Use the word given in capitals at the end of some of the lines to form a word that fits in the gap in the same line. There is an example at the beginning (0).**

AROUND THE WORLD IN 80 DAYS

In Jules Verne's classic adventure novel, the protagonist, Phileas
Fogg, **(0)** ......HAD...... a really difficult time trying to travel **HAVE**
around the world in 80 days. Nowadays **(1)** .... **CIRCUMNAVIGATE**
it is **(2)** .... much easier, all you need is **BECOME**
a round-the-world (RTW) ticket. In fact, a dedicated
(3) .... could probably manage the entire trip in **TRAVEL**
less than a week.

If you have 80 days to spare, however, you have enough
time for a life-changing trip, and the **(4)** .... to **OPPORTUNE**
visit places that will stay with you forever. Careful planning is
essential even if it's easier than it **(5)** .... to be. **USE**

Buying an RTW ticket is less **(6)** .... compared to **EXPENSE**
purchasing separate tickets linking each of your
(7) .... These tickets allow you to visit up to **DESTINY**
16 different places with a minimum of three stops. Decide
whether you plan to travel east or west as you have to head in
one direction or the other and keep **(8)** .... the **MOVE**
same way. Also, just like Phileas Fogg, you have to start and
finish your journey in the same place.

FIRST Reading and Use of English – Part 4

8 **KEY WORD TRANSFORMATIONS. For questions 1-6, complete the second sentence so that it has a similar meaning to the first sentence, using the word given. Do not change the word given. You must use between two and five words, including the word given. Here is an example (0).**

0 When I saw the tourists, they were going in the direction of the Cathedral.
WALKING
When I saw the tourists, THEY WERE WALKING TOWARDS the Cathedral.

1 It's very dark, I hope the mountaineers are able to return soon.
MAKE
It's very dark, I hope the mountaineers .... soon.

2 When he was still at school my dad would make friends very easily.
TO
When he was still at school my dad .... very easily.

3 The cruise ship left ten minutes before we arrived at the port.
ALREADY
When we arrived at the port, ... left.

4 Yesterday my brother and I cycled from London to Brighton for the third time.
HAVE
My brother and I .... from London to Brighton.

5 We usually have holidays by the sea but this year we have chosen the mountains.
HAVING
We usually have holidays by the sea but this year .... in the mountains.

6 My two brothers are constantly arguing.
ALWAYS
My two brothers .... rows.

3 Job opportunities

VOCABULARY ACTIVATOR

Inquadrami per guardare i video e ascoltare gli audio di questa unità

FLIPPED classroom

VIDEO
Jobs and work

WARM-UP

1 MATCH the professions in the pictures to their job titles (1-12).

1 accountant
2 beauty therapist
3 blogger
4 electrician
5 freelance journalist
6 health and safety inspector
7 human resources manager
8 IT consultant
9 laboratory technician
10 marketing manager
11 personal trainer
12 occupational psychologist

2 DISCUSS in pairs. Which of the above professions appeals to you? Which would you like to do in the future?

C Learning to use vocabulary in context

3 2.1 **LISTEN** to six people describing what they do and match them to one of the professions in exercise 1.

1 PERSONAL TRAINER
2 BLOGGER
3 FREELANCE JOURNALIST
4 ACCOUNTANT
5 ELECTRICIAN
6 OCCUPATIONAL PSYCHOLOGIST

FOCUS ON VOCABULARY

4 MATCH the expressions for the workplace (1-12) to their meanings (A-L).

1 ☐ get the sack/be sacked/be fired
2 ☐ get/be promoted
3 ☐ go on strike
4 ☐ resign
5 ☐ retire
6 ☐ apply for
7 ☐ be made redundant
8 ☐ commute
9 ☐ take time/a day off
10 ☐ unemployed
11 ☐ work from home
12 ☐ work/do overtime

A have no job
B work extra hours for extra money
C reach the end of your working life
D lose your job
E accept a leaving offer
F absent yourself from work
G decide to leave your job
H have a rise in salary and responsibility
I do your work without going into an office
J withdraw your labour
K write asking for a specific job
L travel to work every day

5 CHOOSE the more suitable phrase to complete the sentences.

1 After working as a health inspector for forty years, Jamie decided it was time to *be fired* / *retire*.
2 Martin *resigned* / *got the sack* when he was offered a better job in another company.
3 Many students *are unemployed* / *apply for a job* for a while after they leave university.
4 The electricians voted to *have a day off* / *go on strike* in order to get more money and better conditions.
5 When the human resources manager called Judy to her office, she *promoted* / *commuted* her.
6 In order to get a promotion you need to *take time off* / *work overtime*.

WARM-UP

1 **DISCUSS** in pairs. Many students at school now will enter professions in the future that don't yet exist. What do you think these jobs may be? Which jobs might disappear?

2.2

The 'new economy'

Whatever you think of the 'gig' economy (a labour market characterised by the prevalence of short-term contracts or freelance work, as opposed to permanent jobs), it does give us a taste of the jobs we will be doing in the future. Set Sar, of Providence, Rhode Island, for example, earns money by looking at videos and web pages on his computer while having his eyeball movements tracked via webcam. The information this provides is valuable to advertisers – and earns him a dollar every few minutes. The gig economy has already led to a range of jobs with 'consultant' in their title, as people find ingenious ways to help the rich. In New York, for example, 'play-date consultants' charge up to $400 an hour to teach the children of millionaires to share their toys. The bad news (or good, depending on your viewpoint) is that this process will not be slowing down.

Will work be reverting to the previous model? No, work is going to become even more fragmented and insecure. The concept of a 'job for life' will soon have disappeared. In the future, it seems doubtful whether 'jobs' as we know them will exist at all. Many, of course, will have become redundant by the much-prophesied automated takeover of everything from truck driving to brain surgery. But, that is only half the story. After this becomes common, something more basic will change. The old idea of office-based, nine-to-five employment that has defined our working lives for at least a century will have disappeared.

Many jobs – certainly most white-collar ones – consist of a range of different tasks, the majority of which can be performed by anyone with an Internet connection. So why employ one person to do them all, when that also involves renting office space, investing in training, paying benefits and employing managers to supervise? Why not, instead, cut jobs up into their component parts, and contract these out to specialists? In many industries this is already happening, and contractors here will soon have replaced full-time employees.

Such a future will, no doubt, have undesired consequences. When this happens, unemployment will rise and while this is happening, wages will drop. A new model of welfare will have to emerge, to ensure that those pushed out of the workplace can survive. For the unskilled and un-enterprising, the fragmentation of work is especially dangerous. Blue-collar workers are already getting a foretaste of what will be happening as employers extricate themselves from their traditional obligations by forcing employees to work on zero-hours contracts where no particular number of hours or times of work are specified and people can be called in to work at the last minute.

On the other hand, the new order will have its advantages. One, perhaps, will be the demise of office work. Offices are often depressing places, incompatible, for many, with a sense of self-respect. People also dislike having bosses and in the new working world, the old boss will have disappeared as employees become freelance. Many will be enjoying the freedom to work where they want, in their own time, rather than among people and in a place not of their choosing – things that people increasingly value.

(Adapted from an article by William Skidelsky, in the Financial Times, April 2017)

C Reading, understanding and interpreting information

2 **READ** and listen to the article and decide which of the highlighted words has the following meaning:

1 people working in an office
2 people doing manual tasks
3 financial contributions for present or future needs
4 working independently not in a particular company
5 someone who gives professional or expert advice
6 the act of seizing authority or control
7 economic and social assistance given by government
8 the end of something

3 READ the article again and do the following activities.

A1 What does the gig economy give us according to the article?

A The possibility of determining the way the future will change jobs.

B An idea about the new kinds of jobs that we will be doing in the future.

A2 Which two examples does the article give of new jobs?

A3 How will work be changing in the near future according to the article?

A It will revert to a previous model.

B There will be a 'job for life'.

C It will become more insecure.

D The changes will begin to slow down.

A4 Which of the following meanings is closest to the word 'redundant' as used in line 22?

A Repetitive.

B In excess to requirements.

C Necessary.

D Unattractive.

A5 Say whether the following information is true (T) or false (F).

A The pattern of our working lives is changing dramatically. T F

B In the past people wanted the security of fixed working hours and workplace. T F

C Many of the office-based tasks can be done on computers. T F

D Employers prefer having their staff in an office. T F

A6 Which are the two disadvantages of the new economy according to the article?

A7 Which employees are most at risk?

A8 Explain the term 'zero-hours contracts' (lines 48-49) in your own words.

A9 Which two advantages does the new type of working life offer according to the article?

A10 Which of the following best summarises the content of the article?

A The way careers are changing is a challenge that white and blue-collar workers must resist.

B The changes in the working world are happening very quickly and it is important to try to block the consequences.

C The way people work is changing and will continue to change to adapt to the new economy; some changes will be positive but they may also bring problems.

D In the future, the workplace will disappear and humans will no longer have to earn wages.

C Listening and understanding information

4 2.3 **LISTEN to a radio programme about how to be successful in business. Then listen again and decide which of the following is true for which speaker. Write M for Mary, A for Andrew and C for Catherine.**

1 Learn from those who have done the same before you. ......

2 The most important thing is to believe in what you do. ......

3 Don't stick to the idea of a working life of nine-to-five. ......

4 Be prepared to become freelance. ......

5 Be optimistic about the future. ......

6 If you can't find what you want, produce it yourself. ......

Phrasal verbs and collocations for jobs and work

5 MATCH the phrasal verbs and collocations (1-8) in the article to their definitions (A-H).

1 earn money

2 charge (up to)

3 nine-to-five

4 working lives

5 contract out

6 make a living

7 call back

8 job share

A set hours of employment

B return a telephone call

C earn enough money to live on

D receive payment in return for work done

E divide the working week with a colleague

F the phase of your lives in employment

G demand as payment

H use someone external to do a specific task

6 COMPLETE the sentences with the correct form of the phrasal verbs and collocations from exercise 5.

1 In the future, fewer people will be working the traditional ....

2 I'm expecting an important phone call from the human resources manager. If she phones while I'm out tell her I'll .... her .... as soon as I can.

3 Many people have to choose between job satisfaction or .... a lot of ....

4 Consultants can .... £1000 a day for their specialist services.

5 It can be difficult to .... on a part-time job.

6 In the future, ... may last much longer.

7 When the IT consultant wanted a shorter working week, she decided to arrange a .... with a colleague.

8 Rather than keep an office and permanent staff, companies in the future will be .... much of the routine work.

Future tenses

1 READ sentences 1-5 and answer questions A-E.

1 Work **is going to become** even more fragmented and insecure.
2 I don't think this process **will slow down**.
3 My flight for Rome **leaves** at 10 a.m. tomorrow morning.
4 You look tired. Sit down and I'**ll make** you a cup of tea.
5 They **are cutting** jobs up into their component parts in a month.

Which sentence describes
A a regular or time-tabled event?
B a fixed or planned appointment or arrangement?
C a plan or intention?
D a prediction we think, guess or calculate will happen?
E a spontaneous decision?

Grammar reference 3.1

2 COMPLETE the sentences with the correct future form of the verbs in brackets.

1 It's so hot in here! I .... (turn) the air conditioning on.
2 'Next month my sister .... (be) eighteen.' 'What .... (you / organise) for this important occasion?'
3 'What time .... (your train / leave)?' 'It .... (depart) at 7.00 and .... (arrive) at 9.00.'
4 Do you think we .... (have) time to read the whole novel in a week?
5 How long .... (they / stay) at the seaside?
6 Do you think your brother .... (remember) to call Mrs Brown this evening?
7 I think I .... (go) home now. It's getting late.
8 We .... (leave) by the 4 o'clock train.

Future continuous and future perfect

3 READ sentences 1-2 and answer questions A-B.

1 The process of the gig economy **will not be slowing down**.
2 In the future world the old boss **will have disappeared** as employees become freelance.

Which sentence refers
A to an action that will already be completed before another time or event in the future?
B to an action that is going on at a particular time in the future or over a period of time in the future?

Grammar reference 3.2, 3.3

4 COMPLETE the sentences with the future continuous or the future perfect of the verbs in brackets.

1 Mary and Bill .... (live) in Australia this time next year.
2 He .... (run) 26 miles when he finishes the marathon.
3 By the end of today, how many phone calls .... (you / make)?
4 We .... (do) too many exams by the end of our school career!
5 Just think, next Monday you .... (work) in your new job.
6 This time next week, you .... (study) Maths at university.
7 Meet me at the café near our school at 4.00. I .... (sit) at a table outside.
8 The students .... (leave) the classroom by the end of the hour.

FREQUENT MISTAKES **The future with time clauses**

5 READ sentences 1-3 and underline the verbs. Then highlight the time expressions. What do you notice about the tenses?

1 After this becomes common, something more basic will change.
2 When this happens, unemployment will rise.
3 By the time you have finished your work, the football match will have finished.

Remember
You can find either a present tense or a present perfect in the time clause.

Grammar reference 3.4

6 MAKE a single sentence of the following using the time expressions given in brackets.

1 Tom is waiting at the bus stop. He will still be there when the bus comes. (UNTIL)
2 You will have made dinner. Bill will come back home. (BEFORE)
3 My mother will be thinking of me. I will be doing my science exam. (WHILE)
4 First I will finish my homework. Then I will phone my friends. (AFTER)
5 My sister will take the dog out. She will do it the minute she gets home. (AS SOON AS)
6 They will demolish all the houses in the street. The month of October will be over. (BEFORE)
7 I'll come back and I'll do it. (WHEN)
8 I'll have finished my lesson at school by noon. I'll come round. (AFTER)

TIP Before you look at the gaps, you should read through the whole text so that you have a general idea of the content before looking at each individual gap.

FIRST Reading and Use of English – Part 1

1 MULTIPLE-CHOICE CLOZE. For questions 1-8, read the text below and decide which answer (A, B, C or D) best fits each gap. There is an example at the beginning (0).

Interviews

Job interviews can be very **(0)** COMPETITIVE and require careful preparation. First of all, read the **(1)** .... description carefully to think about the questions they will be **(2)** .... you during the interview. Think about where you **(3)** .... be working and who you may be working **(4)** .... and be prepared to answer questions about your feelings on these issues. Find out as **(5)** .... as you can about the company, how it started, how it has grown and what it will **(6)** .... achieved within the near future. Who are its main competitors? Find out about them, too. Remember, they will be asking questions about your qualifications and experience and also about what you think you **(7)** .... have achieved in ten years time. Once you have done the homework about the job, think about your appearance. What clothes are suitable? Discard the jeans and T-shirts you **(8)** .... wear at school and choose something formal and neat but something you feel relaxed in. You want to appear confident and relaxed, so go for sober colours and a clean tidy appearance and if you want, add a bright tie or scarf to give a little personal touch.

	A	B	C	D
0	competing	**competitive**	competed	competition
1	job	work	position	jobs
2	made	had	used to	asking
3	shall	will	going to	are
4	on	in	by	with
5	soon	many	much	little
6	have	has	had	been
7	be	are	will	won't
8	used	used to	wore	will

TIP When you look at the stem word given, think of all the variations that can be formed, remembering also the prefixes and suffixes, before you make your choice. For example, 'employ' gives 'employer', 'employee', 'employment' and also 'unemployment' or 'unemployed'.

FIRST Reading and Use of English – Part 3

2 WORD FORMATION. For questions 1-8, read the text below. Use the word given in capitals at the end of some of the lines to form a word that fits the gap in the same line. There is an example at the beginning (0).

A job for life

Have you ever **(0)** WONDERED what it must be like to be a future monarch? It looks quite **(1)** .... but in reality you will be spending most of your life waiting for your job to begin. Of course, while you are waiting you will be living in luxury, **(2)** .... will be taking pictures of your every move, servants will be attending your every need, but you won't be **(3)** .... the job you were born for and of course it is **(4)** .... for you to know when your real job will begin. When you **(5)** .... make it to the top job, you will have **(6)** .... most of your life doing other things like representing the country abroad, attending official functions and maybe wondering what life is like for most people whose working life is centred around organising work, home and family on a limited wage. We are all fascinated by the idea of **(7)** .... and interested in hearing about their lives and speculating on their actions but would we really like to swap places with them? Maybe not, an **(8)** ...., simple life has a lot going for it.

WONDER
GLAMOUR
PHOTO
DO
POSSIBLE
EVENT
SPEND
ROYAL
COMPLICATE

WARM-UP

1 DISCUSS in pairs. Why do you think the possibility of introducing students into real working environments is considered important? Do you think it is useful or a waste of precious school time?

C Recognising links within a text

2 READ and listen to the blog and say which of the possibilities most appeals to you.

VIDEO
Reading and Use of English Part 7

EXAM DESCRIPTION	
What is there in Reading and Use of English Part 7?	A text or several short texts preceded by ten multiple-matching questions. Candidates must match each question to one of the paragraphs by looking for information in the text.
What do I have to focus on?	Specific information, detail, opinion and attitude.
How many questions are there?	Ten.
How many marks do I get?	One mark for each correct answer.

FIRST Reading and Use of English – Part 7

3 MULTIPLE MATCHING. Read the blog again. For questions 1-10, choose from the people (A-D). The people may be chosen more than once.

Which person

thinks the work experience brings added benefits like increased confidence and new skills? 1

thinks that the placements offer an interesting alternative to being at school? 2

has worked for a newspaper and will be going to a lawyer's office? 3

has doubts about achieving all the promised aims of the placement? 4

says students will have learned useful skills in international operations connected to several countries? 5

thinks it's a good idea to have a variety of experiences? 6

considers the work experience a good way of finding out which career you may go for? 7

talks about the possibility of selecting an area within the company? 8

learnt a lot of practical office skills? 9

thinks Sandie may be interested in a career using Maths? 10

Work experience

2.4

Hi there! I'm looking for advice. I'm currently studying for my A Levels (Maths, English, French and Sociology) but I haven't decided what I will be studying at university. We are being offered various work experience possibilities this year and I was wondering what you out there found interesting or worthwhile or relevant???? **Sandie**

A Megan

Hi Sandie, my view is definitely go for the work experience that appeals to you 🙂 and possibly in two completely different working environments so you have a wide choice when you have to choose what to study at uni. I did work experience at *The Guardian* newspaper last year and we did workshops on video editing and new feature writing. I had to create a short film using material from the Guardian's Katine project in Uganda and also had to research, plan and write a magazine style feature based on the current news agenda. This year I will be applying for a law office placement for a week in June. They have promised that by the end of the week I will have learned to deal with the office routine and practical skills like answering the phone and arranging appointments for the clients.

B Joel

As you're doing Maths you could consider a banking company. Our school has an on-going arrangement with an international banking company where students are introduced to the various aspects of a global investment bank. The chairman of the company gave a presentation to our class last week. Students who go there will be taking part in seminars, interactive presentations, case studies and group exercises. After a week's placement, students will have basically learnt a little about the technology and operational processing needed for global reach and will also have formed invaluable networks for a possible future career in the world of the banker. 🙂

C Vicky

Hi Sandie – you're right, it's not easy to choose where to go but anything is a refreshing change from sitting boringly at a school desk! 🙂 I'm about to go on a week's placement to a technology company. According to their website, students applying to join the Work Experience programme will be working on exciting projects relating to space imaging, the medical industry or ground-breaking work in microwave technology. Sounds good! Whether I manage to do all of that well or not, I guess it will give me an insight into a possible future career.

D **Martin**

One of the best Work Experience programmes I've heard of, is run by a famous pharmaceutical company. They have a Work Inspiration scheme for 14-19-year olds in their Nottingham head office. It's run once a year usually in June and the students accepted onto the scheme will be choosing from a number of areas including, Commercial (branding and marketing), Customer Care, HR (Human Resources), Finance, IT, Manufacturing, Opticians and Group. They will also be receiving inspirational talks from the staff as well as working in teams to complete challenges. Hopefully by the end of the placement, you will have had the chance to develop your skills, grow your confidence and learn about the business world. 🙂 Hope this helps!

4 **FIND** **the words in the text which mean the following:**

1. valuable enough to justify the time or effort spent (para. 1);
2. a column, cartoon, etc., appearing regularly in a newspaper or magazine (para. 2);
3. continuing without ending or without interruption (para. 3);
4. the act of filling a position (para. 3);
5. innovative (para. 4);
6. penetrating mental vision or discernment (para. 4);
7. make a version of a product, as indicated by a trademark (para. 5).

Word formation: adverbs

Adverbs are commonly formed from adjectives by using the suffix ***-ly***: *current* + *ly* = ***currently***.

- In adjectives ending in *-y*, the *y* becomes an ***-i***.
- In adjectives ending in *-able/ -ible/ -le* the *e* is replaced by ***-y***.
- In adjectives ending in *-ic*, add ***ally*** with the exception of *public*.
- Some adverbs remain the same as the adjective, e.g. ***fast***, ***hard***, ***late***. The adverb for *good* is ***well***.
- Some adverbs are formed with the suffix ***-ward***, ***-wards*** or ***-wise***, e.g. *afterward, backwards or clockwise.*

5 **FIND** **the adverbs in the text and say from which words they derive.**

6 **FORM** **adverbs from the adjectives in the box.**

early ▪ beautiful ▪ other ▪ steady ▪ scientific ▪ down ▪ miserable ▪ happy ▪ fatal ▪ noisy

7 **MAKE** **adverbs from the words given to complete the sentences.**

1. Education is not just about academic learning but should help students adapt ......EASILY...... to the working world. (EASY)
2. Whether the experience goes ......WELL...... or ......BADLY...... students in any case have the opportunity to see what a possible job might be like. (GOOD / BAD)
3. Many students found the work experience difficult at first because they weren't used to working ......HARD...... for eight hours a day. (HARD)
4. By the end of the week or two weeks, students will have discovered a lot about their own learning skills and their ability to work ......SYSTEMATICLY...... . (SYSTEMATIC)
5. Companies have commented on the way students take up the challenge of a new environment and often perform ......ABLY...... and ......IMPRESSIVELY...... . (ABLE, IMPRESSIVE)
6. With the possibility of work placements students will also have acquired new relevant experiences to add ......IMMEDIATELY...... to their CVs. (IMMEDIATE)

C Discussing ideas and relating them to personal experience

8 **DISCUSS** **the questions.**

1. What do you see as the possible advantages or disadvantages of work placements?
2. Do you think they should be connected to your future career or not?

9 **WRITE** **a brief paragraph of 10/12 lines about the benefits of work experience. What skills do you think you will have gained from a placement?**

Articles

1 READ sentences 1-4 and answer questions A-D.

1 My view is definitely go for **the** work experience that appeals to you.
2 I had to plan and write **a** magazine style feature based on **the** current news agenda.
3 Students applying to join **the** Work Experience programme will be working on exciting projects.
4 This year I will be applying for **a** law office placement for **a** week in June.

A Does the article in the first sentence refer to something specific or one of many?
B Which article in the second sentence refers to one of many?
C Is 'the Work Experience programme' one specific programme or one possibility among many?
D Which article or articles in the fourth sentence refer to one of many possibilities?

Grammar reference 3.5, 3.6

2 CHOOSE the correct option: *the, a(n)* or – (no article) to complete the sentences.

1 I like *the / a /* – lot of sugar in my coffee and *the / a /* – little milk.
2 On *the / a /* – Continent traffic keeps on *the / a /* – right but in *the / a /* – UK it keeps on *the / a /* – left.
3 He works as *the / an /* – accountant and has recently had *the / a /* – rise in *the / a /* – salary.
4 What *the / a /* – pity you can't take *the / a /* – break. I'm going to have *the / a /* – snack.
5 *The / A /* – Mount Etna is *the / an /* – active volcano in *the / a /* – Sicily.
6 *The / A /* – Thames flows right through *the / a /* – city of *the / a /* – London.
7 *The / A /* – problem for *the / a /* – today's young people is to find *the / a /* – job.
8 They will be going on *the / a /* – cruise in *the / a /* – Mediterranean as *the / a /* – present for their wedding anniversary.

3 COMPLETE the sentences with *the, a(n)* or – (no article).

1 He was .... first man to cross .... Atlantic on .... sailing boat.
2 Susan doesn't like .... work as .... receptionist she does in .... new company. She doesn't like .... answering the telephone at all.
3 We're having .... party on .... Friday. Why don't you come and bring .... friend?
4 'Who was .... cute girl I saw with you .... last night?' 'She was .... new student, you know, ... one who comes from .... France.'
5 'Would you like .... beer with your meal?' 'No, thank you. I prefer .... water.'
6 Paul got .... degree in .... Psychology from .... university of Edinburgh.

FREQUENT MISTAKES Uses of articles

4 LOOK at the sentences and decide which one is correct and which three do not have the correct use of articles. Then explain and correct the mistakes.

1 If the Mr Wilkins calls, tell him I'm not in office.
2 I like my present job but it is not the one I am going to do forever.
3 My sister is the my best friend.
4 The most important things in friendship are the trust and the loyalty.

5 FIND and correct the 12 mistakes regarding the use of articles in the text.

Some jobs are so specific that they need the detailed and specific skills, or some just need someone mad enough to take on job.

Take the tea sampler, for example. Person who does this job for a living needs to know names and flavours of all different varieties of tea. But it goes from the extreme of pet food taster paid at just £20,000 the year to a sublime of bed warmers and professional queuers.

Of course, there are dream jobs children spend their lives wanting to be, including waterslide tester.

Queen's official main piper's duty is to play the bagpipes under her window at the 9 a.m. every weekday for about 15 minutes.

SPEAKING

WARM-UP

1 DISCUSS. In your final years at school, you will be thinking about a future career. What do you think you will have decided by the time you leave?

C Expressing and defending your opinions

VIDEO
Speaking Part 3

EXAM DESCRIPTION	
What is there in Speaking Part 3?	A two-way conversation between the two candidates. The candidates are given spoken instructions as well as written stimuli to be used in a decision-making task.
What do I have to focus on?	The focus is on expressing opinions, exchanging ideas, sustaining the interaction, making and evaluating suggestions and coming to a decision through negotiation and discussion.
How long does it last?	About 4 minutes.
Mark scheme	The mark scheme ranges from 1 (weak) to 5 (excellent).

PROCESS LANGUAGE

Speaking – Part 3

Expressing opinions
I think that ... / In my opinion ...
I would also like to say ...
I'd like to make a further point ...

Agreeing
Of course, ... / You're right but ...
That's a good point ... / I agree ...

Disagreeing
I'm afraid I don't agree ...
That's not how I see it ...

Giving reasons or examples
... because ... / ... such as ... / ... like ... / for example ...

Taking the discussion forward
... on the other hand ..
Don't you think ....
... what's more ...

Speaking reference 195

FIRST Speaking – Part 3

2 COLLABORATIVE TASK. Imagine you are looking at career choices. Here are some possible careers. Talk in pairs about the advantages and disadvantages of the various careers shown (two minutes). Then decide which two you would most like to do (one minute).

lawyer – teacher – physiotherapist – tour guide – chef – sports coach

Which career would give the most satisfaction?

What skills could students learn from these activities?

C Developing social interaction

VIDEO
Speaking Part 4

EXAM DESCRIPTION	
What is there in Speaking Part 4?	A discussion on topics related to the collaborative task (spoken questions).
What do I have to focus on?	The focus is on expressing and justifying opinions, agreeing and/or disagreeing and speculating.
How long does it last?	About 4 minutes.
Mark scheme	The mark scheme ranges from 1 (weak) to 5 (excellent).

Speaking reference 195

FIRST Speaking – Part 4

3 DISCUSSION. In groups of three ask and answer the questions.

1 Is it true that certain jobs are more suitable for women and certain jobs should be done by men?
2 What gives the best job satisfaction? The salary or the usefulness or the stimulating nature of the work?
3 Which professions exist now that weren't here 50 years ago?

1) FREELANCE WRITER JOKES CHRISTMAS CRACKERS FORTUNE COOKIES 300000000 X YEAR
2) QUEUER LATEST COMPUTER GAME, CONCERT, PAID BY THE HOUR / 96 HOURS
3) INSPECTOR AND TASTER BROKEN STRANGE TASTE CLEAN NO TEA OR COFFEE
4) COOL HUNTER PREDICT FUTURE TRENDS NOTICE / FIND INFORMATION CHAT ROOMS AND GATHER INFO

WARM-UP

1 DISCUSS in pairs.

1 Is it possible to create a job based on your own personal interests? Do you have a particular skill or hobby that might become a paid job?

2 What do you think a pet psychologist or a colour consultant do?

C Listening and comparing different options on a given topic

VIDEO Listening Part 3

EXAM DESCRIPTION

What is there in Listening Part 3?

Five short related monologues of approximately 30 seconds each. The multiple-matching questions require the selection of the correct option from a list of eight.

What do I have to focus on?

You are looking for the overall meaning, detail, function, purpose, attitude, opinion, relationship, topic, place, situation, genre or agreement.

How many questions are there?

Five.

How many marks do I get?

One mark for each correct answer.

FIRST Listening – Part 3

5) ADVERTISING SECTION INVENT 100 000 NAMES SUNSET ON THE SEE UNDER THE MOON

2 🔊 2.5 **MULTIPLE MATCHING.** You will hear five different people talking about unusual jobs. For questions 1-5, choose from the list (A-H) the type of activity that each speaker does. Use the letters only once. There are three extra letters which you do not need to use.

TASTE BUDS = PAPILLE

A I do something other people don't have time for.
B I have to be particularly inventive when describing colours.
C I find the job boring but I enjoy earning the money.
D I use my profession to make extra money part-time.
E I'm doing the job now but I'll be looking for a change soon.
F I need to be careful about what I drink.
G I will have worked for the same company for ten years by the end of this year.
H I'm paid to keep up-to-date with what's popular.

Speaker 1	D	1
Speaker 2	A	2
Speaker 3	F	3
Speaker 4	H	4
Speaker 5	B	5

C Discussing ideas and relating them to a specific experience

3 WORK in pairs. Invent an unusual job and decide on what the job would entail. Then write a brief job description.

VIDEO
Running an art gallery

C Watching and understanding a short film

1 BEFORE watching the video, match the words (1-10) to their meanings (A-J).

1 ☐ off the back
2 ☐ carpentry
3 ☐ prior
4 ☐ time-consuming
5 ☐ tricky
6 ☐ free-flowing
7 ☐ loaded
8 ☐ random
9 ☐ juggle
10 ☐ get by

A previous
B difficult
C handle two or more activities
D manage to continue
E together with, meanwhile
F unexpected
G smooth, available
H making things in wood
I busy
J taking a long time

2 WATCH the first part of the video (from 00:00 to 01:45) and write the following information:

1 The speaker's work experience: ....
2 How he started his own gallery: ....
3 His education: ....
4 What he dislikes about his job: ....
5 How many days the gallery is open: ....
6 What he does the rest of the time: ....

3 WATCH the whole video and put Andy's actions in the right order.

A ☐ He sits at his desk in front of his computer.
B ☐ He sees to a visitor who has just gone into the gallery.
C ☐ He works at pictures on his computer.
D ☐ He talks to a visitor of the gallery.
E ☐ He deals with the installation of an artists's work.
F ☐ He opens folders on his computer screen.
G ☐ He talks about a work of art with the artist herself.
H ☐ He hangs a picture on the wall.
I ☐ He walks towards the gallery.

4 WATCH the video again and write the missing words about the way Andy makes decisions.

I generally make decisions based on **(1)** .... I generally find that my first **(2)** .... on an issue is normally the best way of **(3)** .... with it. When it comes to **(4)** .... a show, for example, the kind of first **(5)** .... of images, first idea for the installation, is the one I'd want to **(6)** .... to after. Whether the **(7)** .... agrees or not is a different thing but personally I feel that my instinct is pretty **(8)** ....

5 WATCH the last part of the video (from 02:18 to 03:54) and write down Andy's

1 best career decision: ....
2 greatest strength: ....
3 greatest weakness: ....

6 DISCUSS in pairs. What is Andy's secret of success? Do you find his work experience interesting? Would you like to do a similar kind of job? Why or why not?

7 DISCUSS. Do you think Andy is a flexible person? Why or why not?

BEING FLEXIBLE

Flexibility includes the willingness and ability to respond readily to changing circumstances and expectations. It implies understanding each situation and doing different tasks to reach workable solutions but also being able to deal with praise, criticism and setbacks in a positive way. It finally means acting on feedback effectively.

8 FOCUS on the following questions and answer them.

1 How flexible are you at school, in relationships, in other important aspects of your life?
2 What are the obstacles to being flexible?
3 Do you think being flexible might mean 'being weak or passive'?

9 DISCUSS in groups these tips to expand your capacity for flexibility in your life. Which do you find most effective? Which do you already practise?

1 Let go of your attachment.
2 Be prepared to be wrong.
3 Don't take life too seriously.
4 Go with the flow.
5 Get support and feedback from others.

10 SHARE and compare the opinions of the different groups and vote for the most flexible group in the class.

WARM-UP

1 **DISCUSS.** The list below shows a variety of possible summer jobs for students. Do any of them appeal to you? Why or why not?

- assistant sports trainer
- assistant teacher
- barman
- hotel receptionist
- shop assistant
- summer camp animator
- swimming instructor
- waiter

C Writing a formal letter

2 **READ** the formal letter below and match the various parts (1-10) to their position (A-J) on the layout of the letter.

Formal letters follow a very clear and rigid format:

1 ☐ making a specific request
2 ☐ formal greeting
3 ☐ signature of writer
4 ☐ giving extra information
5 ☐ date
6 ☐ writer's name and address
7 ☐ formal salutation
8 ☐ reference
9 ☐ name or position, company and address of recipient
10 ☐ saying clearly what you are writing about

(A) #5, 4344 Modoc Road
SANTA BARBARA
93110 California
USA

(B) The Manager
Agriturismo Il Borro
125 Località Campogialli
52028 Terranuova Bracciolini
AREZZO
Italy

(C) 14th May 2017

(D) **Reference: Visit to Italy**

(E) Dear Sir,

(F) I am writing to enquire about a stay of two or three nights at your hotel. We will be visiting Italy during the month of September and will be staying in Florence from 10th-11th so we would like to come to you immediately after those dates.

(G) Please let us know about your availability and about the various sports and leisure activities you offer.

(H) We have been given your name by some very good friends who recommend your services highly.

(I) I look forward to hearing from you at the address above,

Yours truly,

(J) *Paul Robinson*
Paul Robinson

VIDEO
Writing Part 2

EXAM DESCRIPTION

What is there in Writing Part 2?	In Part 2, there is a choice of tasks. Questions 2-4 are general questions, based on a range of topics, such as health and fitness, sport, music and so on. The tasks for questions 2-4 may include any of the following task types: an article, a letter/ email, a review, a story. Question 5 is an essay based on a set text.
What do I have to focus on?	Each task gives you a specific purpose and target reader to focus on.
How many questions are there?	The chosen task needs to be between 140-190 words.

FIRST Writing – Part 2

3 **A FORMAL LETTER.** You have been asked to reply to a customer enquiry (see the enquiry attached on the left). Write your letter in 140-190 words making reference to the pictures.

PROCESS LANGUAGE

Writing – Part 2 (a formal letter)

Greetings / Salutation
Dear Sir or Madam, ... Yours faithfully / Yours truly
Dear Mr Brown, ... Yours sincerely

Introduction / Why you are writing
I am writing to enquire about ... / I would like to ...

Further details
The date would be ...
We can discuss further details ...
If you are available and interested ...

Requesting a response
I would be pleased to hear from you at your earliest convenience ...
I look forward to hearing from you ...

Writing reference p. 200

4 The crime scene

Inquadrami per guardare i video e ascoltare gli audio di questa unità

VOCABULARY ACTIVATOR

FLIPPED classroom

VIDEO Crime

WARM-UP

1 DISCUSS in pairs.

1. Make a list of ten actions that might be criminal activities. Then compare your list with another pair of schoolmates.
2. Which crimes would you consider to be relatively new, connected to the Internet or new uses of technology?

C Learning to use vocabulary in context

2 CHOOSE the correct alternative to complete the definitions.

1. Someone who steals from a bank is a *robber* / *burglar*.
2. Someone who steals from a shop is a *pickpocket* / *shoplifter*.
3. Someone who spoils public buildings is a *vandal* / *hooligan*.
4. Someone who kills someone else is a *mugger* / *murderer*.
5. Someone who takes control of a vehicle by force is a *hijacker* / *blackmailer*.
6. Someone who steals someone else's property is a *thief* / *terrorist*.
7. Someone who brings goods or people into a country illegally is a *drug dealer* / *smuggler*.
8. Someone who steals information from your computer is a *kidnapper* / *hacker*.

A

B

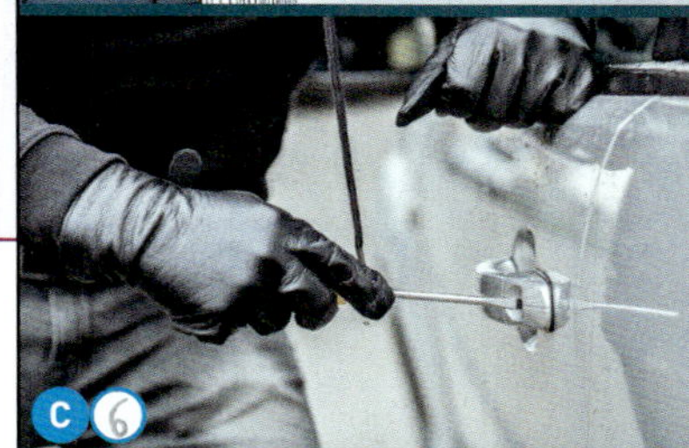
C

D

E

F

3 MATCH the pictures to one of the crimes deriving from the criminals in exercise 2.

4 2.6 **LISTEN** to the description of four famous crimes and match them with the criminals below.

A [ ] a burglar
B [ ] a terrorist
C [ ] a robber
D [ ] a hijacker

FOCUS ON VOCABULARY

5 MATCH the expressions (1-12) to their meanings (A-L).

1. [ ] break the law
2. [ ] confess to (a crime)
3. [ ] get away with
4. [ ] go to jail/be sent to prison
5. [ ] break out (of jail)
6. [ ] be caught red-handed
7. [ ] be found innocent/guilty
8. [ ] track down
9. [ ] let (someone) off
10. [ ] act on (information)
11. [ ] be sentenced to
12. [ ] be convicted of

A be seen committing a crime
B follow the evidence
C admit to doing something wrong
D be given a punishment
E be judged for a crime
F declare someone innocent
G do something illegal
H escape from prison
I be found guilty of a crime
J receive a prison sentence
K take action after hearing something specific
L avoid punishment for what you've done

6 DISCUSS in pairs the difference in meaning for these expressions with 'crime':

- commit a crime
- report a crime
- carry out a crime
- beat crime
- turn to crime
- solve a crime

WARM-UP

1 **DISCUSS** in pairs. Do you download music or films or video games from the Internet? Is it legal to do this or is it a crime? Who is hurt by it?

C Reading, understanding and interpreting information

2 **READ** and listen to the article and decide which of the highlighted words has the following meaning:

1 something serving as a cover or disguise for an illegal activity
2 people selling goods in the street
3 income
4 rules concerning the legal ownership and control of a literary, musical, artistic, or other work

2.7

Intellectual property theft: is it a crime?

Piracy of intellectual property, which is protected by copyright law, is a serious crime. It robs the makers of recordings, videos, movies, games, and other creative works of the money they are entitled to, and it could make thousands of people lose their jobs each year. It can also deprive governments at all levels of essential tax revenue. Piracy itself is illegal, and it may cause an increase in other types of crime. Gangs and organised crime groups are both linked to the piracy of creative work.

Pirated materials are often sold on the streets. Street vendors' stalls lend colour and atmosphere to our city streets, and there are many that might sell CDs and DVDs, but be careful because a few of them may be acting as fronts for criminals that are making money from the goods they may have counterfeited. You can also purchase these pirated materials in stores and on the Web.

Piracy might take place in boarding schools, colleges, bedrooms, and recreation rooms where anyone could illegally download tunes or movies. All that is needed is a computer and access to the Internet. Making unauthorised copies of these creative works is against the law, and breaking it may subject the person who does it to civil and criminal liability – especially if they distribute the stolen product to others. Could you go to jail? The answer is yes, the penalties for first-time offenders include a jail sentence of up to five years and fines of up to $250,000.

The individuals and industries that produce the original goods that are subsequently pirated could be important to national economies. The entertainment industry in the United States, for example, employs 2.9 million people, or 2.1 percent of all US jobs. But each year, more than 300,000 people that depend on copyrighted industries can lose their jobs as a direct result of piracy. This might not just include the authors of creative works, but there must be an effect on all those who derive an income from producing and distributing their work.

The most familiar type of piracy is the illegal copying and distribution of music, movies, and games that individuals have been able to download from the Internet. Downloading these products – if you pay for them or have permission – isn't a crime, but may become a crime if they are sent to others or widely distributed. You can easily post a tune or movie on the Internet where it might live forever – but the artist who created the product may never receive any form of income.

The attraction of piracy is due to its anonymity and the ease with which people manage to make illegal copies of software and succeed in distributing it. However, every person who makes illegal copies could be contributing to the monetary losses caused by piracy. Pirating software costs everyone. The software manufacturers must raise prices because fewer copies of software are sold. This means that the legitimate users pay more due to piracy. In short, piracy is not as 'victimless' a crime as it may seem. Software developers, distributors, and, ultimately, end users, are all hurt by piracy.

3 **READ** the article again and do the following activities.

A1 **Which are the four reasons why piracy of intellectual property is considered a serious crime by the article?**

A2 **Why could it be illegal to buy from street vendors?**

A They sell goods of an inferior quality for exaggerated prices.

B They may be selling goods that have been illegally copied.

A3 **What kind of people download illegally according to the article?**

A All those who stay in boarding schools or colleges.

B Anyone who has access to recreation rooms.

C Anyone with a computer and access to the Internet.

D Those with permission from the owners and sellers.

A4 **Which of the following meanings is closest to the word 'subject' as used in line 24?**

A control

B main part of a sentence

C expose to

D influence by

A5 **Which are the two forms of possible punishment for those committing this crime?**

A6 **Say whether the following information is true (T) or false (F).**

A The industries involved in producing music, films and books provide work and useful revenue. T F

B The entertainment industry in the US accounts for just over 1% of all employment. T F

C Many different kinds of job are affected by piracy. T F

D Piracy does not just affect the original authors and creators of the products downloaded. T F

A7 **Which is the most common type of piracy according to the article?**

A8 **Which two factors make piracy attractive according to the article?**

A9 **Explain the term 'victimless' as used in line 59 in your own words.**

A10 **Which of the following best summarises the content of the article?**

A Piracy has become very popular, especially among young people and actually doesn't really cause any economic problems.

B Illegally downloading music, films, games or books from the Internet may not seem to hurt anyone but the financial consequences can be very widespread.

C Those involved in creating products like music, films, video games and books need to protect their work in a more efficient way.

D The Internet can be seen as an efficient and exciting way to find new audiences for music, films, books and games but it needs to be regulated in a more serious fashion.

C Listening and understanding information

4 2.8 **LISTEN** to a discussion about graffiti. Then listen again and decide which of the following statements is true (T) or false (F).

1 For the local authorities graffiti is a form of vandalism. T F

2 Although it destroys buildings, they do not see it as a crime. T F

3 Many graffiti artists might be first-time offenders. T F

4 Local authorities want more tolerance towards graffiti artists. T F

5 The art teacher disapproves of graffiti as an artistic expression. T F

6 She thinks there may always have been examples of a kind of graffiti. T F

7 She thinks it can be a powerful and peaceful form of protest. T F

8 Local museums might be a good place for graffiti art. T F

Collocations and expressions for crime

5 **MATCH** the highlighted collocations and expressions (1-6) in the article with their definitions (A-F).

1 ☐ victimless crime

2 ☐ illegal counterfeiting

3 ☐ organised crime groups

4 ☐ first-time offenders

5 ☐ (civil and criminal) liability

6 ☐ end users

A organisations that specialise in criminal actions

B those who have not committed any previous offense

C a crime in which no-one suffers

D those who ultimately use the product

E legal responsibility

F make copies without permission

6 **COMPLETE** the sentences with the correct collocation or expression from exercise 5.

1 I truly believe there is no such thing as a ....

2 Downloading illegally is carried out by many individuals for their own use, but .... do it to make money.

3 It is a good idea to try and avoid any activity that might lead to ....

4 Sometimes the .... have no idea where the goods they buy come from.

5 The jail sentence might be short because the robbers are ....

6 It is becoming increasingly difficult for some authors to make a profit on their work because of ....

Modals of ability, possibility and permission

1 READ sentences 1-7 and answer questions A-G.

1 Piracy **can/could** also deprive governments at all levels of essential tax revenue.
2 I have passed my driving test, so I **can** drive on my own.
3 Piracy **may/might/could** take place in boarding schools, colleges, bedrooms, and recreation rooms.
4 The US movie and television industries **could** produce a trade surplus of more than $13 billion in past years.
5 Individuals **have been able to** download from the Internet.
6 When I was six, I **could** surf the Internet.
7 **Can/Could/May** I download the new song by Maroon 5 from your mobile?

Which sentence talks about

A ability in the present?
B possibility in the present, the future or generally?
C ability in the present perfect?
D possibility/probability in the present or generally?
E ability in the past?
F general possibility in the past?
G permission in the present, the future or generally?

Grammar reference 4.1

FREQUENT MISTAKES ***Could / Manage to / Succeed in / Be able to***

2 READ the examples and decide if there is any difference in meaning. What information is given in each sentence?

1 By the time she was ten, my little brother **could download** songs and films from the net.
2 People **manage to make/succeed in making/are able to make** illegal copies of software with great ease.

Grammar reference 4.2

3 COMPLETE the sentences in a positive (+) or negative (-) way.

1 It was very icy, but they (+) .... keep the car on the road.
2 If I keep practising, I know I (+) .... to pass my driving test next year.
3 (+) .... I touch your computer screen to download that file?
4 You (+) .... make money by selling your notes on that novel.
5 I (-) .... understand a word she said because she spoke too quickly.
6 He (-) .... pass the exam. He doesn't feel very confident.

Modals of deduction

4 READ sentences 1-6 and match each modal verb to an explanation A-F.

1 ☐ There **must** be an effect on all those who derive an income from producing and distributing their work.
2 ☐ The artist who created the product **may/could/might** never receive any form of income, but we are not sure about that.
3 ☐ Manufacturers **must have** had to raise prices.
4 ☐ Criminals **may/might/could have** counterfeited those goods.
5 ☐ He **can't** be at school. His bike isn't in the parking place.
6 ☐ My English teacher **can't have** left because her car is still outside the school.

A The speaker thinks it is possibly true, or may be the case.
B Past situations which are possibly correct.
C Past situations which are almost certainly correct.
D The speaker is certain that something is true.
E The speaker is certain that something is not true.
F The speaker is sure that something did not happen in the past.

Grammar reference 4.3

5 COMPLETE the sentences with the verbs in brackets and a modal of deduction.

1 'Why did he leave the lecture suddenly?'
'He .... (feel) sick.'
2 It's not in my bag, it's not on my desk so my phone .... (be) in my pocket.
3 No, it's not possible! I .... (fail) that exam, I knew all the answers.
4 The passengers in the plane .... (be) extremely frightened because of the storm.
5 James looks worried. He .... (lose) his wallet.
6 You .... (see) Hugh yesterday because he is in Sweden on a business trip.

6 CORRECT the mistakes in each sentence.

1 I left my purse at home, so I may not pay.
2 He isn't in his bedroom. He can be in the garden.
3 It can be sunny tomorrow and it can be hot, too.
4 He worked hard and could finish his project.
5 Susan might not speak to David because he had already left for New York.
6 I might swim very fast when I was five.
7 Someone was ringing. It can be my brother. He promised to call.
8 He can have got that job because he looked very pleased.

TIP Although the absence or misuse of punctuation is ignored, spelling, as in all the Use of English parts of the paper, must be correct.

FIRST Reading and Use of English – Part 2

1 **OPEN CLOZE.** For questions 1-8, read the text below and think of the word which best fits each gap. Use only one word in each gap. There is an example at the beginning (0).

Elementary my dear Watson

One of the most famous detectives of all time **(0)** ...MUST... be Sherlock Holmes. I think everyone in the world would **(1)** .... to recognise him even in his American format. *Elementary* is the American drama series based on Sir Arthur Conan Doyle's famous character but with some important differences. **(2)** .... you imagine Sherlock in New York or with a female Dr Watson? Well this is what the popular series is offering. This new Holmes used to be a drug addict and **(3)** .... have been a consultant to Scotland Yard but now assists the New York City Police Department in solving crimes. Of course, being Holmes, he **(4)** .... ignore police procedure and is often **(5)** .... to get into conflict with Captain Thomas Gregson. Dr Joan Watson, who has been helping Holmes get over his drug problem, asks if she **(6)** .... act as his apprentice and companion. You **(7)** .... also enjoy seeing that Holmes's arch-enemy, Moriarty, is part of the series too, as well as a brother you **(8)** .... have heard of before as he was never mentioned and finally Sherlock's father!

TIP It is important to remember that your answer must consist of two to five words. If you write more than five words, you get no marks.

FIRST Reading and Use of English – Part 4

2 **KEY WORD TRANSFORMATIONS.** For questions 1-6, complete the second sentence so that it has a similar meaning to the first sentence, using the word given. Do not change the word given. You must use between two and five words, including the word given. Here is an example (0).

0 It is possible that she is my new neighbour but I'm not certain.
COULD
It COULD BE my new neighbour but I'm not certain.

1 Could he speak German before living in Berlin?
ABLE
Was .... German before living in Berlin?

2 Is it alright if I go out this evening , Mum?
MAY
Mum, ... this evening?

3 I'm sure it isn't Dad in the kitchen, he has just left.
CAN'T
It .... in the kitchen, he has just left.

4 The murderer wasn't the husband or the brother-in-law so it had to be the cook!
MUST
The murderer wasn't the husband or the brother-in-law so .... the cook!

5 The policeman found the robber hiding in a cupboard.
DOWN
The policeman .... hiding in a cupboard.

6 I think the Queen was possibly very shocked to find a stranger in her room.
MIGHT
I think the Queen .... very shocked to find a stranger in her room.

READING

WARM-UP

1 DISCUSS in pairs.

1. What do you think a 'cold case' might be?
2. Can you think of any examples of cold cases?

C Recognising specific information within a text

2 READ and listen to the article and say how Ötzi was killed.

TIP Remember that the 4-option multiple-choice questions are presented in the same order as the information in the text so you can follow the development of the writer's ideas as you work through the questions. The final question may require you to interpret an aspect of the text as a whole.

FIRST Reading and Use of English – Part 5

3 MULTIPLE-CHOICE QUESTIONS. Read the article again. For questions 1-6, choose the answer (A, B, C or D) which you think fits best according to the text.

1 Why did the director of the South Tyrol Museum of Archaeology, in Bolzano, Italy phone Detective Inspector Alexander Horn?

A To offer him a job in the Museum.
B To ask him to undertake an investigation.
C To ask for advice about Ötzi.
D To reveal the nature of Ötzi's death.

2 In which way is Ötzi the coldest of cold cases?

A Because he died in a glacier.
B Because he died in the high mountains where it is very cold.
C Because his body is now preserved in ice in the mountains near Bolzano.
D Because he was preserved in ice for thousands of years.

3 The cause of his death was

A a wound from an arrow in his back.
B a deep wound in his right hand.
C hunger and cold weather.
D a snow storm so that he lost his way in the mountains.

4 Research into his stomach contents showed

A he hadn't eaten for about three days.
B he was a young fit man with blue eyes and short blonde hair.
C he ate three different meals in the two days before he died.
D his normal diet contained a mixture of proteins and grains.

The coldest of cold cases

2.9

When the head of a small Italian museum telephoned Detective Inspector Alexander Horn of the Munich Police, she asked him if he investigated cold cases.

'Yes, if I need to, I do,' Inspector Horn replied, recalling their conversation.

'Well, I have the coldest case of all for you,' said Angelika Fleckinger, director of the South Tyrol Museum of Archaeology, in Bolzano, Italy and we have to find a suitable person to help us.'

The unknown victim, nicknamed Ötzi, is the world's most perfectly preserved Copper Age man. He was frozen inside a glacier along the northern Italian border with Austria until warming global temperatures melted the ice and two hikers discovered him in 1991.

The cause of death remained uncertain until 10 years later, when an X-ray showed an arrowhead in Ötzi's back, just under his shoulder. But Inspector Horn, with a huge amount of new scientific information, thought he had to piece together a more detailed picture of what had happened on that fateful day around 3300 B.C., near the top of the Ötztal Alps.

'When Angelika contacted me with the idea, my instinct told me I should say no, it was too difficult, too much time had passed and I thought to myself I don't have to do this,' said Inspector Horn. 'But actually when I began to examine Ötzi I saw he was in better condition than many recent homicide victims. It was a challenge and I thought: I must try, it is a great opportunity.'

5 Among other information Horn discovered that Ötzi

A lived in the valley below the mountain where he was found.
B had been followed up the mountain and was fleeing for his life when he died.
C had been down in the valley and was involved in a fight.
D had killed a man the day before he died.

6 Which sentence best sums up Horn's findings on Ötzi?

A He was satisfied with all the information about Ötzi and how he died and knew who killed him and why.
B He discovered all Ötzi's movements in the days leading up to the death and how Ötzi died although he knows he mustn't try to arrest his killer.
C In spite of the time difference, he managed to reconstruct Ötzi's lifestyle and how he lived.
D He discovered the cause of his death but he needed further details like the time of year or the kind of diet he ate.

The glacier and the high humidity of the ice kept Ötzi's organs and skin largely intact. 'Imagine, we know the stomach contents of a person 5000 years ago,' Inspector Horn said. 'Something we don't often in modern crimes, or have to apply for special permission for.'

'Those contents were critical in determining what happened to Ötzi,' Horn said. 'You must imagine a man 5 feet 5 inches tall (about average height for his time), who weighed 110 pounds, had brown eyes and shoulder-length, dark brown hair, and a size 7½ foot. He was about 45 and still in his prime. You mustn't think he was old or ill. Someone killed him.'

From the pollen in his digestive tract, scientists were able to place the date of Ötzi's death at sometime in late spring or early summer. In his last two days, they found, he consumed three distinct meals and walked from an elevation of about 6,500 feet, down to the valley floor and then up into the mountains again, where he died at the crime site, 10,500 feet up.

They also found a second, older wound in his right hand. From this, Inspector Horn thinks that Ötzi must have come down to his village where he became involved in a fight. After the fight, he probably had to leave and go back up the mountain. Inspector Horn reckons Ötzi didn't have to hurry. At 10,500 feet, he made what appeared to be a camp in a protected part of the mountain, spreading his belongings around and sitting down to his last meal. About half an hour later the killer arrived and shot him in the back from a distance of almost 100 feet.

'Somebody felt they must kill Ötzi. We will never know for certain why, but he obviously had a reason and my conclusion is that we ought to look at the earlier fight, if we want to find a motive. However,' concludes Horn, 'whatever the reason why the killer needed to kill Ötzi, my employers mustn't ask me to catch the murderer.'

(Adapted from an article by Rod Nordland, in the New York Times, March 2017)

4 **FIND** the words in the text which mean the following:

1 given a different name (para. 2);
2 dissolved (para. 2);
3 important, having great significance or consequences; (para. 3);
4 whole (para. 5);
5 the period or state of greatest perfection or vigor of human life (para. 5);
6 position or location (para. 6);
7 an injury (para. 7);
8 personal possessions (para. 7).

Word formation: negative prefixes

Prefixes can transform the meaning of an adjective or verb: *wise* – ***unwise***, *active* – ***inactive*** – *moral* – ***immoral***, *logical* – ***illogical***, *regular* – ***irregular***, *satisfy* – ***dissatisfy***, *use* – ***misuse***, *conformist* – ***nonconformist***.

5 **FIND** some examples of this use of prefixes in the text and say from which words they derive.

6 **TRANSFORM** the meaning of the words in the box using negative prefixes.

legal ▪ appear ▪ sense ▪ lucky ▪ desirable ▪ relevant ▪ capable ▪ legible ▪ kind ▪ honest ▪ applicable ▪ patient ▪ regular ▪ definite ▪ judge

7 **MAKE** negative meanings from the words given to complete the sentences.

1 One of the problems in making mistakes is that it is .... to .... what you have done wrong. (POSSIBLE/DO)
2 It is .... not to consider downloading as potentially .... (RESPONSIBLE/LEGAL)
3 Some people find it .... that others .... the rules. (ACCEPTABLE/OBEY)
4 There are many .... to breaking the law including a possible .... time in jail. (ADVANTAGE/COMFORTABLE)
5 Our teacher really .... some forms of .... like .... of lessons. (LIKE/BEHAVIOUR/ATTENDANCE)
6 It may well be .... and .... , but I strongly believe in dreams. (RATIONAL/LOGICAL)

C Discussing ideas and relating them to personal experience

8 **DISCUSS** the questions.

1 Why are there so many detective stories and crime series on the television? What is it about crime that fascinates us?
2 Which is your favourite detective or police investigation programme?

9 **WORK** in groups. Find out about the most famous crimes in history and prepare a presentation to the class using Power-Point.

Modals of obligation, necessity and advice

1 READ sentences 1-7 and answer questions A-G.

1 We **have to** find a suitable person to help us.
2 Inspector Horn thought: 'I **must** try, it is a great opportunity.'
3 'I **don't have to** do this,' said Inspector Horn.
4 It's something we **have to** apply for special permission for.
5 You **mustn't** think he was old or ill
6 We **ought to** look at the earlier fight, if we want to find a motive.
7 If I **need** to investigate cold cases, I do.

Which sentence describes
A a self-imposed obligation?
B the absence of obligation?
C an obligation imposed by somebody else, especially authority?
D an action required because of the circumstances?
E a prohibition?
F something that is necessary?
G something that is advisable?

Grammar reference 4.4

2 CHOOSE the correct alternative to complete the sentences.

1 You *should / must* have a driver's licence to drive a car.
2 You *mustn't / don't have to* get any money, I'm going to pay for the dinner.
3 English students *have to / ought to* wear a school uniform.
4 You *shouldn't / don't have to* drive when you have been drinking.
5 They *need to / don't need to* wear a coat, it's getting cold.
6 People *should / have to* cut down on sugar and fats. They may be dangerous for their health.
7 You *mustn't / don't have to* make unauthorised copies of creative works.
8 I *had to / should* fill in a form when I applied for this job.

FREQUENT MISTAKES *Need*

Need is a semi-modal verb because you can use it like a modal verb and like a main verb.

We use ***need* + base form** mostly in the negative form to express absence of necessity to do something.
*You **needn't** investigate any longer.*

Needn't can be replaced by ***don't/doesn't need to*** when it is followed by a verb but not with a noun.
*Mum **needn't buy/doesn't need to buy** any eggs. There are plenty in the fridge.*

But: *Mum **doesn't need** any eggs.*

Grammar reference 4.5

3 COMPLETE the second sentence so that it means the same as the first. Use the correct form of the verb *need*.

1 I had to study very hard before I could take the exam.
I .... before taking the exam.
2 Thanks, but it's not necessary for you to pay for the lunch. I have some money.
Thanks, but .... for the lunch. I have some money.
3 It's not necessary to search the house again! We have enough evidence.
You .... again! We have enough evidence.
4 It's important for her to eat more fruit.
She .... more fruit.
5 The work is very easy, so it's not necessary to stay overtime.
You .... overtime.
6 The police arrested the culprit so it wasn't necessary for the suspect to remain in jail.
The suspect .... in jail.

4 COMPLETE the sentences with the correct modal verb.

1 The police station was very crowded so I .... wait an hour to report the theft.
2 This problem .... be resolved very quickly.
3 You .... see this film! The special effects are stunning.
4 You .... pick me up, I can easily walk there.
5 You .... download tunes or movies illegally.
6 I .... see the doctor about my frequent headaches.
7 You .... be rude to the traffic warden. He is a public official.

5 COMPLETE the second sentence using the word in capital letters so that it has a similar meaning to the first sentence.

1 You aren't careful enough when you drive. BE
You .... when you drive.
2 She cleans the house more than is necessary. HAVE
She .... the house so much.
3 It is necessary to pay the bill before leaving the restaurant. TO
You .... before leaving the restaurant.
4 I recommend using a password to protect your account. MUST
You .... to protect your account.
5 It is forbidden to smoke in public places. NOT
You .... in public places.
6 I think it is wrong for you to trust everybody. OUGHT
You .... everybody.

WARM-UP

1 **DISCUSS** in pairs. Are some crimes more serious than others? Which crime should be put at the top of a list of serious crimes? Compare your answer to others in the class.

C Developing confidence and fluency

2 **LOOK** at the photographs. In pairs, make a list of useful words and phrases to describe them. Then compare your list with the expressions in the Process language box.

TIP Remember to listen carefully to the instructions which follow the words 'and say' and read the question above the photographs carefully. These instructions will give you the focus of the task and help you produce a wide range of language which is necessary in order to speak for the full minute.

FIRST Speaking – Part 2

3 **INDIVIDUAL LONG TURN.** Here are two photographs showing different crimes. Compare them and say which crime can be seen as more serious. You have one minute to do this.

WHICH CRIME MIGHT PEOPLE CONSIDER MORE SERIOUS?

PROCESS LANGUAGE

Speaking – Part 2

Describing pictures in detail
In the first picture there are ... people who are ...
There is a lady/a man wearing ...
The place in the picture looks/appears ...
The man/woman wearing ... could be a robber/criminal ...
The place in the picture must be ...

Comparing pictures
In both pictures we can see ...
The people in the second picture are dressed differently. They are wearing ...
The situation in the second picture is more/less dangerous because ...

Giving your opinion
I think she/he/it is probably ...
I think she/he/it might be ...
I imagine the people are feeling tense/nervous/afraid ...

Speaking reference p. 194

C Talking about and comparing personal experiences on a given topic

4 **CLASS DISCUSSION.** Choose one of the questions to talk about to your classmates.

- What crimes are increasing in your country? What are the main reasons for that?
- Are there any places (in this city, this country or the world) which you would avoid due to fear of crime?
- Do you think the media or politicians unnecessarily increase the fear of crime? What are their reasons for doing so?
- Are there any things which are crimes in this country but shouldn't be?
- Should the police carry guns?

WARM-UP

1 **DISCUSS** in pairs. What is a cyber-attack? Have you heard the term before? Do you know of any examples of cyber-attacks?

VIDEO
Listening Part 4

EXAM DESCRIPTION	
What is there in Listening Part 4?	An interview or exchange between two speakers and lasting 3-4 minutes.
What do I have to focus on?	The questions will be based on the speaker's opinion and attitude. You may also be asked about the main ideas and specific information as well as the general argument.
How many questions are there?	There are seven multiple-choice questions to answer, each with three options.
How many marks do I get?	One mark for each correct answer.

C Listening for specific information

FIRST Listening – Part 4

2 2.10 **MULTIPLE-CHOICE QUESTIONS.** You will hear an interview on a radio programme where a specialist is talking about cyber-crime. For questions 1-7, choose the best answer (A, B or C).

1 Who is Gordon Smith?
- A The announcer for the radio programme *Technology Today*.
- B An expert on Internet security.
- C A cyber-attacker.

2 Who or what did the WannaCry attack affect?
- A It only affected the National Health Service systems in the UK.
- B It paralysed about 20,000 systems all over the world.
- C It affected up to 200,000 computers in well over 100 countries.

3 How was it stopped?
- A It was stopped by the chance finding of a young computer researcher.
- B It was slowed down and stopped by the action of a Californian computer technician.
- C It was stopped through the action of cyber-police in Los Angeles.

4 Why might the young researcher call himself an 'accidental hero'?
- A Because he actually knows very little about cyber-crime.
- B Because he found the 'kill switch' by mistake.
- C Because he was looking for another explanation when he found the problem.

5 What must have been a very exciting moment?
- A The moment he realised he could activate the kill switch.
- B The moment he found the attack.
- C The moment he received a prize of $10,000.

6 What could Microsoft have done to prevent the attack according to the speaker?
- A He thinks Microsoft should not have stopped supporting previous systems leaving them vulnerable.
- B He thinks Microsoft invested too much in Windows XP.
- C He thinks Microsoft should organise proper back-up and viruses.

7 How should computer systems protect themselves against further attacks?
- A They should not use out-dated systems or old software from Microsoft.
- B They should ensure that their data is always backed-up and use the latest anti-virus software.
- C They need to keep up-to-date with all forms of cyber-crime available.

VIDEO
Teenagers about bullying

C Watching and understanding a short film

1 BEFORE watching the video, match the words (1-5) to their meanings (A-E).

1	[D] pick on	A	with evil intent
2	[E] witness	B	unaware of
3	[A] maliciously	C	try to gain
4	[B] oblivious	D	tease
5	[C] pursue	E	hear or see because you are present

2 WATCH the first part of the video (from 00:00 to 00:20) and write down the reasons why the teens are being bullied.

1 FOR BEING SHORT
2 BECAUSE SHE'S DIABETIC
3 STUPID REASONS just to pick on you

3 WATCH the whole video and say if the following sentences are true (T) or false (F). Correct the false ones.

1 Tim has never experienced bullying. T F
2 Lydia wanted to become part of a group she thought was fun. T F
3 The group didn't want her to be part of their group. T F
4 Thalia didn't say anything when she was being bullied. T F
5 Lydia believes there are people who want to be her friends. T F
6 Tim thinks that bullying would exist even if people tried to see the good in everybody. T F
7 Charlie thinks that if you keep it to yourself, the bullies will continue to take advantage of you. T F

4 WATCH the video again and decide who says the following: Will (W), Thalia (T), Charlie (C), Tim (Ti), Lydia (L).

1 They'd start pulling hair, fighting... T
2 I was always made fun of for being short. W
3 As soon as the bullying starts, you need to put a stop to it. C
4 But then I realised that, that I didn't really need to be part of their group. L
5 They were like 'Oh she's diabetic, she can't eat this'. T
6 I try to see the good in everybody. Ti

5 DISCUSS in pairs. Why do you think students bully others? What is the atmosphere like in your school? What can you do when you see another student being bullied? What can teachers do?

LEARN BY DOING

TAKING RESPONSIBILITY

Taking responsibility for someone else helps shape a cultural norm and build values for yourself and others. Rather than minding your own business, it's more about getting involved in a cohesive team effort.

6 WORK in groups. Imagine you have been asked for proposals to help the school reduce bullying.

A proposal is a formal way of putting forth an idea and asking for action to be taken on that idea.

Think about:

1 ways to better supervise students;
2 how families could monitor their children's behaviour or uneasiness;
3 individual responsibility or peer pressure;
4 the punishment options;
5 the possibility to create a team of students to voice teenagers' views.

7 SHARE and compare the findings of the different groups and vote for each final proposal.

8 WRITE a proposal for the school board following these steps:

Step 1 Briefly state your purpose.
Step 2 Provide some information about why you are proposing your suggestion.
Step 3 State your suggestions to the solution of the problem.
Step 4 Conclude with expected results.

WARM-UP

1 DISCUSS in pairs about crime help lines.

1 Who do you think might organise them? Who are they needed for? Who should use them?
2 Have you heard of a local help line? Should there be one in your area? If there is one, can you describe what services it provides?

C Describing and expressing ideas and opinions in an article

2 READ the following article about a new help line in a small British town. Pick out an example of:

- a fact
- a neutral opinion
- a personal opinion

NEW TOWN GAZETTE

We must unite against crime

Our reporter recently visited 'A Helping Hand', our local crime help line to find out how it might help our town. This anonymous service gives everyone the possibility to speak out against crime affecting them, their families or the community. Especially those whose personal circumstances might prevent them from contacting other authorities.

The service believes that individuals and communities should feel safe from crime and safe from the fear of crime. According to the founder, Marie Flynn, 'Our promise of anonymity means everyone can contact us without fear of intimidation or recrimination. We feel we can give vulnerable individuals a voice which could help whole communities to take a stand against crime.' Their mission has to be based on trust: trust that they can protect the anonymity of all callers and trust that the information might be treated properly and discreetly.

'A fundamental point,' says Marie, 'is that we must remain non-judgmental and apolitical. We must never judge our callers or comment on government policy or the police or anyone involved in criminal justice.'

Undoubtedly, the service is valued highly. The help line receives hundreds of calls each day. They say the nature of crime could be changing – there are fewer crimes like burglary but more violent and sexual crimes as well as rising fraud and online crimes.

3 READ the article again and answer the questions.

1 How many paragraphs are there?
2 What is the function of the first paragraph?
3 Which paragraph develops the subject of the article?
4 Which paragraph adds useful information?
5 What is the conclusion of the article and where is it given?

4 DISCUSS. What is the style and register of the article? Give some examples from the text to support your answer and say whether it is appropriate for the readers of a local newspaper.

TIP

First of all, think about who will read the article – this will determine the register (formal or informal or semi-formal).
Think about the organisation. The article should have:

- a title;
- a brief introduction to explain what the article is about;
- a development of clear points – if possible, in separate paragraphs;
- a conclusion, which should have a strong or humorous ending to make the main point.

FIRST Writing – Part 2

5 AN ARTICLE. You recently saw this notice in your local newspaper. You are going to write an article expressing your opinion. Use 140-190 words.

DO WE NEED A CRIME WATCH HELP LINE?

We all want to reduce local crime but sometimes it is difficult to be the one to speak up against criminals.
Can a help line be a good answer?
Write an article giving reasons for or against a crime help line in your area.

PROCESS LANGUAGE

Writing – Part 2 (an article)

Presenting facts
This is ... / There is/are ...
It is clear that ... / Undoubtedly ...

A neutral opinion
Many people say that ... / They say that ...
It has been suggested that ...
Most people might agree that ...

A personal opinion
I think ... / I believe ...
We think ... / We believe ...
I agree that ... / I agree with ...
According to ...

Writing reference p. 198

Review Units 3-4

ZTE ONLINE
Interactive exercises

VOCABULARY ACTIVATOR

1 CHOOSE the correct alternative to complete the sentences.

1 When Tom finishes school next summer he says he will *apply* / *resign* instantly for a job.
2 There is so much extra work in the Christmas period we will all be asked to *commute* / *do overtime*.
3 My colleague takes a lot of time off and I fear he will get *promoted* / *the sack*.
4 My uncle lost his job in a travel agency last year and by this time next week he will have been *on strike* / *unemployed* for 11 months.
5 I often wonder how many years we will have to work before we can *be made redundant* / *retire*.
6 The factory workers decided to *go on strike* / *be fired* rather than face *working from home* / *being unemployed*.

2 COMPLETE the text with a verb from the box in the correct tense.

break out ▪ get away ▪ send ▪ catch (X2) ▪ arrest ▪ break ▪ confess

My brother Jeff wants to write a detective story and says he thinks he will make a fortune. He will invent a fascinating criminal who will **(1)** .... the law constantly but will never be **(2)** .... and never **(3)** .... to a crime even if the police **(4)** .... him red-handed. His criminal will be a James Bond type figure but on the wrong side of the law who will **(5)** .... with loads of crimes but will end up being **(6)** .... and **(7)** .... to jail. The last thing to decide is whether his hero will **(8)** .... of jail or not in the future.

GRAMMAR

3 CHOOSE the correct future form to complete the sentences.

1 We are busy planning our next holiday. We *are going* / *go* to Naples and then we *are visiting* / *are going to visit* Pompeii.
2 Scientists predict that there *won't be* / *isn't going to be* an easy future for the planet unless we *will manage* / *manage* to reduce carbon emissions soon.
3 Do you know what you *will do* / *will be doing* at this time next year? Will you *study* / *be studying* or maybe you *will complete* / *will have completed* your studies and started a job?
4 'Hi Jane, *will you come* / *are you coming* to the drama rehearsal this evening?' 'No, I'm afraid I *am not* / *won't be* there, I'*m having* / *will have* an extra music lesson.'
5 'Oh dear, I feel awful; I think I've got a temperature.' 'Don't worry, I *am going to phone* / *'ll phone* the doctor.'

4 COMPLETE the sentences with a suitable modal verb and say if it is ability (A), possibility (P) or deduction (D).

1 When my dad was younger, he .... run a marathon in 4 hours.
2 We asked the maths teacher if we .... finish the lesson early because of the bus strike.
3 The air quality is pretty awful at the moment, it .... be because it hasn't rained for months.
4 'How many languages .... you speak?' 'I .... speak English and French but I .... speak German.'
5 My friends are meeting up in the centre this afternoon but I .... go, I'm going to see my aunt in hospital.
6 I've been ringing this doorbell for at least half-an-hour and no one is answering; they .... all be out.

USE OF ENGLISH

FIRST Reading and Use of English – Part 1

5 MULTIPLE-CHOICE CLOZE. For questions 1-8, read the blog below and decide which answer (A, B, C or D) best fits each gap. There is an example at the beginning (0).

MY DREAM JOB

My name is Joanne Baker and I **(0)** ....WORK.... for National Geographic. At the moment, I'm training to become an adventure photographer. I am based in Toronto Canada but soon I **(1)** .... all over the world if I succeed in getting the job. Hopefully by this time next month, I **(2)** .... my training and will be out on the road looking for the kind of views everyone dreams of. Photographers **(3)** .... be prepared to move quickly as we **(4)** .... be asked to cover a story anywhere in the world. The photographer I'm training with is an extraordinary man. He got involved in a criminal gang as a teenager and even **(5)** .... a few years in jail. He was **(6)** .... to 6 years but they let him out after three. He loves his job and says he **(7)** .... never offend again. Nothing could ever be as good, according to him, as seeing all the most incredible places he has seen in his **(8)** ....

	A	B	C	D
0	is working	worked	will work	**work**
1	am travelling	will be travelling	travel	to travel
2	will have finished	will finish	finished	was finished
3	have	could	might	must
4	must	have	could	need
5	rested	spent	to spend	will spend
6	sentenced	asked	arrested	had
7	won't	may not	will	will have
8	work life	shared job	earn a living	working life

FIRST Reading and Use of English – Part 2

6 OPEN CLOZE. **For questions 1-8, read the text below and think of the word which best fits each gap. Use only one word in each gap. There is an example at the beginning (0).**

FUTURE CRIME

When software gets smarter, the first effect **(0)** WILL be to empower the already powerful. The fantastic powers available now to Google and Facebook, who **(1)** .... be the publishers of most of what appears on the public Internet, is one example. More sinister is the power given to nation states who **(2)** .... spy on us, manipulate their own citizens, and disrupt the workings of their enemies. But these advantages **(3)** .... last. Soon they will **(4)** .... to be reinforced by law, and ultimately force, as the techniques **(5)** .... fall into the wrong hands.

The speed of technological progress, and the ease with **(6)** .... ideas can now spread, mean that few techniques can long remain the preserve of large firms or entities. Every advance available to the ordinary consumer **(7)** .... soon be available to criminals too. Illegal commerce, whether in drugs, forged documents, stolen credit cards or emails, will be as efficient as the legal sort and it will become increasingly difficult to track **(8)** .... and convict those responsible.

FIRST Reading and Use of English – Part 3

7 WORD FORMATION. **For questions 1-8, read the text below. Use the word given in capitals at the end of some of the lines to form a word that fits in the gap in the same line. There is an example at the beginning (0).**

PREVENTING CRIME AND VIOLENCE IN THE WORKPLACE

From convenience store robberies to teachers being
(0) PHYSICALLY attacked in schools to — PHYSICAL
(1) .... workers bringing guns to the office, workplace — ILLUSION
violence and crime will soon have **(2)** .... street crime — TAKE
as a serious problem.

While no one can predict when a workplace crime might occur,
it's wise to take an **(3)** .... approach to the problem — CONVENTIONAL
and develop a plan to deal with it **(4)** .... before it — EFFICIENT
happens. The scope of the plan should be largely determined by the size and nature of your business.

The easiest and most straightforward part of such a plan is to
protect your physical environment so that **(5)** .... — WANT
intruders cannot physically enter the premises; or if they do, they
can be **(6)** .... spotted, through the use of alarms, — EASY
security cameras, and guards.

Along with taking the standard safety **(7)** .... to — CAUTION
protect your property, you must also protect your employees from both external and internal crime or acts of violence. This might
include issuing **(8)** .... badges, providing training in — SECURE
personal safety, distributing company mobile phones for employees working off-site, and other crime prevention measures.

FIRST Reading and Use of English – Part 4

8 KEY WORD TRANSFORMATIONS. **For questions 1-6, complete the second sentence so that it has a similar meaning to the first sentence, using the word given. Do not change the word given. You must use between two and five words, including the word given. Here is an example (0).**

0 Excuse me, is it possible to use this trolley? All the others are being used.
COULD
Excuse me, COULD I USE THIS TROLLEY? All the others are being used.

1 It is possible that John will come to the concert this evening but I'm not sure.
MIGHT
John .... this evening.

2 We must try to get to the station on time otherwise we will miss the train.
WILL
We must try to get to the station on time otherwise .... left.

3 A lot of the jobs we used to do in the company are now done by others outside.
ARE
A lot of the jobs we used to do in the company .... out.

4 It is difficult to earn enough money to live on from just a part-time job.
MAKE
It is difficult .... from just a part-time job.

5 Where will I be at this time next week? On a train heading for the sea.
TRAVELLING
At this time next week I .... on a train heading for the sea.

6 It isn't necessary to use a password for this computer.
HAVE
You .... a password for this computer.

5 Global issues

Inquadrami per guardare i video e ascoltare gli audio di questa unità

VOCABULARY ACTIVATOR

FLIPPED classroom

VIDEO Global issues

GLOBALISED WORLD — GLOBALLY AWARE → LARGER VIEW — DIVERSITY, IDENTITY — DIVERSE CULTURES — INTERNATIONALLY MINDED — JUSTICE, PEACE, HUMAN RIGHTS — REACH OUT TO OTHER NATIONALITIES — WORLD → INTERCONNECTED — OPEN TO NEW CULTURES

WARM-UP

1 **LOOK** at the diagram and discuss which issues affect you and your community.

A

B

C

D

E

F

2 **LOOK** at the pictures and match them to the corresponding global issues in the diagram above.

FOCUS ON VOCABULARY

Look beyond ⇢ see further.

Identity ⇢ what characterises a person, the qualities that make a person who they are and different to others.

Diversity ⇢ a variety, the realisation of there being many different types of things or people.

Richness of culture ⇢ the wealth of traditions and customs from different nations.

Internationally-minded ⇢ a person who shows an open, positive and curious attitude towards others of different nations and traditions.

An interconnected world ⇢ a world where there is intense and reciprocal dialogue and involvement between different peoples.

See the world through other eyes ⇢ the ability to be aware that there are different ways of understanding and viewing the world.

Knowledge and awareness of the wider world ⇢ having the information and being conscious of the possible questions affecting countries outside your own.

C Learning to use vocabulary in context

3 🔊 3.1 **LISTEN** to a teacher commenting on why students need to learn about global issues and complete the sentence.

'If young people learn about global issues as part of their education, they will discover that knowledge of the wider world is in some ways more important than ...' ACADEMIC DEGREE CLASSIFICATIONS OR A LEVEL RESULTS

4 🔊 3.1 **LISTEN** again and say if the sentences are true (T) or false (F). Correct the false ones.

1 Students need to recognise the incredible opportunities across our planet. T F
2 A growing movement of international educators see global issues as of minor importance. T F
3 Knowledge of global issues is not considered important by business leaders. T F
4 When looking for a job, awareness of global problems is at least as important as academic qualifications. T F

5 **DISCUSS** in small groups why awareness and knowledge of global issues and problems are considered so important for young people. Use the vocabulary from the Focus box.

WARM-UP

1 **DISCUSS** in pairs. Look at the logo of the Sustainable Development Goals (SDGs) including the 17 icons/issues. Can you provide your own definition of sustainable development?

2 **SURF** the net to explain the 17 icons of the SDGs' logo.

C Reading, understanding and interpreting information

3 **READ** and listen to the article and say which goals focus on improving people's quality of life.

Sustainable development

3.2

The world's population of seven billion is likely to increase to more than nine billion by 2050. If it does, the demand for diminishing natural resources will grow. Income gaps are already widening. Sustainable development calls for a decent standard of living for everyone without compromising the needs of future generations. In other words, we must use our resources wisely.

Sustainable development requires us to conserve more and waste less. In industrialised nations, many people live beyond nature's means. For example, one person in a very rich country uses as much energy as 80 people in a very poor country. If we continue to over-consume natural resources like water, which is our most precious but also most wasted resource, it will lead to waste, pollution and we will use up all the resources.

Crushing poverty and growing populations also put great pressure on the environment. When land and forests, which provide food, natural resources and employment, are exhausted, people find it harder to survive. Many go to cities, crowding into unhealthy and unsafe slums.

In September 2015, more than 150 world leaders gathered at the UN Headquarters in New York to adopt an ambitious sustainable development agenda. Signed up to by the 193 Member States of the UN, the new agenda, which officially came into force on 1 January 2016, consists of a Declaration with 17 Sustainable Development Goals (SDGs) and a wide range of targets to be achieved by 2030. Over the next few years, all countries, poor, rich and middle-income, will mobilise efforts to end all forms of poverty, fight inequality and tackle climate change.

Four SDGs focus on improving people's quality of life and their ability to live a dignified life. If there were no conflicts or artificially produced financial and economic crises, there would be enough food for everyone. That is the reason why **goal 1 and 2** require an end both to poverty and hunger and to achieve food security, to improve nutrition and promote sustainable agriculture.

Goal 4 aims to ensure inclusive and fair quality education and promote lifelong learning opportunities for all. Although the world was making progress in the period 2010-2015, it failed to meet the Millennium Development Goal of achieving universal primary education by 2015. If we look at the statistics, we can see that in 2016 about 263 million children and youths were out of school. Estimates show that 1 in 5 of those children had dropped out and the surveys carried out recently have pointed out that 2 in 5 of out-of-school children will never set foot in a classroom.

Goal 5 deals with promoting gender equality and empowering all women and girls. If every form of violence against women and girls represented a violation of their human rights, it would slow down their use and hopefully lead eventually to their elimination.

(Abridged from www.un.org)

4 **READ** the article again and do the following activities.

A1 Why are natural resources said to be 'diminishing' (line 3)?

A Natural resources are essential and unlimited globally.
B The Earth's natural forces are finite and if they aren't protected, they will eventually be exhausted.

A2 Explain the phrase 'live beyond nature's means' (line 10) in your own words.

A3 Which natural resource is the one most wasted according to the article?

A4 Say whether the following information is true (T) or false (F).

A Poverty destroys the environment. T F
B Land and forests can provide only food. T F
C When it becomes almost impossible to live in the countryside, people move to cities. T F
D Slums are dangerous and unsanitary. T F

A5 Explain why the sustainable development agenda signed up to by the 193 Member States of the UN in September 2015 is said to be 'ambitious'.

A6 Which of the following meanings is closest to the verb 'tackle' as used in line 32?

A bring down
B launch
C work on
D catch

A7 The fifth paragraph deals with two Sustainable Development Goals. Summarise them in your own words.

A8 Say which of these data are NOT mentioned in the sixth paragraph.

A In 2016, about 263 million children and youth did not attend school.
B Today we have to feed 795 million hungry people.
C 2 in 5 of out-of-school children will never set foot in a classroom.
D 1 out of every 5 people currently lives on 1.25$ a day or less.

A9 Which of the meanings below is closest to the word 'empowering' in line 52?

A assigning
B permitting
C giving added force to
D delegating

A10 Which of the following best summarises the viewpoint of the article?

A Exploring global realities.
B Reorienting education for a sustainable future.
C Accepting the challenge.
D Understanding sustainable development.

C Listening for specific information

5 3.3 **LISTEN** to two young people talking about sustainable conservation projects. Then listen again and choose the most suitable answer (A, B or C) to the questions.

1 Jodie went to Peru because she wanted
A to volunteer on a conservation project abroad.
B to sign up to a project that focused on physical work.
C to pursue a career abroad.

2 She worked on a project dealing with
A introducing a wonderful and beautiful array of animals and plants.
B discovering another culture while learning about yourself.
C nature conservation and developing the local community.

3 Jonathan's project in South Africa specifically came into force
A to introduce the idea of sustainable tourism.
B to persuade the local farmers not to hunt and kill the cheetahs.
C to introduce large predators onto the nature reserve.

4 He would recommend the experience to anyone especially if
A you have good physical skills and can deal with wild animals.
B you want to go on night safaris and hunt dangerous animals.
C you can adapt to basic conditions and get on well with others.

Phrasal verbs for global issues

6 **MATCH** the highlighted phrasal verbs (1-5) in the article to their definitions (A-E).

1 ☐ call for	**A** agree to
2 ☐ use up	**B** be about
3 ☐ sign up	**C** exhaust
4 ☐ come into force	**D** require
5 ☐ deal with	**E** become effective

7 **COMPLETE** the sentences with the correct form of the phrasal verbs from exercise 6.

1 People must .... for a more comprehensive service that offers more.
2 The new law does not .... until March of next year.
3 The opposition party .... the Prime Minister's resignation last week.
4 The course Jodie chose .... the history of China.
5 They .... the milk when they made the cake.

Zero, first and second conditionals

1 READ sentences 1-3 and answer questions A-C.

1 If the world's population **increases**, the demand for diminishing natural resources **will grow**.

2 If we **look at** the statistics, we **can** see that in 2016 about 263 million children and youths were out of school.

3 If every form of violence against women and girls **represented** a violation of their human rights, it **would slow down** their use and hopefully lead eventually to their elimination.

Which sentence describes

A an unreal or improbable situation?

B a possible future situation?

C a fact or real possibility?

Grammar reference 5.1

2 CHOOSE the correct alternative to complete the sentences.

1 The bus *stops / stopped* at the bus stop if you *will press / press* this button.

2 If there *were / was* no conflicts or artificially produced financial and economic crises, there *would be / will be* enough food for everyone.

3 *Will you / Do you* help me with this itinerary if I *translate / translated* that English passage for you?

4 They hate living in the country; they *would / will* relax more if they *live / lived* in the centre of town.

5 If Joan *opens / will open* that door, she *will get / would get* a nasty surprise.

3 COMPLETE the second sentence using the word in capital letters so that it has a similar meaning to the first sentence.

1 I might become famous and get very rich. IF
I might get very rich ....

2 Mary might go to live in Paris but she'll have to find a job first. WILL
If Mary finds a job first, she
.... in Paris.

3 In India poverty is widespread and many girls under the age of 14 do not go to school. WOULD
If poverty in India were not widespread, many girls under the age of 14 ....

4 Wait until the kettle boils, then make the tea. WHEN
Make the tea ....

5 Protecting the environment should bring governments together to make international laws to solve environmental problems. MADE
If .... international laws to solve environmental problems, they would protect the environment.

4 COMPLETE the sentences using conditionals and the verbs in the box in the correct form.

see ▪ not read ▪ not get ▪ leave ▪ not behave ▪ end up ▪ tell ▪ spend ▪ not find out ▪ care

1 I think I .... if they .... here within the next ten minutes.

2 If my sister and I .... more than two days with our parents, we .... quarrelling.

3 We .... about these famous buildings if we .... the guide book properly.

4 If he .... about other people's feelings, he .... that way.

5 I .... him the news when I .... him.

Unless / In case / As long as / Provided that

5 READ sentences 1-3 and answer questions A-C.

1 These goals wouldn't work **unless** there were also social protection for the poor.

2 I'm going to take an extra bag on holiday **in case** I need it.

3 I'll come to the museum **as long as** / **provided that** I can watch a video later.

Which sentence contains the meaning

A 'if this happens, that can happen'?

B 'if ... not'?

C 'if the possibility arises'?

Grammar reference 5.2

6 COMPLETE the sentences with *unless, in case, as long as* or *provided that.*

1 I won't mention that you've broken the tablet .... someone asks.

2 They'll go riding their bikes in the park .... they get home in time.

3 It's a bit cloudy. Take an umbrella .... it rains.

4 Pam is a sweet person .... you don't contradict her.

5 Take my phone number .... you miss the bus.

6 .... you drive more slowly, you'll have an accident.

7 WRITE sentences using conditionals and the prompts given.

1 Unless / you / finish / your homework / not be able to / watch any television.

2 If / it / rain / we / not go / to the open air concert.

3 When / it / snow / we / usually / drive / to the mountains.

4 If / they / be / rich / they / travel / around the world.

5 I / leave / these videos / here / in case / you / have / time / to watch them.

6 As long as / you / keep / quiet / you / be able / to stay here.

TIP In order to decide whether the missing word needs to be in the plural or in a negative form, it is essential to read the text on both sides of the gap with attention.

FIRST Reading and Use of English – Part 3

1 **WORD FORMATION. For questions 1-8, read the text below. Use the word given in capitals at the end of some of the lines to form a word that fits the gap in the same line. There is an example at the beginning (0).**

There have been huge changes for women
in terms of **(0)** EMPLOYMENT in the past — **EMPLOY**
decades, with women **(1)** .... — **MOVE**
into paid employment outside the home
in ways that their grandmothers and even
their mothers could only dream of. There
are (some) high-profile women chief
(2) .... and there is a small — **EXECUTE**
but increasing number of female presidents.
Women are moving into jobs that used to be
done by men. Even those women working
in factories or sweatshops have more
choice and **(3)** .... than if they — **DEPENDENT**
remained at home.
But although more women are working, they
are often still more **(4)** .... paid — **BAD**
than men, in part-time jobs or in the huge
(5) .... employment sector — **FORMAL**
with little protection and few rights. And at
the top of industry and **(6)** .... — **GOVERN**
the faces remain stubbornly male. In fact,
if we look at the **(7)** ...., we — **EVIDENT**
often see that the numbers of women in
influential positions are **(8)** .... — **ACT**
decreasing.

TIP Remember that abbreviations such as 'I'm' or 'isn't' or 'they're' count as two words with the exception of 'can't' because 'cannot' is just one word.

FIRST Reading and Use of English – Part 4

2 **KEY WORD TRANSFORMATIONS. For questions 1-6, complete the second sentence so that it has a similar meaning to the first sentence, using the word given. Do not change the word given. You must use between two and five words, including the word given. Here is an example (0).**

0 We will be late if he doesn't arrive soon.
UNLESS
We will be late UNLESS HE ARRIVES soon.

1 The world would be a better place if everyone were to respect other cultures and traditions.
RESPECTED
The world would be a better place .... other cultures and traditions.

2 The match will go ahead if it doesn't rain.
THAT
The match will go ahead .... rain.

3 'There will be special protection for refugee children' said the commissioner.
PROMISED
The commissioner .... special protection for refugee children.

4 The law will become official before the next parliament.
FORCE
The law will .... before the next parliament.

5 I think we should bring our coats because it might be cold.
CASE
I think we should bring our coats .... cold.

6 Several nations added their signatures to the petition for equal rights.
SIGNED
Several nations .... to the petition for equal rights.

READING

WARM-UP

1 DISCUSS in pairs.

1. Who are refugees? What is the difference between a political refugee and an economic refugee?
2. Why are there so many refugees in the world today?
3. If you had been born in a war zone, would you have risked everything to escape to another country?

C Recognising links within a text

2 READ and listen to the article and say where Loujean is from and what she is doing now.

TIP Rather than concentrating on individual sentences, you need to be able to follow the development of ideas, opinions and events through the text as a whole, using your understanding of text coherence and cohesion devices.

FIRST Reading and Use of English – Part 6

3 GAPPED TEXT. Read the article again. Six sentences have been removed from the article. Choose from the sentences A-G the one which fits each gap (1-6). There is one extra sentence which you do not need to use.

3.4

Story of a refugee girl

When Lucy Pavia and her husband Will offered Loujean Alsaman, a refugee from Syria, a room in their home, none of them knew what to expect. But over the six months they spent together, the women formed a close, sisterly bond.

Loujean

It was when girls started disappearing that my family decided it wasn't safe for me to stay in Syria any longer. They would be stopped by police at roadblocks and wouldn't return home. Damascus, where I was born and spent my childhood, is one of the safest cities in Syria but the situation there is still very dangerous. **1** At the time I was 20 and studying English literature at the university of Damascus. I remember thinking 'I wish I could stay' but it was impossible.

If I had known how difficult the journey would be, I might not have tried. I still find the experience very hard to talk about. I crossed so many countries. On my arrival in the UK I heard about a charity offering space in UK homes to refugees. **2** If I had been a man, it would have been different. As a woman who had come here without any family, I worried about the safety of living with strangers and also thought my culture could be an embarrassment. I am Muslim. Would they find it strange if they saw me praying?

But then I met Lucy and Will and I stopped worrying. **3** I moved in a few days later. It wasn't always easy. Even though I felt safe I couldn't forget the war, losing sleep worrying about friends and family in Syria. I might be safe, but what about them? If only I could have helped them too. At the darkest times I wondered whether I should have taken the risk and stayed in Damascus.

Lucy

On the evening Loujean moved in with us, she wheeled her huge fuchsia suitcase straight into the kitchen, where she immediately began pulling out carefully wrapped bags of food she had bought that day: rice, chopped lamb, okra and pomegranate syrup. [4 C] Her life had changed unimaginably and I would come to understand how important these dinners were to her, a little way of remembering home.

[5 F] 'Homes For Syrians' recommends hosting for one to six months, enough time to give someone a base and a chance for integration into a country they never expected to end up in. The first week was a bit strange. Loujean spoke little English and we spoke no Arabic so there were a lot of silly hand gestures and unnatural staccato sentences ('Coffee for you?', 'Towels here').

But if we hadn't taken this risk, we wouldn't have this wonderful new member of the family. Getting to know her better meant hearing about the pain she had been through and often her unhappiness when she listened to the news about Syria made her completely inconsolable.

Last summer, Loujean passed her English exam and she's now studying law at university in another town. [6 B] I've told her that if she buys a villa on Lake Como, Will and I expect to have the first invitation.

(Freely adapted from an article in The Guardian, May 2017)

A Our first introduction was by email, then we met and they seemed kind and open-minded.

B One day, she hopes to be a human rights lawyer like Amal Clooney.

C From then on, at least once a week, she would cook one of the recipes her granny had taught her in Damascus.

D Contact between her and her family became increasingly difficult.

E I remember the sound of shells exploding at night and the electricity flashing on and off.

F On that first night, Will and I lay in bed listening to her unpack in the bedroom next door and wondered what on earth we were doing.

G I found the idea of living with strangers frightening.

4 FIND the words in the text which mean the following:

1. an obstruction placed across a road to stop cars usually by the police or military (para. 2); ROADBLOCKS
2. an organisation formed to help others in need (para. 3); CHARITY
3. willing to accept new and different ideas (para. 4); OPEN MINDED
4. moved using wheels (para. 5); WHEELED
5. ridiculous, laughable (para. 6); SILLY
6. impossible to be comforted (para. 7). INCONSOLABLE

Word formation: abstract nouns

Suffixes can be used to form **abstract nouns**: *arrive* – ***arrival***, *appear* – ***appearance***, *efficient* – ***efficiency***, *child* – ***childhood***, *sad* – ***sadness***, *jealous* – ***jealousy***, *excite* – ***excitement***, *wise* – ***wisdom***, *friend* – ***friendship***, *patriot* – ***patriotism***, *revolt* – ***revolution***.

5 FIND some examples of this use of suffixes in the text.

6 TRANSFORM the meaning of the words in the box using the suffixes *-al / -ence / -ty / -ness / -hood / -ment / -ship / -tion*.

DISAPPOINTMENT UN
disappoint ▪ happy ▪ intelligent ▪ explore ▪ relation ▪ cruel ▪ adult ▪ dismiss AL

7 MAKE abstract nouns from the words given to complete the sentences.

1. In a desperate situation there is a need for ...LEADERSHIP... to help those who are weak. (LEADER)
2. A new hostel for refugees is being built in our ...NEIGHBORWHOOD... . (NEIGHBOUR)
3. After the rescue at sea there was a sense of ...HAPPYNESS... and ...CONTENTMENT... among the refugees. (HAPPY/CONTENT)
4. The early history of the United States had elements of ...PURITANISM... and ...SLAVERY... . (PURITAN/SLAVE)
5. Even in difficult situations it is important to believe in the ...POSSIBILITY... of ...SURVIVAL... . (POSSIBLE/SURVIVE)
6. Our ...ADOLESCENCE... can be a period of ...FRUSTRATION... but also of ...FULFILMENT... . (ADOLESCENT/FRUSTRATE/FULFIL)

C Discussing ideas and expressing personal opinions

8 DISCUSS the questions.

1. If there hadn't been so many wars there wouldn't be so many refugees.
2. If you had to leave your country because of fighting or economic hardship, where would you try to go?

9 WRITE a brief paragraph of 8/10 lines about why the refugee problem can be seen as a global issue.

Third conditionals

1 READ sentences 1-2 and answer the questions below.

1 If I **had had** to undertake a journey like that as a child, I **wouldn't have survived**.
A Did the speaker undertake a journey?
B Did she die?

2 If you **had stopped** to think about it, you **would have realised** that the number of children is disproportionate.
A Does this mean you think about it, thought about it or couldn't have thought about it at that time (if they are talking now)?
B Does the sentence express doubt, regret or an impossible past situation?

Grammar reference 5.3

2 REWRITE the sentences using the third conditional and the correct form of the verbs in brackets.

1 If she .... (not tell) me her story, I .... (not know) about it.
2 I .... (forgive) her if she .... (apologise).
3 .... (he / survive) if he .... (be able) to swim?
4 If they .... (not leave) home late, they .... (arrive) in time.
5 If he .... (not go) to the party, he .... (never / meet) his future wife.
6 .... (there / be) fewer wars if nations .... (take) more responsibilities?
7 The accident .... (not happen) if the driver .... (stop) in time.
8 If the students .... (behave) correctly, the teacher .... (not punish) them.

FREQUENT MISTAKES **Mixed conditionals**

3 READ the sentence and decide if the statements are true (T) or false (F).

If we **hadn't had** so many recent wars, we **wouldn't have** these horrific numbers of refugees now.

1 The sentence combines two different types of conditional patterns. T F
2 The *if*-clause contains a type 2 conditional. T F
3 The main clause contains a type 3 conditional. T F
4 The sentence contrasts an imagined or real event in the past with its present result. T F

Grammar reference 5.4

4 CHOOSE the correct option to complete the sentences.

1 I would probably be a refugee if there *had been* / *weren't* / *would be* a war in my country.
2 If they had been born in the USA, they *would need* / *wouldn't need* / *would have needed* a visa to go there.
3 You *would have* / *would have had* / *had* a better chance to get a good job now if you had studied English harder.
4 He wouldn't have a stomach ache now if he *hadn't eaten* / *didn't eat* / *wouldn't eat* so much.
5 We could join the trekking tour now if we *trained* / *would train* / *had trained* harder.
6 If my son had not stayed out late last night, now he *wouldn't have been* / *wouldn't be* / *weren't* tired.

Expressing wishes and regrets: *I wish / If only*

5 DECIDE if sentences 1-3 express a wish or a regret.

1 I wish I were more tolerant.
2 I wish we had had the declaration sooner.
3 We wish this programme would continue.

6 DECIDE which of these sentences expresses the stronger regret.

1 I wish the rich nations took more responsibility
2 If only the rich nations would take more responsibility.

Grammar reference 5.5

7 WRITE a suitable sentence expressing wish or regret for the following situations.

1 You would like your team to win the championship. (win)
2 You can't afford to buy a new car. (have more money)
3 You have run and hurt your foot. (be in such a hurry)
4 Your friend is not listening to what you are saying. (care about what I say)
5 You got sunburnt. (use suntan lotion)

8 COMPLETE the second sentence so that it has the same meaning as the first sentence.

1 I can't find a dress that suits me for the party.
If only ....
2 I treated him rudely, this is why we quarrelled
If only ....
3 I can't stand having to take the bus every morning.
If only ....
4 We are having a test again tomorrow and our teacher often gives tests.
If only ....

WARM-UP

1 DISCUSS. If you had been born in a developing country, you would not have had the opportunities you perhaps take for granted. You may not have had access to school. Think about the advantages of a school education and the possible problems of not having that possibility.

C Developing confidence and fluency

2 LOOK at the phrases in the Process language box used when you are comparing two possibilities and add three more.

PROCESS LANGUAGE

Speaking – Part 2

Comparing possibilities

The first picture contains ..., but the second doesn't ...
On the one hand ..., but on the other hand ...
This is/offers/has ..., but that ...
They both have/show ..., but this one has/shows ... more/better ...
If it were up to me, I would prefer... because ...
I think this one is much more ... because ...
This one seems/looks ..., but I think the other one ...
While I can see that this one ... I believe the other ...
The first picture is probably outside in ...
The second picture is inside a ...

Speaking reference p. 194

TIP Remember it is very important to listen carefully to the instructions and to carry them out as exactly as you can. You will be asked to read the question above the photographs which is there to give the task a focus. Remember to try to produce a wide range of language varying your words as much as possible.

C Organising and carrying out a class discussion on a given topic

4 CLASS DISCUSSION. We are lucky enough to live in a society where education is a priority and a legal right for all, but this is not true in all countries. In many cultures education is not safeguarded and particularly not for girls. Why do you think it is often harder for girls to achieve the right to an education?

5 READ the quotes and write a brief paragraph of 8/10 lines on the importance of education.

When you educate a girl, you educate a family. When you educate a family, you educate a nation. Despite this, millions of girls are denied this basic human right. (*United Nations*)

Education is the most powerful weapon which you can use to change the world. (*Nelson Mandela*)

To be educated means...
I will not only be able to help myself, but also my family, my country, my people. The benefits will be many. (*Meda Wagtole, schoolgirl, Ethiopia*)

No industry or country can reach its full potential until women reach their full potential. (*Sheryl Sandberg, chief operating officer of Facebook, founder of LeanIn.Org*)

FIRST Speaking – Part 2

3 INDIVIDUAL LONG TURN. Here are two photographs showing different life conditions. Compare them and say how the children feel about the way they learn. You have one minute to do this.

How do these children feel about the way they learn?

WARM-UP

1 DISCUSS in pairs.

1 Which are the most serious problems facing the world today? Talk about this with a classmate and then make a list of the three you consider most serious.

2 The world is divided into developed countries and developing countries. Which different problems do they have to deal with? Which problems do they share?

C Listening for specific information

TIP Answers will not exceed three words in length. The word, number or phrase required will be heard on the recording and will not need to be changed in any way. Minor spelling errors are not penalised, but your intention must be clear and unambiguous. You will not be asked to spell words which are above Cambridge English First (B2) level.

FIRST Listening – Part 2

2 3.5 **SENTENCE COMPLETION. You will hear a scientist talking about climate change. For questions 1-10, complete the sentences with a word or short phrase.**

As individuals it's useless to think 'I wish we **(1)** .... the atmosphere.'

If countries want to preserve the natural beauty of their countryside they ought to create National Parks and **(2)** ....

In the United States, for example, there has been **(3)** .... and devastating drought. Tornadoes have hit towns while massive rivers overflowed.

They have had to deal with tornadoes, floods and drought and the ground shook in places like Colorado where **(4)** .... had never happened before.

According to scientists and weather experts there could be **(5)** .... to explain the increase in climate extremes.

Most experts agree that if we had started to study these phenomena sooner we **(6)** .... in this desperate position now.

Scientists and environmentalists agree that we need to limit the amount of **(7)** .... if we want to avoid extreme conditions.

Climate change is not the only factor involved although it is certainly an important element in the magnitude and the number of **(8)** ....

Unless some kind of action is taken to limit global emissions, experts say there could be a **(9)** .... in the region of 4°.

Certainly if we **(10)** .... to prevent global warming in the past, we wouldn't be in such a bad situation now.

C Organising and carrying out a class discussion on a given topic

3 CLASS DISCUSSION.

1 What do you understand by the phrase 'climate change' and 'global warming'?

2 If you were in a position of leadership, what would you do about changing what is happening to the world climatically?

VIDEO
Climate change

C Watching and understanding a short film

1 BEFORE watching the video, match the words (1-8) to their meanings (A-H).

1 ☐ spiral
2 ☐ fossil fuel
3 ☐ gonna
4 ☐ amplitude
5 ☐ pumping
6 ☐ concerted
7 ☐ stark
8 ☐ doom

A going to
B raising
C severe
D any organic combustible derived from the remains of former life
E planned or devised together
F destine to an adverse fate
G rise rapidly
H large measure

2 WATCH the first part of the video (from 00:00 to 00:12) and write down what these images communicate to you.

1 ....
2 ....
3 ....

3 WATCH the whole video and say if the following sentences are true (T) or false (F). Correct the false ones.

1 Today's climate change is only partly due to humans. T F
2 In developing nations, fossil fuel consumption is increasing. T F
3 The nations of the world must act together to face the problem of climate change. T F
4 Climate is changing less rapidly now than in the past. T F
5 It is possible to get rid of CO_2 with new forms of energy. T F
6 If climate change is left unchecked, the death of humans and other species will happen. T F
7 Our planet has never had a global warming. T F

4 WATCH the video again and decide who says the following: Narrator (N), Thompson (T), Overpeck (O), Alley (A).

1 Where's the energy gonna come from in the future? ...
2 The most disturbing thing is the size of CO_2 increases. ...
3 Planned worldwide action could make a difference. ...
4 It's not easy to find a way to generate energy without affecting the world's climate. ...
5 The future may take a major catastrophe before we take the necessary action. ...
6 What would it take to get us all on the same page? ...
7 If we don't learn from our past, we will doom subsequent generations. ...

5 DISCUSS in pairs. How do you know that climate is changing? Why are human activities influencing climate? What could be the impact of climate change in your country?

CREATING NEW IDEAS

Working in teams can be essential to achieve the same goal. Sharing thoughts and beliefs will help you create new ideas and quality work within your team.

6 DESCRIBE the kinds of team work you have done up to now. Which subjects were involved? Did your team manage to create new ideas about a particular given topic?

7 DISCUSS the following in groups.

1 Has the video increased your awareness about the importance of climate change education?
2 Do you think this video may suggest innovative ways to reduce energy consumption?
3 Are you interested in an international climate change forum? If yes, you can work in teams of four:
- each student takes on the role of a country leader;
- each country suggests a strategy to face climate change;
- a discussion of the best strategies follows;
- a summary of the discussion is written and given to the different groups in the class.

WARM-UP

1 **DISCUSS.** Does your school have a Global Awareness Day? What do you think it is? If you had one, what sort of activities should it involve? Or if you have had one, what do you think it should have achieved?

C Communicating in informal emails

2 **READ** the email below and decide which definition (1-11) corresponds with which part of the email (A-K).

1 ☐ topic of the email
2 ☐ developing the ideas of the email
3 ☐ final salutation
4 ☐ additional information and requests
5 ☐ signature
6 ☐ person the email is addressed to
7 ☐ introducing the topic of the email
8 ☐ sender
9 ☐ an extra person or people who receive a copy of the email
10 ☐ the opening greeting
11 ☐ closing remarks and request for reply

(A) From: Anna Morley
(B) To: sara.brown@bcnet.com
(C) Cc: Tom Wilkinson, Paul James
(D) Subject: **Global Awareness Day**

(E) Hi Sara,
(F) as promised, here are some details about our class's part in the Global Awareness Day.

(G) There have been several ideas mentioned but all in all if we want to raise a decent amount of money, I feel we should concentrate our efforts on one project. Of the different options I think the water project sounds the most interesting and most accessible for us to deal with. If you agree, then I think we should arrange a preliminary meeting and I'm copying in Tom and Paul who have also volunteered to help.

(H) Let me know whether you agree about the choice of project and whether you have any ideas about how we can present our chosen project and of course how we can raise the money. So far I have thought of a lottery with prizes, a lucky dip, a competition – something like guess the weight of a cake (and the cake can be the prize). If you have any better ideas please let me know.

(I) Hope to hear from you asap.
(J) Bye for now.
(K) Anna

3 **READ** the email again and answer the questions.

1 Why is Anna sending an email?
2 Why is she copying in other people?
3 Does Anna know the person she is sending the email to well?
4 What information does Anna expect in Sara's next email?
5 What is the style of the email?

TIP Because there is a choice of questions with different topics in this part of the writing paper, make sure you choose a task or topic suited to your interests and experience. You will write more effectively if you write about something that genuinely interests you.

FIRST Writing – Part 2

4 **AN INFORMAL EMAIL.** As part of Global Awareness Day at your school, your class has decided to raise funds for a water distribution programme in a village in Kenya. Read the email on the left and write a reply of 140-190 words containing the following information:

- Agreeing to a meeting and suggesting a time and place
- Agreeing with the project
- Choosing one of the fund raising ideas and offering two more

PROCESS LANGUAGE

Writing – Part 2 (an informal email)

Greeting
Dear ... (name) / Good morning ... (increasingly used) / Hi ... (for a friend)

Why you are writing
You asked me to ...
I've found some information about ...
As promised, I'm writing ...
About your trip, ...

Salutation
Regards. / With best wishes. (more formal)
Cheers. / Bye for now. (informal)
Hope to hear from you soon.
Looking forward to hearing from you. (formal)

Writing reference p. 199

5 **CLASS ACTIVITY.** Make a poster for a Global Awareness Day. Use images of children and people in need and make it personal by asking questions like: 'If you had been born into poverty with little hope for the future, what kind of help would you most want to receive?'

6 Meet the Arts

Inquadrami per guardare i video e ascoltare gli audio di questa unità

VOCABULARY ACTIVATOR

FLIPPED classroom

VIDEO The Arts

A

B

WARM-UP

1 DISCUSS the following questions.

1 What kind of art do you relate to?
2 Do you like looking at paintings?
3 Are you interested in modern art or modern architecture?
4 Is music important to you? Have you been to a music concert?

C

D

E

F

G

C Learning to use vocabulary in context

2 3.6 **LISTEN** to a talk about different forms of artistic expression and look at the pictures. Match each picture to its description (1-7).

1 Television programme
2 Modern painting
3 Classical painting
4 Sculpture
5 Modern architecture
6 Pop concert
7 Urban Art

3 3.6 **LISTEN** again and complete the sentences.

1 Art is any creative expression or interpretation of ....
2 We cannot say that any particular form is better or worse ....
3 There are so many exciting forms of .... that are .... at the same time.
4 Many young people prefer pop .... or inventive .... based on fantastic tales.
5 Basquiat's paintings are less .... but more ....
6 Some forms of art require more .... and more .... but there is no doubt about the .... and .... of artistic expression around us.

4 DISCUSS in small groups which form of artistic expression you prefer. Use the vocabulary from the Focus box.

FOCUS ON VOCABULARY

Performing Arts ···> cinema/television, circus, dance, music, theatre, opera, ballet

Visual Arts ···> drawing/graffiti, architecture, painting, sculpture

Interactive Arts ···> interactive film/video, interactive architecture, installation art

Literature ···> prose, poetry, drama

Useful expressions for the Arts

- appreciate/enjoy/prefer/get pleasure from
- find difficult to understand
- be creative
- inspire/stimulate/provoke/express/interpret
- form of entertainment

WARM-UP

1 **LOOK** at the pictures in these pages and discuss in pairs. Have you ever been to a festival? Was it in the open air or indoors? Was it a music, theatre, book or film festival?

C Reading, understanding and interpreting information

2 **READ** and listen to the article and decide which of the highlighted words has the following meaning:

1 any place where an organised gathering is held
2 the finest or most flourishing period
3 created bit by bit
4 a source, usually sudden and unexpected, of luck or wealth

3.7

Every summer the capital city of Scotland is transformed into a living bonanza of entertainment. The Edinburgh International Festival began in 1947 in a post-war effort to 'provide a platform for the flowering of the human spirit'. The original organisers were convinced that a festival of music and theatre was needed to restore the artistic heritage of Europe after six years of devastation. Edinburgh was more suitable than many other European cities because of its cultural prestige, its picturesque location and the larger than usual number of theatres and hotels that could accommodate hundreds of performers and thousands of visitors.

The Edinburgh Festival is actually a collective term for several arts and cultural festivals that take place each summer, mostly in August. Though the festivals are put on by various organisations unrelated to each other, and so they are officially separate events, they are more and more regarded as part of the same event and together they form the largest annual cultural festival in the world.

From the start, there were two main festivals: the official Edinburgh International Festival, which was as important as the unofficial Edinburgh Festival Fringe. These two festivals continue to run side-by-side though they have separate programmes covering theatre, comedy, circus events and much more. The official festival has built up a reputation for virtuosity and originality, inviting some of the finest creators and performers from the world of theatre, music, opera and dance to offer a unique experience for audiences.

The Fringe Festival, on the other hand, has a policy of open-access and includes in its programme anyone with a story to tell and a venue willing to host them. They are less official but more innovative, offering a range of cultural events from theatre, comedy, dance, circus, cabaret, children's shows, physical theatre, musicals, opera, music, spoken word, exhibitions and more. The Fringe events happen on the streets, in pubs, in galleries – anywhere and everywhere – giving the city an atmosphere of constant and continuous performance. Every street in town becomes a live stage or concert hall. In fact, the Fringe has created by far the biggest and most dynamic international arts market in the world. It has never avoided political commitment and one of the latest slogans was 'Taking a stand by taking a seat'. In fact, the Fringe has always dealt with the most controversial issues of the day. A few years ago, mental health was the most prominent theme whereas more recently the emphasis has been more about transgender and racial equality.

One of the most striking performances I've ever seen was by a black woman, Selina Thompson, who grew up in Birmingham, but is inevitably asked where she's 'really from'. In 2016, she embarked on a journey from the UK to Ghana by cargo ship, then from Ghana to Jamaica and back, retracing old slave routes.

This Festival City has recently been celebrating its 70th anniversary with many more ticket sales than ever and huge audience numbers. The audience is more and more international and the shows on offer more and more numerous. The greater the variety of events the greater the numbers that want to see them.

(Freely adapted from an article by Griselda Murray Brown, in The Financial Times, August 2017)

3 **READ** the article again and do the following activities.

A1 Why did the first Edinburgh Festival take place?

A As an antidote to the destruction of the war years.

B As a way of reminding people that violence isn't the answer to everything.

A2 Name three reasons why Edinburgh was more suitable than other European cities.

A3 In which way can the festival be seen as a 'collective term'?

A It collects people together.

B It unites many different festivals.

C It provides a collection of different objects.

A4 Which of the following meanings is closest to the expression 'open-access' as used in line 32?

A no door available

B free entry to all

C doors are left permanently open

D unlimited possibilities

A5 Say whether the following information is true (T) or false (F).

The Fringe Festival

A allows anyone to perform if they have a place to perform in. T F

B offers a tremendous variety of different cultural events. T F

C is in direct competition with the official festival. T F

D offers every type of entertainment except ballet. T F

A6 Explain in your own words what the slogan 'Taking a stand by taking a seat' (lines 45-46) means.

A7 Which social or political issues have been emphasised recently in the festival?

A8 Give two reasons why Selina Thompson was qualified to present a show about the history of slavery.

A9 The Edinburgh Festival has recently celebrated its 70th anniversary. What evidence is there that it is continuing to grow in popularity?

A10 Which of the following best summarises the viewpoint of the article?

A The writer explains the background of the festival and is obviously impressed with the variety and range of events that make up the various festivals.

B The writer emphasises the international character of the festival and suggests other countries should be more involved.

C The writer talks about the festival from a very personal point of view and shows his own preferences in the type of entertainment described.

D The writer criticises the choices made for the different festivals and considers that there could be a greater number of more varied events.

C Listening and understanding information

4 3.8 **LISTEN** to five different entertainment options for Saturday evening. Listen again and choose the most suitable one for each.

A ☐ A musician who enjoys an intimate atmosphere and playing with fellow musicians.

B ☐ Two friends who enjoy a live performance which holds their attention.

C ☐ A student who wants to take her parents out for an evening with the calm beautiful music they love.

D ☐ A father and his teenage son who like watching something with action.

E ☐ A young couple who enjoy light music and something amusing.

Phrasal verbs and expressions for the Arts

5 **MATCH** the phrasal verbs and expressions (1-5) in the article to their definitions (A-E).

1 ☐ cultural prestige

2 ☐ put on

3 ☐ artistic heritage

4 ☐ live stage

5 ☐ build up a reputation

A stage/produce for a performance

B traditions from the past connected to the Arts

C a performance physically happening at that moment

D gradually obtain a good name

E high reputation based on cultural events

6 **COMPLETE** the sentences with the correct form of the phrasal verbs and expressions from exercise 5.

1 An Australian acting company .... a new play about racism at the drama festival.

2 Many of the festival events were performed on a .... in the open air.

3 The festival is based on its .... from the past seventy years and the .... of its contemporary events.

4 It took time but eventually the dance troupe .... an international ....

Comparatives

1 READ sentences 1-5 and explain how comparatives are formed in English.

1 The Edinburgh Festival's picturesque location **is better than** usual theatres.
2 Edinburgh was **more suitable than** many other European cities.
3 They are **less official** but **more innovative**.
4 There were **fewer** performers from the world of music last August **than** in the previous year.
5 The Edinburgh International Festival was **as important as** the unofficial Edinburgh Festival Fringe.

2 DECIDE if these statements are true (T) or false (F) to revise your knowledge about comparatives.

A All adjectives and adverbs add the ending 'er' to form majority comparisons. T F
B One- or two-syllable adjectives add 'er' to make a comparison otherwise they use 'more'. T F
C There are some irregular adjectives like 'good' and 'bad'. T F
D The structure of minority comparative is as follows: T F
Less + adjective/countable noun + *than*
Fewer + singular noun + *than*

Grammar reference 6.1

3 COMPLETE the sentences with the comparative form of the adjectives in brackets. Use *than* when necessary.

1 It's too noisy here. Can we go to a .... (quiet) place?
2 Yesterday's performance at the Fringe was .... (amusing) today's.
3 In the last few months, competition has become much .... (tough).
4 His results were not .... (good) his colleagues'.
5 I like living in the country; there are .... (little) cars and the air is .... (polluted).

4 COMPLETE the second sentence so that it has a similar meaning to the first sentence.

1 The performance was not as great as we expected.
We enjoyed the performance ....
2 Jennifer did not expect the film to be so good.
The film .... expected.
3 She hasn't got as much money as you, but she doesn't care.
She has .... but she doesn't care.
4 George's new bike is faster than his old one.
George's old bike .... his new one.
5 The weather this summer is not as bad as it was last year.
This summer the weather .... last year.

Superlatives

5 READ sentences 1-4 and explain how superlatives are formed in English.

1 The official Edinburgh International Festival invites some of **the finest** creators and performers from the worlds of theatre, music, opera and dance.
2 The Fringe has created **by far the biggest** and **most dynamic** international arts market in the world.
3 One of **the best** performances of all was by a black woman.
4 It was **the least interesting** performance of the festival.

6 ANSWER questions 1-2 to revise your knowledge about superlatives.

1 What do we use after superlatives?
2 What do we use to emphasise superlatives?

Grammar reference 6.1

7 COMPLETE the sentences with the correct superlative form of the adjectives in brackets.

1 The day of the exhibition was .... (happy) of their lives.
2 Transgender and racial equality are .... (important) themes of the Edinburgh International Festival.
3 Is this .... (big) statue you have ever seen?
4 The journey was so long and tiring. It is .... (comfortable) flight I've taken so far.
5 .... (simple) ideas are sometimes .... (successful).
6 Those sleeping giants are .... (unusual) urban project I've seen up to now.

8 COMPLETE the second sentence so that it has a similar meaning to the first sentence.

1 We have never seen better graffiti than these ones.
These ones .... we have ever seen.
2 That artist has never had a worse reception than this.
It is .... he has ever had.
3 There is no earthwork more famous in the world than *Spiral Jetty*.
Spiral Jetty is .... in the world.
4 He paints more traditionally than any other painter of that movement.
He is the .... movement.
5 None of us is as skilful at sculpture as Mary.
Mary is .... us all.
6 I've never heard stories as funny as the ones Chris told me last night.
Chris's stories are .... I've ever heard.
7 Mark is not as tall as his classmates.
Mark is .... in his class.

TIP A good knowledge of prepositions is fundamental to do well in this exercise. As revision, you could revise the prepositions of time and place. Remember that certain verbs are always followed by particular prepositions e.g. 'to go + to'. Also revise phrasal verbs and their meanings.

FIRST Reading and Use of English – Part 1

1 MULTIPLE-CHOICE CLOZE. For questions 1-8, read the text below and decide which answer (A, B, C or D) best fits each gap. There is an example at the beginning (0).

GAME OF THRONES

Game of Thrones, the American fantasy drama series adapted **(0)** ....FROM.......... George R.R. Martin's novels *A Song of Ice and Fire* has been **(1)** .... popular than anyone imagined. The series is considered to be more interesting **(2)** .... many similar historical dramas and has won the largest audiences and the **(3)** .... awards for the acting and its 'medieval realism'. The plot **(4)** .... the continual drama of alliances and conflicts between the noble families around the throne in an imaginary medieval kingdom. To many it reflects the real-life world of the English Wars of the Roses between the families of York and Lancaster. However, the series has received criticism for more **(5)** .... nudity and violence.

The first series followed the original plot of the novels closely, but then the story line became wider and more attuned to modern ideas. George Martin wanted to put **(6)** .... a production based on historical fiction with **(7)** .... emphasis on magic and more attention to real-life drama like battles and political intrigue. According to Martin the **(8)** .... horrors come from within us rather than from any 'dark lord'.

0	**A** to	**B** for	**C from**	**D** by
1	**A** more	**B** much	**C** many	**D** as
2	**A** as	**B** more	**C** from	**D** than
3	**A** prestigious	**B** as prestigious	**C** most prestigious	**D** more prestigious
4	**A** builds of	**B** builds on	**C** builds for	**D** builds
5	**A** and more	**B** and less	**C** more	**D** than
6	**A** of	**B** on	**C** in	**D** to
7	**A** more little	**B** least	**C** smaller	**D** less
8	**A** worst	**B** worse	**C** as bad as	**D** as bad

TIP Remember to read the whole text before you begin to fill in the gaps. It is important to have a complete idea of the text. Also remember to read the complete sentence before and after the gap for each question.

FIRST Reading and Use of English – Part 2

2 OPEN CLOZE. For questions 1-8, read the text below and think of the word which best fits each gap. Use only one word in each gap. There is an example at the beginning (0).

Jean-Michel Basquiat

The graffiti artist Basquiat, **(0)** ....WHO.......... became a famous painter, was the star of the 1980s New York art scene. Since his early death, aged 27, his reputation has grown **(1)** .... and more and art critics say he was responsible **(2)** .... an increased interest in painting. What was he really like? Basquiat the man and Basquiat the painter are hard to separate. He lived **(3)** .... and died harder, from an unintentional heroin overdose, and had more of the rock-star persona **(4)** .... the art aesthete about him, a cool celebrity sparkle that he couldn't always rely **(5)** .... to keep him out of trouble. Some art connoisseurs find his work hard to take seriously; others, though, have an immediate, almost visceral response. To many, non-art critics, his work is fantastic: it feels contemporary, with a chaotic, musical sensibility. It is full of opposites, beautiful and hectic, young and **(6)** .... , graphic, arresting, packed with ambiguous codes; there's a questioning of identity, especially race, and a sampling of life's stimuli that takes in music, cartoons, commerce and institutions, as well **(7)** .... celebrities and art greats. You could spend hours in front of a Basquiat painting and like me find it the **(8)** .... fascinating modern painting you have ever seen.

READING

WARM-UP

1 DISCUSS in pairs.

1. Have you heard of Urban Art? What do you think it might be? Can you think of any examples?
2. What about Land Art? Can using natural forms or transforming existing features be considered as art?

C Recognising links within a text

2 READ and listen to the texts about different forms of Urban and Land Art and match them to the pictures.

> **TIP** You need lots of practice in skimming and scanning for this activity, reading quickly and looking for specific information. Remember to ask yourself why a particular part of the text matches a question before you answer. This will help check your choices. Be careful not to choose an answer on the basis of similar vocabulary alone.

FIRST Reading and Use of English – Part 7

3 MULTIPLE MATCHING. Read the texts again. For questions 1-10, choose from the paragraphs (A-D). The same paragraph may be chosen more than once.

Which paragraph

discusses how art that began as political or social statements is now accepted as mainstream?	1
explains that this form of art was once seen as vandalism?	2
talks about artists who produce their art works at a higher level than most?	3
mentions two particular artists who have used natural surroundings in their work?	4
shows how art can make pictorial comments on overcrowding in cities?	5
gives an example from a street in New York?	6
says that this art form is characterised by bright colours and painted signatures?	7
introduces two different forms of artistic expression?	8
explains how the impossible was made possible in an unexpected way?	9
shows how concepts of space can be viewed in a different light?	10

1

2

Forms of artistic

3.9

A Urban Art

This is an art form that started as Street Art and Graffiti. The inspiration grew from modern city landscape as a social and political comment on urban life-styles. Originally criticised as vandalism, it is now an accepted art form and appears more and more in the best-known galleries around the world. Most Urban Art is created to be seen by as many people as possible in public locations and is usually unofficial. This form of art includes spray paint graffiti, stencil graffiti, poster art, sticker art, street installations, and sculpture. Well-known examples include wall poetry like *Broken Promises* by John Fekner in New York's Bronx or the *Fearless Girl* statue on Wall Street by artist Kristen Visbal, which has become the most famous example of female equality.

B Street Art

A French couple, she works as a comedian and he as a graffiti artist, have been raising Street Art to a higher and higher level – to the rooftops! Ella and Pitr began working together in France on various urban projects painting on walls and then roofs and parking spaces. Their project entitled *Sommeils Lourds* ('Deep Sleep') is about space or rather the less and less space we have in our cities. Their enormous sleeping giants, more like ordinary people than the worst fantasy monsters, are crushed into limited spaces, often bent and uncomfortable and are meant to be a comment on the smaller and smaller spaces around them. They are sleeping in the midst of the greatest urban noise, traffic, buildings and pollution. Because they are seen from above, these images give a new perspective on urban life and emphasise how much more vulnerable we are.

C Graffiti

This form of art first began in New York in the Seventies when young people used spray paint or other art material to create images on walls, buildings and subway trains. Their works were characterised mainly by their brightly coloured images known as 'wildside' or their use of stylised

expression

monograms called 'tags'. Famous New York pioneers were Jean-Michel Basquiat and Keith Haring. Haring's work and imagery expressing concepts of birth, death, sexuality and war, are highly political and have become among the most widely recognised visual languages of the 20th century. Some of the best-known recent graffiti artists, like Banksy and Barry McGee, are accepted as mainstream now and exhibited in the most prestigious art galleries around the world.

D Land Art

This form of artistic expression, also called Earth Art or Environmental Art, has grown as a rejection of the commercialisation of art and the emergence of a strong environmental movement which became less and less enthusiastic about urban living. Artists like Eduardo Sanguinetti, the Latino-American philosopher and land-artist, used natural materials like soil, rocks, vegetation and water. They used natural spaces in such a way that they could also become functional as plants or habitats for animals. Another of the most interesting environmental artists is Christo, who first with his wife and then on his own, transformed buildings and public spaces so that the more people looked at them the more they realised they could see them in a different light. One of his most recent art works was to create walkways across Lake Iseo in Italy enabling more and more people to perform the 'miracle' of walking across the lake to the island of Monte Isola.

4 FIND the words in the texts which mean the following:

1. deliberate destruction or damage of private or public property (para. A); VANDALISM
2. a professional entertainer or actor particularly one who makes an audience laugh (para. B); COMEDIAN
3. pressed or squeezed so as to change the shape (para. B); CRUSHED
4. a design made up of combined letters, normally a person's initials (para. C); MONOGRAMS
5. the most commonly accepted group or style (para. C); MAINSTREAM
6. any form of passage used for walking (para. D). WALKWAYS

Word formation: compound words

Compound words are formed from two words that are next to each other, joined together as one word or joined with a hyphen.

5 FIND some compound words from the texts.

6 FORM compound words by joining a word from list A to a word from list B.

A		B	
old	some	time	quake
life	grand	tree	stop
bus	apple	light	port
earth	air	board	fashioned
moon	skate	mother	bag
paper		where	

7 COMPLETE the sentences with a suitable compound noun from the texts.

1. Graffiti art began as a protest against uncomfortable forms of .... in cities around the world.
2. There are some works of art specifically made to remain in a chosen ....
3. The .... paintings by the French artists, Ella and Pitr, are made to be seen from the air.
4. Some famous graffiti has been painted on the walls or on the trains in the New York ....
5. There is now a frightening .... made of transparent glass above the Grand Canyon in Colorado.
6. One of the most famous .... is in the Great Salt Lake in the USA.
7. .... is a well-known form of graffiti made by spraying bright colours on walls or buildings.
8. Christo has become a more famous .... than his wife.

C Discussing ideas and relating them to personal experience

8 DISCUSS the questions.

1. Can the Arts be an effective form of protest or social comment? Give examples.
2. Should Street Art or Land Art be seen in a similar way as traditional or classical art?

9 WRITE a brief paragraph of 10/12 lines about any particular artwork you have seen which could be classified as Urban or Land Art. Describe it, say what you think the artist's message or intention might be and whether in your opinion it is effective or not.

Expressions using comparatives

1 READ sentences 1-3 and match the comparative expressions to the correct meanings A-C.

1 ☐ Graffiti appears **more and more** in the best-known galleries around the world.

2 ☐ **The more** people looked at them **the more** they realised they could see them in a different light.

3 ☐ Earth Art has grown as a rejection of the commercialisation of art and the emergence of a strong environmental movement which **became less and less enthusiastic** about urban living.

A A comparison that leads into another.
B A considerable decrease.
C An increasing amount.

Grammar reference 6.2

2 COMPLETE the sentences with the correct comparative expression using the adjectives in brackets.

1 Finding the tickets for the festival is getting .... (hard) every year.
2 The .... (much) you pay, the .... (good) service you get.
3 My grandad's health is getting .... (good) thanks to the medicine.
4 The .... (long) we waited for him to arrive, the .... (worried) we felt.
5 The job market is becoming .... (competitive) for young people.
6 The .... (little) mistakes my students make, the .... (high) their marks are.
7 *The Lord of the Rings* is a difficult book to read, but once you get into it, it becomes .... (interesting).
8 My mother works all day, that's why she has .... (little) time to cook.
9 We are going to move house because our street is getting .... (noisy).
10 The .... (many) pages of this book you read, the .... (involved) you'll get.

FREQUENT MISTAKES **Modifiers of comparatives**

You cannot use *very* to modify comparatives and superlatives. To add emphasis to comparatives use ***much/ far/ a lot*** + adjectives, adverbs, uncountable nouns and ***many/ far*** + plural nouns.

*You are **far more** tolerant than I am.*
*There are **many more ticket** sales than ever.*

Grammar reference 6.3

Linkers of manner: *like / as*

3 READ sentences 1-4 and explain the different function of *like* and *as*.

1 Originally criticised **as** vandalism, it is now an accepted art form.
2 She works **as** a comedian.
3 Their enormous *Sleeping Giants* are more **like** ordinary people.
4 Artists **like** Eduardo Sanguinetti used natural materials **like** soil, rocks, vegetation and water.

4 CHOOSE the correct answer to revise your knowledge about *like* and *as*.

1 They express *similarity / difference*.
2 *Like / As* is a conjunction.
3 *As / Like* is a preposition.
4 You can use *like / as* before a noun to refer to an occupation.

Grammar reference 6.4

5 COMPLETE the sentences with *like* or *as*.

1 Most people are keen on team games .... football and rugby.
2 Tell Joan how dreadful she is dressed .... that famous actress.
3 The train was late, ... everyone expected.
4 You must write this email .... this.
5 He had a part .... a merchant in that play.
6 You can do .... you like.
7 She is described .... a promising pianist.
8 Your attic is so hot! It's .... an oven.

6 COMPLETE the sentences with the correct comparative expression of the adjectives in brackets or *like/as*.

1 There is an increase in the world population, that's why there are .... (many) people.
2 I like your perfume, it smells .... oak and roses.
3 Rugby is getting .... (popular) among young people.
4 He works .... a sculptor and exhibits his works in the best-known galleries.
5 .... (hard) he works .... (little) free time he has.
6 The situation of the weather is very serious .... we heard on TV last night.
7 The children are driving me mad! It seems that .... (happy) they are, ... (loud) they scream.
8 That artist uses a great variety of materials .... wood, rock and steel.

WARM-UP

1 **DISCUSS** in pairs. Do you think the Arts should be taught at school? Is it important for children to receive an education in music, art and drama? Should this be part of the curriculum or an outside activity?

C Expressing and defending your opinions

TIP This part of the exam is testing your ability to comprehend and carry out a task, but also your ability to interact with others. Remember not just to concentrate on your opinion, but also to listen attentively to the other candidate and where necessary encourage them to contribute to the discussion.

FIRST Speaking – Part 3

2 **COLLABORATIVE TASK.** Imagine that your school has decided to introduce some after-school activities. Here are some possible options. Talk in pairs about the different new skills the various activities would teach (two minutes). Then decide which two you think would teach the most useful skills (one minute).

- playing a musical instrument
- drawing and painting
- theatre and drama
- a school choir
- learning about different cultures
- creating fashion – sewing and knitting

What skills could students learn from these activities?

Which two activities would teach the most useful skills?

PROCESS LANGUAGE

Speaking – Part 3

Bringing someone else into the discussion
What do you think about ... ?
Wouldn't you say that ... ?
Do you agree?
Isn't it true that ... ?

Explaining your point
What I wanted to say was ...
But that's not what I meant.
Perhaps I didn't express that point clearly.
I don't think you understand what I was saying.

Speaking reference p. 195

C Talking about and comparing personal experiences on a given topic

TIP It is very important to give full answers to the questions asked in this section. Never limit your answers to the minimum of 'yes' or 'no'. It may help you to think of the question words 'Why?', 'How?', 'When?', 'Where?' when answering the interlocutor. If he or she asks 'Do you like the idea of after-school clubs?', you shouldn't merely say 'yes' or even 'yes, I do' but explain why and when and where they are or should be held. Use your own personal experience as much as you can – it is always the most interesting way to carry on with the discussion.

FIRST Speaking – Part 4

3 **DISCUSSION.** In groups of three ask and answer the questions.

1 What benefits can you gain from acting in a school drama production?
2 How might studying music enrich other areas of your life?
3 Do you have to have special talents to be good at painting or drawing?
4 Is fashion art? Can designing clothes and following the latest trends be a legitimate area of study?
5 Should the study of culture, both traditional and contemporary, be an obligatory subject at Secondary School?

WARM-UP

1 DISCUSS in pairs. Are you interested in design? Does the external appearance of an object or a building matter? Can you think of any exceptional examples of successful designs?

2 LOOK at the following pictures of iconic designs and match the objects to the names (A-H).

- **A** ☐ British telephone box
- **B** ☐ All Star sneakers
- **C** ☐ Skateboard
- **D** ☐ Apple iPod
- **E** ☐ Rubik's cube
- **F** ☐ Mini Minor
- **G** ☐ Lego
- **H** ☐ Vespa

3 ADD a further two design items that you know of.

C Listening for specific information

TIP

Remember to listen carefully to catch the complete meaning in the listening text, and those words similar to ones in the questions may be mis-matches, distractions rather than the correct answers.

FIRST Listening – Part 1

4 3.10 **EXTRACTS WITH MULTIPLE-CHOICE QUESTIONS. You will hear people talking about eight different design icons. For questions 1-8, choose the best answer (A, B or C).**

1 You hear a young man talking about the Rubik cube.
What are players of the Rubik's cube trying to achieve?

- **A** They want to return the six faces back to their original colours in the quickest time possible.
- **B** They want to twist the cube into different shapes and numbers of sides.
- **C** They want to return to the success of the original cube.

2 You hear a girl talking about the Mini Minor.
Why did the Mini influence car manufacturers?

- **A** Because of its attractive design.
- **B** Because it replaced the unpopular Ford Model T car.
- **C** Because the new design gave more space inside the car.

3 You hear two friends talking about the skateboard.
Why was the skateboard invented by Frank Nasworthy faster than previous models?

- **A** He wanted his board to look like a Cadillac car.
- **B** He changed the material the wheels were made of.
- **C** He improved the quality of the iron wheels.

4 You hear a grandfather talking to his grandson.
Why is the telephone box not used as much as before?

- **A** Because it is no longer useful.
- **B** Because its designer made more important designs.
- **C** Because it became too old.

5 You hear a young man talking about Lego.
Who owns the current Lego company?

- **A** A grandson of the original owner.
- **B** An international Toy company.
- **C** A Danish company based in Switzerland.

6 You hear two girls talking on the phone.
Why does Katie know all about the Vespa scooter?

- **A** Because it has been in so many films and fashion photos.
- **B** Because she spoke about it at an art class.
- **C** Because she owns one herself.

7 You hear a boy talking to his mum.
What makes the iPod different from other digital devices?

- **A** The range of things you can do.
- **B** The pleasing appearance.
- **C** The original model has remained the same over time.

8 You hear a man talking about one of his most prized possessions.
Who designed the famous All Star sneakers?

- **A** The founder of the Converse footwear company.
- **B** A man working for Nike.
- **C** A basketball player who had sore feet.

5 DISCUSS in pairs. What can be considered design features of your town or area? Consider statues, buildings, Street Art and fashion in your discussion.

VIDEO
Making art

C Watching and understanding a short film

1 WATCH the whole video about artist Jack West and say if the following sentences are true (T) or false (F). Correct the false ones.

1 Jack decided that art was more than a passing passion after university. T F
2 Creativity is to do with big objects. T F
3 He uses laser to cut the materials. T F
4 He thinks machines are sculptures. T F
5 He believes machines are only objects. T F
6 One of the biggest difficulties in being an artist in London is moving heavy objects. T F
7 He is very proud of the works of his that are exhibited in public places. T F
8 He is aware it will take him a long time to create works with permanence and public relevance. T F

2 WATCH the second part of the video (from 00:32 to 00:58) and complete with the missing words.

For me being **(1)** .... is mostly about having the time and **(2)** .... and space, to explore new **(3)** .... or explore new **(4)** .... or having a **(5)** .... in which I have an idea and it **(6)** .... and it **(7)** .... and becomes something bigger than it is. And I think that's when I find that I'm most creative is when I am kind of developing new things and looking for new ideas and exploring in an **(8)** .... way.

3 WATCH the third part of the video (from 00:59 to 03:10) and write:

1 the materials he uses;
2 his method of work;
3 his practical difficulties when working;
4 the two ways he conceives of the machine;
5 the biggest reward for him.

4 DISCUSS in pairs. How does Jack's creativity lead to innovation? Why does he make art? What do you think of his works? Do you like them? What do they communicate to you?

LEARN BY DOING

THINKING CREATIVELY

5 DISCUSS in groups.

1 Why do you think people are reluctant to have an opinion about art?
2 What makes an object a piece of art?
3 Is it worth spending some time looking at a work of art? Why or why not?
4 Can art change somebody's understanding of the world?

6 LOOK at the work below by French street artist JR.

Portrait of a Generation: Braquage, Ladj Ly, Les Bosquets, Montfermeil, France, 2004

Describe it and your reaction to it. Do you think that a work like this may change the way we assume things about people?

7 CARRY out a survey about your classmates' favourite work of art and create a virtual art gallery for your class. Follow these steps:

Step 1 Allow each student one week to think about their favourite work of art.
Step 2 Each student prepares a slide describing the artwork.
Step 3 Divide the class into groups. Each group will create a room in the gallery by inserting their chosen artworks.
Step 4 Use one of the many templates available on the net to create your virtual art gallery.
Step 5 Comment on what your virtual art gallery tells about you as a class.

WARM-UP

1 DISCUSS. Where was your last school trip? Did you visit a city of historic interest? Did you visit an art gallery or museum? Do you ever go on school outings to museums in your own town or area? Talk about what you liked or didn't like about the visits.

C Expressing personal opinions on a specific experience

2 READ the review of a visit to a museum and decide which number (1-5) corresponds to which part of the review (A-E).

(1) Our class has recently visited the museum in the Sforza Castle in Milan.

(2) This imposing castle, built and rebuilt from the fourteenth to nineteenth centuries, houses nine different museums and we visited four: the museums of ancient art, of applied arts, musical instruments and the Rondanini Pietà.

(3) I found that the exhibits were well spaced out and well lit and every room had information sheets in various languages. There was an impressive variety of objects on show, from statues to paintings to tapestries as well as a very interesting display of furniture and musical instruments from all ages and countries.

(4) In my opinion there was too much to take in during a single visit and the information sheets were far too detailed. I think they should have a shorter alternative with less information for those who want an overall view. Also some of the indications were difficult to follow.

(5) In conclusion, I would say it was a stimulating experience with the best part being the very moving Pietà in a separate museum at the end.

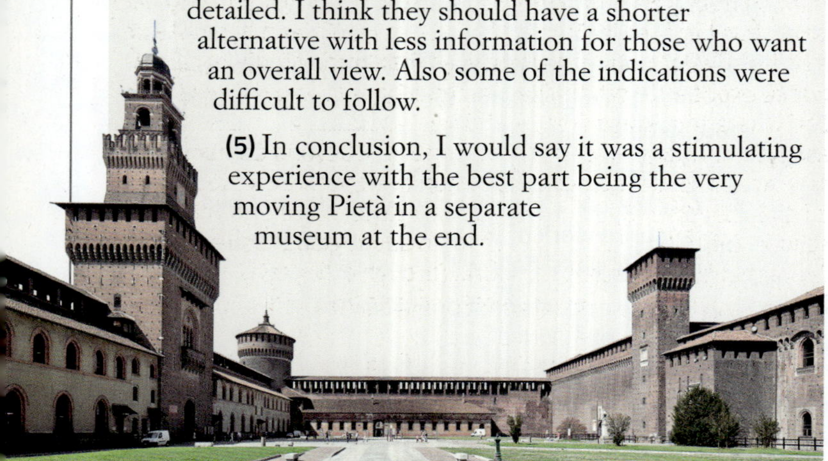

- **A** ☐ Positive points
- **B** ☐ Concluding personal opinion
- **C** ☐ Negative points
- **D** ☐ Some information about the place visited
- **E** ☐ Introduction – describing where the visit was

3 READ the review again and answer the questions.

1. Where was the visit to?
2. Which museums did the class visit?
3. What did the reviewer praise about the visit?
4. What did the reviewer criticise about it?
5. What was the highlight of the visit?
6. What was the overall impression of the reviewer?

TIP One of the choices in Part 2 can be a review. You will normally be asked to write a review for a magazine or website about either a book, film, holiday or school trip. It is important to give information about what you are reviewing but also express your opinion giving positive and negative points. The review should end with a personal recommendation.

FIRST Writing – Part 2

4 A REVIEW. An international arts website is looking for reviews of local museums for a new section called 'Making the most of our culture'. You have decided to write a review of a museum you've recently visited. Describe the visit and say what you think about it. Would you recommend this museum to others?

PROCESS LANGUAGE

Writing – Part 2 (a review)

Expressing positive opinions
I found the ... better/more interesting/more stimulating ...
I've never seen a more well-spaced/well lit ...
There was an impressive selection/range/display/ variety of exhibits/paintings/statues ...
Overall, I enjoyed the visit because ...

Expressing negative opinions
I thought the ... were worse/not as interesting as/less stimulating than ...
There was too much/not enough ...
I think the museum/gallery should ...

Expressing concluding opinions
On the whole, I think that ...
In conclusion, I found that ...
Finally, I believe that ...

Writing reference p. 202

5 CLASS ACTIVITY. Make a review board in the classroom where students can post reviews of films, books, exhibitions, visits or holidays. To make it more visually exciting, the different reviews can award stars from one to five.

Review Units 5-6

ZTE ONLINE
Interactive exercises

VOCABULARY ACTIVATOR

1 CHOOSE the correct alternative to complete the sentences.

1 Everyone using a computer is obviously concerned about the issues of *identity* / *diversity* theft.
2 A person used to travelling and open to new cultures and ideas is someone *nationally* / *internationally* minded.
3 *Architecture* / *Painting* is becoming increasingly popular as beautiful new buildings are built in public places where everyone can see them.
4 Of all the different aspects of literature, I personally find *sculpture* / *poetry* the most difficult.
5 Film, dance and opera are among the many forms of *entertainment* / *drama* on offer in the city centre.
6 *Awareness* / *Interaction* refers to the ability to find out about possible questions affecting the contemporary world.

2 COMPLETE the paragraph with a suitable phrasal verb from the box in the correct tense.

call for ▪ use up ▪ sign up ▪ deal with ▪ put on ▪ build up

Art and creativity have often been used in the past to **(1)** .... greater understanding and more cooperation within communities and even as a way to get countries to **(2)** .... to peace treaties. A visual message can **(3)** .... action on a local problem that many might never have otherwise been aware of. Street Art is a common way of drawing attention to problems affecting the environment. A graffiti artist who paints a child in a gas mask near a power station is giving a very clear message. The performing arts have often been used for such messages. Dance companies have **(4)** .... many productions about war and conflict. Dramatists too **(5)** .... difficult issues about race and gender in their plays. When politicians **(6)** .... all the possibilities for talks and discussions, perhaps they should turn to art for help in solving tricky questions.

GRAMMAR

3 MATCH a beginning (1-5) with a suitable ending (A-E).

1 ☐ I always feel very emotional
2 ☐ Tom will definitely play in the match on Saturday
3 ☐ I would look for a job in journalism or photography
4 ☐ If only I had listened to the history of art teacher more,
5 ☐ If he hadn't had such brilliant ideas,

A if I had already finished school.
B the scientist wouldn't have become so famous.
C then I might have understood the modern art show.
D if I see a particularly moving art exhibition.
E if he manages to finish all his homework by Friday.

4 COMPLETE the sentences with the adjectives in brackets in the comparative or superlative form.

1 Bob is not as clever as his sister, she is much .... (intelligent) than him.
2 What a great film! It was the .... (good) action film I've ever seen.
3 The world is getting .... (warm) and there are more and more problems with the climate.
4 That Maths test was simple, in fact I think it's the .... (easy) test we've had so far this year.
5 I didn't like that concert at all, I thought it was the .... (interesting) concert of the season.
6 Don't you think Banksy is one of the .... (controversial) street artists around at the moment?

USE OF ENGLISH

FIRST Reading and Use of English – Part 1

5 MULTIPLE-CHOICE CLOZE. For questions 1-8, read the blog below and decide which answer (A, B, C or D) best fits each gap. There is an example at the beginning (0).

GLOBAL AWARENESS AND SCHOOLS

If sixth formers at Impington Village College are more accustomed **(0)** .... most students to questioning their place in the world, there is good reason. The popular comprehensive school just outside Cambridge is one of the pioneers of the International Baccalaureate in the UK and its sixth form attracts young people from all over the world. This year, 57 overseas students have **(1)** .... for the two-year IB diploma programme making the school's international sixth form centre seem **(2)** .... like a mini United Nations than a traditional English state school. Their presence is invaluable because it **(3)** .... greater awareness of a wide range of cultural perspectives that home students would not be exposed to otherwise. Students have to know themselves and where they come from – and **(4)** .... is always important – but if they learn to look beyond Cambridge and recognise the incredible opportunities that are created by diversity they **(5)** .... global citizens. If more schools **(6)** .... children about global issues and encouraged them to see the world through other eyes, there **(7)** .... fewer global issues to **(8)** ....

0	A than	B with	C of	D because
1	A put on	B signed up	C dealt with	D called for
2	A much	B less	C most	D more
3	A calls for	B signs up	C deals with	D puts on
4	A identify	B identification	C identity	D diversity
5	A would become	B will become	C became	D become
6	A would teach	B teaches	C had taught	D taught
7	A would be	B will be	C were	D won't be
8	A call for	B put on	C deal with	D sign up

FIRST Reading and Use of English – Part 2

6 OPEN CLOZE. **For questions 1-8, read the text below and think of the word which best fits each gap. Use only one word in each gap. There is an example at the beginning (0).**

BAND AID 30

Band Aid 30 is the 2014 incarnation of the charity supergroup Band Aid. The group was re-formed by Bob Geldof and Midge Ure. Geldof later said that **(0)** ....WHEN.... the United Nations contacted him, saying help was urgently needed to prevent the Ebola crisis in Western Africa spreading throughout the world, he had to help. 'If I **(1)** ....HAD.... not done something, I couldn't **(2)** ....HAVE.... lived with it,' he declared. As in previous incarnations, the group covered the track *Do They Know It's Christmas?*, written in 1984 by Geldof and Ure.

The song was recorded by some of the **(3)** ....BIGGEST.... selling current British and Irish pop acts, including One Direction, Sam Smith, Ed Sheeran, Emeli Sandé, Ellie Goulding and Rita Ora, Bastille and Guy Garvey of Mercury. Prize-winning band Elbow were also on board, along with Chris Martin (Coldplay) and Bono (U2) – who has probably done more **(4)** ....THAN.... any other singer to help on global issues.

Footage of the recording session in Sarm West Studios in Notting Hill, London, was streamed live on an official app, forming the basis for the music video. The record was produced by Paul Epworth, who has worked with some of the **(5)** ....MOST.... famous pop artists like Adele and One Direction.

The video was introduced by Geldof on the X Factor television show and began with shots of victims of Ebola. 'It was difficult viewing not meant for an entertainment show,' he commented 'but if we hadn't shown the reality of the problem, people **(6)** ....WOULD.... not have felt the need to contribute. All contributions went towards battling the Ebola virus epidemic in West Africa.'

The next day the BBC reported that the song was the **(7)** ....QUICKEST.... selling single of the year so far, with 206,000 copies sold in one day. Martin Talbot, Chief Executive of the Official Charts Company, said: 'Everyone expected a strong start from Bob Geldof and his team, but they have done **(8)** ....MORE.... than anyone imagined.'

FIRST Reading and Use of English – Part 3

7 WORD FORMATION. **For questions 1-8, read the text below. Use the word given in capitals at the end of some of the lines to form a word that fits in the gap in the same line. There is an example at the beginning (0).**

ARCHITECTURE AS A 'SOCIAL ART'

Challenging the preconception that good design costs more and
illustrating the ways in which the lives of the **(0)** ....POOREST.... **POOR**
people on Earth can be improved through successful building and
design, Article 25's 'Art for Architecture' exhibition features works,
(1) ....OLD-FASHIONED.... and modern, donated by many top architects and **FASHION**
artists. Demonstrating the way in which design can be a real force for
good while working on the ground alongside aid agencies, NGOs (ONG), grass
roots **(2)** ....COMMUNITY.... organisations, and humanitarian charities, **COMMUNE**
Article 25 have a **(3)** ....REPUTATION.... for quality, innovation, and **REPUTE**
integrity in bringing award winning architectural design to benefit those
most in need.
'As a designer I have always been driven by a **(4)** ....BELIEF.... **BELIEVE**
that the quality of our surroundings directly influences the quality
of our lives, whether in the **(5)** ....WORKPLACE...., at home or in the **WORK**
public spaces that make up our cities,' explains the celebrated architect
Norman Foster, who has donated a piece to the auction. 'Architecture
is a social art – a **(6)** ....NECESSITY.... and not a luxury. It is generated **NECESSARY**
by the needs of people, both spiritual and physical. It has much to do
with **(7)** ....OPTIMISM...., joy and reassurance – of order in a **OPTIMIST**
(8) ....DISORDERED.... world, of privacy in the midst of many, of light on a **ORDER**
dull day.'

FIRST Reading and Use of English – Part 4

8 KEY WORD TRANSFORMATIONS. **For questions 1-6, complete the second sentence so that it has a similar meaning to the first sentence, using the word given. Do not change the word given. You must use between two and five words, including the word given. Here is an example (0).**

0 He thought that if he had a lot of money, he would buy an island in the Pacific Ocean.
WERE
He thought that IF HE WERE RICH, he would buy an island in the Pacific Ocean.

1 He drove too fast and had an accident.
MIGHT
If he hadn't driven so fast he ....MIGHT NOT HAVE HAD.... an accident.

2 I regret being rude to the policeman who gave me a fine.
WISH
I ....WISH I HADN'T BEEN.... rude to the policeman who gave me a fine.

3 The music became increasingly loud, so I asked the band to stop playing.
LOUDER
The music became ....LOUDER AND LOUDER.... so I asked the band to stop playing.

4 If the weather doesn't improve, we won't think about having a barbeque on Saturday.
UNLESS
We won't think about having a barbeque on Saturday ....UNLESS THE WEATHER.... improves.

5 The new regulations about identity cards will become obligatory from March 1st.
FORCE
The new regulations about identity cards ....WILL COME INTO FORCE.... from March 1st.

6 They had never seen such a wonderful firework display in their lives.
THE
It was ....THE GREATEST FIREWORK DISPLAY.... they had ever seen.

DULL = NOIOSO

7 A techno world

Inquadrami per guardare i video e ascoltare gli audio di questa unità

VOCABULARY ACTIVATOR

FLIPPED classroom

VIDEO Technology

WARM-UP

1 LOOK at the pictures and discuss in pairs.

1 How important is technology in your life?
2 Which of the objects in the pictures do you use every day and which could you not do without?

C Learning to use vocabulary in context

2 4.1 **LISTEN to four people describing technical devices and match them to one of the following objects.**

A [1] cash machine
B [4] smartphone
C [3] GPS
D [2] microwave oven

FOCUS ON VOCABULARY

3 MATCH the words or expressions (1-10) to their meanings (A-J).

1 [B] gadgets/devices
2 [C] app (application)
3 [G] profile
4 [I] a post/to post
5 [J] back up
6 [F] log on/sign in (LOG IN)
7 [E] log out/sign off
8 [A] tap/key in
9 [D] upload/download
10 [H] keep in touch

A use the keyboard to type in what is required
B something made for a particular purpose, especially a mechanical or electric invention
C a download that allows special or particular use for a computer or smartphone
D put or take information or photos or music onto/from your computer
E end a work session using a multiuser system, or a connection to such a system
F use a system that permits a user to enter a name and password in order to access multiple applications
G a concise informal outline of a person
H maintain a connection through frequent communication
I send a message to a group on a computer
J make a copy of what you have on the computer in case of a crash

4 COMPLETE the paragraph with words or phrases from exercise 3.

I have just had delivered an extraordinary **(1)** ....GADGET.... to attach to my computer. It communicates with an **(2)** ....APP.... on my smartphone and can automatically **(3)** ....DOWNLOAD.... photos and music from the phone onto a tablet or laptop. I **(4)** ....LOGGON.... on this morning straightaway and the first thing I did was create a new **(5)** ....PROFILE.... before **(6)** ....POSTING.... all my friends. I'm so pleased, it works really well and can also keep **(7)** ....IN TOUCH.... with my messages or I can **(8)** ....TAP IN.... texts to send out. It doesn't lose anything when I **(9)** ....LOG OUT.... because it has a feature that automatically creates a **(10)** ....BACK UP.... of everything.

5 DISCUSS. Look up the different definitions of the word 'smart' and say why it is or isn't a suitable word for smartphones and other devices.

WARM-UP

1 **DISCUSS** in pairs. What do you understand by the term 'artificial intelligence'? Can you think of any examples? How have our lives been affected by AI?

C Reading, interpreting and understanding information

2 **READ** and listen to the article and decide which of the highlighted words has the following meaning:

1 wound or cause harm to
2 logical, strong
3 draw into
4 recommended strongly
5 inserted, attached
6 injury or demage

4.2

How to regulate artificial intelligence

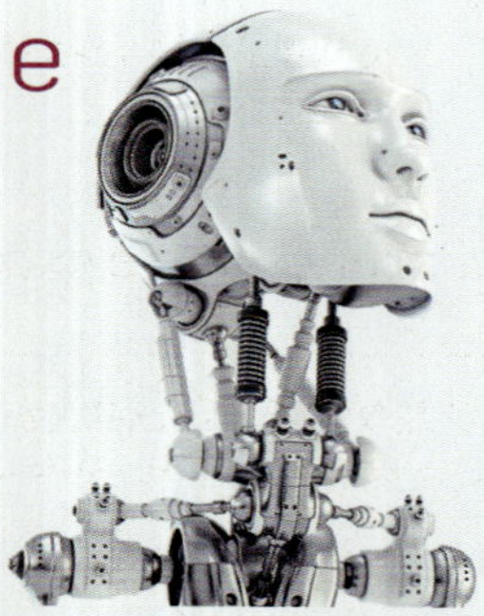

The technology millionaire Elon Musk recently urged leaders to regulate the use of artificial intelligence (AI) 'before it's too late.' Mr Musk insists that artificial intelligence represents an 'existential threat to humanity,' an alarmist view that confuses AI science with science fiction. Nevertheless, even AI researchers like me recognise that there are valid concerns about its impact on weapons, jobs and privacy.
As a researcher, I believe that of course AI must be developed but, shouldn't steps be taken to at least slow down progress in the interest of caution? My belief is that AI systems need to be regulated. However, it would be totally wrong to try to slow down or stop progress in this rapidly developing and fascinating field.

I propose three rules inspired by the 'three laws of robotics' that were introduced by the writer Isaac Asimov in 1942.

1. A robot may not injure a human being or, through inaction, allow a human being to come to harm.
2. A robot must obey the orders that are given it by human beings, except when such orders would conflict with the previous law.
3. A robot must protect its own existence as long as such protection does not conflict with the previous two laws.

These three laws are elegant but ambiguous. I suggest a more concrete basis for avoiding AI harm, based on three rules of my own.

My first rule is that an AI system needs to be controlled under the same laws that apply to its human operator. This rule would cover private, corporate and government systems. In this rule, AI won't be allowed to engage in cyberbullying, stock manipulation or terrorist threats; the FBI couldn't release AI systems that entrap people into committing crimes. Autonomous vehicles mustn't be allowed to drive through red lights, or worse, international treaties can't be violated by AI weapons.

My second rule is that it must be clearly stated that an AI system is not human. As we have seen in the case of bots — computer programmes that can engage in increasingly sophisticated dialogue with real people —, society needs assurances that AI systems are clearly labelled as such.
My rule would ensure that people know when a bot is impersonating someone. AI systems don't just produce fake tweets; they also produce fake news videos. A fake video of former President Barack Obama has been recently released by researchers at the university of Washington where he convincingly appeared to be speaking words that had been grafted onto a video of him talking about something entirely different.

My third rule is that an AI system cannot retain or disclose confidential information without explicit approval from the source of that information. Because of their exceptional ability to automatically elicit, record and analyse information, AI systems are in a prime position to acquire confidential information. Think of all the conversations that Amazon Echo — a 'smart speaker' present in an increasing number of homes — hears. Even seemingly innocuous housecleaning robots create maps of your home. That is information that shouldn't be controlled by anyone else but you.

My three AI rules are, I believe, sound but far from complete. I introduce them here as a starting point for discussion. Whether or not you agree with Mr Musk's view about AI's rate of progress and its ultimate impact on humanity, it is clear that AI will be brought into our lives. Society needs to get ready.

(Adapted from an article by Oren Etzioni, in The New York Times, September 2017)

3 READ the article again and do the following activities.

A1 Why does the technology entrepreneur, Elon Musk, think the nation's governors should regulate AI?

A Because he thinks the technology is too sophisticated.
B Because he feels it could become dangerous.
C Because at the moment there are too many rules about AI.

A2 Which of the following meanings is closest to 'before it's too late' on line 3?

A Before other people do it.
B Before it becomes impossible.
C Before something disastrous happens.
D Before the present time.

A3 What point is the writer making in paragraph 1?

A Progress on AI should be stopped for the time being.
B AI should be regulated but not stopped.
C AI should be slowed down gradually and eventually stopped.
D There should not be any regulations regarding AI.

A4 Which are the three laws introduced by Asimov in 1942?

A5 Which of the following meanings is closest to the phrase 'elegant but ambiguous' on line 26?

A Smart and open to interpretation.
B Sophisticated and intelligent.
C Look good but don't have a clear meaning.
D Refined and open.

A6 Say whether the following information about the writer's first rule is true (T) or false (F).

A The same rule should apply to the AI system and the person controlling it. T F
B The rule should apply to all private and corporate uses but not to use by the government. T F
C The threat of cyberbullying and terrorist threats would not be covered by this rule. T F
D The use of AI should not interfere with international treaties. T F

A7 Explain the writer's second rule in your own words.

A8 Which two possibilities of uncontrolled private information does the writer give in his third rule?

A9 Which of the following best summarises the content of the article?

A The writer believes that the future of AI is potentially very dangerous and urges complete control.
B The writer sees the possible advantages of AI but warns of the possible dangers if the future use of AI is not regulated.
C The writer of the article is enthusiastic about the possibilities of AI in the future and wants to encourage its wide and indiscriminate use.
D The writer would like to see the formation of a controlling body to oversee the future development of AI and its use.

C Listening for specific information

4 4.3 **LISTEN** to four people giving their views on technology. Listen again and complete the sentences with one-three words.

1 In some ways technology has made our lives simpler, but it has also made them more .... and stressful.
2 With email and mobile phones, we are .... which is fine if we want to be in contact.
3 Using technology means we save a lot of time when we .... or buy goods online.
4 It is impossible now to imagine how life was before mobile phones ....
5 There is a danger, if we overuse technology, of becoming .... from the real world.
6 We frequently see people in restaurants or on the street talking on the phone instead of talking to the person ....
7 Jill's first laptop was given to her ....
8 She wasn't always in favour of technology, but now feels we must all .... into our lives.

Collocations and expressions for technology

5 MATCH the collocations and expressions (1-7) in the article to their definitions (A-G).

1 [ ] take steps
2 [ ] acquire, retain or disclose confidential information
3 [ ] engage in
4 [ ] rate of progress
5 [ ] fake tweets
6 [ ] cyberbullying
7 [ ] labelled

A speed at which something is advancing
B take part in something
C put into a specific category
D aggression towards others using the Internet
E carry out necessary actions
F get, keep or reveal secret information
G false messages

6 COMPLETE the sentences using the correct form of the collocations and expressions from exercise 5.

1 Experts in the field of technology must find ways to prevent the .... unless people give their permission.
2 It is certainly not easy and perhaps counter-productive to try to slow down the .... in developing AI projects.
3 Authorities should .... to regulate what is happening in the field of AI.
4 Misinformation and false news or .... have caused serious problems.
5 .... and other negative aspects of the Internet need to be monitored carefully.
6 The students were enthusiastic about being .... projects concerning future technology.
7 Experts in AI don't like being .... as interfering in the right to privacy.

Passives

1 READ sentences 1-3 and answer questions A-C.

1. The rules for artificial intelligence systems **are inspired by** the 'three laws of robotics'.
2. They **were introduced by** the writer Isaac Asimov in 1942.
3. A robot must obey the orders that **are given** to it **by** human beings.

A What is the subject in each sentence?

B What is the activator or agent of the verb?

C Which preposition introduces the agent?

2 MATCH each of the following examples (1-5) to one of the explanations (A-E) below.

1. My second rule is that it **must be** clearly **stated** that an AI system is not human.
2. Reports say that exams **were marked** too strictly this year.
3. An important painting **has been stolen** from the National Gallery.
4. **Shouldn't** steps **be taken** to at least slow down progress in the interest of caution?
5. It's natural to ask how and why AI **should be developed**.

The passive is used when

A [ ] the action is more important than the agent.

B [ ] the performer of the action, or agent, is unknown.

C [ ] it is not important to know who the agent is.

D [ ] the agent has already been mentioned.

E [ ] the agent is obvious to the reader or listener and therefore unnecessary.

Grammar reference 7.1

3 READ the sentences and underline the passive forms. Then rewrite them in the active form.

1. AI won't be allowed to engage in cyberbullying, stock manipulation or terrorist threats.
   Human beings ....
2. International treaties can't be violated by AI weapons.
   AI weapons ....
3. A fake video of former President Barack Obama has been recently released by researchers.
   Researchers ....
4. The 'three laws of robotics' were introduced by the writer Isaac Asimov in 1942.
   Asimov ....
5. I should have received the letter by now. It might have been sent to the wrong address.
   I should have received the letter by now.
   Someone ....
6. If you had locked the car, it wouldn't have been stolen.
   If you had locked the car, someone ....

FREQUENT MISTAKES

Be supposed to, be expected to, be asked to, be allowed/permitted to, be told to are very frequently used in the passive. They are followed by the infinitive.

*John **has been asked to** make a speech at the meeting.*
*You **are supposed to** wear a uniform.*
*You **are expected to** arrive by 8 o'clock.*

Grammar reference 7.2

4 FIND and correct the mistakes in the sentences. One of the sentences is correct.

1. Problems as well as advantages have brought into our lives with technology.
2. Closed Circuit Television Cameras will install on buses next month.
3. People request not to smoke anywhere in the building.
4. Job applicants informed of the result of the interview yesterday.
5. Examination candidates are expected to arrive ten minutes before the start of the test.
6. This dictionary often uses by our students.
7. Has your motorbike repaired yet?
8. You would not allow to arrive so late if you attended my school.

5 COMPLETE the second sentence using the word in capital letters so that it has a similar meaning to the first sentence.

1. The students are using the computers to carry out a history project. COMPUTERS
   The .... the students to carry out a history project.
2. My friend has given me this new gadget for my computer. BY
   This new gadget has .... my friend.
3. Researchers believe that AI systems will be the key to progress. IS
   Technology .... the key to progress.
4. The Prime Minister will make a statement shortly. BE
   A statement .... the Prime Minister shortly.
5. We haven't seen good manners for a very long time. BEEN
   Good manners .... for a very long time
6. They expect the plane from London to arrive on time. ARRIVE
   The .... on time.
7. The police officer saw the robber. WAS
   The robber .... the police officer.
8. The US Government is discussing changes in AI systems. ARE
   Changes in AI systems .... the US Government.

TIP Remember you can only use ONE word to fill each of the gaps. You cannot use abbreviations and you can't fill any of the gaps with a contraction like 'didn't' or 'he'll' because these count as two words. The only exception is 'can't' as 'cannot' is one word.

FIRST Reading and Use of English – Part 2

1 OPEN CLOZE. For questions 1-8, read the text below and think of the word which best fits each gap. Use only one word in each gap. There is an example at the beginning (0).

The Circle

The Circle is a gripping modern techno-thriller film based **(0)** ....ON.... a book of the same name by Dave Eggers. Both the book and the film **(1)** ....ARE.... expected to show the possible evils of over-using social media. The main character, Mae (Emma Watson) **(2)** ....IS.... given a job in a powerful tech and social media company. She is soon encouraged **(3)** ....BY.... the company's founder, Eamon Bailey (Tom Hanks) to take part in an experiment that touches the delicate area of privacy and ethics and will ultimately violate her **(4)** ....OWN.... freedom. Although the film has an impressive cast and attempts to deal with a particularly topical question, it received mixed reviews and **(5)** ....WAS.... criticised for being monotonous and lacking in originality. For some the film lacked interest because there was no build up and the evil of the tech company is made obvious from the beginning. There have **(6)** ....BEEN.... a lot of films made as warnings of the information age like the psychological thriller of *Mr. Robot* or the extremes of *Silicon Valley*. *The Circle* comes somewhere in **(7)** ....BETWEEN.... because it is an Orwellian drama about the dangers of a surveillance society but also tries to raise a genuine debate about young adulthood and its relationship with **(8)** ....SOCIAL.... media.

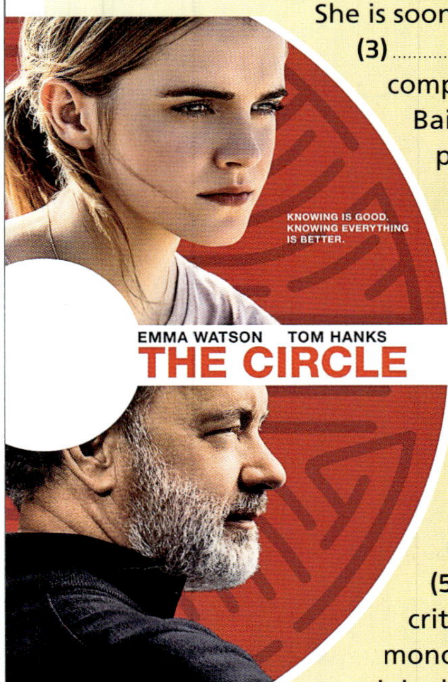

TIP Think carefully about whether the word required is a verb, noun, adjective or adverb – it could be any of these. Also think about the possibility of it being negative. Remember to read through the whole sentence before making a final decision.

FIRST Reading and Use of English – Part 3

2 WORD FORMATION. For questions 1-8, read the text below. Use the word given in capitals at the end of some of the lines to form a word that fits in the gap in the same line. There is an example at the beginning (0).

Drones

Drones were first **(0)** ....USED.... in World War I in developing automatic, unmanned airplanes, but their use has multiplied and drones are now widely used in many areas. **USE**

Drone technology has developed and prospered in the last few years. Individuals, commercial entities, and **(1)** ....GOVERNMENTS.... have come to realise that drones have multiple uses, which include aerial photography for **(2)** ....JOURNALISM.... and film as well as express shipping and **(3)** ....DELIVERY.... . They are used for gathering information or supplying essentials for disaster **(4)** ....MANAGEMENT.... and thermal sensor drones are used for search and rescue operations. **GOVERN** **JOURNAL** **DELIVER** **MANAGE**

Uses include geographic mapping of **(5)** ....INACCESSIBLE.... terrain and locations, law enforcement and border control surveillance. They are involved in safety inspections, crop **(6)** ....MONITORING.... and forecasting hurricanes and tornadoes. **ACCESS** **MONITOR**

Moreover, the **(7)** ....DEVELOPMENT.... of hundreds of more uses of drones is underway due to the multiple investments pouring into this **(8)** ....PROMISING.... industry everyday. **DEVELOP** **PROMISE**

(From www.businessinsider.com)

WARM-UP

1 DISCUSS in pairs.

1 Which apps do you have on your phone?
2 Do you have a fitness app or one to do with being healthy?
3 Do you think an app could help keep you fit and healthy?

C Recognising specific information within a text

2 READ and listen to the blog and say which of the apps or devices interests you most.

TIP Remember that it can be misleading to think an answer is correct simply because it contains the same word as one used in the text. It is the entire meaning of the phrase or sentence that is important, not just similar words.

FIRST Reading and Use of English – Part 5

3 MULTIPLE-CHOICE QUESTIONS. Read the blog again. For questions 1-6, choose the answer (A, B, C or D) which you think fits best according to the text.

1 Dave is enthusiastic about health apps and devices but
- A thinks there needs to be a wider choice available.
- B considers the ones currently available too complicated.
- C thinks there are so many it makes the selection difficult.
- D hasn't had any fitted recently.

2 Kate has recently had an app downloaded that
- A can be used to give nutritional information about the food she is eating.
- B can read food labels and rate the healthiness.
- C gives suggestions about what to eat each day.
- D tells her which food products to buy and which to avoid.

3 What could be surprising about the information from the sleep monitor apps?
- A The number of hours spent in a light sleep compared to those in a deep sleep.
- B The fact that most of us suffer from some sort of insomnia.
- C That it is better to wake up from a deep sleep rather than a light one.
- D The fact that most of us actually sleep more than we think.

4 What information is NOT available to runners from a fitness wrist watch?
- A The speed that you are currently running at.
- B The suitability of the running shoes you are currently wearing.
- C How your current speed relates to other runs you have already done.
- D Your pulse and heart rates.

5 Why does Dave think you can use the phobia apps with confidence?
- A Because they have been proved to be effective.
- B Because they are available on the national health service.
- C Because they have been put together by professionally trained specialists.
- D Because Dave has used them himself and speaks from personal experience.

6 In general the opinions on the forum concerning apps and devices can be described as
- A generally positive but with some reservations about the cost.
- B mixed, with some in favour and some suggesting alternative ways of checking up on health and fitness.
- C mostly enthusiastic and informative but with a lack of detailed information about personal use.
- D very positive and given from personal experience of using the apps or devices.

Healthcare and technology – friend or foe?

4.4

Get someone to fix you up with health apps, they're great! Hi everyone, this is Dave and today's forum is going to chat about health apps and devices. I don't know about you, but I reckon that smartphones are possibly the most dramatic advance in healthcare in living memory. Through one small device or app, we have access to a technological wonderland. The only problem is that there are so many apps to choose from. Has anyone out there had an app fitted recently? Or maybe you've had someone recommend a particular device. **Share with us!**

Hey Dave, and all of you following the forum. I have just had an app downloaded to help with checking what I eat. Each time I eat something I tap in the info and I've had the app programmed to work out the calories and nutritional value and tell me how much more I can eat without going into overload! I was told that after a while the app will learn my eating habits and make suggestions about a daily diet. There's also another I'm considering where I can have food products rated from 0 (unhealthy) to 10 (very healthy) by an app that scans food labels and uses an algorithm to analyse the ingredients and tell me the nutritional value. It's such a cool idea. **Kate**

Hi everyone, one of my personal favourites is an app to monitor sleep behaviour. Whether you have insomnia or not you can have your sleep patterns checked by one of several sleep apps. These apps are so sophisticated that they can tell you how long you have slept and how many hours were in deep sleep and how many in light sleep. Do you have to have special equipment fitted? No, all you need is to have a sensor applied to your finger. It was such a surprise for me to learn I actually sleep longer than I thought. If you want, you can also have yourself woken while you're in the lightest phase of sleep so that you feel readier to face the day! **Bob**

I'm into keeping fit and it has never been so easy with the myriad of fitness apps and devices. You can get fitted up with an app on your phone or have someone advise you on the best wrist fit watch. It's not really a watch at all, it's a mini computer that tells you all you want to know about your progress in a particular sport. There are so many functions. If you're running, it will tell you how fast you are going, how this works out as an average over your chosen distance and how this compares with your previous runs. It will also tell you your pulse and heart rate and if you want, it can let you listen to your favourite music while you run. Such devices can be used for walking, biking, even swimming. Julie

---

This is Dave again, I've had such fun reading your posts. I've heard of apps that can tell you about your mood changes, about your energy levels, apps to keep a check on blood pressure and blood sugar levels but one I want to share is one that helps with phobias. I have always suffered from arachnophobia but got someone to help me choose an app. With this, sufferers like me are shown a series of pictures of spiders from tiny ones to an interactive tarantula. You don't have fears treated irresponsibly as the apps are created by psychiatrists and officially approved by the national health service and I tell you – it works.

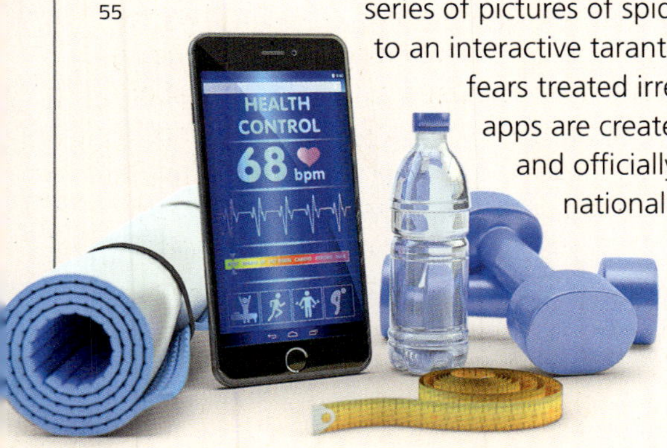

4 READ the text again and find the words which mean the following:

1. an object made for a particular purpose (para. 1);
2. a place of fantastic marvels (para. 1);
3. too much (para. 2);
4. whatever is required for a certain purpose or activity (para. 3);
5. a quantity intermediate to a set of quantities (para. 4);
6. fear of spiders (para. 5).

Word formation: prefixes

Prefixes can add to the meaning of a word: ***counter*** – *counterproductive*, ***down*** – *downgrade*, ***fore*** – *forehead*, ***out*** – *outlaw*, ***over*** – *overcome*, ***re*** – *return*, ***under*** – *undervalue*, ***inter*** – *interview*, ***trans*** – *transcontinental*.

5 FIND some examples of this use of prefixes in the text and say from which words they derive.

6 TRANSFORM the meaning of the words in the box using the prefixes above.

estimate ▪ size ▪ set ▪ national ▪ act ▪ value ▪ port ▪ see ▪ grow

7 MAKE suitable words using prefixes and the words given to complete the sentences.

1. Many of the apps to help keep you healthy or fit can be .... free. (LOAD)
2. .... flights are usually much longer than national ones. (CONTINENT)
3. The London .... is one of the most complex in the world. (GROUND)
4. The financial .... was so complicated I had it done by an adviser at the bank. (ACTION)
5. The model we made for our science project was a disaster and we had to .... everything from the beginning. (THINK).

C Discussing ideas and relating them to personal experience

8 DISCUSS the questions.

1. Can you foresee a time when apps and devices replace doctors? Why or why not?
2. Could these apps be considered dangerous? Why or why not?

9 WRITE a brief paragraph of 10/12 lines describing the kind of app or device that you would like to use. Describe what its functions should be and why you would like to use it.

Have/Get something done

1 READ sentences 1-2 and underline the form using *have/get* + the past participle. Who does the action in the sentences?

1 Has anyone out there had an app fitted recently?
2 All you need is to get a sensor applied to your finger.

Remember
When using the form *have/get something done* it is very rare to include the activator of the verb unless it is unexpected:
I'm having my hair cut by my sister this evening.

Grammar reference 7.3

2 WRITE sentences with the correct form of *have/get something done* and the prompts below.

1 I / get / the new table for the living room / deliver / last week.
2 The school / have / all its computers / update / next month.
3 He finds it difficult to read the newspaper. He / must have / his eyes / test.
4 They / ever / have anything / steal / from their flat?
5 Tina / have / her wedding dress / make / in Milan at the moment.
6 Our neighbours / get / a new garage / build / at the back of their house / recently.

3 COMPLETE these pairs of sentences with a suitable second sentence using the verbs given.

1 His beard is far too long. CUT
He needs ....
2 My car has been making strange noises. REPAIR
I'll have to ....
3 He fell over and spilt some coffee on the carpet. CLEAN
Don't worry, I'll ....
4 I like the new colour of the walls in your bedroom. REDECORATE
We've just ....
5 Her son's trousers are far too long. SHORTEN
She'll have to ....
6 The battery on my mobile phone doesn't last very long. CHECK
Why don't you .... ?

Expressing emphasis with *so* and *such*

4 READ sentences 1-5 and complete the rules A-E using *so* and *such*.

1 **Such** devices can be used for walking, biking, even swimming.
2 The only problem is that there are **so** many apps to choose from.
3 These apps are **so** sophisticated that they can tell you how long you have slept.
4 It's **such** a cool idea.
5 I've had **such** fun reading your posts.

A You use .... + adjectives/adverbs (+ *that* ...)
B You use .... + plural noun (+ *that* ...)
C You use .... + uncountable noun (+ *that* ...)
D You use .... + *a/an* + singular noun (+ *that* ...)
E You use .... + quantifiers (+ *that* ...)

Grammar reference 7.4

5 COMPLETE the sentences using *so* and *such*.

1 Artificial intelligence is .... a challenging field of study.
2 I think the whole matter is .... difficult to understand that it requires more study.
3 There is .... beautiful weather that we can go for a walk.
4 The novel has a very complicated plot. There are .... many different characters.
5 Robotics is .... an interesting subject that I want to become a specialist.

6 JOIN the two sentences together using *so* or *such*. You may need to make changes.

1 The tree in the garden has many branches. We must have it pruned.
2 The weather was wonderful. They decided to have a picnic.
3 The room is very dark. It's impossible to see where the furniture is.
4 There are good arguments against the building of the new factory. We have decided to vote against it.
5 It was a beautiful surprise. She burst into tears.

7 COMPLETE the second sentence using the word in capital letters so that it has a similar meaning to the first sentence.

1 She spoke very softly and I couldn't hear her. SO
She .... couldn't hear her.
2 This meat is delicious. I think I'll have some more. SUCH
This is .... that I think I'll have some more.
3 The children ate a lot and all got a stomach ache. MUCH
The children ate .... they all got a stomach ache.
4 What a wonderful journey, I'll always remember it! THAT
It's .... I'll never forget it!
5 She's read a lot, she's a real expert in literature. SO
She's read .... a real expert in literature.

SPEAKING

WARM-UP

1 DISCUSS. Which are the three most important technical devices in current use? Compare your ideas with your classmates.

2 LOOK at the phrases below to continue a discussion and write three sentences based on the discussion in exercise 1 using phrases from the box.

PROCESS LANGUAGE

Speaking – Part 3

Linking words to continue a discussion

Positive
as well as … / besides … / furthermore … / moreover … / what's more … / in addition … / therefore … / so … / obviously … / this is why …

Negative
but … / however … / on the other hand … / unfortunately … / alternately … / nevertheless … / another option would be …

Speaking reference p. 195

C Expressing personal opinions

TIP It is important to remember that this task is opinion based and there is no right or wrong answer. The task gives you the opportunity to show your range of language and your ability to invite the opinions and ideas of the other candidate. You are expected to share the interaction in this way and to initiate and respond appropriately.

FIRST Speaking – Part 3

3 COLLABORATIVE TASK. Imagine you are looking at different technological devices. Talk in pairs about the advantages and disadvantages of the different devices shown (two minutes). Then decide which two you would most like to have (one minute).

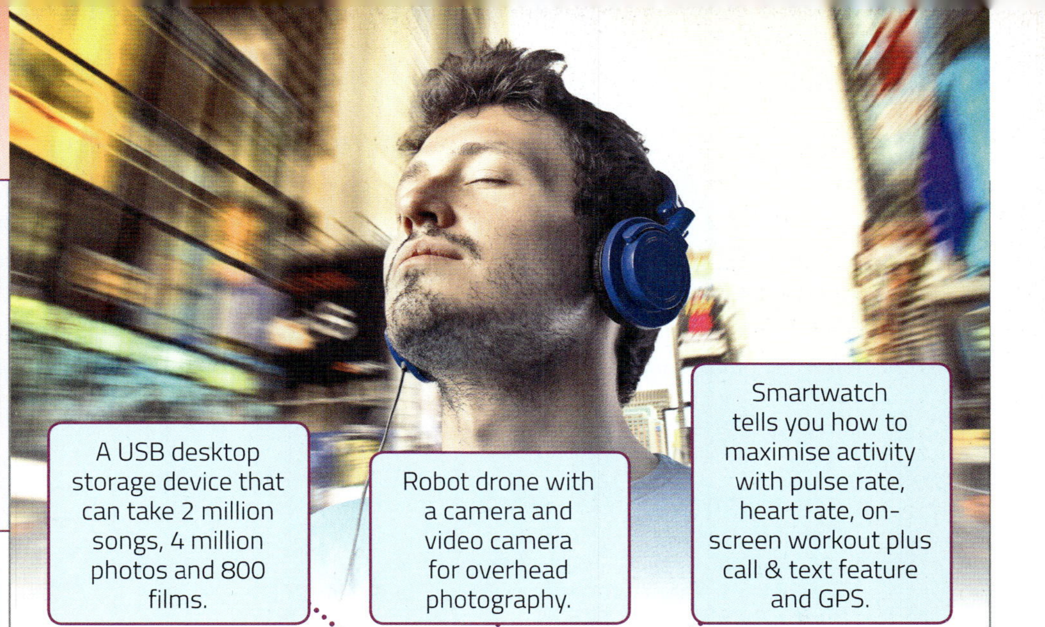

A USB desktop storage device that can take 2 million songs, 4 million photos and 800 films.

Robot drone with a camera and video camera for overhead photography.

Smartwatch tells you how to maximise activity with pulse rate, heart rate, on-screen workout plus call & text feature and GPS.

How essential are these types of devices in your everyday life?

In-ear microphones let you hear by capturing the human voice and lessening other noise. Also let you listen to music from bluetooth devices.

Atomic alarm clock displays time, day, date, temperature, humidity and moon phases. It also acts as mobile phone charger.

Wireless bluetooth speaker you can connect to WiFi for music, news, weather reports or even order a pizza. Press the microphone button and say what you want!

Which two devices would you choose to have?

C Talking about and comparing personal experiences on a given topic

TIP Remember that this part of the exam is an extension of Part 3 and is designed to give you the opportunity to expand your vocabulary and show your fluency. You can refer back to the discussion in Part 3 and reuse the vocabulary adding further examples.

FIRST Speaking – Part 4

4 DISCUSSION. In groups of three ask and answer the questions.

1 Which devices do your parents use?
2 Which devices do your grandparents use?
3 Which devices that haven't been mentioned would you find useful?
4 Which devices do you think your children may use?

WARM-UP

1 **DISCUSS** in pairs. How have our lives been changed by the Internet, smartphones and the World Wide Web? Think of five different ways and compare your list with other classmates.

C Listening for specific information

TIP Always listen carefully to instructions as to write too little or too much can lose marks. In this part of the listening test the gaps only require a maximum of three words. If you write more you will lose marks. The answers are one, two or three words and are always the same as they appear in the listening text.

FIRST Listening – Part 2

2 4.5 **SENTENCE COMPLETION.** You will hear an interview about how the Internet has transformed our lives. For questions 1-10, complete the sentences with a word or short phrase.

How have our lives been changed by the Internet?

25 YEARS INTERNET CAME

Jane Barton has just written a book about **(1)** THE INTERNET GENERATION.

It is not easy to say how our lives have been changed by the Internet because we don't know how they **(2)** WOULD HAVE BEEN without it.

REVOLUTIONAL COMMUNICATION

The Internet has multiple uses like **(3)** CHATTING FRIENDS, SENDING PICTURES, ordering food, buying shopping and instant messaging.

Jane looks on the Internet if she needs to have her **(4)** HAIR CUT, her car washed or alterations done to her house.

ACCESS TO INFORM.

According to Jane, the Internet has made our lives easier and **(5)** LESS STRESSFUL.

Communication is now **(6)** INSTANT and from anywhere to anywhere.

Young people use their phones as watches, cameras, navigators and also to watch films or listen **(7)** TO MUSIC / VIDEOS.

The Internet generation have no **(8)** DEAD TIME because they are constantly using their phone wherever they are.

WE NEED TO TAKE TIME TO REFLECT

Because of the Internet we all expect everything instantly so that concentration levels **(9)** ARE DROPPING.

PATIENCE IS RUNNING OUT

According to Jane, we have been brought great benefits by the Internet but should be aware of the dangers of **(10)** OVERDEPENDENCE.

C Interacting in a discussion on a topical issue

3 **CLASS DISCUSSION.** How has the Internet affected education? Has it changed the way students study or the way teachers teach? Think of the benefits brought and any downsides.

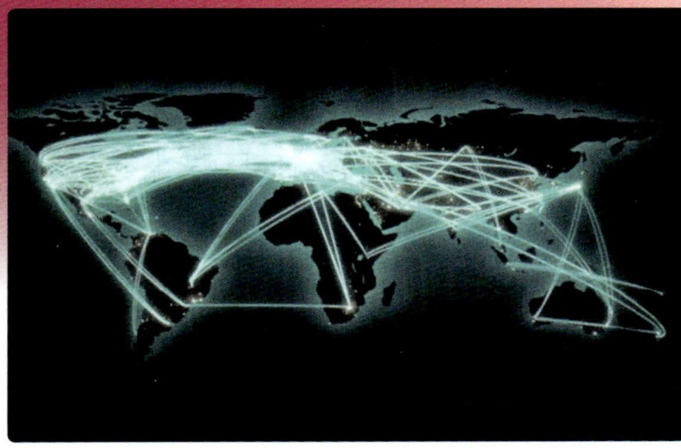

VIDEO
The Internet revolution

C Watching and understanding a short film

1 BEFORE watching the video, match the words (1-6) to their meanings (A-F).

1 ☐ emboldening
2 ☐ ebb
3 ☐ flow
4 ☐ wake
5 ☐ allegiances
6 ☐ cul-de-sac

A decline, decay
B trail, aftermath
C impasse, road to nowhere
D loyalty of a citizen to his/her government
E encouraging
F movement in

2 WATCH the video and say if the following sentences are true (T) or false (F). Correct the false ones.

1 Our world was transformed by the World Wide Web ten years ago. T F
2 The Internet will have a greater impact on civilisation than the printing press. T F
3 Ordinary people have not been encouraged to fight for freedom and democracy by the web. T F
4 A flow of winners and losers in the fight for power has been created by the Internet virtual revolution. T F
5 The web provides us with traditional allegiances. T F
6 The web is able to reinvent warfare and to create a cultural impasse. T F

3 WATCH the video again and decide who says the following: Al Gore (AG), Jeff Bezos (JB), Tim Berners-Lee (TB), Clay Shirky (CS), Stephen Fry (SF), Narrator (N).

1 Will the web help us achieve greater global understanding? ...
2 The web is a huge powerful tool for the state to control us. ...
3 It makes openness easy. ...
4 It represents the emergence of a completely new information ecosystem. ...
5 It's driving the perfection of information. ...
6 Anyone who wants to participate has the means to participate. ...

4 LOOK at these online logos. Can you identify them?

5 DISCUSS these questions in groups.

1 What activities do you generally do online?
2 Which social networks do you prefer? Why?
3 What are the advantages and disadvantages of social networks?
4 Do you believe all the information you see online?
5 Do you think carefully before sharing a photo or information online?
6 Would you give out your private passwords/codes?
7 What rules should you keep in mind when online?
8 Have you ever come across any online danger signs? Can you describe them?

LEARN BY DOING

ANALYSING MEDIA

6 READ the following tips to help you create the poster for exercise 7.

Learn more, get involved and do your part to make the Internet more secure for everyone by making research posters with your **top tips for staying safe online**. To help you with this task, you can follow these steps:

Step 1 Choose a short title to attract interest.
Step 2 Present your ideas in a logical order. You can divide your poster into three columns:
- introduction and objectives of your topic;
- results of your group's discussion;
- conclusion containing the main points of your research.

Step 3 Don't fill every inch of your poster but focus on your most important messages.
Step 4 Don't use full sentences but employ bullet points, numbers, and headlines.
Step 5 Use effective pictures/graphs to illustrate your ideas.
Step 6 Don't use too many colours (from three to five) and employ white for the background.
Step 7 Don't include too many different fonts.

7 CREATE in groups a poster to illustrate how to be safe on the web. Stand by your poster display while you present your research to the rest of your class.

WARM-UP

1 DISCUSS in pairs.

1 Have you ever been disappointed by something you have bought? Was it broken or just didn't work? Did you take it back? Or send it back if it was something you bought online?

2 How did you complain? Did you speak to someone, write an email or write a letter?

2 DISCUSS in pairs when or where it is appropriate:
▪ to speak to someone ▪ to write an email ▪ to write a letter

C Expressing a complaint in a letter

3 READ the letters A-B. Chris ordered a new wireless speaker online but he is very disappointed with the product and wants to return it. Letter A is Chris's letter and letter B is his dad's corrected version.

Letter A

24/5/18

Dear Mr, or Mrs

The speaker I ordered from you last week was delivered today and it is not what I wanted so I'm sending it back. It's really disappointing for me. If you haven't got a better one I want my money back.

Cheers

Letter B

12, Rockford Avenue
Acton
London W3 5FD

Innovative Technology
78, Industrial Road
Guildford
Surrey RH3 2AF

24th May 2018

Dear Sirs,

I am writing to say how disappointed I am with the speaker that has just been delivered from your company. I ordered the speaker online ten days ago and have to say the product is not at all what I expected.

There are two serious problems. First of all, the speaker arrived with a definite dent in the side and consequently doesn't stand up independently and secondly the battery runs out after less than an hour of listening to music. On your website it is clearly stated that the speaker can run for up to ten hours before re-charging is necessary.

I am therefore returning the speaker to you and would like to receive a complete refund. I look forward to hearing from you very soon.

Yours faithfully,

Christopher Pitchford
Christopher Pitchford

4 DISCUSS what Chris's dad changed with a classmate. Consider the following points:

- Does he know the address and the name of the person he is writing to?
- Which letter is more formal?
- Should he use contractions?
- Does he give details of the problem?
- What is his complaint?
- Does he mention any positive characteristics?
- Does he expect a response?
- What action does he expect?

TIP A formal letter is a kind of presentation and the lay-out is extremely important. If the letter is not presented in the correct formal way, it will not be taken seriously and the requested action will not be considered.

FIRST Writing – Part 2

5 A FORMAL LETTER. You have recently bought an expensive new fitness training wrist watch but the first time you tried to use it, you found the display was faulty and difficult to read and the pulse rate information kept changing. Moreover, the ear plugs that came with the watch only work intermittently. Write a letter of complaint to the shop where you bought it, listing the reasons for your dissatisfaction and ask for a replacement or a total refund. Write your letter in 140-190 words.

PROCESS LANGUAGE

Writing – Part 2 (a formal letter)

Formal language
Formality in English is not obtained from over officious language but from clear concise language. Avoid: jargon, abbreviations, colloquial English, slang and clichés.
No: *We acknowledge receipt of your letter.*
Yes: *Thank you for your letter.*

Making formal complaints
With reference to ...
I would be grateful if ...
I am sorry to say ... / Unfortunately ...

Writing reference p. 200

8 A sporting life

VOCABULARY ACTIVATOR

Inquadrami per guardare i video e ascoltare gli audio di questa unità

FLIPPED classroom

VIDEO Sport

WARM-UP

1 **LOOK** at the list below and discuss in pairs which of the sports appeal to you.

1 free climbing
2 jogging
3 paragliding
4 sailing
5 mountaineering
6 zorbing/sphering
7 surfing
8 darts
9 skateboarding
10 baseball
11 white-water rafting
12 cricket

2 **DISCUSS** in pairs. Have you tried any of them? What was it like? Which do you think might be dangerous to do?

C Learning to use vocabulary in context

3 4.6 **LISTEN** to six people describing the way they keep fit and match them to one of the pictures.

FOCUS ON VOCABULARY

4 **LOOK** at the groups of words related to sports challenges and decide which word or phrase doesn't fit.

Verbs

- enter, participate in, join in, accept
- turn down, refuse, take up, decline
- take on, face up to, accept

Nouns

- opportunity, present, possibility, challenge
- exam, race, contest, test
- participant, opponent, challenger, enemy
- match, test, game, competition

5 **CHOOSE** the more suitable alternative to complete the sentences.

1 At the end of the match, the winner congratulated his *opponent* / *loser* on such a good performance.
2 Mountaineering can be a difficult and dangerous sport suitable for those who enjoy facing a *possibility* / *challenge*.
3 The *race* / *game* began well but finished in a disaster as so many runners fell over.
4 The weather was hot and sunny and the waves perfect for *free climbing* / *surfing* and sailing.
5 The park was full of people jogging and *sailing* / *skateboarding*.
6 *Zorbing* / *Paragliding* is a sport that requires courage and not being frightened of heights.

WARM-UP

1 **DISCUSS** in pairs. What are the benefits of keeping fit? Does doing sport only improve our muscle strength and our general health or does it also improve our ability to study and do well at school?

C Reading, interpreting and understanding information

2 **READ** and listen to the article and decide which of the highlighted words has the following meaning:

1 placing at intervals among other things
2 curved
3 centre
4 bending or tightening by contraction
5 not prearranged
6 short periods of time

A sporting brain

4.7

The brain is often described as being 'like a muscle'. It's a comparison that supports the brain training industry and keeps school children bent over desks. We judge literacy and numeracy exercises as more beneficial for your brain than running, playing and learning on the move.

But the brain-as-muscle analogy doesn't quite work. To build up your muscles, you can't avoid flexing them. When it comes to your brain, an oblique approach can be surprisingly effective. In particular, working your body's muscles can actually benefit your grey matter. A wave of studies exploring the unexpected links between mental and bodily fitness is emerging from labs. This research might give you the impetus to get more active. It can also help you choose the best ways to prepare physically for mental challenges such as exams, interviews and creative projects.

The part of the brain that responds strongly to aerobic exercise is the hippocampus. Well-controlled experiments in children, adults and the elderly show that this brain structure grows as people get fitter. Since the hippocampus is at the core of the brain's learning and memory systems, this finding partly explains the memory-boosting effects of improved cardiovascular fitness. As well as slowly improving your memory hardware, exercise can have a more immediate impact on memory formation. German researchers showed that walking or cycling during, but not before learning, helped new foreign language vocabulary to stick. So don't forget to exercise while you revise. Don't push it too hard, though: vigorous workouts can raise your stress levels, which can block your memory circuits.

Besides improving memories, exercise can help you focus and stay on task. The best scientific evidence comes from testing school children, but the same most likely applies to us all. Interspersing lessons with 20-minute bouts of aerobics-style exercise improved the attention spans of Dutch school pupils. Meanwhile, a large randomised controlled trial in the US looked at the effects of daily after-school sports classes over a school year. The children, of course, got fitter. Less predictably, their executive control improved. They became more adept at ignoring distractions, multitasking, and holding and manipulating information in their minds.

And if that all sounds like hard work, you may not have to get out of breath to achieve the attention-improving effects of exercise. Just 10 minutes of playful coordination skills, like bouncing two balls at the same time, improved the attention of a large group of German teenagers.

Love it or hate it, bouts of physical activity can have potent effects on your mood. The runner's high – that feeling of elation that follows intense exercise – is real. Thoreau, Nietzsche and many other creative types have also claimed that walking gives wings to the imagination.
What you do with your body influences your mental faculties. Sitting still all day, every day, is dangerous. So don't lose time wondering about what form of exercise to do. Find something you enjoy, then get up and do it.

(Adapted from an article by Ben Martynoga, in The Guardian, June 2016)

3 **READ** the article again and do the following activities.

A1 **What type of exercise is considered more beneficial to the brain according to the first paragraph?**

A Literacy and numeracy.

B Running and playing.

A2 **What kind of conclusion about the brain is emerging from lab studies?**

A3 **Which three mental challenges does physical activity help you prepare for?**

A4 **What happens to the hippocampus part of the brain as you get fitter?**

A It expands.

B It reduces in size.

C It becomes more central.

A5 **Say whether the following information is true (T) or false (F).**

A Physical exercise before learning improves the memory. T F

B The more energy you use in your fitness routine, the better your memory will function. T F

C Attention spans improve if students have aerobics-style exercises between lessons. T F

D A year's attendance of daily after-school sports classes in the USA had no effect on students' minds. T F

A6 **Which of the following meanings is closest to the word 'trial', as used in line 39?**

A process of justice

B experiment

C attempt

D project

A7 **Explain in your own words whether even playful activity can have an effect on the brain.**

A8 **What other benefit is there from physical exercise?**

A9 **What did some philosophers mean by the phrase 'gives wings to the imagination' in lines 56-57?**

A10 **Which of the following best summarises the content of the article?**

A The writer is cynical about the academic benefits that can arise from physical activity.

B If the brain can be considered a muscle, it is one that benefits from physical exercise as well as learning.

C According to the writer, the only benefits from physical exercise are those of making you fitter.

D The article concludes that the brain is not a muscle that can be exercised in physical activity.

C Listening and understanding information

4 🔊 4.8 **LISTEN** to a sports journalist talking about danger in sports. Then listen again and decide which of the following statements is true (T) or false (F).

1 Anna lost consciousness and was taken up high into the air while training in New Zealand. T F

2 Although she was frightened, she thought she had a good chance of surviving. T F

3 She was rescued by her ground team in a small farm. T F

4 Abby was trying to sail around the world when her boat was overturned by high waves. T F

5 She was eventually rescued by a Quantas airplane. T F

6 Jordan Romero, from California, almost became the youngest person ever to climb Everest. T F

7 He and his father climbed from the Chinese side of the mountain. T F

Collocations and expressions for sport

5 **MATCH the collocations and expressions (1-6) in the article with their definitions (A-F).**

1 ☐ on the move	**A** remain focused
2 ☐ flex your muscles	**B** exaggerate
3 ☐ push (something) too hard	**C** find it difficult to breathe
4 ☐ stay on task	**D** the length of time you can concentrate
5 ☐ attention span	**E** while physically moving
6 ☐ get out of breath	**F** bend or use your muscles

6 **COMPLETE the sentences using the correct form of the collocations and expressions from exercise 5.**

1 I find it hard to .... for more than an hour without a break.

2 Scientists claim that too much screen time is lowering our .... considerably.

3 New technology means we can listen to music or hear the radio while ....

4 We don't have to .... too much as even playful activity will help our mental powers.

5 It is important to pace yourself while climbing a mountain and not .... too quickly.

6 Runners have to learn not to .... too .... if they want to win.

Gerunds and infinitives

1 READ sentences 1-10, then match the examples to the rules A-J below.

1 The brain is often described as **being** 'like a muscle'.
2 **To build up** your muscles, you can't avoid **flexing** your muscles.
3 This research might **give** you the impetus **to get** more active.
4 Besides **improving** memories, exercise can help you **focus**.
5 **Walking** or **cycling** during, but not before **learning**, helped new foreign language vocabulary **stick**.
6 The children became more adept at **ignoring** distractions.
7 You may not have **to get out** of breath **to achieve** the attention-improving effects of exercise.
8 **Wondering** about what form of exercise **to do.**
9 Don't forget **to exercise** while you revise.
10 It can also help you **choose** the best ways **to prepare** physically for mental challenges such as exams.

Gerunds

A follow a preposition;
B follow certain verbs;
C can be the subject of a sentence;
D can be used as an object;
E can serve as an object after a preposition.

Infinitives

F mean 'in order to';
G follow the superlative + a noun;
H follow certain nouns or verbs;
I can be used as adjectives modifying a noun;
J Which sentence/s show/s an infinitive without 'to'? What does it follow?

Grammar reference 8.1

2 CHOOSE the correct alternative to complete the sentences.

1 *Sitting* / *To sit* still all day is dangerous.
2 They became good at *multitask* / *multitasking*.
3 Margaret hates *to run* / *running* in the park, because there are so many people.
4 Don't forget *to pick up* / *picking up* some milk on your way home.
5 The teacher helped Sarah *studying* / *study* History.
6 They were afraid of *lose* / *losing* the match.
7 She trained very hard *to win* / *for winning* the world cup.
8 I think you should *knowing* / *know* the truth.
9 I tried to sell my car, but nobody was interested in *buying* / *buy* it.
10 We ran ten kilometres without *stop* / *stopping*.

3 COMPLETE the sentences using the correct form of the verbs in brackets.

1 I don't mind .... (say) I was wrong.
2 Policemen didn't allow people .... (park) in front of the building.
3 They were used to .... (take) me around to cycle in races.
4 I've never been to Hong Kong, but I'd like .... (go) there.
5 After .... (climb) Mount Everest and .... (sail) round the world, what can you .... (achieve) next?
6 I want .... (try) paragliding even though I'm frightened of .... (fall).
7 He refused .... (answer) any more questions.
8 It was the best play .... (be performed).
9 I feel lazy. I don't feel like .... (do) any work.
10 We are looking forward to .... (go) to Greece.

FREQUENT MISTAKES Verbs + both *-ing* and infinitive

4 LOOK at sentences 1-2 and decide on the difference in meaning of the verb *stop*. Then answer questions A-B.

1 I **stopped drinking** coffee.
2 He **stopped to buy** a coffee on the way to work.

Which one means
A ☐ 'to stop for a short time'?
B ☐ 'to give up'?

Grammar reference 8.2

5 CHOOSE the correct alternative to complete the sentences.

1 I stopped *to do* / *doing* exercise for about a year and it was bad for my health.
2 Sorry, I'm late! I stopped *helping* / *to help* a man cross the street.
3 I don't regret *to leave* / *leaving* the paragliding team, I only regret *not to do* / *not doing* it sooner.
4 Please don't forget *reading* / *to read* the feedback of the test once you have finished the quiz.
5 I still remember *to be* / *being* nervous on my first day at school.
6 I was very tired. I tried *keeping* / *to keep* my eyes open, but I couldn't.
7 If you try *using* / *to use* the correct ingredients, I'm sure the recipe will work.
8 I promise I'll remember *calling* / *to call* Tom.
9 I'll never forget *meeting* / *to meet* the famous marathon runner.
10 We regret *to inform* / *informing* you that your application has been unsuccessful.

TIP This exercise often tests collocations and phrasal verbs. It may test your knowledge by requiring the right preposition as in 'to take UP a challenge' or the complete phrase 'to TAKE UP a challenge'.

FIRST Reading and Use of English – Part 1

1 MULTIPLE-CHOICE CLOZE. **For questions 1-8, read the text below and decide which answer (A, B, C or D) best fits each gap. There is an example at the beginning (0).**

Zorbing: a new sport

It's great **(0)** ......TO TRY...... something different and a bit **(1)** ......CHALLENGING...... . So when my friend Jimmy and I saw an ad for zorbing, we decided not **(2)** ......TO LOSE...... any time and give it a go. What is zorbing? It's a new sport also called 'sphering' where you and a partner are strapped into a large sphere. It began in New Zealand and is becoming more and **(3)** ......MORE...... popular. The round sphere is made up of two chambers; the inner one where you and your partner are strapped in, and an outer sphere **(4)** ......WHICH...... is a protective outer circle. The sphere is 3.6 metres in height and the outer circle is big enough **(5)** ......TO TAKE...... all the pressure from any bumps. When you are secure, the instructor will set the ball in motion and the **(6)** ......ROLLING...... begins. The adrenalin will start immediately as you begin **(7)** ......TO ROLL...... and spin and the speed gets really fast up to nearly 50 kilometres an hour. We came out after just twenty minutes feeling very disoriented but we stayed **(8)** ......ON...... task and we laughed a lot! This hilarious new experience has become a 'must-do' and guarantees an exciting thrill for you and a friend.

0	**A** trying	**B to try**	**C** tried	**D** tries
1	**A** to challenge	**B** challenged	**C** challenging	**D** has challenged
2	**A** to lose	**B** lost	**C** losing	**D** loses
3	**A** much	**B** many	**C** less	**D** more
4	**A** when	**B** which	**C** where	**D** who
5	**A** taking	**B** took	**C** to take	**D** taken
6	**A** rolling	**B** rolled	**C** to roll	**D** had rolled
7	**A** rolled	**B** rolling	**C** rolls	**D** to roll
8	**A** at	**B** to	**C** on	**D** in

TIP The given word in this exercise must be used as it is and not altered in any way. Failure to use it or altering it will lead to a loss of marks.

FIRST Reading and Use of English – Part 4

2 KEY WORD TRANSFORMATIONS. **For questions 1-6, complete the second sentence so that it has a similar meaning to the first sentence, using the word given. Do not change the word given. You must use between two and five words including the word given. Here is an example (0).**

0 The children couldn't concentrate for more than ten minutes.
SPAN
The children's ATTENTION SPAN was limited to ten minutes.

1 Sport keeps your body fit but also improves your mental wellbeing.
BESIDES
Sport, ...BESIDES KEEPING YOUR BODY FIT......, also improves your mental wellbeing.

2 Can you call in at the supermarket before you come home this evening?
COMING
Before ......COMING HOME THIS EVENING......, can you call in at the supermarket?

3 Did you post the letter on your way to school this morning?
REMEMBER
Do you ......REMEMBERED TO POST THE LETTER...... on your way to school this morning?

4 The umpire congratulated the team and said they'd played very well.
FOR ARBITRO
The umpire congratulated the team ......FOR PLAYING...... very well.

5 The teacher greeted her students in the street outside the school.
STOPPED
The teacher ......STOPPED TO GREET...... her students in the street outside the school.

6 He was embarrassed because his phone rang during the concert.
OFF
He was embarrassed because he forgot ......TO TURN OFF THE PHONE...... during the concert.

WARM-UP

1 DISCUSS in pairs.

1 What sports do you practise? Where and when do you practise?

2 Do you watch the Olympic Games? Do you know where the last games were held and where the next ones will be?

C Recognising links within a text

2 READ and listen to the texts about new Olympic sports and say which you already know and which you would like to know more about.

TIP Read through all the texts before beginning to link statements to a specific text. Only then should you read each text on its own and match possible statements to it before moving on to the next text.

FIRST Reading and Use of English – Part 7

3 MULTIPLE MATCHING. **Read the texts again. For questions 1-10, choose from the descriptions (A-E). The descriptions may be chosen more than once.**

Which sport

has a variant that is simpler and played by female teams?	1 B
uses a graded system of ability shown through different coloured belts?	2 C
requires water, wind and waves?	3 D
has champions who learned their skills on the streets?	4 A
is not as stressful and requires simpler equipment than the original version?	5 E
can be practised indoors with artificial waves but is more thrilling outside?	6 D
has two teams who alternate between using a bat or running after the ball?	7 B
was made popular through the cinema?	8 C
develops endurance as well as gymnastic ability?	9 E
was considered controversial until recently?	10 A

New Olympic sports

4.9

The International Olympic Committee has recently agreed to add a further five sports for the Tokyo Summer Olympics in 2020. These are:

A Skateboarding

A popular recreational and professional sport, skateboarding is an action sport which involves riding and performing jumps and turns using a skateboard. Since the 1970s specific parks for skateboarders have been built and competitions organised, which involve freestyle BMXers and aggressive skaters. Skateboard champions, whose skills and tricks were learned on the streets, have helped to transform this sport into an accepted Olympic one. In the past it was considered controversial because of the damage to public places which was attributed to skateboard users.

B Baseball/Softball

Baseball and softball, which is a variant of baseball, are not new Olympic sports but have returned after being voted out in 2008 probably because of concerns about building suitable stadiums, a lack of professional players, and doping. It is particularly popular in the USA where it is considered a national sport. It is a bat-and-ball game played between two teams of nine players who take turns batting and fielding. The batting team can score runs by hitting the ball hard and running between bases before the fielding team gets the ball back. The team with the highest score wins. Softball is played with a larger ball on a smaller field. As it is played by women, it is also called ladies' baseball.

C Karate

Karate is a martial art which was developed in Japan, but the time when it became internationally known, was in the 1960s and 1970s through popular martial arts movies. Karate schools, where the sport was practised and taught, began to appear across the world. Karate competitors may enter competitions either as individuals or as part of a team. Sparring matches are typically divided by weight, age, gender, and experience. Karate has a Dan system based on belt colours rising to the highest which is a black belt. The first five to six Dans are given for stance, balance, and coordination with speed and power added at the higher grades.

D Surfing

After many years as a casual sport and pleasure activity, surfing is finally getting recognition as an Olympic sport. Surfing is a surface water sport in which the wave rider or surfer, rides on the forward curve of a moving wave which is usually heading towards the shore. The waves considered best for surfing are found in the sea or ocean, especially when wind forces are strong and heading inland. Suitable waves can also be found in lakes or in rivers but this is rarer and the waves are normally weaker. Surfers who want to practise in a safe environment can also use artificial waves in wave pools but nothing can compare with the thrill of riding huge waves in the ocean.

E Sport climbing

Sport climbing is a type of rock climbing but one that uses permanent anchors in the rocks unlike traditional climbing where climbers have to put in, use and then remove protection as they climb. It is a sport that develops strength, endurance, gymnastic ability and technique offering a simpler experience which requires less equipment than traditional climbing. Its popularity, which is encouraged by the inclusion of indoor and outdoor climbing walls in sports centres, has grown considerably. In fact, many climbers now enter the sport through gyms and purpose-built climbing walls rather than mountain climbing. This is also because sport climbing is less stressful and carried out in a safe environment.

4 **FIND** the words in the texts which mean the following:

1 some form of injury, harm, or destruction (para. A);
2 absence of something necessary or needed (para. B);
3 the use of drugs (para. B);
4 the team using the bat (para. B);
5 the team covering the playing field where the game is played (para. B);
6 the way the body is held up while standing (para. C);
7 a bending line (para. D);
8 moving in the direction of (para. D);
9 devices for support and security (para. E).

Word formation: word families (1)

Many English words are part of a 'word family' where **nouns, adjectives and verbs can be formed from the base word**: ***teach*** *– teacher, teaching, taught*; ***act*** *– actor, acting, action.*

5 **COMPLETE** the table with words from the texts.

Base word	Noun	Adjective	Verb
	skateboarding/ skateboarder		
play			
			to compete
field			
		surf/surfing	
gym			
	performer		
		developing	

6 **MAKE** suitable variations of the words given to complete the sentences.

1 The .... and .... entered the arena from opposite ends. (COMPETE/SPECTATE)
2 The most experienced .... are the ones who have practised in the open air. (CLIMB).
3 Lots of young people are thrilled to see one of their .... in the next Olympic Games. (FAVOUR/PLAY)
4 During the baseball game, the .... found it difficult to return the ball quickly to the bases. (FIELD)
5 One of the most beautiful sights in the harbour are the .... ships. (SAIL)
6 The young athlete, when he held up his gold medal, was congratulated on his terrific .... (ACHIEVE).
7 I am not usually an .... as I like joining in and find .... more fun than watching. (OBSERVE/ PRACTISE).
8 My best friend runs in .... races and is becoming a really proficient .... (COMPETE/RUN)

C Discussing ideas and relating them to personal experience

7 **DISCUSS** the questions.

1 Do you agree with including new sports in the Olympic Games or should they only allow traditional sports?
2 Can activities like skateboarding and surfing really be considered sports?

8 **WRITE** a brief paragraph of 10/12 lines about the reasons why sport is so popular to perform and to watch. Why do supporters become so emotionally involved with their teams or favourite athletes or players?

Relative clauses

1 LOOK at the following sentences from the texts and decide if the underlined part is essential to the meaning of the sentence or not.

1. Skateboarding is an action sport which involves riding and performing jumps and turns using a skateboard.
2. Baseball and softball, which is a variant of baseball, are not new Olympic sports.
3. Surfers who want to practise in a safe environment can also use artificial waves in wave pools.
4. Since the 1970s specific parks for skateboarders have been built and competitions organised, which involve freestyle BMXers and aggressive skaters.
5. Sport climbing is a type of rock climbing but one that uses permanent anchors in the rocks.
6. The skateboard champions, whose skills and tricks were learned on the streets, have helped to transform this activity into an accepted Olympic sport.

2 DECIDE which of the following statements are true (T) or false (F). Correct the false ones.

Defining relative clauses

1. The pronouns 'which' and 'that' are used for people and things. T F
2. A defining relative clause gives essential information and cannot be left out of the sentence. T F
3. In a defining relative clause the relative pronoun can be omitted if the clause has a different subject to the main clause. T F

Non-defining relative clauses

4. In a non-defining relative clause the pronouns 'which' and 'who' can be omitted. T F
5. A non-defining relative clause gives additional information and the sentence does not make sense without it. T F
6. We usually put a comma before and after a non-defining relative clause. T F

***Whose* + noun**

7. *Whose* + noun is used both in defining and non-defining relative clauses to express possession. T F

Grammar reference 8.3

3 UNDERLINE the relative clauses in the sentences and say which are defining (D) and which are non-defining (ND).

1. The skater over there, who is wearing a helmet for head protection, is the new athlete in our team.
2. He took part in the latest Olympic Games that were held in Brazil.
3. The local swimming pool, which has artificial waves, is near the station.
4. The place where I love surfing is Hawaii.
5. That skateboarder, whose style is very aggressive, is taking part in the competition.

4 COMPLETE the text with suitable relative pronouns.

There may be people for **(1)** .... practising a sport could be difficult. Among them are those **(2)** .... work long hours or have shifts, or even the young couples **(3)** .... children are too little to be left alone. There are also people **(4)** .... take on too many responsibilities, **(5)** .... means they do not have the time and energy to join a team **(6)** .... trains regularly during the week. Of course, there are gyms **(7)** .... you can practise all day long, but they are not easy to find in little towns in **(8)** .... small communities live. However, there may be moments during the day **(9)** .... you might have some free time. One solution is an app **(10)** .... is becoming more and more popular because it acts as a trainer and has lots of exercises suitable for the busiest people.

5 JOIN these pairs of sentences using a relative clause.

1. Skateboarders are always trying new figures. They are very creative sportsmen.
2. The programme about the new Olympic Games was broadcast on TV last night. It is the one I was telling you about yesterday.
3. Our volleyball team won the first set. It played against Nottingham College.
4. I saw a book at the library. It explained all about the rules of baseball.
5. The red and blue outfit was the best. The one my team was wearing.
6. The gym at the end of the sports centre is very well equipped. It is where the national champions train.

FREQUENT MISTAKES

6 FIND and correct the mistakes in the sentences.

1. My new knee pads, which I have just bought them, have a hole in them.
2. The team, where my brother played there last year, has been sold to a Chinese investor.
3. All the equipment which you recommended it to me has arrived!

7 CROSS out the word/s in the sentences that is/are not necessary.

1. The tennis player whom the public loved won the tournament.
2. The stadium, whose seats of which were all taken, was very crowded.
3. They enjoyed the cricket match that they saw last Sunday.
4. Toronto is where the defenseman of the hockey team was born there.
5. The team which we played against was the strongest of all.
6. Ice hockey, which is my favourite sport, it is very popular in Norway.

WARM-UP

1 **DISCUSS.** Does sport have a place in your life? What is the difference between individual or team sports? What different benefits can you obtain from them?

C Developing confidence and fluency

2 **WRITE** four sentences, two positive and two negative, about a sporting experience. Use the Process language box below. Then share your sentences with a partner.

PROCESS LANGUAGE

Speaking – Part 1

Talking about personal experiences
I have never ... / I often ... / I really enjoy ...
At my school we ... / I normally do/don't ...
I find it very exciting to ... / I love doing ...
My favourite ... is/has always been ...
What I enjoy most is ...

Adjectives to describe experiences
Positive:
terrific, great, stimulating, exciting, fantastic, exhilarating
Negative:
frightening, disappointing, dangerous, awful, dreadful

Speaking reference p. 194

TIP

Part 1 is designed to be a gentle introduction into the Speaking test. It is meant to give you the opportunity to show your ability to use general, social and interactional language while giving basic personal information. The questions relate to areas such as family, school, leisure time and future plans. In this part of the test, interaction between the candidates is not expected. You just have to respond to the interlocutor's questions, and to listen to what the other candidate has to say.

FIRST Speaking – Part 1

3 **INTERVIEW.** Form groups of four in which two students are the examiners and two students are the candidates. Use the role cards to role-play Part 1 of the Speaking exam. After three minutes, exchange roles. Use the Process language box.

Examiner 1

Introduce yourself with your name and surname and introduce the second examiner. Explain that you will be asking questions and your colleague will just take notes. Ask the candidates their names and then ask the candidates questions in turn. Begin with general questions about their family, their likes and dislikes and then ask about sport. Ask about sport in school and out of school, whether they practise or enjoy watching sport on television. Ask about which sports they like or dislike and why. Encourage them to give full answers.

Examiner 2

Your role is to listen and take notes while the other examiner is asking the candidates questions. Listen and make notes on how complete and interesting the candidates' answers are. Do they respond with full answers, do they use interesting vocabulary? Have they understood the questions fully? Do the candidates listen to each other? Be prepared to give feedback at the end of three minutes.

Candidate 1

Imagine you are really taking the Speaking exam. Smile and try to look relaxed. Listen carefully to the questions and try to give complete, interesting answers. Try to use a variety of vocabulary and avoid giving brief 'yes', 'no' answers. Wherever you can, give examples of your own experiences. Listen with interest to the other candidate while they answer the examiner's questions. Look straight at the examiner while answering your questions and remember to smile and look interested and involved.

Candidate 2

Try to appear bored and uninterested in the exam. Spend time looking at the floor or around you but not directly at the examiner. Listen to the questions but give very brief answers, sometimes answering with just 'yes', or 'no'. Only say the minimum in your answers and don't add any extra information or any description of personal experience. Repeat the same vocabulary. Look distracted and bored while the other candidate is answering questions.

4 **CLASS DISCUSSION.** Talk as a class about how to give a good or bad impression in an oral exam. Talk about the importance of body language as well as the quality of spoken answers.

WARM-UP

SOME IDEAS

1 **DISCUSS** in pairs. Have you ever tried any unusual sports? Did you do it alone or with a partner? Did it take courage? If you've never done any unusual or dangerous sport, would you like to? Which would you choose?

C Listening and comparing different options on a given topic

TIP If you are unsure about an answer, you should wait for the second time you hear the listening text before making your decision. Making a quick decision may mean using an answer incorrectly that belongs to another speaker.

FIRST Listening – Part 3

2 4.10 **MULTIPLE MATCHING.** You will hear five different people talking about unusual sports. For questions 1-5, choose from the list (A-H) the type of activity that each person has experienced. Use the letters only once. There are three extra letters which you do not need to use.

ZAP CAT

- **A** It is practised in small rafts containing two people.
- **B** It gives an intense feeling of flying.
- **C** It requires intense concentration as well as mountaineering skills.
- **D** It is not the sport for you if you don't enjoy being in water.
- **E** It requires you to perform difficult athletic stunts.
- **F** It is on water and uses a very powerful engine.
- **G** It is a team sport rather than an individual sport.
- **H** It can give you fantastic views if you have the courage to do it.

Speaker 1	F	1
Speaker 2	A	2
Speaker 3	H	3
Speaker 4	E	4
Speaker 5	C	5

C Discussing ideas and relating them to personal experience

SOME IDEAS

3 **WORK** in pairs. Decide which of the sports described in the listening exercise you would like to try and which you absolutely wouldn't.

VIDEO
Free climbing

C Watching and understanding a short film

1 BEFORE watching the video, match the words (1-7) to their meanings (A-G).

1 [E] rumour
2 [G] awesome
3 [A] limestone
4 [F] spotted
5 [B] overhanging
6 [D] tufas
7 [C] smooth

A a rock made up of calcium carbonate
B being suspended over
C not rough
D a soft, porous rock
E something said which is not known to be true
F located, identified by seeing
G impressive

2 WATCH the video and identify the functions of the close-ups which open the sequence.

1 00:01-00:02: ....
2 00:05-00:12: ....
3 00:13-00:17: ....

3 ANSWER these questions about the short film.

1 Which means of transport did you recognise in the sequence? AIRPLANE – MOTORBOAT
2 Why were Chris Sharma and his friend flying north to Kalymnos, a Greek island? WALL IT'S FULL OF LIMESTONES GOING ON THE OCEAN
3 What could they perceive while flying over the Cyclades?
4 What did they reach at the end of the first day? A OVERHANGING WALL, VERY CLEAN ROCK WITH PERFECT TAPE
5 What was Chris's climbing like according to his friend, Sam Whittaker? VERY SMOOTH
6 What can we admire nearly at the end of the sequence? CHRIS ~~SLIPPERING~~ SLIPPING
7 How does the sequence end? WITH CHRIS EXULTING

4 WATCH the video again and complete these sentences about what climbing is to Chris.

1 Climbing is a CREATIVE PROCESS.
2 It opens your perception to WHAT IS POSSIBLE AND WHAT ATTRACTS YOU.
3 Climbing is AN EXPERIENCE, it means travelling and encountering ~~UNEXPECTED~~ UNEXPECTED THINGS
4 It's an ADVENTURE. You may find something AMAZING, you MAY NOT FIND anything at all, but you STILL HAVE TO GO OUT THERE and try.
5 The ROCK was red with stalactites and tufas and its HEIGHT was PERFECT.
6 As the water was cold, Chris knew he didn't have many times TO FALL ON THE WATER before he would get too cold to CLIMB ANYMORE. But he started and he IS ONE OF THE MOST AMAZING FREE CLIMBERS I'VE EVER SEEN

5 DISCUSS in pairs. Have you ever had a true passion for a particular activity? Have you ever worked hard towards sports challenges keeping up your effort and interest despite obstacles or failures?

ADAPTING TO CHANGE

6 IN GROUPS discuss the following:

1 What emotions did you feel while watching the video?
2 Were you impressed by Chris's decisions while climbing? Or do you feel he was going too far? What would you have done in his place after the first fall?
3 **If you practise a sport**
- Think about how you felt when you first started. Did you feel you would never learn, never become good?
- Was there a situation where you felt things were getting out of hand? What did you do?

4 **If you don't practise any sports**
- Think about why you have decided not to try. Are you afraid of not being able to do well?
- Do you not want to put yourself in a difficult position?

7 DISCUSS in pairs the changes that have happened in your life so far. Did you find it difficult to adapt to them? How did you cope with the new situation?

8

WARM-UP

1 LOOK at the pictures and discuss in pairs what might have happened. Use the Process language box.

C Writing a story

PROCESS LANGUAGE

Writing – Part 2 (a story)

Linkers

At the beginning … / At first … / Firstly …
Then … / After that … / Secondly …
Finally … / At the end/In the end … / Eventually

Writing reference p. 203

2 REORDER the paragraphs so that they form a story.

A ☐
The game began, the baseball bat was swinging, the fielders were running and our supporters who were watching from the stands, were cheering. Their team batted first and scored 80 runs. Then it was our turn.

B ☐
We had been waiting for the moment for so long, it seemed incredible to think it was here at long last. Here we were at the beginning of the most important match of the season. The Schools' Cup depended on the outcome of this game.

C ☐
It was close but we did it in the end – we won! The best part of all was that I didn't fall, which is what I'd been frightened of, and I actually scored 40 runs. That's my record. I was proud and happy and the coach congratulated me on a fantastic game.

D ☐
Then we all got into position and each of us thought about all the training we had done and the coach who had helped us all so much.

TIP The time allowed for the Writing paper (1 hour 20 minutes) is designed to be sufficient for you to make brief plans and then write two answers. Time spent planning your answer is time well spent and allows you to produce a clear organised piece of writing. Remember that a good story must have a clear storyline which is linked to the opening sentence, successfully uses the prompts provided and shows good effective use of linkers and narrative tenses.

FIRST Writing – Part 2

3 A STORY. You have seen this announcement on your school website.

SPORTS STORIES WANTED FOR NEXT MONTH'S SCHOOL MAGAZINE

Write about an interesting, terrific or dreadful experience connected to sport for our next edition.
Your story must begin with this sentence:

My friend and I were looking for a new challenge.

Your story must include:
- a disappointment
- a surprise

Write your story using 140–190 words.

Review Units 7-8

ZTE ONLINE Interactive exercises

VOCABULARY ACTIVATOR

1 **FIND the right piece of technology according to the definitions.**

A A machine that allows us to see programmes and films and with modern technology is getting bigger and bigger.

B This little machine holds all our personal contacts, our messages and can carry out all the functions of a mini computer.

C This machine enables a family to eat at different times, it cooks and defrosts and warms up food quickly.

D A machine that carries out numerous functions especially in the fields of work and communication.

E This machine enables us to obtain cash from our bank account at any time of the day or night.

F Without this device we might easily get lost; it gives us our bearings and helps us get to where we want to be.

2 **COMPLETE the sentences with suitable sports taken from the box.**

free climbing ▪ jogging ▪ paragliding ▪ sailing ▪ mountaineering ▪ zorbing/sphering ▪ surfing ▪ darts ▪ skateboarding ▪ baseball ▪ white-water rafting ▪ cricket

1 .... is a traditional English summer ball game, whereas .... is more popular in the States.

2 There are so many sports to do in the mountains; apart from .... , there is .... up the rocks and .... for those who want the sensation of flying.

3 The seaside offers great opportunities for sports like .... if you have a boat, and .... if you enjoy riding on the waves.

4 In the park yesterday there were lots of activities, I saw people running and .... as well as teens .... on a specially built course.

5 My local pub has the best .... team in the area.

6 The school is organising an activity day in the country next week and we can choose between .... in huge transparent balls or .... down the fast-flowing river.

GRAMMAR

3 **COMPLETE the second sentence using the prompts so that it has the same meaning as the first.**

1 A painter will come to paint the sitting room next week. I'm having ...
2 A gang of robbers robbed the main post office. The main post office ...
3 Someone is cutting the grass in the park. The grass in the park ...
4 This isn't the first time they have drawn graffiti. This isn't the first time graffiti ...
5 A dance company will perform a modern ballet. A modern ballet ...
6 I have booked the hairdresser to cut my hair. I'm having ...

4 **COMPLETE the text with the correct alternative.**

This is a photograph of the young man I met **(1)** *jogging / to jog* in the park. He is the one **(2)** *who / which* remembers **(3)** *to meet / meeting* his future wife while **(4)** *to work / working* in America. He had been there just a few days **(5)** *which / when* he bumped into her in an office lift in the building **(6)** *that / where* they both worked. They stopped **(7)** *talking / to talk* and arranged **(8)** *meeting / to meet* later for lunch in the bar round the corner **(9)** *where / which* they both knew. The wedding, **(10)** *who / which* was in Hawaii, took place six months later.

USE OF ENGLISH

FIRST Reading and Use of English – Part 1

5 **MULTIPLE-CHOICE CLOZE. For questions 1-8, read the blog below and decide which answer (A, B, C or D) best fits each gap. There is an example at the beginning (0).**

SPORTS AND TECH

Running is one of the fastest growing sports in the world. In Europe 50 million people do it on a regular basis and nearly €10 billion a year is **(0)** ......SPENT...... on shoes, clothes and related technology. Two out of five Europeans now claim **(1)** .... a sport on a regular basis, with running and cycling at the top of the list. The motivation is clear, an active and healthy life is increasingly **(2)** .... in our society and equipment available is **(3)** .... to increasingly sophisticated standards. Amateur athletes now **(4)** .... steps to use high-tech materials that were until recently available only to professionals. Meantime, the pros have improved their **(5)** .... thanks to materials like fibreglass, carbon fibre and polyurethane. Data analysis helps reduce the risk of **(6)** .... but even when they occur, new therapies and prostheses accelerate the healing process. Anyone who doubts the radical impact that technology can have **(7)** .... sport should consider the swimming contests at the 2008 Olympics in Beijing. Professional swimmers had new all-in-one swimsuits known as the LZR Racer made from polyurethane. The new swimsuit was said to increase swimmers' speed and also boost the oxygen flow to the muscles. It proved a stunning success: **(8)** .... wearing the suit at Beijing scooped 94 per cent of the swimming gold medals.

	A	B	C	D
0	spend	**spent**	spends	spending
1	to practise	practising	practised	practises
2	value	to value	valued	valuing
3	making	being made	were made	make
4	take on	turn	join in	take
5	possibilities	matches	tests	competitors
6	danger	hurts	injuries	wounds
7	of	on	by	in
8	competitors	athletes	opponents	sports

FIRST Reading and Use of English – Part 2

6 OPEN CLOZE. For questions 1-8, read the text below and think of the word which best fits each gap. Use only one word in each gap. There is an example at the beginning (0).

TOP TECH CITIES

In less than 35 years, the World Health Organisation estimates that two-thirds of the world population will be living in urban areas. The cities that will flourish the most are those that rely on cutting-edge technologies and create opportunities for people to take **(0)** ......ON...... new ones.
To get a sense of which cities face **(1)** .... to the tech challenge best, a list of the most high-tech cities in the world has **(2)** .... created with information from a research firm that specialises in analysing innovative cities.
The top tech city is no surprise to anyone who keeps in **(3)** .... with technology. San Francisco is the undeniable epicentre of all things tech, from its gigantic startup culture to its venture capital scene to its population of designers and programmers. This Californian city is followed **(4)** .... London, which has more startups and programmers than almost any other city in the world. It **(5)** .... estimated by some that there are more IT jobs in London than in all of California. Another city joining **(6)** .... the tech revolution is Boston, Massachusetts. The city has several venture capital firms that pour money into innovation labs and university startups, and important research and development offices **(7)** .... been set up there by big-name companies like Facebook and Amazon **(8)** .... tap into this growing pool of talent.

FIRST Reading and Use of English – Part 3

7 WORD FORMATION. For questions 1-8, read the text below. Use the word given in capitals at the end of some of the lines to form a word that fits in the gap in the same line. There is an example at the beginning (0).

HOW TO START A SPORTS BLOG

Before **(0)** ......GETTING...... started with your sports blog, you need	**GET**
to make sure the foundation for your site is put in place. First of all	
choose a **(1)** .... blogging platform. The majority of	**RELY**
blogs on the Internet today are **(2)** .... through free	**POWER**
software which is easy to use and most web hosting services offer	
one-click installation to set this up.	
You are **(3)** .... to set up your own domain name and	**ADVISE**
premium web hosting when you register, so you are free to use your	
blog as you want and **(4)** .... possible interference.	**COME**
Choose the topic of your site carefully. It is better to concentrate on a	
specific sport or sportsperson as trying to cover all sports is	
(5)	**PRODUCE**
Once the blog is up and running you need to **(6)**	**PUBLIC**
through social profile pages. You probably already have social	
accounts for yourself, but this is a great **(7)** .... and	**OPPORTUNE**
would be a huge benefit to your blog if you set them up for your blog	
as well.	
The secret to creating a successful sports blog is to continually	
produce content that people are **(8)** .... in and want	**INTEREST**
to see.	

FIRST Reading and Use of English – Part 4

8 KEY WORD TRANSFORMATIONS. For questions 1-6, complete the second sentence so that it has a similar meaning to the first sentence, using the word given. Do not change the word given. You must use between two and five words, including the word given. Here is an example (0).

0 Norman Foster designed the Millennium Bridge to celebrate the beginning of a new millennium.
WAS
The Millennium Bridge WAS DESIGNED BY NORMAN FOSTER to celebrate the beginning of a new millennium.

1 The young man was embarrassed because his phone rang during the lecture.
TURN
The young man forgot .... during the lecture.

2 The local authorities will build three new sports centres within the next five years.
BE
Three new sports centres .... within the next five years.

3 Tim has arranged for a gardener to come next Saturday to cut the grass.
HAVING
Tim .... next Saturday.

4 My coach has asked me to participate in the training session this evening.
JOIN
My coach has asked me .... the training session this evening.

5 The television is showing the royal wedding at the moment, come and see!
SHOWN
The royal wedding .... at the moment, come and see!

6 The policeman gave the motorist a fine for speeding.
BY
The motorist .... the policeman for speeding.

9 Saving our planet

Inquadrami per guardare i video e ascoltare gli audio di questa unità

VOCABULARY ACTIVATOR

FLIPPED classroom

VIDEO The environment

WARM-UP

1 DISCUSS how 'green' you are by answering the following questions.

1 Do you come to school by bike or on foot?
2 Do you recycle paper and plastic?
3 Do you love animals?

C Learning to use vocabulary in context

2 READ the list below and decide what is positive and what is negative for the environment. Then look at at the pictures and match them to the right words (1-12).

1 deforestation	7 recycling
2 earthquake	8 solar panels
3 flood	9 tornado
4 ice melting	10 tsunami
5 pollution	11 waste
6 public transport	12 wind power

3 5.1 **LISTEN** to a group discussion on environmental problems and possible solutions. Match each speaker (1-4) to an opinion (A-D).

1 ☐ John
2 ☐ Marilyn
3 ☐ Steve
4 ☐ Frances

A wants more done to find alternative sources of energy.
B is concerned about the huge amount of waste that is dumped.
C thinks climate change has given rise to global warming.
D agrees with Al Gore that if we don't act soon about pollution, it will be too late.

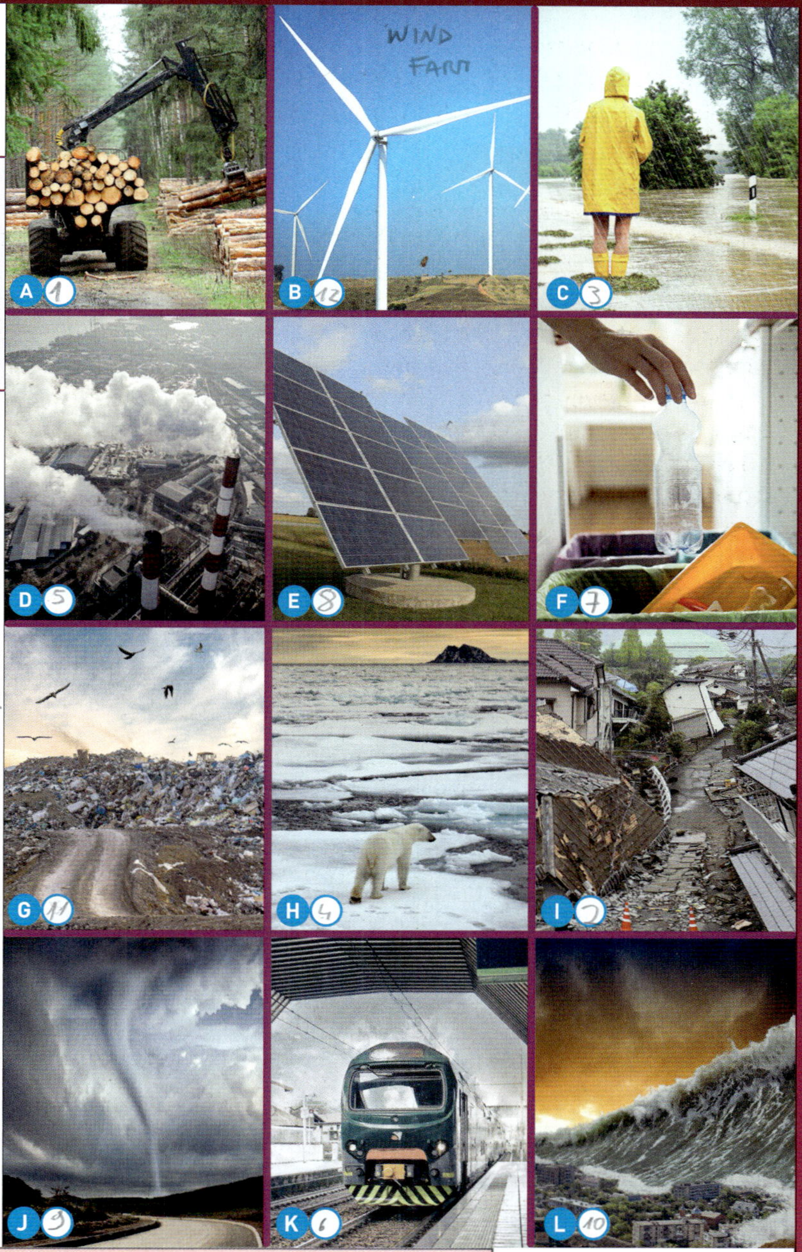

FOCUS ON VOCABULARY

Cause	Effect
Pollution ⇢	greenhouse effect global warming ice caps/glaciers melting rising sea level
Climate change ⇢	heatwaves natural disasters drought famine (starvation)

Useful expressions for the environment

endangered species, congestion charge, ozone layer, carbon footprint, dumping, contamination, biodiversity, ecosystem, alternative energy

4 DISCUSS in small groups. Is the climate really changing? Is global warming a reality? What evidence is there to prove it is or isn't?

WARM-UP

1 LOOK at the picture below and discuss in pairs.

1 How much plastic do you use in your daily life?
2 What do you think happens to the plastic bottles and containers when they're thrown away?
3 Have you heard of the plastic island? What do you think it is?

C Reading, understanding and interpreting information

2 READ and listen to the article and decide which of the highlighted words has the following meaning:

1 the period of time during which something or someone is expected to function LIFESPAN
2 bringing or easing slowly to an end PHASE OUT
3 an undesired flow or escape LEAKAGE
4 pure SHEER
5 overtaken in speed, development, or performance OUTPACED
6 area where waste material is disposed of by burying it under layers of earth LANDFILLS

5.2

91% of plastic isn't recycled

Mass production of plastics has accelerated so rapidly that it has created billions of metric tons, most of it in disposable products that end up as waste. If that seems like an incomprehensible quantity, it is. Even the scientists who set out to conduct the world's first count of how much plastic has been produced, discarded, burned or put in landfills, were horrified by the sheer size of the numbers.

'We all knew there was a rapid and extreme increase in plastic production, but actually quantifying the cumulative number for all plastic ever made was quite shocking,' said last month Jenna Jambeck, a University of Georgia environmental engineer who specialises in studying plastic waste in the oceans. She went on to say that this kind of increase would 'break' any system that was not prepared for it, and that was why we have seen leakage from global waste systems into the oceans. Plastic takes more than 400 years to degrade, so most of it still exists in some form. Only 12 percent has been incinerated.

The prediction that by mid-century the oceans will contain more plastic waste than fish, ton for ton, has become one of the most-quoted statistics and a desperate cry to do something about it. The problem of plastic pollution is becoming ubiquitous in the oceans, with 90 percent of sea birds consuming it and over eight million tons of new plastic trash finding its way into the oceans every year. Henderson Island, located in the South Pacific region, was recently crowned the most plastic-polluted island on Earth, as researchers discovered it is covered in roughly 38 million pieces of plastic waste.

If present trends continue, by 2050 there will be 12 billion metric tons of plastic in landfills that will eventually end up in the oceans. That amount is 35,000 times as heavy as the Empire State Building. Roland Geyer, the study's lead author and an engineer by training, has studied various metals and how they're used and managed. The rapid acceleration of plastic manufacturing, which so far has doubled roughly every 15 years, has outpaced nearly every other man-made material. And, it is unlike virtually every other material. Half of all steel produced, for example, is used in construction, with a decades-long lifespan. Half of all plastic manufactured becomes trash in less than a year, the study found.

Gaining control of plastic waste is now such a large task that it calls for a comprehensive, global approach, Jambeck says, which involves rethinking plastic chemistry, product design, recycling strategies, and consumer use. 'We as a society need to consider whether it's worth trading off some convenience for a clean, healthy environment,' Geyer concludes that for some products that are very problematic in the environment, we should think about using different materials – or, phasing them out completely.

(Adapted from articles in the National Geographic, July 2017)

3 **READ** the article again and do the following activities.

A1 What was the scientists' reaction to the amount of plastic waste they discovered?

A They were shocked and dismayed at the quantity involved.
B They were not surprised; it was exactly what they had predicted and expected.

A2 Why is Jenna Jambeck's opinion regarding this problem particularly important?

A3 According to Jenna, what percentage of plastic is destroyed by burning it?

A Less than 10%.
B Nearly half.
C Just over 10%.
D As much as 80%.

A4 Which statistic is frequently quoted according to the article? Use your own words.

A5 Say whether the following information is true (T) or false (F).

Henderson Island

A is an island made up entirely of plastic waste. T F
B is situated in the South Pacific region. T F
C has an enormous amount of plastic waste. T F
D is covered in about 20 million tons of plastic. T F

A6 Which of the following meanings is closest to the expression 'roughly' as used in line 31?

A violently
B not smoothly
C more or less
D less than

A7 What is the amount of plastic waste compared to?

A8 What are the two reasons Geyer gives to explain why plastic is a greater problem than other metals?

A9 Explain the meaning of 'trading off' as used in the last paragraph.

A10 Which of the following best summarises the viewpoint of the article?

A The writer gives a series of explanations about why plastic waste is the most important environmental issue the world has to deal with currently.
B The article points out the serious nature of the environmental issues connected to the huge amount of plastic waste produced in the world and suggests there should be a global solution.
C The article is designed to explain the findings of the recent study carried out by environmental scientists and how the solutions proposed can be put to use.
D The writer discusses the progress and strategies currently employed to become more efficient at recycling plastic.

C Listening for specific information

4 5.3 **LISTEN** to a teacher talking to a class about microplastic contamination and complete the sentences.

1 Microplastic contamination refers to .... of plastic suspended ....
2 Scientists have found this contamination in .... of the samples taken.
3 Plastic fibres were found in .... taken from the Congress building in the US and .... in New York.
4 European nations have a lower .... but it is still a worrying ....
5 People have been eating microplastic in ....
6 In Germany fibres were found in all of the .... brands as well as in ....
7 Scientists see these findings as a .... of warning.
8 The experts agree that we need .... in our lives, but must stop discarding it in ....

Phrasal verbs and expressions for the environment

5 **MATCH** the phrasal verbs and expressions (1-8) in the article to their definitions (A-H).

1 [C] mass produce
2 [F] disposable products
3 [A] end up
4 [G] set out
5 [H] waste systems
6 [D] plastic pollution
7 [E] man-made materials
8 [B] recycling strategies

A reach a final state or condition
B plans or methods to do with recycling
C manufacture goods in large quantities
D pollution caused by plastic waste
E things made by humans
F goods designed to be thrown away
G try
H different ways of disposing of waste

6 **COMPLETE** the sentences using the correct form of the phrasal verbs and expressions from exercise 5.

1 Most plastic products are ....DISPOSABLE.... which lead to the serious problem of ....PLASTIC POLLUTION.
2 Environmentalists are looking for new ....RECYCLING STRATEGIES.... that can help with their future ....WASTE SYSTEMS.
3 Although people don't ....SET OUT.... to cause more pollution, they ....END UP.... doing so because of the increased use of plastic.
4 Plastic is one of the ....MAN MADE MAT..... and unfortunately is increasingly ....MASS PRODUCED.... so there is more and more plastic waste.

Reported speech

1 MATCH direct sentences 1-4 to reported sentences A-D.

1 He stated: 'If present trends continue, by 2050 there will be 12 billion metric tons of plastic in landfills.'
2 A researcher said: 'This year we've hit the limits of nature.'
3 Lindy to her friend: 'Tomorrow I'll have an English test.'
4 He said: 'I want to attend this conference about climate action.'

A Lindy announced to her friend that she **would have** an English test on the following day.
B He said that he **wanted** to attend that conference about climate action.
C He stated that if the present trends **continued**, by 2050 **there would be** 12 billion metric tons of plastic in landfills.
D A researcher stated that that year they **had hit** the limits of nature.

2 READ the sentences in exercise 1 and list the three things that change when you report what someone has said.

1 ....
2 ....
3 ....

Grammar reference 9.1

3 REPORT the following statements using the prompts.

1 'We only accept new clients by appointment.'
He explained ....
2 'I'll travel round the world if I win the lottery.'
He declared ....
3 'You should help your mother with the housework.'
Mr Leighton told his daughter ....
4 'The President is holding a press conference tomorrow.'
The spokesman said that ....
5 'Guests can use all the facilities of the hotel.'
The receptionist told the guests that ....
6 'The Antarctic may be at risk.'
A scientist stated that ....

4 REPORT the following statements making all the necessary changes. Begin each reported statement with 'He said...'.

1 'Stop annoying me and complaining about everything!'
2 'The combination of effects has played a major role in the alarming rise of sea levels in the past ten years.'
3 'I'll come and help you on Saturday.'
4 'I was waiting for the bus when Nick arrived.'
5 'I'd never been here before.'
6 'We are convinced that you will like the innovations such as three-dimensional figures on birthday cards.'

FREQUENT MISTAKES ***Say* and *tell***

5 READ sentences 1-2 and complete the rules A-B with *say* or *tell*.

1 'What did she **say** (to you)?' 'She **said** (to me) she would be late.'
2 'What did she **tell** you?' 'She **told** me she would be late.'

A When using the verb .... it is necessary to have an object.
B When using the verb .... it is necessary to use a preposition when there is an object.

Grammar reference 9.2

6 COMPLETE the sentences with the correct form of *say* or *tell*.

1 If you .... me what he .... yesterday, I'll keep the secret.
2 The sign .... 'silence' but nobody was taking any notice of it.
3 Unfortunately, she .... what she wanted and I brought her the wrong thing.
4 Why.......... (you) you wanted to leave her?
5 .... (you) me that you have made a mistake?

7 READ the text and underline all the examples of reported speech. Then turn those sentences into direct speech.

Mr Irons, a scientific researcher, told his students that last year on 22nd April, hundreds of thousands of people around the world gathered to celebrate Earth Day. He also stated that the celebration had become an opportunity to raise the awareness of threats to our planet and to learn how to protect the environment.
Scientists stated that humans caused that warming because they burnt fossil fuels such as coal, oil and gas for their cars, houses and factories. They went on saying that it would take time to educate people about environmental problems properly.
Mr Irons also told us that the Earth Day had started in 1969 when a massive oil spill in Santa Barbara had destroyed the environment and killed sea life. In 1990, Earth Day developed into a global event; now, 141 countries participate in it.
He also explained that in 2017, for the first time, another event had happened on the same day: the International March for Science. In London, thousands of people had marched from the Science Museum to Parliament Square to draw attention to the importance of science. There had also been big crowds in Edinburgh, Scotland, Sydney, in Australia, and Washington DC, the capital of the USA. There, the organisers of the march had declared that science had been under attack from some politicians.

TIP Remember that you are required to use just ONE word for each gap. Using more than one word will lose the mark.

FIRST Reading and Use of English – Part 2

1 **OPEN CLOZE. For questions 1-8, read the text below and think of the word which best fits each gap. Use only one word in each gap. There is an example at the beginning (0).**

He said we must save the bees!

In a time of global **(0)** ....WARMING.... where nature's needs come behind economic growth, we must all learn to protect endangered **(1)** .... One of these is the bee. Bees pollinate a third of everything we eat and play a vital role **(2)** .... sustaining the planet's ecosystems. Almost all of our food, including most fruits and vegetables, many nuts, and plants such as rapeseed and sunflowers that are turned into oil, as well as cocoa beans, coffee and tea, rely on pollination from bees.

Bees also make an invaluable contribution to ecosystems around the world. Seeds, fruits and berries eaten **(3)** .... birds and small mammals are all from **(4)** .... pollinated by bees, making **(5)** .... guardians of the food chain and the biodiversity of our species.

But intensive farming, insecticide use and climate **(6)** .... are threatening bees. A combination of parasites, viruses, poor nutrition and pesticides are the reason for the widespread death of honeybees. A recent study shows nearly one in 10 of Europe's wild bee species could end **(7)** .... being extinct.

John Muir, a giant of the conservation movement, summed up the importance of bees to the human race when he **(8)** .... : 'When one pulls at a single thing in nature, you find it attached to the rest of the world.'

(Adapted from www.theguardian.com)

TIP Each of the transformations is based on a particular grammar structure or transformation e.g. active into passive, direct speech into indirect speech. If you recognise the structure being tested, it will help you formulate the correct transformation.

FIRST Reading and Use of English – Part 4

2 **KEY WORD TRANSFORMATIONS. For questions 1-6, complete the second sentence so that it has a similar meaning to the first sentence, using the word given. Do not change the word given. You must use between two and five words including the word given. Here is an example (0).**

0 'There will be more and more plastic islands in the ocean,' said the recycling expert.
WOULD
The recycling expert said there WOULD BE MORE AND MORE plastic islands in the ocean.

1 'We must tell manufacturers to produce fewer disposable plastic containers,' said the environmentalist.
HAD
The environmentalist said that we .... to produce fewer disposable plastic containers.

2 'No, it definitely wasn't me who dumped,' said the young man.
NOT
The young man said he .... all that e-waste in the river.

3 Unfortunately, a huge percentage of plastic waste eventually gets to the ocean.
ENDS
Unfortunately, a huge percentage of plastic waste .... the ocean.

4 Megan said: 'My idea is to open a recycling station for plastic, glass and paper.'
HER
Megan said .... a recycling station for plastic, glass and paper.

5 'I think climate change is to blame for all the flooding,' said the scientist.
WAS
The scientist said he thought .... for all the flooding.

6 We certainly don't need so many manufactured products.
MASS
We certainly don't need so many .... products.

WARM-UP

1 DISCUSS in pairs.

1 Do you feel involved and responsible towards the environment?

2 Is there anything you personally feel you could do to protect the environment more?

C Recognising links within a text

2 READ and listen to the texts about recycling and care for the environment and match the pictures to the texts.

TIP Read the complete article before you begin looking at the individual gaps. Also read all the sentences. Then read the text again and at each gap try out the sentences. Do they follow the sentence before? Are they connected to the sentence after?

FIRST Reading and Use of English – Part 6

3 GAPPED TEXT. Read the texts again. Six sentences have been removed from the texts. Choose from the sentences A-G the one which fits each gap (1-6). There is one extra sentence which you do not need to use.

A Unable to race, he realised just how much he loved the sport.

B After hearing about the mass of trash that's twice the size of Texas floating in the Pacific Ocean, they agreed to create The Plastic Patrol, beginning their global effort to make a difference, one kid at a time.

C This 16-year-old first learned about the environmental problems associated with e-waste after reading a Wall Street Journal article on the subject.

D She learned about the importance of mangroves in preventing damage during natural disasters and refused to do nothing about it.

E Her ideas have been presented in schools and she was invited as a delegate by the United Nations Environment Programme (UNEP).

F By the end of the first year, he was able to collect and clean-up more than 500 pairs of running shoes, which were sent to kids in inner-city Los Angeles, as well as overseas to Sudan, Uganda and Kenya.

G No one can deny that these young people have made a considerable contribution to this cause.

A

B

How kids are saving the planet

1 Alex Lin - Team WIN

To suggest that the work of Rhode Island teen Alex Lin is impressive would be an understatement. **1** Since then, he and his student-led community service team, Team WIN, have organised the recycling of 300,000 pounds of e-waste, successfully lobbied the Rhode Island state legislature and have asked them to pass a statewide bill banning the dumping of e-waste. They have also created media centres in developing countries using refurbished computers, secured grants to fund the projects and created a national PSA (parent student association) on the subject of e-waste.
In fact, a representative of Team WIN insisted that manufacturers take back their computers and televisions and pay for their collection and recycling.

2 Greg Woodburn, non-profit founder and president

Greg Woodburn was a national track and cross country runner when an injury suddenly stopped him running in his freshman year of high school. **2** He complained that while running was hard, not running was harder. He said he didn't accuse anyone of preventing him from running and took the opportunity to think of underprivileged kids who couldn't enjoy the sport – not because of injury, but because they didn't have the money to buy the shoes.
We asked him what he had done next and he explained that he had started Give Running, a non-profit organisation, when he was just 15 years old. The organisation collects and donates used running shoes, in good condition, to underprivileged young people and orphans. **3** He went on to say that the reason he keeps doing more and more is because the feedback from youth in Africa had been especially moving. He claimed that for many these were not just the first running shoes they had owned, but they were also the first shoes many of them had ever had. When asked if he would continue, Greg immediately confirmed.

3 Adeline Tiffanie Suwana

Twelve-year-old Indonesian student Adeline Tiffanie Suwana became concerned for the environment after seeing the effects of natural disasters and flooding on her country. 4 ___ She accused the local authorities of doing too little. So she formed a community of young people called Sahabat Alam, which means 'Friends of Nature'. The community now has thousands of members throughout Indonesia.

Adeline organises students to plant coral reefs, help with fish breeding and turtle protection, plant mangrove trees and engage in environmental cleanups and education activities. Adeline and Sahabat Alam also operate the Electric Generator Water Reel project where they connect remote villages to an electric grid, providing potential economic growth to villagers and improving health and education facilities. They apologise only that they can't do more.

Adeline denied being a heroine but she has become internationally recognised. 5 ___ In 2009, she received the Action for Nature International Young Eco-Hero award for her efforts.

4 Peyton_Leighton

Seven-year-old Merit Leighton and five-year-old Marlowe Peyton of California were watching Oprah's Earth Day show when they learned about the impact of plastic pollution on the planet's oceans. 6 ___ When asked how the girls were helping the environment, they insisted that they were raising awareness. They said that the smallest of actions made a big difference – picking up a plastic wrapper, making sure parents bring reusable bags to the market or even bringing reusable utensils and cups to eateries that use plastic ware.

The Plastic Patrol is currently filming a series of Webisodes to provide kids with simple ways to help reduce plastic marine pollution. They suggest learning to make craft items out of recycled plastic and hope to raise money to combat ocean pollution with the sales of these items.

(Adapted from www.earth911.com)

4 FIND the words in the texts which mean the following:

1 tried to influence the actions or votes of politicians (text 1);
2 getting rid of, throwing away (text 1);
3 a student in the first year (text 2);
4 children who have lost both parents (text 2);
5 a great amount of water (text 3);
6 reproduction (text 3);
7 a covering or cover (text 4);
8 restaurants (Am. Eng.) (text 4);

Word formation: word families (2)

5 COMPLETE the table where you find words from the texts.

Base word	Noun	Adjective	Verb
		impressive	
organise			
	wrapper		
			create
		privileged	
	manufacturer		
environment			
		preventing	

6 MAKE suitable variations of the words given to complete the sentences.

1 Many young people, even those from .... backgrounds, have become committed .... (PRIVILIGE/ENVIRONMENT)
2 We need to ask .... to produce less plastic and fewer plastic .... (MANUFACTURE/WRAP)
3 If each one of us .... in the .... of the environment, it could make a .... (PARTICIPATE/PROTECT/DIFFER)
4 The two .... teenagers formed an .... to deal with e-waste. (IMPRESS/ORGANISE)
5 They suggested an interesting .... for our lunch. (EAT)

C Discussing ideas and relating them to personal experience

7 DISCUSS the questions.

1 What of the initiatives described in the texts do you consider the most valid? Why?
2 Which other ideas do you have of ways to protect the environment?

8 WRITE a brief paragraph of 10/12 lines about environmental problems in your area and what you think could be done to solve them.

Reporting verbs

1 READ sentences 1-4 and answer questions A-D.

1 A representative of Team WIN **insisted** that manufacturers take back their computers and televisions.
2 They **agreed** to create The Plastic Patrol, beginning their global effort to make a difference.
3 They **suggest** learning to make crafts out of recycled plastic.
4 She **accused** the local authorities of doing too little.

Which reporting verb
A is followed by the *-ing* form?
B is followed by the infinitive?
C is followed by a preposition + the *-ing* form?
D takes a direct object + infinitive?

Grammar reference 9.3

2 MATCH each reported sentence (1-5) with the corresponding direct sentence (A-E).

1 ☐ The teenager admitted that he might have been wrong.
2 ☐ She absolutely refused to hear her father's words.
3 ☐ The director regretted that they had rejected my application.
4 ☐ The advertising manager expected the company to try a different course of action.
5 ☐ My mum reminded me to buy some pizza on my way home.

A 'We're sorry but we have decided not to accept your application for the course.'
B 'OK, perhaps I was wrong after all.'
C 'I won't listen to you!'
D 'I thought we were going to propose this new product.'
E 'Don't forget to buy some pizza, Meg!'

3 REPORT the following sentences using the prompts and one of the reporting verbs given in the box.

suggest ▪ warn ▪ invite ▪ apologise ▪ deny ▪ complain ▪ explain ▪ threaten

1 'We're sorry, we kept you waiting.' (shop assistant)
2 'Why don't you take the plastic bottles to the recycling bin?' (your friend)
3 'I can't finish the report on time because it's too long.' (Tom to his colleague)
4 'If the press treats me unfavourably, I won't give any more interviews.' (actress)
5 'Make sure you avoid taking the underground at the rush hour.' (my father)
6 'Would you and your wife like to come to have dinner with us next Saturday.' (Mrs Smith to Mr Brown)
7 'We have too much homework to do!' (the students)
8 'I didn't eat all the biscuits in the jar.' (the child)

Reported questions

4 READ the following examples, then say whether the statements below them are true (T) or false (F).

'What did you do next?' we asked him.
We **asked** him what he had done next.

'Will you continue?' we asked Greg.
We **asked** Greg if/whether he would continue.

1 In reported questions the question word disappears. T F
2 In questions requiring a 'yes' or 'no' answer a question word is added. T F
3 In questions requiring a 'yes' or 'no' answer *if* or *whether* is used to report the question. T F
4 The construction of the sentence remains interrogative. T F

Grammar reference 9.4

5 CORRECT the mistakes in the sentences.

1 I asked her why was she crying.
2 They asked Susan she needed help.
3 She wanted to know how long the film did last.
4 He wondered whether was there another way to reach the station.
5 We asked the traffic warden when left the next bus.

6 COMPLETE the second sentence using the word in capital letters so that it has a similar meaning to the first sentence.

1 'Why do you behave like this?' THAT
His father asked ....
2 'Did the teacher explain how to do it?' WHETHER
He asked .... how to do it.
3 'What was he throwing into the bin?' BEEN
The policeman enquired .... into the bin.
4 'Can you turn the TV volume down?' IF
My mother asked .... the TV volume down.
5 'Have you ever been interested in conservation projects before?' asked the reporter. EVER
The reporter wanted to know ....
interested in conservation projects before.
6 'Who will you meet tomorrow?' NEXT
She asked me who I ....

7 TURN the following sentences into direct speech.

1 The young girl wondered what the ending of the book would be like.
2 He suggested choosing that area for a picnic.
3 They wanted to know if he was going to volunteer to clear the beaches of rubbish.
4 The girl asked why they hadn't filmed any tutorials to teach how to reduce pollution before.
5 They warned the students not to smoke inside the school.

SPEAKING

WARM-UP

1 **DISCUSS** in pairs.

1 Do you think the control and improvement of the environment we live in is the responsibility of the local or national governments?

2 Should the local community be involved in this? Can individuals make a difference?

C Expressing and defending your opinions

TIP While discussing the different options given, try to mention something about all of them. See if you can think of a positive point and a possible negative point for each one. Keep focused on the task by referring back to the question given in the centre.

FIRST Speaking – Part 3

2 **COLLABORATIVE TASK. Here are six different ways in which we can contribute to preserving or improving the environment. Talk in pairs about the different options and how they could help the environment (two minutes). Then decide which two you think would help the most (one minute).**

- Looking for alternative energy supplies like wind turbines or solar panels.
- Recycling paper, glass and plastic efficiently.
- Making public transport obligatory in cities and banning cars.
- Reducing the amount of air travel.
- The use of mass media to keep people informed of environmental issues.
- Involving as many people as possible in environmental operations like clearing rivers and planting trees.

In which ways do these activities help the environment?

START WITH MORE GENERAL
NOT SO FLUENT
FOCUSED TOO MUCH ON TWO OF EM

Which two activities are the most effective in helping the environment?

PROCESS LANGUAGE

Speaking – Part 3

Comparing options

This possibility is interesting because ..., but ...
This option would mean ...
I think the possible problems with this idea are ...
The advantages of this type of solution are ..., but there are also disadvantages like ...
All things considered, perhaps the worst ...

Giving examples from your own experience

In my experience ...
I have seen this type of solution ...
I remember once seeing ... / being near... / reading about ... in a newspaper/on the Internet
I believe this has been tried and it was/wasn't ...

Speaking reference p. 195

C Developing social interaction

TIP The questions asked in this section will be connected to Part 3, but may not be asking the same things. Read carefully and make sure you are answering the question, not merely continuing the discussion from Part 3.

FIRST Speaking – Part 4

3 **DISCUSSION.** In groups of three ask and answer the questions.

1 What changes should be made in the way we use energy?
2 Do you know about bike-sharing and car-sharing schemes? Do you think they are useful?
3 Do you think recycling is necessary?
4 Where does most of the pollution come from?
5 What about nature in your area? Is it protected?

WARM-UP

1 LOOK at the following pictures of endangered species and discuss in pairs.

1 How does the pollution in sea and in the air affect wildlife?
2 Which animals suffer from the effects of climate change?

C Listening for specific information

TIP Choose your answer after you have listened to the extract twice. Read the questions then listen for the first time and then read the questions again before listening for the second time and choosing your answer.

FIRST Listening – Part 1

2 5.5 **EXTRACTS WITH MULTIPLE-CHOICE QUESTIONS. You will hear people talking about endangered species. For questions 1-8, choose the best answer (A, B or C).**

1 You hear a conversation about the tiger.
Why did the class start discussing tigers?
- A Because they were studying the history of South China.
- B Because they read a poem about a tiger in their English lesson.
- C Because they had a geography lesson instead of an English lesson.

2 You hear a talk about the blue whale.
What are the current dangers that put the whale at risk?
- A Being hunted for their meat and oil.
- B Their huge size and the amount of noise they make which attracts hunters.
- C Collision with ships and becoming caught in fishing nets.

3 You hear an interview with a nature conservationist.
What does the speaker say about animals in danger of extinction?
- A That action needs to be taken in climate change and habitat.
- B That the most important animals in danger are the panda and the tiger.
- C That there are many less attractive animals, just as much in danger, but less talked about.

4 You hear an Indian talking about the importance of elephants in his culture.
Why are elephants considered sacred in India?
- A Because they are connected to a religious belief.
- B Because their precious tusks can be sold for ivory.
- C Because their habitat is needed for the growing human population.

5 You hear a biology teacher talking about the orang-utan.
What do orang-utans have in common with gorillas and chimpanzees according to the teacher?
- A They make nests in trees and sleep during the day.
- B They all are capable of using equipment.
- C They all live in lowland forest areas.

6 You hear two friends talking about a snow leopard.
Why was the snow leopard known as the 'king of the mountains'?
- A Because it is a very strong and agile animal.
- B Because it can be hunted, poached or shot.
- C Because it lives in both China and Mongolia.

7 You hear part of a radio programme about the Hawksbill turtle.
How do you recognise a Hawksbill turtle?
- A Because it lives in tropical oceans and in coral reefs.
- B Because of its highly-valuable tortoiseshell.
- C Because of its characteristic beak and shell.

8 You hear a brother and sister talking about different species of dolphin.
What has happened to the Baiji dolphin in the Yangtze River?
- A It has become famous for its smile and intelligence.
- B It no longer exists because of human activity.
- C It is one of two species of dolphin that live in the Yangtze River.

C Expressing personal opinions on a given topic

3 DISCUSS in pairs. What do you feel about the animal kingdom? Is it our responsibility to preserve the natural habitat that supports the lives of animals? Is it a problem if animals become extinct? Why or why not?

VIDEO
The Panda Project

C Watching and understanding a short film

1 BEFORE watching the video, match the words (1-5) to their meanings (A-E).

1 ☐ breeding
2 ☐ picking
3 ☐ cubs
4 ☐ chase off
5 ☐ civet cat

A offspring, the young
B make or cause to run away
C causing animals to reproduce
D cat-like mammal
E choosing, selecting

2 WATCH this shot (from 00:00 to 00:18). What does this animal communicate to you?

3 WATCH the whole video and identify:

1 the different settings in place;
2 who Papa Panda is;
3 what he says about the breeding of pandas;
4 what the name of his project is;
5 what his project deals with;
6 what it includes.

4 WATCH the video again and complete these sentences about the Panda Project.

1 Papa Panda is .... giant panda.
2 Preparing these animals born in captivity for .... is an ....
3 Papa Panda has discovered how .... to teach .... necessary to survive in the wild.
4 The baby pandas are watched while:
- they .... or
- when they try to .... animals and .... avoiding .... to escape from predators.
5 Director Zhang is aware that pandas can only survive in the wild with ....

5 DISCUSS in pairs. Have you ever heard of conservation animal projects around the Globe? Have you ever seen documentaries about endangered animals? Share your findings with the rest of the class.

6 SURF the net to discover where these conservation projects may take you.

MANAGING PROJECTS

7 DESCRIBE what kinds of projects you have been involved in up to now. How did you deal with them and what results did you achieve?

8 READ the chart about the phases of a project. Then explain each step with your own words referring to your personal experience.

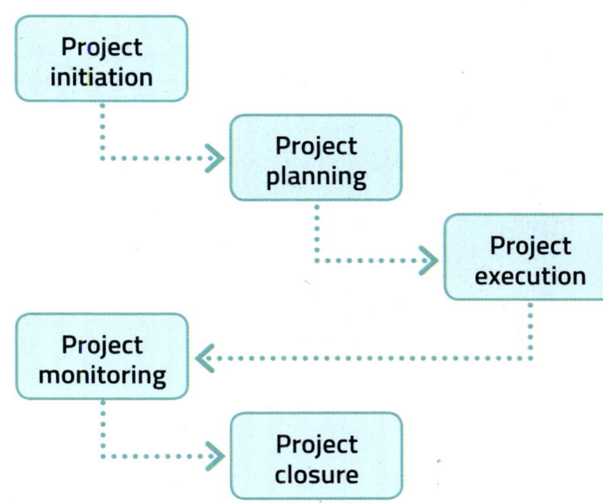

9 DISCUSS the following in groups.

1 What do you think the priorities of the Panda Conservation Project were?
2 Do you admire Papa Panda or do you think he was too devoted to his project?
3 What would you have done with the great sum of money granted him by the Government for his project?
4 Are you interested in wildlife and conservation volunteer programmes abroad? Think about your online research in exercise 6.
- Will these projects really offer you the chance of working under professional conservationists?
- Will they give you the opportunity of a lifetime to learn the basics of wildlife conservation techniques?

WARM-UP

1 DISCUSS in pairs. Nature, the air we breathe, the source of food and water, is essential to our well-being and yet we as a human race seem to be doing as much as possible to destroy it. Do you agree? What further steps should be taken?

C Expressing ideas and opinions in an essay

2 LOOK at the essay below about the environment and put the paragraphs in the correct order. Then add the correct label to each part.

Is the environment really getting **worse** or are we just more **aware** than before?

A ☐ On the other hand, we are also more aware of the possible consequences and I refuse to believe it is not possible to persuade people to change. Although change is never easy, we can all try to reduce our carbon footprint by using public transport rather than cars and reducing unnecessary use of energy – turning off lights, lowering the central heating.

B ☐ Some people claim that the environment we live in is no worse than in the past and actually many claim that we are living longer so obviously we must be healthier. But I don't agree.

C ☐ I am convinced that if everyone makes more effort, we can stop the process of harming our world and start to make it a better place to live.

D ☐ It is clear that we are polluting our atmosphere more than in the past. Just look at the increase in traffic in cities, and it cannot be denied that we use much more energy than ever before. Just consider the number of houses that use air-conditioning.

- **Introduction** Paragraph: ....
- **One side of the argument** Paragraph: ....
- **The other side of the argument** Paragraph: ....
- **Conclusion** Paragraph: ....

TIP Before you begin writing, read the title carefully and underline what you consider to be the key words. This will focus your mind on the key issues. Then spend at least five minutes brain-storming ideas. Then select and organise the ideas into possible paragraphs.

FIRST Writing – Part 1

3 AN ESSAY. In your geography class, you have been talking about nature and the ways we are failing to maintain and preserve our planet. Now your teacher has asked you to write an essay of between 140-190 words. Write your essay using all the notes and giving reasons for your point of view.

A cleaner environment is essential for our health and well-being. Are we doing enough to preserve it?

Notes
Write about:

1 what is being done to use alternative energy
2 how recycling and other initiatives are helping the environment
3 .... (your own idea)

PROCESS LANGUAGE

Writing – Part 1

Reporting information
It is clear that ...
People claim that ...
Some insist that ...
It cannot be denied that ...
I refuse to believe it is not possible to ...

Linkers
Moreover ... / On the other hand ... / Although ... / Nevertheless ... / However ...

Writing reference p. 196

C Organising a class discussion on a given topic

4 CLASS DISCUSSION. As an experiment, go around your school and see how much rubbish you find in the way of paper, plastic, cans or anything else. If you have recycling bins, check that the contents match what they should contain. Then have a class discussion on how 'green' your school is. If necessary, make notices about how rubbish should be dealt with more efficiently.

10 Money and business

VOCABULARY ACTIVATOR

Inquadrami per guardare i video e ascoltare gli audio di questa unità

FLIPPED classroom

VIDEO
Money and business

WARM-UP

1 DISCUSS. Do you have a set amount each week or month from your parents? Do you have your money in a bank account? Do you have a budget for your expenses?

C Learning to use vocabulary in context

2 5.6 **LISTEN** to a phone conversation about opening a bank account and complete the sentences.

1 A current account comes with a .... and .... statements.
2 A .... account doesn't have a cheque book but has monthly ....
3 There is a .... with the current account and also a ....
4 The debit card acts as a .... in any ATM machine.
5 After a year as a bank customer, you are allowed to begin .... where payments and .... can be done from any computer.

FOCUS ON VOCABULARY

Nouns
bank/current/savings account, bank statements, interest rates, credit/debit card, cheque book

Verbs
borrow, lend, cash in, save/spend money on, pay for (something), pay (someone) back

Collocations
fixed-rate/variable rate interest, cash machine, financial advisor, bank transfers, online banking

Expressions
be worth, bear an interest, pay a deposit, deposit money, withdraw money, fill in a cheque, open a bank account

3 LOOK at the list of departments in companies and organisations (1-8) and match them to the right picture (A-H).

1 Human Resources/ Personnel Department
2 Marketing
3 Product Design
4 Research and Development
5 Sales Department
6 Customer Services
7 Finance/Accounting Department
8 Production/Manufacturing Department

4 CHOOSE from the list above the right word or phrase to complete the sentences.

1 The .... is the division of a business that is responsible for selling products or services.
2 An accountant works in a .... to organise the financial and accounting affairs of a company.
3 Generally speaking, a .... manager investigates and produces new products.
4 In large offices there is a .... that deals with the selection of new staff.
5 Working in the .... means helping to advertise and sell the products produced.
6 One of the most interesting jobs in manufacturing concerns the development and .... of new goods.
7 When there are complaints or problems about a product it is normally the .... that has to deal with them.
8 Once a new product has been designed and approved, it is the .... that takes over.

WARM-UP

1 DISCUSS in pairs. What is a startup? Have you heard this expression? What do you think it means and can you name any startups that you know?

C Reading, interpreting and understanding information

2 READ and listen to the article and decide which of the highlighted words has the following meaning:

1 made specifically for an individual
2 with little or no experience
3 endurance, ability to continue in spite of difficulties
4 strength and firmness of character
5 rise very quickly
6 brought forward / come up with

5.7

Startups

The number of new startups in the UK continues to soar as more aspiring entrepreneurs, people of all ages and backgrounds, take the plunge. In 2015, the Centre for Entrepreneurs and StartUp Britain reported over six hundred thousand new incorporations. In the first four months of 2017 more than two hundred thousand new startups were created.
Sadly, for many, their entrepreneurial journey will be short-lived. After five years, just four in ten small businesses will be allowed to continue trading, according to research from Ormsby Street.
Should we let this pessimistic view deter new entrepreneurs? Not according to these successful small business owners who started out five years ago, with no previous business experience, but plenty of stamina and staying power and have made the business world work for them.

Sam Bruce, Alex Narracott, and Guy Bowden are the founders of *Much Better Adventures*, a travel platform they launched in 2012 after graduating from university. Their idea, hatched in a cabin in the Alps, allowed them to promote amazing global outdoor experiences and let the best local guides and hosts turn them into simple, logistics-free adventures. Five years on, they've sold over £7m worth of holidays and have had their company register a consistent 45% year-on-year growth. Surviving the crucial first five years, says Bruce, came down to three things: developing one new product at a time with a scalable business blueprint, building a passionate team with industry expertise, and having a clear destination but allowing people to be flexibile. What you don't necessarily need is previous experience.

Unseasoned entrepreneurs in more traditional service sectors have also shown what hard work and sacrifice allow people to achieve. In 2012, Dave and Anna France gave up their jobs with the Royal Mail and took redundancy to start their home-based dog walking and boarding business *Best Paw Forward*.
'The demand is there, and it lets us work from home surrounded by dogs, which is very appealing,' says Anna. 'But the reality is very different; you are out walking several hours a day in all weathers, and if you are boarding dogs, it is a 24/7 business, which means you have to make sacrifices. But the hard work has paid off for us, and the word of mouth recommendations we get from customers who love the service we provide, have allowed our business to grow and succeed.'

Another very traditional, but much more lucrative market, the jewellery industry, was where entrepreneurs and school friends David Sutton and Nikolay Piriankov had set their sights when they launched their online custom designed engagement rings startup, *Taylor&Hart*.
Their biggest challenge, Piriankov says, was getting people to lend them funds while they were still unprofitable. 'Selling the business vision took a long time to master,' says Piriankov. 'I dealt with rejection so many times, I lost count.' Nevertheless, they eventually secured £500,000 via crowdfunding which allowed them to start. Piriankov sums up the lesson for all would-be startuppers: 'At the start, it's just you, and the only way is up, so survival is really about whether you have the motivation, stamina and grit to keep going, and the ability to come up with good ideas and learn lessons quickly.'

(Adapted from www.theguardian.com, June 2017)

3 **READ** the article again and do the following activities.

A1 According to the article, who are the people going into startups?

A Many people of varied age groups and backgrounds.
B Mainly young people fresh out of university.

A2 Is the number of new startup businesses going up or down according to the article? Justify your answer.

A3 What is the meaning of 'short-lived' as used on line 9?

A Without much hope.
B Destined to last for a short time only.
C Renewable after a brief period of time.

A4 Which of the following are NOT necessary for a successful business according to the article?

A energy
B persistence
C previous experience

A5 Say whether the following information is true (T) or false (F).

A *Much Better Adventures* was launched by three young graduates. T F
B The idea came to them while on holiday in Scotland. T F
C They wanted to allow local experts to participate in organising the holidays. T F
D Their idea was focussed on relaxing, hotel-based holidays. T F

A6 What proof is there of the success of the enterprise?

A7 What are the three fundamental characteristics that enable startup hopefuls to survive according to the article?

A8 Which other successful businesses are cited as examples in the article?

A9 Explain the expression 'crowdfunding' (line 59) in your own words.

A10 Which of the following best summarises the content of the article?

A The easiest way to form new and successful businesses in today's world is to form startups.
B There are so many new startup companies now that it is becoming increasingly difficult to be successful.
C There are only a few areas left where there is a realistic possibility to do well in startup businesses.
D In an age of increasing attempts to form successful startups it is fundamental to have the right qualities and strength of character to carry your ideas forward.

C Listening and understanding information

4 5.8 **LISTEN** to how four successful teenage millionaires made their money. Then listen again and match each speaker to their company or profession.

This person
A showed business selling skills from a very young age and has been successful in a variety of ways. ....
B set up their own website based on characters he/she had seen in a cartoon. ....
C has made a successful business out of a personal enthusiasm. ....
D made a business out of frustration at losing too much time looking for information. ....

Speaker 1: Tony
Speaker 2: Julia
Speaker 3: Martin
Speaker 4: Annie

Phrasal verbs and collocations for business

5 **MATCH** the phrasal verbs and collocations (1-8) in the article with their definitions (A-H).

1 ☐ take the plunge	**A** the ability to keep going
2 ☐ staying power	**B** aim towards, focus on
3 ☐ turn into	**C** be basically
4 ☐ come down to	**D** throw yourself into something
5 ☐ pay off	**E** have an idea
6 ☐ set your sights (on)	**F** be unable to keep an accurate record
7 ☐ lose count	**G** transform
8 ☐ come up with	**H** be successful

6 **COMPLETE** the sentences using the correct form of the phrasal verbs and collocations from exercise 5.

1 Starting your own business obviously requires .... to keep going and the courage to ....
2 Successful entrepreneurs are those who .... an interesting idea and manage to .... it .... a business.
3 Success in business fundamentally .... courage and the ability to .... on realistic goals.
4 Hopefully all the hard work eventually .... even if you .... of all the sleepless nights and anxieties.

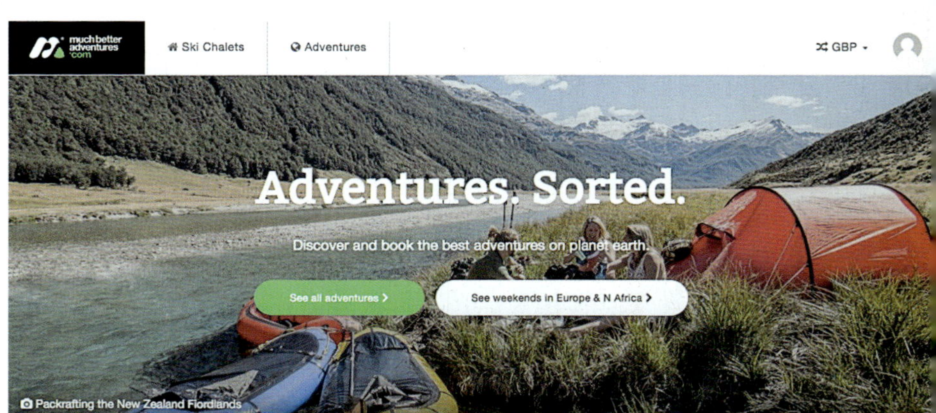

Award-winning adventures with the best local guides and hosts around the world

Causative verbs

1 READ sentences 1-5 and answer questions A-C.

1 Their idea **let** the best local guides and hosts turn them into simple, logistics-free adventures.
2 His jokes always **make** me laugh.
3 My father won't **allow** me to come home late.
4 I'll **have** my assistant call to reschedule the appointment.
5 Their biggest challenge, he says, **was getting** people to lend them funds.

A Which verb in **bold** has the same meaning as:
ask ....
oblige ....
persuade ....
permit ....
B Which phrases use causative verb + object + infinitive with *to*?
C Which phrases use causative verb + object + infinitive without *to*?

Grammar reference 10.1

2 CHOOSE the correct alternative to complete the sentences.

1 Public opinion will *make* / *let* the government modify its policy.
2 I must *have* / *let* a taxi driver collect us.
3 My father *made* / *let* me apologise for what I said.
4 All that heavy rain *made* / *allowed* the river overflow its banks.
5 I can't believe she *had* / *made* you look at her holiday pictures again last night.
6 When my mother had flu, we *got* / *had* the local supermarket deliver the weekly shop.
7 Andrew thinks television is a waste of time, so he won't *let* / *allow* his children watch it.

3 COMPLETE the sentences with the correct form of the causative verbs in the box.

let ▪ allow ▪ make (X2) ▪ have (X2) ▪ get

1 We .... a professional photographer take pictures of everyone who attended our wedding.
2 My teacher .... me re-write my essay because it was full of mistakes.
3 Jamie had a terrible backache yesterday, so he .... his twin brother Tim go to the lesson in his place.
4 The teacher .... the students leave earlier than usual as there was a school football match to watch.
5 The Browns .... some kids in the neighbourhood to cut the grass in their garden last week.
6 Sad movies .... me cry.
7 My parents never .... me to go out during the week.

4 WRITE two answers using causative verbs for each of the following questions.

1 What makes you laugh?
2 What makes you cry?
3 What allows you to relax?
4 What lets you feel good about yourself?

FREQUENT MISTAKES **Uses of *get***

Get is probably the most used verb in English and it can have various uses and meanings.

5 REPLACE the expression using *get* in the sentences with the correct form of one of the verbs in the box.

persuade ▪ begin ▪ rise ▪ listen to ▪ prepare ▪ understand ▪ be on friendly terms ▪ arrive ▪ receive ▪ manage to deal with

1 Did you *get* what the teacher was saying?
2 What time do you usually *get up* in the morning?
3 We both *got* really good marks in our English test.
4 The refugees will need help to *get through* the winter.
5 Could you possibly *get* supper *ready* this evening? I'm going to be late.
6 I didn't like the new girl at first, but now I'm *getting* to know her better and I like her a lot.
7 What time do your parents *get* here this evening?
8 *Get* this! According to the newspaper, my favourite football team have won the cup.
9 My dad always *gets* me to finish my homework – even when I really don't want to.
10 Amy and Nick really *get on very well*.

Grammar reference 10.2

6 MATCH each question (1-8) with the suitable answer (A-H).

1 ☐ How do you and Jake get on?
2 ☐ Will you manage to get home by 8 o'clock?
3 ☐ Why aren't you laughing?
4 ☐ What time do you get there?
5 ☐ Why did you arrive at school so late?
6 ☐ Did you manage to get through the first part of your speech?
7 ☐ Did it take you a while to get to know the city?
8 ☐ What did the starter shout at the beginning of the race?

A I was so tired that I couldn't get up on time.
B At tea-time.
C Yes, I did and then I was fine.
D Of course!
E It took me one month!
F Get ready!
G I didn't get the joke!
H We are great friends.

TIP Take time in your decision about the correct answer, as the different words may have a similar meaning. You need to decide the number and tense if a verb is required, and you need to think about number and appropriateness for an adjective, adverb or noun.

FIRST Reading and Use of English – Part 1

1 MULTIPLE-CHOICE CLOZE. For questions 1-8, read the text below and decide which answer (A, B, C or D) best fits each gap. There is an example at the beginning (0).

SHOP TILL YOU DROP

One of the many ways I fail at **(0)** ....BEING.... a proper woman is that I loathe shopping. Walking wearily in and out of sweaty changing rooms with friends, as they try on clothes which you are meant to oooh and aaah over, is my idea of hell. I am like those blokes who sit outside looking bored saying: 'Yeah, that looks alright. Buy that.' If I can't **(1)** .... them to buy something in 20 minutes, I'm gone.

Supermarkets overwhelm me and Ikea produces such bizarre mood swings that I have calculated the psychic damage is not worth the money you **(2)** .... When I eventually find the till holding two dozen egg cups, some box files and a bargain bath mat, I have to **(3)** .... someone revive me with water.

Oh yes, I know I should go around with an air of superiority looking like someone in a **(4)** .... of authority, taking a basket to organic markets and buying stuff from artisanal producers. But I would still prefer to **(5)** .... stuff from a neighbour. This is not some pure, ideological position. I like having nice things and I have worked in shops. When I was younger, my mother **(6)** .... me buy 'working clothes' to look good in.

What I deeply resent is the idea that shopping – especially for women – is some kind of leisure activity. Something that all women set their **(7)** .... But shopping to feed and clothe a family is often hard work and definitely not a hobby. As for window shopping? Looking at stuff you can't **(8)** .... the plunge and buying is just culturally legitimated masochism.

0	**A** to be	**B** are	**C** been	**D** **being**
1	**A** get	**B** have	**C** make	**D** let
2	**A** saving	**B** need	**C** save	**D** paying
3	**A** get	**B** have	**C** allow	**D** made
4	**A** air	**B** look	**C** position	**D** place
5	**A** borrow	**B** lend	**C** take	**D** save
6	**A** got	**B** had	**C** let	**D** made
7	**A** selves	**B** sights on	**C** needs	**D** money on
8	**A** bring	**B** have	**C** take	**D** put

TIP Remember that the spelling of the word may change if you have to add a prefix or a suffix to transform the word into what is required in the text.

FIRST Reading and Use of English – Part 3

2 WORD FORMATION. For questions 1-8, read the text below. Use the word given in capitals at the end of some of the lines to form a word that fits the gap in the same line. There is an example at the beginning (0).

Smart money

The way we pay is **(0)** ....CHANGING.... .	**CHANGE**
Long gone are the days in which everyone had to carry cash around for all their	
(1) .... requirements. Getting	**SHOP**
something **(2)** .... from another	**DELIVER**
town was complicated because of the payment and buying something expensive was a	
(3) .... problem.	**SECURE**
Gradually everything has changed. The first big change came from using plastic money – credit cards and debit cards and cash cards enabling	
you to make **(4)** .... or take out	**PAY**
cash at any time. Suddenly it was possible to buy over the phone, or online without moving from your home. The next big change is already here. It's paying with your smartphone. Those wallets, full of cards, paper money and coins have become	
(5) ...., we just need the phone.	**NECESSARY**
There are various ways you can choose to use your phone. Payments can be made with SMS, direct mobile billing, PayPal or	
(6)	**CONTACT**
Constant access to your bank is also possible through the phone. In fact, all the big banks and credit cards have their own mobile apps, which allow you to check your balance and transfer funds at any time. Of course you have to get the security right and make sure you are using	
a safe password but **(7)**	**GENERAL**
speaking, using mobile payments is convenient	
for **(8)** .... and is being used	**CONSUME**
more and more all over the world. Soon the wallet will be a thing of the past.	

WARM-UP

1 DISCUSS in pairs.

1. What skills do you have that you could offer others? Do you play a musical instrument, speak another language or maybe know how to sew?
2. Have you ever volunteered in your neighbourhood to help those in need with shopping or gardening? Would you do so if it was organised efficiently and safely?

C Recognising specific information within a text

2 READ and listen to the text about Time Banking and say which activities are mentioned as skills.

TIP Remember that the questions are always in the order in which the information appears in the text, so you don't have to keep going backwards and forwards looking for information.

FIRST Reading and Use of English – Part 5

3 MULTIPLE-CHOICE QUESTIONS. Read the text again. For questions 1-6, choose the answer (A, B, C or D) which you think fits best according to the text.

5.9

Time Banking

Not so long ago we all knew our neighbours and knew which of them would do us a favour if we asked them for one – and our neighbours knew if we would be happy to do them a favour in return. Life has changed because our friends and family do not always live nearby and it is not so easy to ask neighbours for help these days, also owing to the fact that we do not know if we can ever pay them back.

Time Banking is a non-profit company that is organising this rewarding and enjoyable way to bring people together once again to strengthen the feeling of community and share their skills. With time banking, people of all ages and all abilities can utilise and exchange a whole range of skills, consequently everyone feels valued. It is a type of skills-swapping – a person can cash in the credit earned from an hour of volunteering for an hour of learning a new skill such as being taught how to play the guitar.

So how does it work?

1 People list the skills and experience which they can offer and those that they may need.
2 Everyone's skills are valued equally, therefore one hour qualifies for one time credit.
3 Everyone agrees to both give and to receive help, to earn and to spend their time credits.
4 A record is kept of all the time credits earned and spent, ideally on computer using the 'Time Online' system.
5 Everyone is authorised and encouraged to spend their time credits to allow others the chance to make a difference and feel needed.

A typical example is Ian Toplis, from Gloucester, who says: 'I really hate gardening and the fact that I can do some IT for someone and have my garden done is a huge incentive. I helped a lot of elderly residents during the digital switch-over and as a result, I have a lovely garden.'

The Time Banking organisation feels that the real wealth of any society is its people since every individual has valuable experience, skills and connections to contribute to the wellbeing of others in their local community. Activities such as bringing up children, acting as a carer for older people, keeping communities safe, fighting injustice and making democracy work have to be recognised and rewarded as real work. Thus, belonging to a mutually supportive and secure social network brings more meaning to our lives, due to the new opportunities to rebuild our trust in one another, just as it was in the past.

The more people share their time and skills, the healthier and happier your neighbourhood will become. With time banking, everyday acts of kindness are recognised as the important contribution they are to everyone's wellbeing.

(From www.timebanking.org.uk)

1 In which way has life changed according to the text?
- A Neighbours have all moved away from each other.
- B There aren't neighbours any more.
- C Neighbours don't know each other as well as they used to.
- D Neighbours nowadays are unlikely to be friendly.

2 Time Banking is an organisation that
- A arranges for people in the same neighbourhood to exchange services.
- B acts as a form of banking and money exchange for the local community.
- C introduces new neighbours to each other.
- D encourages people in the community to learn new skills.

3 What do participants in time banking have to agree?
- A That they will not abuse the system.
- B That they will keep a record of all the services they receive.
- C That they will only use a computer-based programme to organise their services.
- D That they will offer their services and use other services in return.

4 The phrase 'digital switch-over' on line 36 means
- A changing from a non-digital system to a digital one.
- B changing equipment to introduce new technology.
- C changing one digital system for another.
- D dumping or throwing out older equipment.

5 What incentive did Ian Toplis give as an example of successful time banking?
- A He could do more gardening and less IT.
- B He could get help with a job he hated by doing something he was good at.
- C He could help older people with their gardening in return for help on the computer.
- D His incentive was to help others and not expect anything in return.

6 What are the social benefits of time banking according to the article?
- A There are several benefits involving greater justice and democracy as well as safety.
- B The benefits need time and commitment but will eventually result in a richer community.
- C It is a way of restoring trust and good neighbourliness making the local community a happier and healthier place.
- D It is a way of reintroducing services like bringing up children and caring for older people.

4 FIND **the words or phrases in the text which mean the following:**

1. in exchange (para. 1); IN RETURN
2. close (para. 1); NEARBY
3. due to (para. 1); OWING
4. providing satisfaction (para 2); REWARDING
5. written account (para. 3); RECORD
6. something that encourages a person to do something (para 4); INCENTIVE
7. a condition of good health and contentment (para 5); WELLBEING
8. someone who takes care of an old or sick person (para. 5). CARER

Word formation: suffixes to form verbs

Many **English verbs** are formed by adding a **suffix** to nouns and adjectives. The most used suffixes are: ***-en*** (*dark* – ***darken***), ***-fy/-ify*** (*intense* – ***intensify***, *simple* – ***simplify***), ***-ise*** (*terror* – ***terrorise***, *memory* – ***memorise***).

5 FIND some examples of this use of suffixes in the text and say from which words they derive.

6 TRANSFORM the following into verbs using the suffixes above.

horror ▪ white ▪ character ▪ electric ▪ economy ▪ sharp ▪ apology ▪ beauty ▪ thick ▪ note ▪ critic

7 MAKE verbs in a suitable tense from the words given to complete the sentences.

1. Some people .... others when they are only trying to help. (FRIGHT)
2. To help others well it is important to .... the needs of each person and .... with their problems. (INDIVIDUAL/SYMPATHY)
3. An organisation can help you .... what is really necessary in a community. (IDENTITY)
4. In the summer, when the days ...., it is easier to .... what outside help is needed. (LENGTH/QUANTITY)

C Discussing ideas and relating them to personal experience

8 DISCUSS the questions.

1. What do you think about the skills-swapping idea?
2. Can you see the advantages and disadvantages?
3. Would it work in your community? Why or why not?

9 WRITE a brief paragraph of 10/12 lines giving your views on this form of time banking or using services rather than money to pay for things you need.

Linkers of reason and result

1 READ sentences 1-7 and answer questions A-B.

1 Life has changed **because** our friends and family do not always live nearby.
2 People of all ages and all abilities can use and exchange a whole range of skills; **consequently**, everyone feels valued.
3 It is not so easy to ask neighbours for help these days, also **owing to the fact** that we do not know if we can ever pay them back.
4 I helped a lot of elderly residents during the digital switch-over and **as a result**, I have a lovely garden.
5 The Time Banking organisation feels that the real wealth of any society is its people **since** every individual has valuable experience, skills and connections.
6 Everyone's skills are valued equally, **therefore** one hour qualifies for one time credit.
7 Thus, belonging to a mutually supportive and secure social network brings more meaning to our lives, **due to** the new opportunities to rebuild our trust in one another.

Which word in bold
A is a linker of reason?
B is a linker of result?

Grammar reference 10.3

2 COMPLETE the sentences using the linkers from the box. You can use more than one linker in some sentences.

owing to ▪ therefore ▪ thus ▪ consequently ▪ since ▪ because (of) ▪ so ▪ as a result ▪ due to

1 Tim has joined the photography club .... he wants to become a reporter when he grows up.
2 .... Ben worked very hard, he had little difficulty in getting a promotion.
3 The vacuum cleaner broke down .... we had to buy a new one.
4 I think people are reluctant to have face-to-face relationships these days .... the excessive use of social networks.
5 She was aware she couldn't perform well in the race. .... she didn't take part in it and started to train hard for the next one.
6 .... a traffic jam, we couldn't reach the airport in time for our flight.
7 It snowed heavily, ... there were avalanches in the area.
8 .... I wanted to improve my Spanish, I spent six months in Madrid.
9 The Time Banking organisation is very useful, ... a lot of people have become members.
10 The football match had to be postponed .... the thick fog.

3 CHOOSE the correct linker to complete the sentences.

1 People of all ages participate in Time Banking *therefore / due to the fact that* they have several skills and time to offer.
2 There was a protest march organised by the consumer association *due to / owing to the fact that* the price increase.
3 I felt sick last night, *so / since* I'm not sure I'll come to school today.
4 They can't leave today *due to / because* the train strike.
5 Do you mind if we pass by the grocer's *since / therefore* I need to buy some flour.
6 The company's most important designer could not attend the meeting. *Because / Therefore*, the project general manager decided to postpone it until next week.
7 Thousands of people lost their homes *thus / owing to* a terrible earthquake.
8 The band's frontman couldn't sing in the concert *because of / since* his sore throat.
9 She thought nobody had liked her performance in the school play. *Consequently / Owing to the fact that*, she was caught by surprise when she got a prize for being the best actress in the school.
10 It's my turn to do the shopping *because / so* you have done it for the past two weeks.

4 REWRITE the following sentences. Replace *because* and *so* with other linkers of reason or result.

1 She needs to buy a very elegant dress because she has just received an invitation to a wedding.
2 The student cheated in the test. So the teacher put him in detention.
3 We have decided to buy a bigger house because we are expecting our fourth baby.
4 The thief was caught red-handed. So he was arrested by the police.
5 We don't think the young woman would be a good candidate for this job because she is not self-confident enough.
6 My son has long been interested in economics. So he has decided to study finance at university.
7 The government does not provide enough relief money. So the number of poor people is increasing.
8 I like the view of life young people have because they always see the bright side.

WARM-UP

1 DISCUSS in pairs.

1 Are you a saver or a spender? Have you ever saved for something that was quite expensive like a holiday or a new phone? Or do you spend your money as soon as you get it?
2 Have you ever bought a lottery ticket or a scratch card hoping to get more money?

C Developing confidence and fluency

2 LOOK at the photographs. In pairs, make a list of useful words and phrases to describe them.

TIP Talking without interruptions for a minute is longer than you think! To get a good idea of the length of time you should keep talking, practise by describing pictures from your textbooks or from the web and time yourself. Practise by comparing two pictures on a similar topic.

FIRST Speaking – Part 2

3 INDIVIDUAL LONG TURN. Here are two photographs showing different ways of dealing with money. Compare them and say which way you consider a good way to use your money and why. You have one minute to do this.

Which is the best way to use your money?

PROCESS LANGUAGE

Speaking – Part 2

Describing the people in the pictures
The girl/boy/lady/man in the first/second picture has ... hair, ... eyes and a ... mouth.
They look happy/sad/angry/disappointed/ frustrated ...
I think they are interested/not interested in ...
In my opinion the man/woman/girl/boy is probably feeling ...

Describing the atmosphere in the pictures
The background is important/not important in this picture because ...
Behind/To the left/To the right/In front of the lady/man/girl/boy we can see ...

Describing what the people are doing
The lady/man/girl/boy in the first picture is holding ... because ...
The lady/man/girl/boy in the second picture is ... probably because ...

Speaking reference p. 194

C Talking about and comparing personal experiences on a given topic

4 CLASS DISCUSSION. Choose one of the questions to talk about to your classmates.

- How do you spend your money? What are your expenses?
- Do you make yourself a weekly or monthly budget?
- Do you get your parents to help you out?
- Do you use a credit or debit card and do you worry about over-spending and getting into debt?
- Is buying lottery tickets a good way of trying to make more money?

WARM-UP

1 DISCUSS in pairs.

1 Look at the picture and say what you think the World Savings Day may be about.

2 How do you save your money? Do you have a money box, a piggy bank or a bank account?

C Listening for specific information

TIP Read the question carefully and think about the answer in your own words before reading the options given. This will help you choose the correct one.

FIRST Listening – Part 4

2 5.10 **MULTIPLE-CHOICE QUESTIONS. You will hear an interview on a radio programme where a banker is talking about World Savings Day. For questions 1-7, choose the best answer (A, B or C).**

1 Where and when did the idea of a World Savings Day begin?
- A In Rome, Italy, in October 1921.
- B At an international conference in Turin, Italy, in 1931.
- C In Milan, Italy, in October 1924.

2 Where did the conference suggest that people keep their savings?
- A In banks or savings institutions.
- B Hidden in the house or under the mattress.
- C In responsible places but not in banks or financial institutions.

3 When was the day most popular?
- A During the difficult times of the war.
- B Immediately after the war when many saw their savings vanish.
- C During the Sixties.

4 Why was the day also called 'Thrift Day'?
- A Because people were forbidden to spend money on that day.
- B Because people were encouraged not to spend on that day.
- C Because retailers and shops closed on that day and it was impossible to spend money.

5 How can everyone contribute to global development according to Mary Shannon?
- A By making the public aware of the importance of saving.
- B In modern economics savers are as important as bankers.
- C Every individual who puts money into a savings account is helping development.

6 What role does the World Savings Bank have?
- A Its role is to encourage local institutions in their support for local individuals and companies.
- B It acts as a central reference for countless individuals and local communities.
- C It plays an active role locally in encouraging communities to save rather than spend.

7 What have some countries developed to celebrate World Savings Day?
- A Nearly 80 countries all over the world have developed a 'happy saver' to represent World Savings Day.
- B The headquarters of the World Savings Bank have developed and distributed mascots to local banks all over the world.
- C Some countries, like Austria, have developed mascots to represent happy savers.

C Expressing personal opinions on a given topic

3 WORK in pairs. **Decide if a Savings Day is a good idea or not. Is it necessary to persuade people to spend less?**

VIDEO
PayPal
A global currency

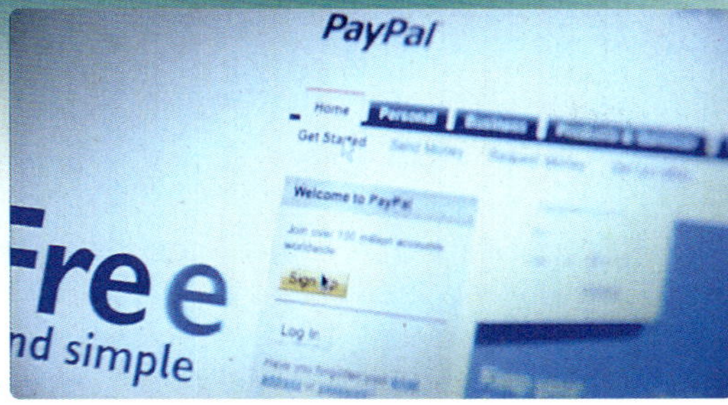

C Watching and understanding a short film

1 **BEFORE** watching the video, match the words (1-5) to their meanings (A-E).

1	☐ harness	A	understand, solve
2	☐ handling	B	got on well
3	☐ figure out	C	controlling, managing
4	☐ hit it off	D	unprepared
5	☐ on the hop	E	gain control over something

2 **WATCH** the video and identify the functions of these shots at the beginning of the sequence.

1 00:08-00:12: ....

2 00:16-00:23: ....

3 00:40-00:42: ....

3 **ANSWER** these questions about the short film.

1 Where did a new kind of global awareness come through?
2 Who are Bill Gates and Tim Berners-Lee?
3 Who is Peter Thiel? Is he as famous as the people above?
4 What does PayPal allow people to do?
5 Where and when was PayPal founded?
6 Who did Thiel meet at Stanford?
7 What did Thiel see in PayPal?

4 **WATCH** the video again and complete these sentences about the features of PayPal highlighted by Peter Thiel.

1 He wanted to .... to allow people .... around the world.
2 The slogan of PayPal is that it was ....
3 PayPal was going .... the way the world thought ....
4 It was going to give ....
5 PayPal changed ....
6 It also gave people .... in a completely different way.
7 PayPal's system lets ordinary people .... internationally.

5 **DISCUSS** in pairs. Have you ever heard of PayPal? What do you know about the methods of payment supported by PayPal? You can surf the net to look for more information about it.

6 **DISCUSS** the following questions in groups.

1 What emotions did you feel while watching the video?
2 Were you impressed by Peter Thiel's wish to get globalisation to work?
3 What was his relationship with Max Lefchin like? Was Peter a follower of Max's or a leader within their team?
4 Do you think Thiel could have managed to create PayPal by working alone? Or, were his collaboration and leadership within his team the winning tools to reach success?

LEARN BY DOING

GUIDING AND LEADING OTHERS

To guide and lead others means being experimental, open to changes and innovative. You must inspire others to reach their very best by managing yourself and giving them examples. You must also be respectful of your colleagues' ideas and opinions and encourage them to collaborate within your team.

7 **WORK** in groups. Imagine you have been asked to create a digital newspaper and periodical library for your school. Write the 'business plan' for your project.

Think about:
1 the copyright of newspapers and magazines your school must pay to have access to the various articles;
2 the newspapers/magazines which might be interested in becoming your project sponsors;
3 the advantages and disadvantages.

8 **WRITE** a business plan for your project following these steps:

Step 1 Write down a brief summary of your plan specifying its goals.
Step 2 Give a profile of your High school – its strong points (an example: in the top ten list of the best schools), management structure (headmaster, teachers, technicians), competitors (other High similar schools in the area), the services your school offers.
Step 3 Funding request – how much money your digital library will need for the next three years and how to cover the expense by launching a crowdfunding on the web.
Step 4 Explain why you care about this project (this could create an emotional connection with your customers).

WARM-UP

1 DISCUSS the following questions.

1. Look at the advertisement below for a brief course about how to deal with your personal finances. Do you think a course like this one could be useful? Would you consider going? Why or why not?
2. What should a course like this one deal with according to you?

Come and join our 'Learning to deal with money' course designed for young people who are starting out in the economic world.

LEARN ABOUT

- WHICH ACCOUNTS TO OPEN
- WHICH SAVINGS ACCOUNTS OR OPTIONS TO CHOOSE
- HOW TO USE CREDIT CARDS SENSIBLY WITHOUT RUNNING INTO DEBT
- THE MEANING OF TERMS LIKE 'FIXED INTEREST', 'MORTGAGE' OR 'RATING' AND 'SPREAD'

ALL ABOUT

- HOW TO UNDERSTAND YOUR PAYCHECK

It's a weekend course you will never regret!

EMAIL US AT:
financialcourses@freenet.com for the attention of Dave Turner

C Communicating in formal emails

2 LOOK at the advertisement again and say

- who the courses are for.
- how long they last.
- what will be taught.

PROCESS LANGUAGE

Writing - Part 2 (a formal email)

Greeting
Dear ... (*full name*), Dear Sirs (*if you don't know the name*)

Why you are writing
I have seen your advertisement for ...
and I would like to know ...
I am writing for information about ...
Can you also let me know ...
I would be grateful if you could email me ...

Salutation
Looking forward to hearing from you ...
Yours sincerely / Yours truly

Writing reference p. 200

TIP Although this is an email, the rules about formal language still apply as though it were a letter, so don't use abbreviations or informal language.

FIRST Writing – Part 2

3 A FORMAL EMAIL. Your economics teacher has shown the class an advertisement for courses that teach young people about money. The teacher has asked you to write an email of 140-190 words asking for the following information:

- Dates and times of the courses
- Parts of the course you are particularly interested in
- Costs of the courses
- Location and possible transport
- Whether there is an attendance certificate
- Ages and numbers of participants
- Other

C Organising a class activity on a given topic

4 CLASS ACTIVITY. Make a poster containing essential financial information about banking services, plastic money, saving possibilities and explaining terms like variable or fixed interest rates, mortgage, rating and spread.

Review Units 9-10

ZTE ONLINE Interactive exercises

VOCABULARY ACTIVATOR

1 CHOOSE the correct alternative to complete the sentences.

1 There has been such heavy rain in the last few days, there is a real risk of *pollution* / *floods*.
2 Weather extremes like *dumping* / *tornados* and *tsunami* / *deforestation* are happening more frequently.
3 We need to change to alternative *system* / *energy* and reduce our carbon *contamination* / *footprint*.
4 Global *heating* / *warming* and the greenhouse *effect* / *affect* are responsible for *earthquakes* / *ice melting*.
5 The *falling* / *rising* sea levels and the *contamination* / *waste* in the oceans are causing more and more concern among environmentalists.
6 The lack of rain and *drought* / *famine* are one of the reasons for a greater number of *endangered* / *recycling* species.

2 MATCH a sentence from the first list (1-6) to one in the second (A-F).

1 ☐ You need to speak to someone about a problem with a product you have recently bought.
2 ☐ Your brother has just applied for a job.
3 ☐ Sally wants a bank account with a cheque book and credit card.
4 ☐ You enjoy meeting people and are good at persuading.
5 ☐ The students find it difficult to understand the difference between fixed and variable interest rates.
6 ☐ Josey and I have decided to borrow some money from the bank to buy a car.

A You should think about working in a Sales Department.
B You should call the Customer Services Department.
C He has sent his CV to the Human Resources Department.
D Think carefully because you'll have to pay interest on the loan.
E She needs to open a current account in a bank.
F They should speak to a financial advisor.

GRAMMAR

3 REWRITE the sentences as direct or reported speech.

1 'Can Mary come to the fashion show tomorrow?' asked Sue.
2 The Personnel manager informed us that the company were looking for new sales staff that week.
3 'What interest is there on a savings account at the moment?' asked the customer.
4 The young man denied taking the silver cups from the sports centre display.
5 'Will there be a vacancy in the Research and Development Department next month?' asked Jim.
6 The manager said that unfortunately there was nobody in the Customer Services Department that day.

4 COMPLETE the sentences with a suitable causative verb: *let, allow, make, have, permit, get*.

1 We are absolutely not .... to smoke in the classroom.
2 It is really difficult to .... my dad to .... me meet my friends on a weekday evening.
3 I love films that .... me laugh, but I enjoy films that .... me cry too!
4 Please don't .... the dog out into the garden, we can't .... it back in again.
5 It .... me feel sad to see how many animals are .... to suffer because of environmental problems.
6 My financial advisor .... me change my account because the new one .... me more interest.

USE OF ENGLISH

FIRST Reading and Use of English – Part 1

5 MULTIPLE-CHOICE CLOZE. For questions 1-8, read the blog below and decide which answer (A, B, C or D) best fits each gap. There is an example at the beginning (0).

HOW GREEN ARE YOU?

The environment is a hot topic these days. We are continually being asked **(0)** ....WHETHER.... we recycle efficiently, use **(1)** .... transport, and try to use alternative energy. There are numerous articles that **(2)** .... to inform us about endangered species that need support or **(3)** .... disasters that require international aid. The richer developed countries are accused of contaminating and polluting the atmosphere, weakening the ozone **(4)** .... and causing global warming and the greenhouse effect. It all makes us feel as though our world **(5)** .... in danger of collapse. Luckily there are also positive innovations to improve the ecosystems and introduce more biodiversity allowing us to accept initiatives like the **(6)** .... charge in our cities and making us aware of limiting our **(7)** .... footprint. So let's talk less about the problems and think about alternative energy like **(8)** .... power that will let us be more optimistic about the future.

	A	B	C	D
0	that	**whether**	which	so
1	personal	car	public	carbon
2	set out	set on	put up	take on
3	human	unnatural	alternative	natural
4	cloud	layer	atmosphere	charge
5	could end up	can end	can end up	could be
6	pollution	contamination	endangered	congestion
7	personal	carbon	eco	greenhouse
8	sun	rain	wind	snow

FIRST Reading and Use of English – Part 2

6 **OPEN CLOZE.** **For questions 1-8, read the text below and think of the word which best fits each gap. Use only one word in each gap. There is an example at the beginning (0).**

SMART BANKING

There is a new generation of digital banks for people who **(0)** ......ALLOW...... smartphones to rule their lives. They typically have catchy one-word names and claim **(1)** .... they are redefining what a bank should be. They also insist that they are a genuine alternative with more staying **(2)** .... than the big high street banks.

These new banks are all trying to **(3)** .... us to use the rapidly increasing digital technology as bank branches close and turn **(4)** .... restaurants. But what benefits do they really **(5)** .... up with for potential customers? Do they offer enough in financial terms to allow us to leave our existing bank? What are the downsides?

(6) .... these banks typically have no costly branch networks or vast call centres to maintain, it's all about the app. However, many aren't fully up and running, and as a **(7)** .... , some have quite substantial charges for ATM withdrawals or for simply holding an account. **(8)** .... , the advice is to ask yourself what is being offered and look carefully for any hidden costs before moving your account.

FIRST Reading and Use of English – Part 3

7 **WORD FORMATION.** **For questions 1-8, read the text below. Use the word given in capitals at the end of some of the lines to form a word that fits in the gap in the same line. There is an example at the beginning (0).**

THE WAR AGAINST PLASTIC

The EU is waging war against plastic waste as part of an urgent plan to clean up Europe's act and ensure that every piece of
(0) ...PACKAGING... on the continent is **PACKAGE**
(1) .... or recyclable by 2030. **USE**
Following China's decision to ban imports of foreign recyclable material, Brussels launched a plastics strategy designed to change minds in Europe, tax damaging behaviour, and
(2) .... plastic production and collection. **MODERN**

The vice-president of the commission, Frans Timmermans, said Brussels' priority was to reduce single-use plastic that takes five seconds to produce, five minutes to use and gives 500
years of **(3)** .... to the environment. According to **CONTAMINATE**
Timmermans, we need to **(4)** .... our efforts to **INTENSE**
reduce the use of throw-away items such as drinking straws, bottles that do not degrade, coffee cups, cutlery and takeaway packaging.
He added that if children knew what the effects were of using
single-use plastic straws they might **(5)** .... and **CONSIDER**
use paper straws or no straws at all.

The EU wants an **(6)** .... 55% of all plastic to be **IMPRESS**
recycled by 2030 and for member states to reduce the use of bags per person from 90 a year to 40 by 2026. He also stated that additional money would be made available for research
into better designs, durability and **(7)** .... and EU **RECYCLE**
member states will be put under an **(8)** .... to **OBLIGE**
'monitor and reduce their marine litter'.

FIRST Reading and Use of English – Part 4

8 **KEY WORD TRANSFORMATIONS.** **For questions 1-6, complete the second sentence so that it has a similar meaning to the first sentence, using the word given. Do not change the word given. You must use between two and five words, including the word given. Here is an example (0).**

0 In fairy tales, the frog will transform into a handsome prince if kissed by a beautiful girl.
INTO
In fairy tales, the frog WILL TURN INTO a handsome prince if kissed by a beautiful girl.

1 Tom was sorry about being late for his lesson.
FOR
Tom .... for his lesson.

2 'I won't be available for an appointment until this afternoon' said Mrs Jones.
SHE
Mrs Jones said .... until that afternoon.

3 The bank was closed owing to strike action by the employees.
DUE
The bank was closed .... by the employees.

4 'Why did you arrive so late Stephen?' asked the teacher.
HE
The teacher asked Stephen .... so late.

5 The umpire allowed the players to replay the final point in the match.
LET
The umpire .... the final point in the match.

6 In spite of being afraid of the challenge, the investors decided to give it a go and put money into the new company.
TAKE
In spite of being afraid of the challenge, the investors decided .... and put money into the new company.

DOSSIERS and 21ST-CENTURY SKILLS

21ST-CENTURY THEMES
Interdisciplinary themes to weave into key subjects

MANAGING LANGUAGE SKILLS
Language skills as part of lifelong learning

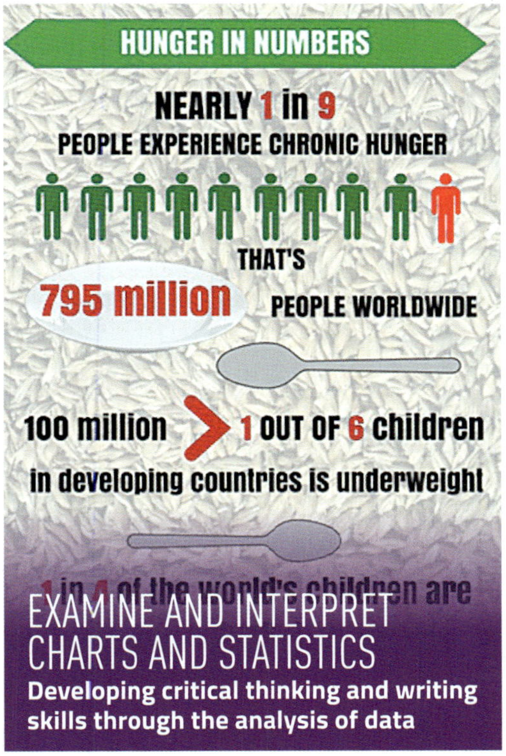

EXAMINE AND INTERPRET CHARTS AND STATISTICS
Developing critical thinking and writing skills through the analysis of data

TOWARDS INVALSI
Training for the INVALSI Test through reading and listening skills

CLASS DEBATE
Debating 21st-century issues within the class

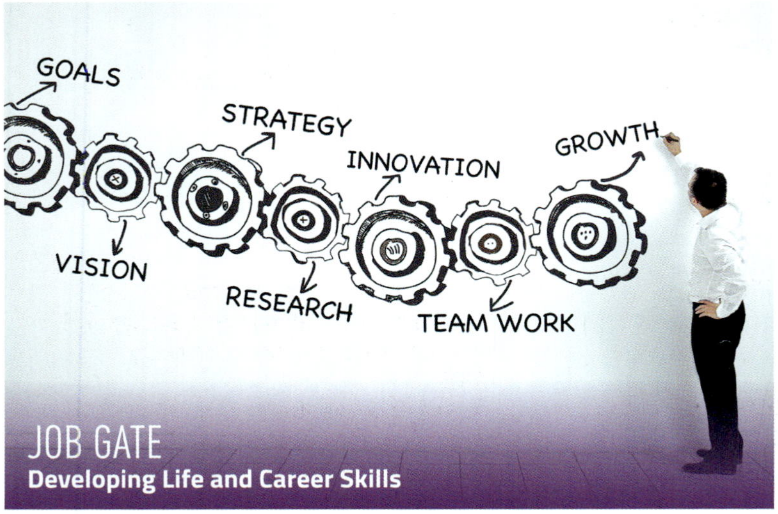

JOB GATE
Developing Life and Career Skills

LEARN BY DOING
The creation of situations or problems for which the student should find a solution using his/her competences. The task must be operative and requires a final product

DOSSIER 1

21ST-CENTURY SKILLS
GLOBAL AWARENESS

Global ambassadors

Inquadrami per ascoltare gli audio di tutti i dossier

WHAT IS GLOBAL AWARENESS?

Global awareness involves a recognition and appreciation of the dynamic complexity and the diversity of peoples and cultures on the earth conceived as a single entity. Global awareness fosters our understanding of the lives of people around the globe and enhances our understanding of our roles in the world.

Global awareness affects people's ability to:

- explore the reasons why learning about the international community matters;
- learn about major global issues – including education, global conservation and environmentalism, global health, and human rights;
- understand other nations and cultures;
- learn from and work collaboratively with individuals representing diverse cultures, religions and lifestyles in a spirit of mutual respect and open dialogue.

SPEAKING

1

MATCH the acronyms (1-6) with their definitions (A-F). Then discuss the goals of these organisations.

1 [F] FAO
2 [E] UNHCR
3 [A] UN
4 [B] WFP
5 [C] MTF
6 [D] OXFAM

A United Nations
B World Food Programme
C Make Trade Fair
D Oxford Committee for Famine Relief
E United Nations High Commission for Refugees
F Food and Agricultural Organisation

LISTENING

2 6.1

LISTEN to a talk about celebrities as global ambassadors. Match them to the pictures and complete the table below.

Celebrity	Organisation/ Campaign	Issue supported	Action taken
Name: Picture: 4	OXFAM MTF	MIGRANTS FORCED TO FLEE THEIR LANDS DUE TO NATURAL DISASTERS EXTREME HARDSHIP AND BRUTAL CONFLICTS	DONATED AN ACOUSTIC VERSION OF THEIR SONG AGAINST LANDGRABBING
Name: Picture: 2	UN HCR	HELP REFUGEES MAJOR CRISIS THAT CAUSE MASS POPULATION DISPLACEMENT	60 FIELDMISSIONS
Name: Picture: 3		ELIMINATE HIV/AIDS IN AFRICA	PARTNERSHIP WITH NIKE TO SUPPORT PROGRAMMES WHO OFFER MEDICATION AND EDUCATION ABOUT IT
Name: Picture: 5	UN LEONARDO DI CAPRIO FOUNDATION	CLIMATE CHANGE PROTECTING BIODIVERSITY OCEAN AND FORESTS CONSERVATION	
Name: Picture: 1	WFP	GLOBAL HUNGER	TRAVELLED TO GUATEMALA

1

2

3

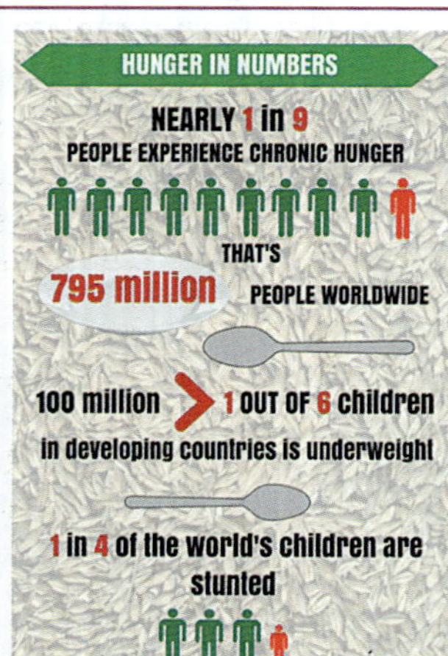

WRITING

3

LOOK at the chart showing hunger in numbers. Summarise the information by highlighting and reporting the main features.

ALMOST 795 MILLION PEOPLE WORLDWIDE EXPERIENCE CHRONIC HUNGER AND IN THE DEVELOPING COUNTRIES 1 OUT OF 6 CHILDREN IS UNDERWEIGHT AND 1 OUT OF 4 CHILDREN WORLDWIDE IS STUNTED AND STARVING

4

5

STUNTED = RACHITICO

Zero hunger challenge

SPEAKING

4

DISCUSS in pairs how we can fight poverty also in our everyday life.

READING 6.2

The year 2015 marked the end of the monitoring period for the two internationally agreed targets for hunger reduction. The first was the World Food Summit (WFS) goal set in 1996 whose aim was '... to eradicate hunger in all countries, with an immediate view to reducing the number of undernourished people to half their present level no later than 2015'. The second was the formulation in 2000 of the eight Millennium Development Goals (MDGs), the first of which included among its targets 'cutting by half the proportion of people who suffer from hunger by 2015'.

The global mobilisation behind the Millennium Development Goals has produced the most successful anti-poverty movement in history. The MDG target of reducing by half the proportion of people living in extreme poverty was achieved in 2010, well ahead of the 2015 deadline. One in seven children worldwide are underweight, down from one in four in 1990. However, a lot more work needs to be done.

Food is at the core of the Sustainable Development Goals (SDGs), the UN's development agenda for the 21st century. The second of the UN's 17 SDGs is to 'end hunger, achieve food security and improved nutrition and promote sustainable agriculture'. Achieving this goal by the target date of 2030 will require a profound change of the global food and agriculture system. Some of the components of this goal are ending hunger and ensuring access by all people to safe, nutritious food; ending all forms of malnutrition; doubling the agricultural productivity and income of small-scale food producers; increasing investment in sustainable food production systems; adopting measures to ensure the proper functioning of food commodity markets to avoid mono-culture crops and damage to the eco-system.

It is time to rethink how we grow, share and consume our food. If done correctly, agriculture, forestry and fisheries can provide nutritious food for all and generate decent incomes, while supporting people-centred rural development and protecting the environment. A change of the global food and agriculture system is needed if we are to nourish today's 795 million hungry and the additional 2 billion people expected by 2050.

(Adapted from www.un.org)

TOWARDS INVALSI

5

READ and listen to the article and do the following activities.

A1 What was the internationally agreed target for hunger by 2015? *TO CUT BY HALF THE PROPORTION OF PEOPLE WHO SUFFER FROM HUNGER*

A2 What did the Millennium Development Goals create? *THE BIGGEST ANTI-POVERTY MOVEMENT IN HISTORY*

A3 One ... children were underweight in 2015.

A in ten **B** in seven **C** in four

A4 Which of the following does the word 'sustainable' in line 15 mean?

A Causing little damage to the environment.
B Bearable.
C Long-lasting.

A5 'Improved nutrition' goes hand in hand with

A small-scale food producers.
B biodiversity.
C sustainable agriculture.

A6 Say whether the following information about UN's 2 SDGs is true (T) or false (F).

A Its target date is 2050. T F
B It wants to eradicate hunger. T F
C Its aim is to increase the agricultural output. T F
D It encourages more investment in the food commodity market. T F

MATERIE PRIME

A7 List the advantages of better food growth and consumption.

A8 By 2050, the number of hungry people in the world will increase by about

A 50%. **B** 150%. **C** 250%.

DOSSIER 1

The challenge of integration

SPEAKING

6

DISCUSS in groups.

1 Can you think of any synonyms for 'integration'?
2 What forms may it take?
3 How does your community face the problem of integration?
4 What do you personally think?

READING 6.3

CLASS DEBATE

The integration of migrants and refugees is one of the most complex challenges of our era. Effective integration policies can enrich countries economically, socially and culturally, generating new opportunities for development. There are many stories of successful integration around the world, however, looking at recent campaign speeches and referendum and election outcomes, reading the newspapers, or watching the news, you may get the impression that international migration is out of control, that governments are feeble in the face of unstoppable movements, and that migrants are threatening the social fabric of many countries.

International migration through legal channels has increased dramatically. Migrants and refugees are often vulnerable people fleeing war, violence or extreme hardship. They may have endured great trials, crossing continents, and losing relatives and friends. Nonetheless, many in host countries view them as a threat, fearing the burden they may impose on taxpayers, local values and cultures.

Migration itself is a fact of life, one of the oldest human phenomena. But numbers are likely to increase further due to large political, demographic and economic imbalances and climate change. This increase in legal flows has been overshadowed by the mass inflows of asylum seekers and humanitarian migrants, who represent only a fraction of total migration flows. The vast majority of migrants are trying to find work, study, or reunite with their families. In OECD countries, local people think that there are two or three times as many immigrants as there really are. There is an exaggerated perception of how much migrants cost and how much they access social benefits. The evidence reported annually by OECD shows that migrants are productive members of society who work in various sectors, set up businesses and have innovative ideas.

Addressing this challenge depends on international efforts to reinforce co-operation on migration issues. There are common rights for all refugees and migrants. Xenophobia and discrimination must be fought just like smuggling and corruption and the illegal employment of foreign workers.
Setting internationally adopted standards would allow countries to focus on integration, because the domestic issues related to the lack of integration – economic costs, political costs, instability, and the erosion of social cohesion – have international implications.

As well as recognising qualifications, we need early and intensive efforts to improve literacy and language proficiency, and provide adult education and vocational training. Host countries also need to build ties between migrant and host country communities.
We need both global and local migration policies for the 21st century. Global, because no country can deal with large flows in isolation. And local, because policies must promote quick and effective integration for better lives.

(Adapted from oecd.org)

7

READ and listen to the text and answer the questions.

1 How could good integration policies improve the life of a country?
2 What is the current general impression about international migration according to the speaker?
3 Who are migrants and how are they perceived in most host countries?
4 What is the ratio between legal and illegal flows of migration?
5 What is the difference between public perception and the evidence provided by accredited organisations?
6 What attitudes and behaviours should be fought at local and international levels?
7 How are national communities affected by the issue of migration?
8 What should national integration policies aim at?

8

DIVIDE the class into groups to debate the following issue:
Is migration a threat or an opportunity?
Then choose two speakers with different opinions who will carry out a debate about the problem of integration. Each of them will stick to four points:

- a claim
- a comment
- evidence or data to support the argument
- a conclusion

Job gate

INFORMATION, MEDIA AND TECHNOLOGY SKILLS
• Access information

CREATING AN INTERVIEW

An essential skill is to access information efficiently (time) and effectively (sources) in order to use and manage it critically and competently. Research can be carried out with different methods, mostly through the net but also through interviews or focus groups.
Interviewing is the most common format of data collection in qualitative research. Most of the qualitative research interviews are either semi-structured, lightly structured or in-depth. Semi-structured interviewing is best used when you won't get more than one chance to interview someone and when you will be sending several interviewers out into the field to collect data.

Semi-structured interview

A semi-structured interview is a qualitative method of inquiry that combines a pre-determined set of open-ended questions to prompt respondents to think, express values and provide answers in their own words.
Unlike a structured questionnaire, a semi-structured interview does not limit respondents to a set of pre-determined answers.

Prepare for the interview	Make sure that you are clear as to what information you want to obtain.
Information and consent	It is ethically important to be open and transparent with the interviewee as to why you want to speak to them, and how the information will be used. If recording the interview, it is important that you gain consent.
Recording answers	Recording answers can be done through taking notes, audio-recording, or both.
Carry out the interview	• Determine the order of the questions. • Start with some warm-up questions to help the participants feel comfortable. • Begin with simpler topics and move to those that are more complex.
Type of questions	• Phrase questions so that they lead the respondents to provide detailed answers, rather than simple 'yes' or 'no' answers. • Keep the questions as short and specific as possible. • Use terms that participants can understand. • Avoid questions with a strong positive or negative association. • Avoid phrasing questions as negatives.
End of the interview	When you end an interview, a good practice is for the interviewer to summarise the key points that they feel the respondent has provided, as this gives the respondent a final chance to expand or clarify any points.
Analysis	Review interview responses and observational data for insights and patterns. A computer database may be used to analyse patterns and relationships.
Report	The research can either end at this point with a report on the data analysis, or it can be used to build up another survey.

9

PREPARE a semi-structured interview to gather data for the following research:

My school/town as a place for integration

Carry out the interviews, record them, analyse and report the results.

DOSSIER 2

21ST-CENTURY SKILLS
CIVIC LITERACY

Youth's rights and responsibilities

What is civic literacy?

While civic responsibility is the act of fulfilling duties such as serving on a jury, paying taxes, and obeying laws, civic literacy is

- participating effectively in civic life through knowing how to stay informed and understanding governmental processes;
- knowing how to exercise the rights and duties of citizenship at local, state, national and global levels;
- understanding the local and global implications of civic decisions.

To be civically literate, people must show the basic civic skills:

- respect and tolerance of others, so differences are valued and not feared;
- civility, that is listening to different points of view and finding a common ground;
- humility, so we can always keep in mind that we might be wrong about something;
- honesty, so our common considerations are open and straightforward;
- resolution to overcome setbacks and challenges.

SPEAKING

1

LOOK at the pictures and express your personal opinions about youth's rights and responsibilities.

1

2

3

4

LISTENING

2 6.4

LISTEN to a conversation about the rights and responsibilities of children and young people. For questions 1-6, choose the correct answer (A, B or C).

1 According to Jamie, which of the following is NOT linked to the children's right to education?
- **A** Children have the right to education.
- **B** They have the duty to attend school.
- **C** Compulsory education is not free.

2 A child
- **A** has the duty to respect only the opinions of other children.
- **B** has the right to free speech.
- **C** is allowed not to take care of other children's honour.

3 Discrimination of any kind to children and youth
- **A** is prohibited.
- **B** is not given any attention.
- **C** means that only certain groups of children are granted special protection.

4 ... must guarantee a child a friendly society.
- **A** Governments
- **B** Governments, employees, unions and members of society
- **C** Unions

5 The primary obligation of parents is to guarantee their children's
- **A** education.
- **B** healthcare.
- **C** growth and the realisation of their talents and skills.

6 Children's and youth's opinions must
- **A** be heard and taken into consideration.
- **B** only be heard.
- **C** be avoided since they do not have any experience.

WRITING

3

LOOK at the graph below. It shows the negative trend of the decline in political rights, civil liberties and freedom in the period 2006-2013. Summarise the information by highlighting and reporting the main features.

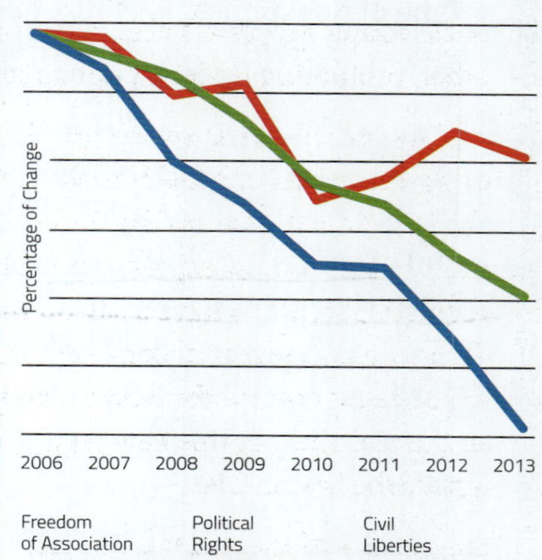

Young people, social media and civic literacy

SPEAKING

4

DISCUSS in pairs.

1 List your rights and match them with a corresponding responsibility. An example has been provided for you:
I have the right to privacy in my bedroom but I have the responsibility to keep my room tidy.

2 Choose a right and think about what can be done to protect it. Consider others who are responsible for protecting rights: community, local government, central government and the international community.

READING 6.5

The European Commission's General Data Protection Regulation aims to give consumers more control over their personal information and more transparency on how their information is used by companies and governments.
This regulation originally reflected the status quo in most of Europe, the US and other regions, by requiring parental consent before commercial services could process personal information from children under 13. But, at the last minute, the age was raised to 16, effectively banning children from accessing Facebook, Snapchat, Instagram and other services without parental consent. After an outcry from technology companies and child protection organisations, this rule was watered down with the condition that member states can lower it back to 13.

We don't yet know how individual countries might respond to the age condition in the regulation. Social media, even when they are operated by private companies, are where young people go to express their opinions, interact with peers and family, learn about the news, as well as obtain health information and access to services. Depriving youth of this access, violates their rights of expression and information as well as their ability to participate in civic engagement.

A lack of access to the Internet could interfere with the ability of some youths to assimilate into new environments and to explore social, political and religious values. This is a time when we should be breaking down barriers to interaction and social engagement among young people, not erecting new ones. Young people are able to use online platforms to connect with each other, promoting understanding rather than violence and extremism.

The reality is that young people have rights and it is the responsibility of governments to protect those rights. In Europe, countries have ratified the UN Convention on the Rights of the Child which grants children 'the right to freedom of expression', and there is nothing in that convention that requires parents to have a say on those rights.
There are also practical considerations. The current law is ignored by millions of pre-teens around the world who lie about their age to access social media, so the real effect of this new regulation is to encourage European teens to ignore the law, and lie.

(Adapted from The Guardian, December 2016)

TOWARDS INVALSI

5

READ and listen to the article and do the following activities.

A1 **What is the aim of the European Commission's General Data Protection Regulation?**

A2 **Say whether the following information is true (T) or false (F).**

A The regulation of the Commission generally concerned the US. T F
B At first, children under 13 needed their parents' consent to give personal information on the net. T F
C Later young people under 16 were banned from accessing the net without parental control. T F
D Technology companies accepted this regulation. T F

A3 **Which of the following meanings is closest to the word 'watered down' as used in line 11?**

A Weakened with water.
B Modified to be less severe.
C Moderated.

A4 **Why do young people use social media?**

A5 **What could 'a lack of access to the Internet' NOT interfere with?**

A Interaction and social engagement among youth.
B Taking action against injustice.
C Breaking down barriers among young people.

A6 **What is the responsibility of governments?**

WRITING

6

WRITE a paragraph about your classmates' behaviour while using social media.

DOSSIER 2

Young people and their right to vote

SPEAKING

7

DISCUSS. What is the voting age in your country? Are you old enough to vote? Are there any European countries where you are allowed to vote at 16? Do you think that 16- and 17-year-olds are too young to be trusted? Are you interested in political issues?

READING 6.6

CLASS DEBATE

It is not the lack of knowledge that stops young people voting. Rather it is the absence of any way for the great majority of citizens of any age to be involved in policymaking.
Young people want to know how they will be able to contribute their ideas and experience, as well as protect their own interests, in the development of policies in the society where they live. Many of them have grasped the fact that even voting may be a waste of time and effort, as only a small number of voters in a small number of marginal seats decide who will form the next government.

It is not surprising that many young people have felt alienated and see politics as a game being played by MPs, opinion pollsters and media operators to their own financial, economic and personal benefit, which has nothing to do with them. The current political system in several European countries has to be judged as unfit for its purpose and in need of change.
Three actions may boost political education: give the subject the status it deserves, and students' political organisations the training and support to do it well; give 16-year-olds the vote, so that they have an incentive to learn and participate; set up a commission on learning for democracy, to build cross-party support of traditional parties, based on evidence of what works. We put great effort into teaching sport as a way of forming young people's characters but we are unable to raise their interest in politics. Yet political decisions directly affect their future life. It's time to act.

A knowledge of constitutional politics is well worthwhile because it is the foundation our society is built on and introduces us to civic life. If the best learning is 'learning-by-doing', why not add the study of political sciences to school curricula? The elections of fellow pupils, or even staff, to class and school bodies, referendums on changes to school rules etc., all impart some practical understanding of what political participation in democracy means. Who knows, such initiatives might even develop wider support for dealing with the present democratic deficit in national policies. Incidentally, during the referendum for Scottish independence, where 16 year-olds were given the vote, only a quarter of the millions in the lower age groups voted.

The gap between what the young are being taught about our complex society and what they need to know to stimulate their civic activism, is enormous. As schools are production factories for future literate citizens and managerial classes, they should help students acquire the knowledge, skills and will to own, connect and engage with their communities and society.

(Adapted from The Guardian, November 2017)

8

READ and listen to the article and answer the questions.

1 What stops young people voting?
2 What do young people want to know?
3 What have many of them understood?
4 What actions may boost political actions?
5 What initiatives might develop a wider support for dealing with the present democratic deficit in national policies?
6 How many young people did not bother to vote in the past referendum for Scottish independence?
7 What should schools help students do?

9

DIVIDE the class into two groups. One group, as happens in Parliament, has to express the opinions of the majority, and the other, as representative of the opposition, debates about these topics.

- The request to the Mayor to have lower public transport fares.
- The possibility to rent the school gymnasium to local sports organisations in the late afternoon and evening to increase the school's income.
- Allowing students to park their bicycles and motorbikes in the school courtyard to avoid thefts.

Then choose a speaker in each group who will deliver a speech to the class about the issues above.

Job gate

LEARNING AND INNOVATION SKILLS
• Communication and collaboration

CREATING A COMMUNITY CAMPAIGN

21st-century learners must be able to communicate clearly in different environments
- articulating thoughts and ideas using oral, written and nonverbal communication skills;
- listening effectively;
- using communication for a range of purposes (to inform, instruct, motivate and persuade);
- employing different kinds of media and technologies.

They must collaborate with others
- demonstrating the ability to work effectively and respectfully with different teams;
- exercising flexibility and willingness to be helpful to reach a common goal;
- reflecting critically on past experiences in order to inform future progress.

A **community campaign** includes all these skills and helps you spread your message to the public raising awareness and provoking reflection.

It is linked to the following steps:
1 plan a programme analysing the needs and setting your goals;
2 become an expert (do some research before your campaign: you need to have detailed information about your subject);
3 identify your priorities (think about what you want to achieve);
4 create a resource pool (look for support and resources to give your campaign more impact);
5 know your stakeholders and possible opponents;
6 establish a budget (think about what needs to be done, who should be responsible for it in your team, and what the deadline should be);
7 establish how to get your message across: the most important communication elements are a poster/leaflet with headlines or claims, and visuals to catch people's attention, call to action (like organising a flash mob, payoff, logo, and possible sponsor/s);
8 reflect on your performance and assess your campaign.

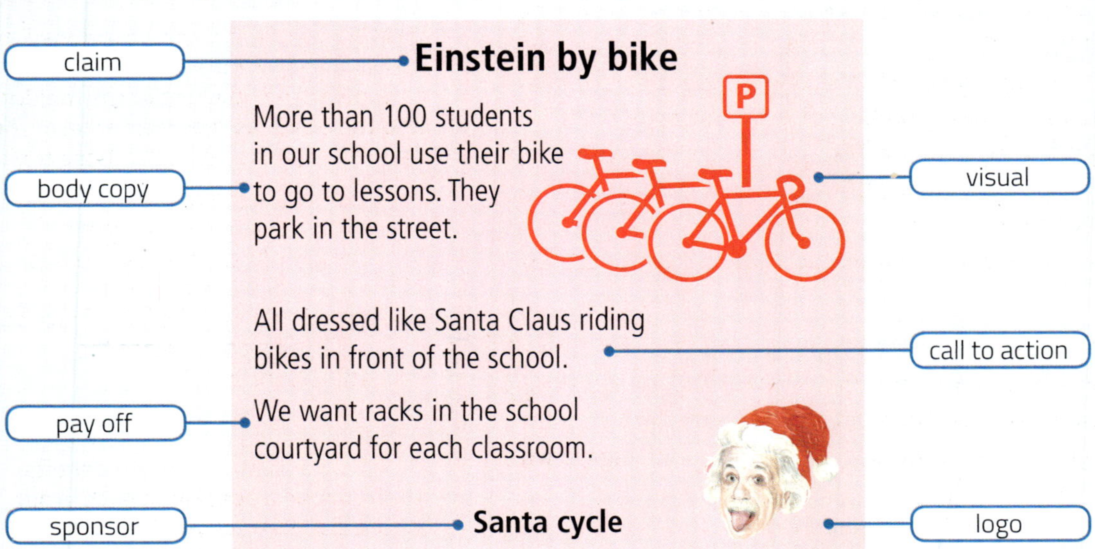

10

PLAN a campaign to let the school courtyard become a parking area for the students' bicycles. Write down your ideas in a leaflet/poster.

1 Analyse the needs of the stakeholders/clients.

2 Become a researcher, before your campaign: you need to have detailed information about your subject.

3 Identify your priorities.

4 Create a team to work together.

5 Know your possible opponents.

6 Establish a budget (think about what amounts are needed and look for possible sponsor/s).

7 Establish how to get your message across.

8 Reflect on your performance, redemption (the results obtained) and assess your campaign.

DOSSIER 3

21ST-CENTURY SKILLS
HEALTH LITERACY

How to plan a healthy diet

WHAT IS HEALTH LITERACY?

Health literacy has been defined as the cognitive and social skills which determine the motivation and ability of individuals to gain access to, understand and use information in ways which promote and maintain good health. It implies understanding preventive physical and mental health measures, including proper diet, nutrition, exercise, risk avoidance and stress reduction.

Health literacy affects people's ability to:
- navigate the healthcare system, including filling out forms and locating providers and services;
- share personal information, such as health history, with providers;
- engage in self-care management;
- understand mathematical concepts such as probability and risk.

SPEAKING

1

LOOK at the pictures and discuss which behaviours belong to a healthy diet and which do not.

1

3

5

2

4

LISTENING

2 6.7

LISTEN to a talk about healthy eating. For questions 1-5, choose the correct answer (A, B or C).

1 What is healthy eating to do with?
   A Achieving a steady mood and a lot of energy.
   B Giving up your favourite foods.
   C Sticking to a strict diet and watching your weight to keep thin.

2 Amanda recommends that you should
   A reduce pre-prepared food.
   B increase proteins and vitamins.
   C eat only real food.

3 Which is the benefit of proteins?
   A They prevent kidney disease.
   B They let us get up and go and sustain the brain functions.
   C They are high-quality nutrients.

4 What advice does Amanda give about the consumption of carbohydrates?
   A You should eat bread, cakes and sugar to keep your energy high.
   B You should eat them regularly to avoid fluctuations in blood sugar levels.
   C The majority of your intake should come from unprocessed carbs.

5 About calcium, Amanda says that
   A it works better together with magnesium and some vitamins.
   B it keeps the nervous system strong.
   C you may find it difficult to sleep if you take too much of it.

WRITING

3

LOOK at the table. It shows blood sugar levels. Summarise the information by highlighting and reporting the main features.

BLOOD GLUCOSE CHART

Mg/DL	Fasting	After eating	2-3 hours after eating
Normal	80-100	170-200	120-140
Impaired glucose	101-125	190-230	140-160
Diabetic	126+	220-300	200 plus

Emotional eating

SPEAKING

4

ANSWER the questions in pairs to find out if you are an emotional eater.

1 Do you eat to feel better when you're stressed, sad, bored, anxious or disappointed?

2 If you're not hungry or you're full, do you eat anyway?

3 Do you consider food as a reward?

4 Do you feel out of control with some kinds of food?

READING 6.8

People don't always eat just to satisfy hunger. Many also turn to food to relieve stress or cope with unpleasant emotions such as sadness, loneliness, or boredom. And after eating, they often feel guilty for overeating.

Emotional eating is using food to make yourself feel better – eating to satisfy emotional needs, rather than to satisfy physical hunger.
Occasionally using food as a pick-me-up, a reward, or to celebrate isn't necessarily a bad thing. But when eating is your primary emotional coping mechanism, you get stuck in an unhealthy cycle where the real feeling or problem is never addressed.

Emotional hunger can be powerful, so it's easy to mistake it for physical hunger. But there are clues you can look for to help you distinguish physical from emotional hunger.
Emotional hunger comes on suddenly. It hits you in an instant and feels overwhelming and urgent. Physical hunger, on the other hand, comes on more gradually.
When you're physically hungry, almost anything sounds good – including healthy stuff like vegetables. But emotional hunger craves junk food or sugary snacks that provide instant pleasure. You feel like you need cheesecake or pizza, and nothing else will do.
Before you know it, you've eaten a whole bag of chips or an entire pint of ice-cream without really paying attention or fully enjoying it. When you're eating in response to physical hunger, you're typically more aware of what you're doing.
Emotional hunger isn't satisfied once you're full. Physical hunger feels satisfied when your stomach is full.

Common causes of emotional eating include: stress, which leads to high levels of the stress hormone, cortisol. Cortisol triggers cravings for salty, sweet, and fried foods. Other unconfortable emotions, including anger, fear, sadness, anxiety, loneliness, resentment, and shame can be temporarily silenced through eating.
In order to stop emotional eating, you need an alternative to food that you can turn to for emotional fulfilment.

(Adapted from Harvard Women's Health Watch, 2016)

TOWARDS INVALSI

5

READ and listen to the article and do the following activities.

A1 What are the reasons why people turn to food?

A2 What is the problem about emotional eating as a primary coping mechanism?

A3 How can you distinguish real hunger from emotional hunger?

A Real hunger is overwhelming.
B Emotional hunger comes on slowly.
C Emotional hunger comes on all at once.

A4 Which of the following meanings is closest to the word 'craves' as used in line 17?

A impresses **B** desires **C** digs

A5 Say whether the following information is true (T) or false (F).

A Vegetables are appealing when you feel very hungry. T F
B Emotional eating looks for sugary stuff. T F
C You are conscious of what you're eating when you practise emotional eating. T F
D People always stop eating when they feel full. T F

A6 Which is NOT a common cause of emotional eating?

A hurry
B cortisol
C displeasure
D unhappiness

DOSSIER 3

Stress management

SPEAKING

6

DISCUSS how you currently manage and cope with stress in your life. Are your strategies healthy or unhealthy, helpful or unproductive?

READING 6.9

CLASS DEBATE

It may seem like there's nothing you can do about stress. However, the foundation of stress management lies in the simple realisation that you can regain control of your life by taking charge of your lifestyle, thoughts, emotions, and the way you deal with problems. The ultimate goal is a balanced life, with time for work, relationships, relaxation, fun and the resilience to hold up under pressure and meet challenges ahead.

Stress management starts with identifying the sources of stress in your life. While it's easy to identify major stressors such as changing jobs, moving, or going through a relationship breakdown, understanding the sources of chronic stress can be more complicated. Keeping a stress journal can help you identify the regular stressors in your life and the way you deal with them.

Some stressors arise at predictable times, for example, your commute to school or work, an important meeting, or family gatherings. When handling such predictable stressors, you can either change the situation or change your reaction. When deciding which option to choose in any given scenario, it's helpful to think of the four A's: avoid, alter, adapt, or accept. Learn how to say 'no' and avoid people who stress you out. Drop tasks that aren't necessary to the bottom of the list or eliminate them entirely. If you can't avoid a stressful situation, try to alter it. Rather than complaining about a traffic jam, look at it as an opportunity to pause, listen to your favourite radio station, or enjoy some alone time.

When you're stressed, the last thing you probably feel like doing is getting up and exercising. But physical exercise releases endorphins that make you feel good. Also, there is nothing more calming than spending quality time with another human being who makes you feel safe and understood. So make it a point to connect regularly and in person with family and friends. The people who care about you will be flattered by your trust and this will strengthen your bond.

The hustle and bustle of life can make you forget to take care of your own needs, but nurturing yourself is a necessity, not a luxury. It is vital to make time for fun and relaxation regularly and keep one's sense of humour. This includes the ability to laugh at yourself. Finally, it is essential to get enough sleep because adequate sleep fuels your mind, as well as your body.

(Adapted from Harvard Women's Health Watch, 2016)

7

READ and listen to the article and answer the questions.

1 What are the basic steps to manage stress?

2 Where can stress originate from?

3 What is the first piece of advice given by the writer to deal with stress?

4 What do the first two A's refer to?

5 What other five healthy habits are suggested in the text to fight stress?

8

DIVIDE the class into groups to debate the following issues. Always discuss the argument and the counterargument.

- Why most people do not exercise.
- You need safety rules when you exercise.
- Stress is not always negative.

Then choose a speaker in each group who will deliver a speech to the class about the issues above.

Job gate

LIFE AND CAREER SKILLS
• Initiative & self-direction

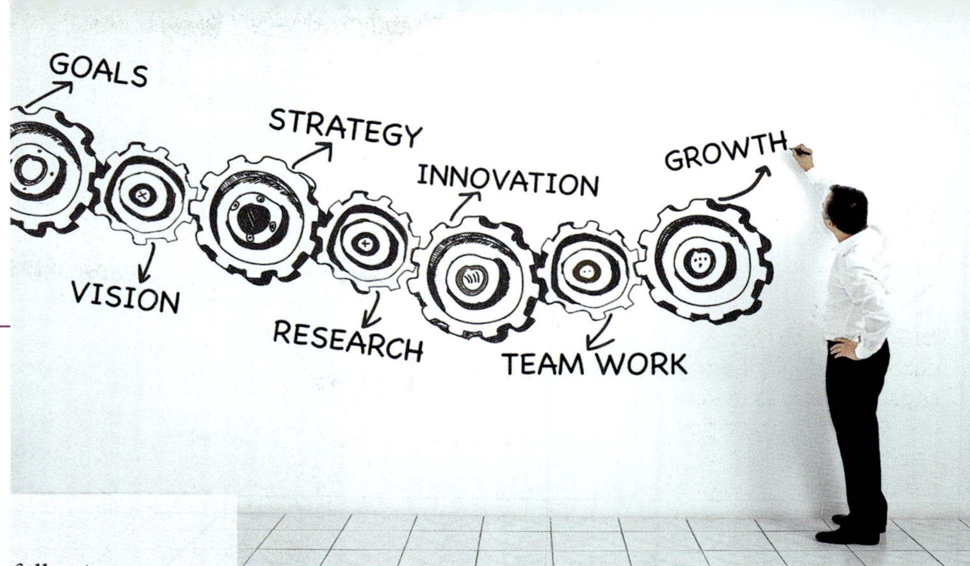

DEVELOPING PERSONAL GOALS

The development of personal goals involves the following stages:
- identifying personal goals (and strategies to achieve them);
- monitoring progress;
- reporting on progress made;
- refining or developing new goals.

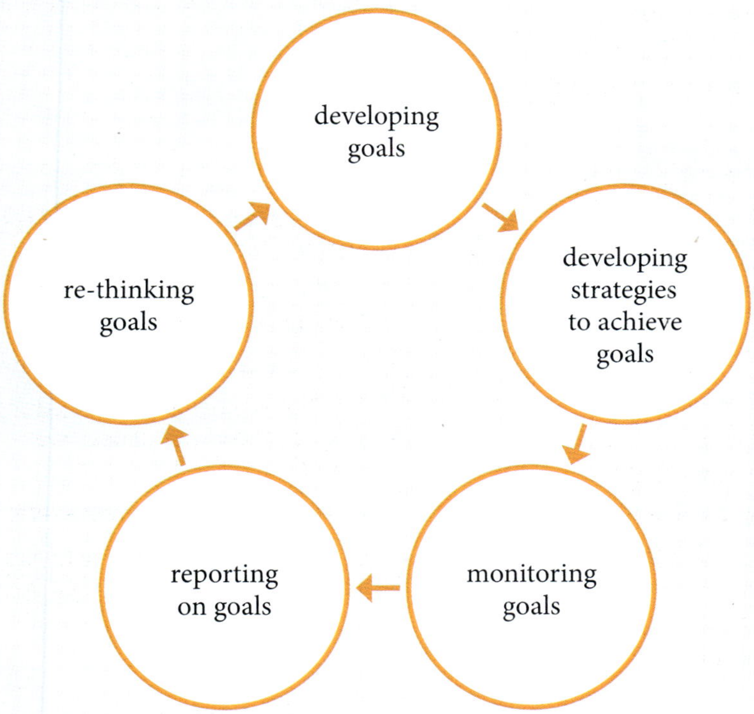

All the stages of the cycle are important, and in practice they overlap. As the diagram above demonstrates, the process is ongoing and cyclical.
The acronym **SMART** could provide a common schema to determine the goals you wish to attain. Try to evaluate your goals in terms of whether they are:

Specific
Meaningful
Action-based
Realistic
Time-based

9

REVIEW your medical history and consider your current lifestyle. Then plan your personal health and fitness goals.

1. Break them into small, specific and achievable mini-goals.
2. Be specific and make them measurable.
3. Set a reasonable timeframe.
4. Keep a diary to monitor your progress.
5. Always see your doctor for a medical check-up before starting any new nutrition or fitness program.
6. Adapt to changing circumstances and think how to cope with them.

10

WRITE a letter to the teachers and administrators of your school to give advice on how to increase health literacy among adolescents.

- Suggest possible ways to develop this topic further in future.
- Highlight the benefits of implementing this part of the school curriculum.

DOSSIER 4

21ST-CENTURY SKILLS
ENVIRONMENTAL LITERACY

The increase of greenhouse gases

WHAT IS ENVIRONMENTAL LITERACY?

Environmental literacy is the knowledge and understanding of the natural world and the circumstances and conditions affecting it, particularly those related to air, climate, land, food, energy, water and ecosystems. It also includes a broad understanding of society's impact on the natural world, that is, population growth and development and resource consumption rate.

Environmental literacy affects people's ability to
- identify and analyse environmental issues;
- investigate them by gathering new information;
- evaluate and make personal judgments about these environmental issues;
- create and evaluate plans to resolve environmental issues by assuming the responsibility of acting with others.

1

SPEAKING
1
LOOK at the pictures and express your personal opinions about the effects of human activities upon the environment.

2

3

4

LISTENING
2 6.10
LISTEN to a lecture about rising CO_2 levels. As you listen, complete the notes below. Write no more than three words for each answer.

Global emissions
The world is far from achieving **(1)** .... to limit global warming in this decade.
Declines of global emissions have been due to the **(2)** .... in developing countries.

The 2015 Paris agreement
The countries that signed it discussed **(3)** ....
their efforts to prevent climate change.
Global emissions from **(4)** ...., factories, cars and trucks **(5)** .... to zero by the end of the century.

New industrialising countries
China and India mainly use **(6)** .... and there is a dramatic increase of vehicles on the roads.

Wealthier countries
The reduction of CO_2 emissions has **(7)** ....
notwithstanding their economic development.
These countries have invested in **(8)** .... and the use of cleaner energy.
In the USA, emissions from sectors like **(9)** ....
remain high.
In the European Union, emissions are expected to **(10)** .... percent this year, but it is a smaller decrease than the previous decade.

WRITING
3
LOOK at the graph below. It shows the annual CO_2 emissions in the most industrialised countries in the period 1960-2010. Summarise the information by highlighting and reporting the main features.

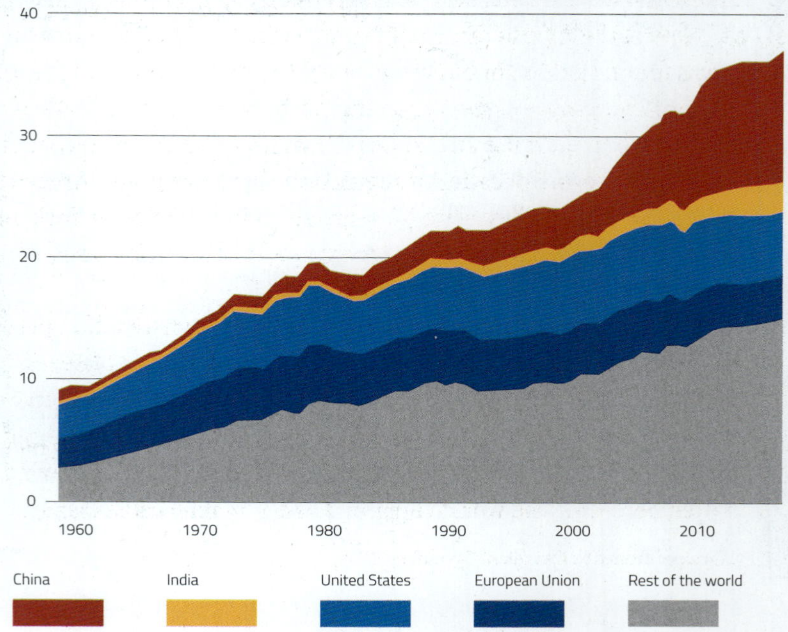

Breathe less... or ban cars

SPEAKING

4

ANSWER the questions in pairs to express your personal opinions.

1 What is air pollution like in the area where you live?

2 How does air pollution affect you, your family and the people around you?

3 What are you, your neighbourhood or your city government doing to improve air quality?

4 Are the measures that have been introduced to tackle air pollution working?

5 What suggestion would you add to solve this problem?

READING 6.11

When a thick cloud of air pollution settled over London last week, experts warned those with health problems and children to avoid going out. The advice to Londoners was 'breathe less'.

Meanwhile, as Paris suffered a similar pollution episode, the Mayor decided to restrict the number of cars allowed on the roads and to get all diesel vehicles off the roads by 2025. Diesel is highly polluting. Despite this health damage, governments across Europe, including Britain's, offered motorists tax incentives in the past that effectively encouraged the use of diesel, on the assumption that it produced less planet-warming carbon dioxide than petrol.

But the attitude towards diesel has changed. The Mayor of London has announced a doubling of funding for reducing pollution. His planned measures include charges for the dirtiest diesel cars entering central London from 2017, an expansion of the Ultra-Low Emission Zone, and a cleanup of buses.

Berlin is an exception to the story of the diesel problem. It cleaned up its public fleet, installing pollution filters on buses and garbage trucks, and imposed tough rules on heavy goods vehicles. As a result, the levels of the tiniest, most dangerous particles, ultrafine PM10, fell 70% in just three years.

New York has also targeted heating systems. After careful analysis, it was found that 1% of buildings burnt the dirtiest kinds of fuel oil. As this produces more carbon than the city's traffic, officials made plans to gradually ban their use and to help landlords convert to cleaner alternatives. In addition to the decades of regulation that have made American cars 99% cleaner than they were 40 years ago, cities like New York and LA have benefited from American motorists' distaste for diesel, which accounts for only about 2% of cars in the US.

Even China, whose atrocious air killed more than a million people in 2012, has begun to confront this crisis. Beijing has used licence plate restrictions to limit the number of cars and set out plans to keep the oldest and most polluting vehicles off the roads when the air quality is especially bad. More importantly, the government has invested billions of dollars in wind and solar power, becoming the world's biggest investor in renewable energy.

(Abridged from The Guardian, December 2016)

TOWARDS INVALSI

5

READ and listen to the article and do the following activities.

A1 Who was given the advice 'breathe less' in London last week? Why?

A2 Say whether the following information is true (T) or false (F).

A The Mayor of Paris restricted the number of cars on the roads. T F

B Diesel vehicles will be allowed to circulate in Paris only after 2025. T F

C Motorists all over Europe are offered tax incentives to discourage the use of diesel. T F

D New charges for the dirtiest diesel cars entering central London were introduced. T F

A3 Which of the following meanings is closest to the word 'Ultra-Low Emission Zone' as used in line 14?

A An area where only diesel cars are allowed to travel.

B An area where you have to pay a daily charge to drive.

C An area only for the public fleet.

A4 How has Berlin solved the diesel problem?

A5 What is/are the main cause/s responsible for air pollution in New York?

A Private traffic. **B** Public transport. **C** Heating systems.

A6 How has China coped with air pollution?

WRITING

6

WRITE a paragraph where you explain and judge the rules about the congestion charge.

DOSSIER 4

Less air pollution in towns

SPEAKING

7

DISCUSS the life styles which can help the reduction of air pollution in towns.

READING 6.12

CLASS DEBATE

High-rise forests in Milan

As air pollution is the biggest environmental health risk the world faces today, it is no wonder designers and engineers are racing to come up with all kinds of air-purifying solutions, from the use of bikes to moss-covered walls. But one of the most impressive ideas so far can be found in Milan, one of the most polluted cities in Europe. The Italian architect Stefano Boeri designed two towers, called 'Bosco Verticale', with over 100 apartments together with nearly 500 medium and large trees, 300 small trees, 5,000 shrubs, and 11,000 plants. The science is simple: trees are the cheapest and most efficient way to absorb carbon dioxide. The 20,000 trees and plants across this pair of towers can transform approximately 44,000 pounds of carbon dioxide into oxygen each year. Trees can also keep temperatures cool indoors and filter out fine dust particles and noise pollution from the traffic below. The logistics of making it all happen, however, were a lot more complex. The process began with bringing together experts in structural engineering and botany to answer all the essential questions. As cities continue to deal with air pollution, housing shortages and climate change, these 'vertical forests' could be the residential typology we need for the future.

Bike sharing: an aid against town air pollution

Twenty-five towns and cities in the UK have signed up to bike-sharing schemes, more than double the number of two years ago. The growing popularity of bike sharing is driven, in part, by a generation that is less into ownership and more into 'service provision'.

However, there may be significant barriers that could prevent people from accessing this sharing economy. These are often financial, language-related or simply due to a lack of confidence.

To encourage the community to use bikes, the price of annual membership for Nextbike, Glasgow's bike-share provider, was reduced from £60 to £3. It was so successful that subscriptions sold out in a matter of days. Special events such as cycle-in movie nights, group rides and road skill courses also helped break down the social barriers that saw bike schemes as the exclusive preserve of the better off. It is innovative projects like these that have made the UK the fastest growing place in Europe for bike sharing.

Bike sharing is here to stay and the next big change will come with the introduction of electric bikes. They will give more and more people the possibility to cycle.

(Abridged from The Guardian, November 2017)

8

READ and listen to the article and answer the questions.

1 What are designers and engineers looking for to combat air pollution?

2 What did the architect Stefano Boeri do in Milan?

3 What scientific principle was Boeri inspired by?

4 What are the main features of the two towers called 'Bosco Verticale'?

5 What has caused the growing popularity of bike sharing in the UK?

6 What are the main problems of the sharing economy?

7 What innovative projects have made the UK the fastest growing place for bike sharing?

8 What will the next change for bike sharing be?

9

DIVIDE the class into groups. Each group has to choose one of the following topics and debate it.

- Is the building of your school oriented to energy saving? Is it possible to make it more energy efficient?
- Do you know the Government incentives for sustainable mobility?
- Is there a bike-sharing service in your town or nearby? Is it an opportunity or a problem?

Then choose a speaker in each group who will deliver a speech to the class about the issues above.

Job gate

LIFE AND CAREER SKILLS
- Initiative & self-direction

CREATING A PERSONAL DEVELOPMENT PLAN

Today's greatest success stories are not about people who are the smartest, but those who can communicate a vision to others and lead them in its implementation. They are able to

- work independently, monitoring, defining, prioritising and completing tasks without direct oversight.

They are self-directed learners because they can

- demonstrate initiative to advance skills to a professional level;
- demonstrate commitment to learning as a lifelong process;
- reflect critically on past experiences in order to inform future progress.

A **Personal development Plan (PdP)** includes all these skills and helps you structure your thinking. It is a process that consists of defining what is important to you, what your goals are, what you need to achieve them and to improve and develop them with time.

The Personal development Plan is linked to a cyclical process and involves the following steps:

- establishing your goals (what you want to achieve);
- identifying development needs (what your strengths are);
- identifying learning opportunities (what you need to know, update and improve);
- formulating an action plan (remember it must be SMART – Specific, Measurable, Achievable, Realistic and Timely);
- undertaking development (put your plan into action: specify what you do and how you do it);
- recording outcomes (keeping records reminds you what you have done);
- reviewing and evaluating (reflect upon whether your activity has been appropriate and worthwhile).
- All the stages of the cycle are important, ongoing and cyclical.

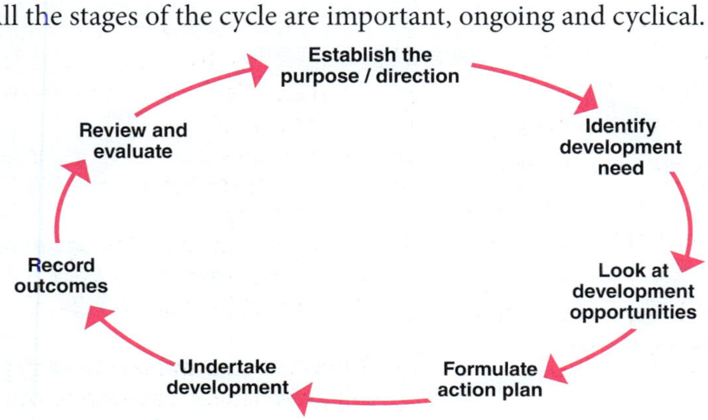

10

IMAGINE a project linked to sustainable mobility in the area you have decided to analyse. Then plan your personal proposal.

1 Analyse the needs of the area and carry out a test.

2 Study what resources technology can offer you.

3 Formulate an action plan (timing, costs and the administration rules you have to follow).

4 Choose if you want to start either from the simplest or the most difficult goal.

5 Start to record your outcomes.

6 Evaluate what you have achieved and the difficulties you have been able to overcome.

11

PREPARE a communication plan for the stakeholders, that is, a group interested in what your plan proposes.

DOSSIER 5

21ST-CENTURY SKILLS
ECONOMIC LITERACY

Why study economics?

WHAT IS ECONOMIC LITERACY?

Economic literacy has been defined as the ability to identify economic problems, alternatives, costs, and benefits; examine the consequences of changes in economic conditions and public policies; weigh costs against benefits.

Economic literacy affects people's ability to:
- know how to make appropriate personal economic choices;
- understand the role of the economy in society;
- use entrepreneurial skills to increase productivity and career options.

SPEAKING

1

DISCUSS your money management skills.

Do you know how much your family spends on food or bills a month? What about their saving plans?

Do you know the basics of budgeting, saving and spending?

Are you informed about the national economy and how it affects jobs and prices?

Do you have a bank account, a debit card or even a controlled credit card?

2

MATCH the words and expressions (1-5) with their definitions (A-E).

1 ☐ Game theory
2 ☐ Econometrics
3 ☐ Equity or stock market
4 ☐ Mortgage
5 ☐ Deadweight loss

A A legal agreement by which a bank, building society, or similar, lends money at interest in exchange for taking title of the debtor's property.
B The loss of economic efficiency in terms of utility for consumers/producers such as the loss of total welfare or the social surplus due to reasons like taxes.
C In mathematical economics, the process of modelling the strategic interaction between two or more players in a situation containing set rules and outcomes.
D A market that gives companies a way to raise needed capital and gives investors an opportunity for gain by allowing those companies' stock shares to be traded.
E The branch of economics concerned with the use of mathematical methods (especially statistics) in describing economic systems.

LISTENING

3 6.13

LISTEN to a talk about economics. For questions 1-5, choose the correct answer (A, B or C).

1 According to the speaker, what is economics to do with?
A Econometrics.
B Civil service.
C Political science.

2 The speaker recommends the study of economics
A to study different topics.
B to learn skills applicable in other jobs or personal life.
C to open a lot of doors.

3 What is the benefit of studying economics according to the speaker?
A To get mortgages from the bank.
B To use the computer more efficiently.
C To be aware of secondary effects and make better decisions.

4 What skill does the speaker believe the study of economics gives?
A Evaluating costs, benefits, and the limitations of resources.
B Understanding the benefits and costs of national and international policies.
C Being able to describe various public and private economic institutions.

5 By learning more about economics you will become
A a better politician.
B a successful entrepreneur.
C a better-informed consumer and voter.

A beginner's guide to economics

READING 6.14

Economics is divided into two general categories: microeconomics and macroeconomics. The first looks at the individual markets, while the second looks at an entire economy. Economics can then be further subdivided into other areas of study. These include econometrics, economic development, agricultural economics, urban economics, and many more. Much of what we study in economics has to do with money and financial markets. Common questions economists examine include: What price are people willing to pay for something? Which industries are performing best? What is the economic future of a particular country or the world?

To understand economics you need to know some basic concepts. The concept of supply and demand is one of the first things you learn in economics. Supply is the quantity of something that's available for sale while demand refers to the willingness to purchase it. If the supply is higher than the demand, the market is thrown off balance and costs typically decrease.
The opposite is true if demand is greater than the supply available, because that commodity is more desirable and harder to obtain.
Elasticity is another key concept in economics. Essentially, it is about how much the price of something can fluctuate before it has a negative impact on sales. Elasticity ties into demand and some products and services are more elastic than others.

One question that many investors have is: 'What happens to my money when stock prices go down?' The answer is not easy. Before diving into the stock market, it's essential to know how it typically works. However, certain economic situations, like a recession, can complicate things. For instance, if an economy goes into recession, it doesn't necessarily mean that all prices will fall. In some areas, like housing, the opposite can be true. Here prices can go up because supply is down and demand may rise. If there is a steady rise in prices, it is known as inflation.
Interest rates and exchange rates also cause fluctuations in the financial markets. You will often hear economists express concern over these. When interest rates go down, people tend to buy and borrow more. Yet, this can cause interest rates to rise in the long term. Exchange rates are another key component in the global economy. These refer to how the currency of one country compares to that of another.

Whether on a national or global scale, measuring the health of the economy is not easy. We can look at factors like GDP, which stands for Gross Domestic Product. This refers to the market value of a country's goods and services. Each country's GDP is analysed by global organisations like the World Bank and the International Monetary Fund (IMF).
Every now and then, you will hear government officials discussing fiscal stimulus. This is an approach for encouraging economic growth, particularly in more difficult times. But again, it's really not as easy as creating jobs that will lead to more consumer spending.
As with all things in economics, nothing is simple. That is precisely why this topic is so intriguing. With so many variables that come into play, economics is an ever-evolving field of study.

(Adapted from www.thoughtco.com)

TOWARDS INVALSI

4

READ and listen to the article and answer the following questions.

1 What is the difference between microeconomics and macroeconomics?

2 How are supply and demand related?

3 What exactly is elasticity?

4 What can recession bring about?

5 How do interest and exchange rates affect the market?

6 What does GDP mean?

7 What is meant by fiscal stimulus?

DOSSIER 5

Assessing soft skills

SPEAKING

5

DISCUSS. Do you know what 'soft skills' are? Do you think employers care about them? If so, why?

READING

CLASS DEBATE

6

READ and complete the self-evaluation questionnaire about your skills. The assessment score ranges from 1 (low) to 5 (high).

Social skills	**Score**
▪ I start interaction with peers.	....
▪ I offer help or assistance to peers.	....
▪ I join in discussions with peers.	....
▪ I can carry out leadership activities.	....
▪ I provide peers with positive feedback.	....
▪ I engage in positive social behavior.	....
Self-management	
▪ I accept rules.	....
▪ I respect the teachers and other members of the school staff.	....
▪ I can manage anger.	....
▪ I try to avoid conflict through compromise.	....
▪ I can bear criticism from others and respond appropriately.	....
▪ I cooperate with others.	....
▪ I can stay focused on tasks.	....
Academic soft skills	
▪ I always bring the required materials to school.	....
▪ I am always on time and complete assigned tasks.	....
▪ I listen and follow the teachers' instructions.	....
▪ I ask for assistance if I need it.	....
▪ I can work independently.	....
▪ I can produce quality work for ability levels.	....
▪ I use study skills suitable to the situation.	....
Approaches to learning	
▪ I am often anxious.	....
▪ I enjoy school.	....
▪ I work hard.	....
▪ I like challenges.	....
▪ I have confidence in my abilities.	....
▪ I get involved with extracurricular activities.	....

7

DIVIDE the class into groups to debate the results of the questionnaire. Discuss what you have achieved in the course of your studies up to now as regards each area of the test. Then choose a speaker in each group who will deliver a speech to the class about the 'soft skill profile' of the group.

Job gate

LIFE AND CAREER SKILLS
• Initiative & self-direction

DEVELOPING SELF-DIRECTION
→ BE SELF-DIRECTED LIFELONG LEARNERS

The development of initiative and self direction goes beyond the basic mastery of skills and the curriculum in order to explore and expand your lifelong learning and chances to get expertise.
At the end of your studies you will be applying for a job. When you apply for a job you normally send your CV accompanied by a cover letter in which you introduce yourself and the reasons why you are applying.

8

WRITE a cover letter for your CV using the following steps.

First paragraph → Explain why you are applying for this particular position.

Second paragraph → Briefly describe your studies and work experience. Focus on the skills and experience you have that suit the job you are applying for. Remember that this is just an introduction to your CV, not a repetition.

Third paragraph → End you letter by thanking the employer for taking your application into consideration. Include information on how to be contacted.

9

WRITE your CV. Many companies require the Europass European Standard Format (you can download the template at http://europass.cedefop.europa.eu). You may decide to use this format or create your own CV. Here are some principles before you start.

Five basic principles for a good CV

1 Focus on the essentials

- Employers generally spend less than one minute reading a CV before deciding to reject it, or to shortlist it for detailed consideration.
- Be brief: two A4 pages are usually more than enough. Do not exceed three pages. If you hold a degree, include your Secondary School qualifications only if relevant to the job in question.
- If your work experience is limited, describe your education and training first; highlight volunteering activities and traineeships.

2 Be clear and concise

- Use short sentences.
- Give specific examples. Quantify your achievements.
- Update your CV as your experience develops. Don't hesitate to remove old information if it does not add value for the position.

3 Adapt your CV to suit the position you are applying for

- Highlight your strengths according to the needs of the employer and focus on the skills that match the job.
- Do not include work experience or training which is not relevant to the application.
- Explain any breaks in your studies or career giving examples of any skills you might have learned during your break.

4 Pay attention to the presentation of your CV

- Present your skills and competences clearly and logically.
- Put the most relevant information first.
- Print your CV on white paper (unless you are asked to send it electronically).
- Use the suggested font and layout.

5 Check your CV once you have filled it in

- Correct any spelling mistakes, and ensure the layout is clear and logical.
- Do not forget to write a cover letter.

Grammar reference

1.1 Present simple

USE

- It expresses general statements of a fact or a permanent situation that is unlikely to change.
  *Most animals **kill** only for food.*
- It expresses repeated or usual actions.
  *He **always eats** a sandwich for lunch.*
- It expresses scheduled events in the near future (public transport, shows, etc.).
  *The film **begins** at 9.*

» SPELLING -*S*

When adding -*s* in the third-person singular:

- verbs ending in consonant + -*y* → *stud**ies***
- verbs ending in -*o* → *go**es**, do**es***
- verbs ending in -*sh*, -*ch*, -*s*, -*z*, -*x* → *wash**es**, watch**es**, buzz**es***

» FREQUENCY ADVERBS

Frequency adverbs like: *always, often, sometimes, usually, hardly ever, seldom, never,* etc. have a specific place in the word order:

- They follow the subject with simple tenses.
  *He **never** forgets birthdays.*
- They come after the simple tenses of the verb *be*.
  *I am **rarely** angry.*
- With interrogative phrases they come after the subject.
  *When does the train **usually** leave?*

1.2 Present continuous

USE

- It expresses actions taking place or in progress at the moment of speaking.
  *I **am studying** right now.*
- It expresses actions taking place only for a limited period of time that is still in progress.
  *I **am taking** five courses this semester.*
- It expresses actions that are arranged for the near future; there is an indication of time, either direct or implied by the context.
  *Sam **is leaving** at noon tomorrow.*
- It expresses complaints, annoyance or anger. In these cases it is used with the adverb *always*.
  *Mary **is always leaving** her dirty socks on the floor.*

» SPELLING -*ING*

When adding -*ing*:

- verbs ending in single -*e* → *argu**ing***
- verbs of one syllable ending in vowel + consonant → *stop**ping***
- verbs of two or more syllables ending in vowel + consonant with stress on the last syllable → *admit**ting***
- verbs ending in vowel + -*l* → *travel**ling*** (BrEn)
- verbs ending in -*ic* → *panic**king***

» PRESENT SIMPLE VS PRESENT CONTINUOUS

Present simple	Present continuous
habitual actions	actions happening at this moment
*She **reads** exciting novels;*	*right now she **is reading** a sci-fi story.*
*My parents normally **drink** tea,*	*but now they **are drinking** coffee.*
*What **do** you **do**? (What's your job?)*	*What **are** you **doing**? (At the moment.)*

1.3 Dynamic and stative verbs

USE

Some verbs, called 'stative verbs', are not used in the continuous tenses and, therefore, in the case of the present tense they only have the present simple form. They describe states and not dynamic activities. Verbs which describe actions or activities are called 'dynamic verbs', and they have both a simple and a continuous form.

COMMON STATIVE VERBS

Mental activity	*agree, appreciate* (= understand), *assume, believe, doubt, expect* (= think), *feel* (= think, sense), *forget, guess, imagine, know, mean, perceive, realise, recall, recognise, recollect, remember, remind, see* (involuntary action), *suppose, think* (= have an opinion), *understand*
Feelings and emotions	*admire, adore, appreciate* (= value), *desire, detest, dislike, fear, hate, like, loathe, love, mind* (= care), *need, prefer, respect, value, want, wish*
Possession	*belong, have, owe, own, possess*
Sense perceptions (normally used with *can*)	*feel, hear* (involuntary action), *see, smell* (= perceive a scent or an odour), *taste*
Other existing states	*appear, be, concern, consist, contain, cost, depend, exist, hold, keep, matter, resemble, seem, signify, sound, weigh*
Auxiliaries	*be, have*

» STATIVE VERBS WITH A CONTINUOUS FORM

Some stative verbs can be commonly used as continuous with a difference in meaning. Here are some examples:

- *Hear*: listen formally to complaints. → *The court **is hearing** evidence this afternoon.*
- *Think*: use one's mind, no opinion is given or asked for. → *'What **are** you **thinking** about?' 'I'**m thinking** about my boyfriend.'*

- *See*: meet by appointment. → *I **am seeing** my solicitor tomorrow.*
- *See*: visit. → *The doctor **is seeing** a patient.*
- *Smell*: sniff at. → *Don **is smelling** the roses.*
- *Feel*: when followed by adjectives such as *angry/ pleased, happy/ sad, hot/ cold, tense/ relaxed, nervous/ confident*, can be used both in simple and continuous tenses with little or no difference in meaning. → *'How **do** you **feel**/ **are** you **feeling**?' 'I **feel**/ **am feeling** better.*
- *Feel*: touch. → *Sue **is feeling** the fur.*
- *Have*: take (*a meal, food* or *drink, a bath, a lesson*), give (*a party*), encounter (*trouble/ difficulties*), experience, enjoy (usually with an adjective). → *They **are having** a party tomorrow.*
- *Be*: with certain adjectives (*quiet/ noisy, good/ bad, wise/ foolish, clever/ stupid, generous/ mean, kind, lazy, nice, patient, rude*, etc.) to imply a temporary characteristic of the subject. → *Tom **is being** foolish.*

1.4 Present perfect simple

USE

- It expresses the idea that something happened (or never happened) before now, at an unspecified time in the past. The exact time is not important.
  *They **have moved** into a new apartment.*
- It expresses the idea that the past action involved has results in the present.
  *The lift **has broken** down. (We have to use the stairs.)*
- It expresses the idea that a past action can be repeated in the present time.
  *I **have seen** wolves in that forest. (It is still possible to see them again).*
  *James Cameron **has made** many films. (He still makes films.)*
- It is used for actions occurring in an incomplete period of time which may be indicated by *today, this morning/ week/ month/ year/ century, lately, recently, in the last few days/ weeks/ months/ years* or *before*.
  *I **haven't seen** Tom this afternoon. (It's 3 p.m.)*
- It is used for the repetition of an activity before now.
  *We **have had** four tests so far this semester.*
  *I **have flown** on an airplane many times.*

» SPELLING -*ED*

When adding -*ed*:

- verbs ending in single -*e* → *argu**ed***
- verbs of one syllable ending in vowel + consonant → *stop**ped***
- verbs of two or more syllables ending in vowel + consonant with stress on the last syllable → *admit**ted***
- verbs ending in vowel + -*l* → *travel**led*** (BrEn)
- verbs ending in -*ic* → *panic**ked***
- verbs ending in consonant + -*y* → *stud**ied***

» PRESENT PERFECT WITH ADVERBS OF TIME

- The present perfect is often used with indefinite time adverbs such as *already, always, ever, just, never, often, rarely, seldom, still, yet*.
  *I have **already** finished this book.*
  *I have **not** finished this book **yet**.*
  *Has the postman arrived **yet**?*
  *Have you **ever** been to England?*
  *I've **just** washed my scooter.*
  *We've **never** changed a tyre before.*
- It is also used with phrases such as *so far, up to now, this is the first/ second time that ...* and with superlatives.
  *I haven't learnt much in the course **so far**.*
  ***This is the first time** I've met Tom.*
  ***That is the most interesting** museum I've **ever** visited.*
- Where to place adverbs:

Before the past participle	At the end of the sentence
already, ever, just, never, still	*once, twice, three/many/several times*
almost, nearly	*so far, up to now, recently, lately, in the last few days, before*
always, often, rarely, seldom	*yet*

» *BEEN* AND *GONE*

- ***Gone*** is used when someone has left to go somewhere, is still there visiting and hasn't returned.
- ***Been*** is used when someone visited somewhere, possibly more than once, and also returned.

*They have **gone** to Rome. (They are in Rome or on their way there, and they haven't come back yet.)*	*They have **been** to Rome. (They went to Rome and they have already come back.)*
*Paul has **gone** to the hospital this morning. (He is still there or on his way there.)*	*Paul has **been** to the hospital this morning. (He went and has come back.)*

1.5 Past simple

USE

- It is used to express that an activity or situation began and ended at a particular time in the past.
  *I **bought** a new car three days ago.*
- It is also used for an action whose time is not given but which occupied a period of time now finished.
  *He **lived** in Paris for ten years, but now he lives in Rome.*
- Sometimes a definite time in the past is stated or the time is asked about.
  *He arrived **a minute ago**.*
  *I saw my cousin **yesterday/last week**.*
  ***When** did you meet him?*
- Time needn't be mentioned if it is clear when the action took place.
  *I bought this car **in Montreal.***

- It is used to describe completed actions which happened in sequence.
  When Jane arrived, we watched TV. (= Jane arrived ***and then*** *we watched TV.)*
- It is used with the expression *It's time ... / It's high time ... / It's about time ...*
  It's time *we* ***left****.*
  It's about time *you* ***started*** *recycling.*

» IRREGULAR VERBS

When studying the simple past, remember that there are regular and irregular verbs.

☞ For a list of irregular verbs see pages 191-193

☞ For spelling rules for *-ed* see 1.4

PRONUNCIATION

-ed is pronounced:	
/t/	after voiceless sounds: /k/, /p/, /f/, /s/, /tʃ/, /ʃ/ ➔ *watched* /wɒtʃt/; *washed* / wɒʃt/
/d/	after voiced sounds: /b/, /l/, /n/, /v/, /z/, ➔ *loved* /lʌvd/; *cleaned* /kliːnd/
/ɪd/	after /t/ and /d/ ➔ *wanted* /wɒntɪd/; *ended* / endɪd/

1.6 Present perfect simple vs past simple

	Present perfect simple	Past simple
Time of action	undetermined: what has happened is more important than when or where it has happened *Somebody* ***has stolen*** *my bike.*	determined: we know exactly when or where in the past the action took place *I* ***saw*** *Tom at the disco yesterday.*
Relationship to present time	the effects of the action often have results in the present *John* ***has broken*** *his leg.* *(Effects on the present = Now he can't walk.)*	none *John* ***broke*** *his leg.* *(No effects on the present because his leg is now OK.)*
Expressions of time **and adverbs**	either no past time is mentioned or use of adverbs (☞ See 1.4) undetermined time: *recently, ever, never, just, already, so far, up to now*, etc. *I* ***have*** *already* ***studied*** *this rule.* time not yet concluded: *today, this morning, this year*, etc. *(It's 11 a.m.) I* ***haven't done*** *much this morning.* repeated action: *twice, a few/ several times*, etc. *I****'ve been*** *to London twice.*	definite (☞ See 1.5) determined time: *yesterday, last year, in 1992, two days ago, when I was born*, etc. *I* ***studied*** *this rule a week ago.* time already concluded *(It's 3 p.m.) I* ***didn't do*** *much this morning.* singular action: *once, one time*, etc. *I* ***went*** *to London once.*
Particular constructions	***It's the first time*** *I have seen this film.* *This is* ***the only*** *film he has seen.* *This is* ***the best*** *film I've* ***ever*** *seen.*	***It's time*** *we saw that film.*

» USING BOTH TENSES

Questions and answers in the present perfect can often lead to answers and other questions in the past simple.

*'****Have*** *you ever* ***been*** *to England?'*

'Yes, I ***have****. We* ***went*** *last year.'*

*'****Did*** *you* ***enjoy*** *it?'*

1.7 Present perfect continuous and duration form

USE

- The present perfect simple and continuous are used to express duration. The present perfect continuous looks at the continuous situation itself, while the present perfect simple usually describes something that is completed or achieved or has only just finished.
  I ***have been*** *in the army for three years. (I'm still in the army.)*
  He ***has had*** *this car since June. (He still has the same car.)*
  *I****'ve been teaching*** *English since I left university. (Teaching is my present job.)*
  I'm sorry I'm late. ***Have*** *you* ***been waiting*** *long?*
- As regards the situation expressed by these two tenses, particular attention must be paid to dynamic and stative, positive and negative verbs.

	Present perfect simple	Present perfect continuous
In general The differences represent the usual distinctions between simple and continuous tenses.	*I **have read** that Harry Potter book. (I read the book at some unspecified time in the past.)* *I **have lived** in London since I was born. (It is a permanent situation.)*	*I **have been reading** that Harry Potter book. (I am currently reading the book.)* *I **have been living** in London since February. (It is probably not a permanent situation.)*
Dynamic verbs When the action is still in progress.	✗	*I **have been playing** tennis a lot this week. (I'm going to play again.)* Compare to: *I have played tennis a lot this week. (I'm probably not going to play again before the week is over.)* *I **have been studying** English since 3 o'clock. (I am still studying.)*
Dynamic verbs When the action was continuing up to this moment and has literally just finished.	✗	*I **have been studying** English since 3 o'clock. (I just stopped.)* *'Why are you so sweaty?' 'I **have been running**.' (The focus is on an action that has just finished, whose effects are still visible in the present.)*
Time expressions When we want to imply a duration.	*for, all day/ night/ week, all one's life, all the time, since* + past simple	
Questions	***How long** have they been married?*	***How long** have you been watching TV?*
Negative statements The present perfect continuous is not generally used in negative sentences. The simple form is preferred.	*I **haven't studied** English for three years.*	✗

» ALTERNATIVES FOR EXPRESSING DURATION

*I **haven't seen** Tom for two weeks.*	
***It is** two weeks **since** I saw Tom.*	***The last time** I saw Tom was two weeks ago.* *I (**last**) saw Tom two weeks ago.*
***How long is it since** you (**last**) saw Tom?*	***How long ago** did you see Tom?* ***When** did you **last** see Tom?*

- These are the only possible constructions when there are verbs that refer to a completed action and there is no continuity in time. Such verbs include, for example, ***arrive***, ***begin***, ***die***, ***finish***, ***leave***, ***start***, ***stop*** and with them the present perfect simple/continuous + *for/ since* cannot be used.

1.8 *For* and *since*

USE

The present perfect simple and continuous are used with two prepositions to speak about the time during which the action takes place.

For	*Since*
It is used with a period of time that can be quantified (seconds, minutes, hours, days, weeks, months, years, etc.): *for three hours, for two days, for ages, for ten years, for a long time, for long,* etc.	It is used with a point in time that is the starting moment of the action: *since 2 o'clock, since May, since 1990,* etc.
It is omitted with expressions beginning with ***all***. *They have been singing **all** night.*	It can also be used with a **clause + simple past.** *I haven't seen him **since I was a child.***

» FOR A LONG TIME AND FOR LONG

For a long time	*For long*
It is used in **affirmative** sentences. *They have been in Rome **for a long time.***	It is used in **interrogative** sentences. *Have they been in Rome **for long**?*
It is used in the **negative** when **a long period of time** is implied. *They haven't been to Rome **for a long time.** (Their last visit to Rome was a long time ago.)*	It is used in the **negative** when **a short period of time** is implied. *They haven't been in Rome **(for) long.** (They have just arrived in Rome.)*

2.1 Past continuous

USE

- It can be used to express an action that was in progress at a particular time in the past. The action began before, was in progress during, and continued after that particular time in the past.
  *He **was sleeping** at 10 p.m. last night.*
- It is also used to express an action that was in progress when another event took place (normally in the past simple).
  *He **was sleeping** when I arrived.*
- As it is a continuous tense, it can only be used with dynamic verbs. (See 1.3)
- When it is used without a time expression, it indicates a gradual development or a description.
  *The sun **was rising**.*
  *A girl **was playing** the piano.*
- It indicates two actions occurring at the same time and covering a certain period of time.
  *I **was watching** TV and Tom **was reading** a book.*

2.2 Past simple vs past continuous

Past continuous	Past simple
When, *while* and *as* can be used with the past continuous in the longer of two actions, to mean 'during that time'. They suggest that the action took enough time to complete to allow something else to happen while it was going on.	But only *when* can be used with the simple past to express either: a) the action interrupting the one in the past continuous; b) or an action followed by another action. In this case, it means 'at that time'.
When/ While/ As *I was walking home,* I was planning my holiday.*	a) *He was talking on the phone*** ***when*** *I arrived.* b) ***When*** *it began to rain,* I stood under a tree.*

» PUNCTUATION

*A comma is used when the adverbial clause precedes the independent clause.

**When the adverbial clause follows the independent clause, usually no comma is used.

2.3 *Used to* and *would* + bare infinitive

USED TO

- It expresses a past habit or state that is in contrast with the present.
  *I **used to** have long hair, but now it is short.*
- This habit can be an activity.
  *When I was a child, my father **used to** read me a story before I went to bed.*
- Or it can be a situation.
  *Jack **used to** live in Chicago, he **used to** be a tennis player and he **used to** have a Ford.*

WOULD

- Gives the same idea as *used to* but only when actions are involved. It cannot be used for situations.
  *When I was a child, my father **would** read me a story before I went to bed.*
  Jack used to live in Chicago. NOT *Jack ~~would~~ live in Chicago.*
- It usually suggests that the action was deliberate, and the time when it happened is in some way mentioned or suggested.
  ***When I was a child**, my father would read me a story before I went to bed.*

2.4 *Be used to / Get used to*

BE USED TO

- It means 'be accustomed to' and can be followed either by a noun or by an *-ing* verb form.
  *Mary **is used to cold weather**. (= Mary is accustomed to cold weather.)*
  *Mary **is used to living** in a cold climate. (= Mary is accustomed to living in a cold climate.)*

GET USED TO

- It means 'get accustomed to' and gives the idea of the process between 'not being' and 'being used to'.
  *He is not used to a lot of noise, but as he has moved to the centre of the city, he will soon **get used to** it.*

2.5 Past perfect simple

USE

- It expresses an action that happened before something else occurred.
  *When I left the house, I discovered that somebody **had stolen** my bike. (The bicycle was stolen while I was in, and so when I went out, I realised that someone had stolen it.)*
- It expresses an action that happened before another period of time in the past or at a time farther back than a certain point in the past.
  *Until yesterday I **had** never **heard** about it.*
- Certain expressions, such as *after*, *already*, *as soon as*, *before*, *by the time*, *when* are followed by the past perfect when there is the need to emphasise that the action expressed had happened (or the state had existed) at an earlier time than another action or state in the past.
  *Sam **had already left** when we got there.*
  *When she **had sung** her song, she sat down.*
  *My parents **had eaten** by the time I got home.*
- With *before* or *after*, the past perfect is often not necessary because the time relationship is already clear. In these cases the simple past may be used.
  *The film **had started** before we arrived at the cinema = The film **started** before we arrived at the cinema.*
  *After the guests **had left**, we went to bed = After the guests **left**, we went to bed.*
- The past perfect is also used when the sentence starts with *It was the first/second/... time.*
  *It was the second time he **had broken** his leg.*
- It is also used when a sentence contains a superlative to talk about the past.
  *That was **the worst** film I **had** ever **seen**.*

2.6 Past perfect continuous

USE

- It refers to actions or events in progress up to another time in the past. Expressions like *for* and *since* can be used with this tense.
  *Sean finally arrived at 6 o'clock. I **had been waiting** for him **since** 4.30 in the afternoon.*
- It can also express an action as a process going on before a past event.
  *She **had been swimming** so her hair was wet.*

3.1 Future tenses

PRESENT SIMPLE

- (See 1.1) It can be used with adverbs which have a future time reference when the action or event is part of a fixed timetable. Verbs normally used in this way are those associated with timetables, schedules and organised events, such as *begin, end, leave, depart, arrive, come, open, close, stop, go.*

*The museum **opens** at 10 tomorrow morning.*
*Classes **begin** next week.*
*My plane **arrives** at 9:05 in London.*

PRESENT CONTINUOUS

- (☞ See 1.2) It can be used with future time adverbs: the action or event expressed is pre-arranged. It is different in meaning from the present simple as the present continuous implies personal agreement and planning on the part of the subject, while the present simple does not.
  *I have already made my plans; **I'm leaving** at 4 tomorrow.*
  *Jim has an appointment. He **is seeing** Dr Smith next Wednesday.*
- A future time must be given or indicated by the context.
  *After dinner, **I'm meeting** a friend of mine.*

BE GOING TO

- It expresses a prior plan or intention, something the speaker is determined to do in the near future.
  *'Why did you buy this paint?' '**I'm going to paint** my bedroom tomorrow.'*
- It can also express a prediction which is based on present evidence or knowledge.
  *Look at those black clouds! **It's going to rain**.*

» PRESENT CONTINUOUS VS *BE GOING TO* FOR THE FUTURE

Present continuous	***I'm meeting** John at the station at 6 p.m.*	It implies an arrangement with John.
Be going to	***I'm going to meet** John at the station.*	No arrangement has been made. John may get a surprise.

WILL

- It expresses a future action which is totally independent from the speaker.
  *People **will spend** their holidays on the Moon in the future.*
- It can also express a prediction one thinks, guesses or calculates will happen. No particular time is implied as it could also refer to the remote future, and verbs such as *be afraid, be sure/ certain, believe, expect, hope, suppose, think* can introduce the sentence.
  *I don't think they **will come** back soon.*
- It is also used to express a decision which is made at the moment of speaking about an immediate future.
  *'The phone's ringing.' '**I'll answer** it.'* (Here the speaker is not making a prediction and he has made no prior plan to answer the phone. He is showing his willingness to do the action.)
  Note: if after the speaker's decision the action is mentioned again, *be going to* or the present continuous must be used.
  Waiter: What would you like to drink?
  *Sheila: **I'll have** a coffee, please.*
  (Tom joins Sheila before her coffee has arrived.)
  *Tom: What **are** you **going to have**?*
  *Sheila: I'**m having** a coffee.*
- It is also used to express promises, opinions, determination and probability. In these cases, expressions such as *perhaps, probably, it is likely/ unlikely, definitely* and verbs such as *promise, think, expect, hope* are used.
  ***I'll stop** smoking, I promise.*
  *They**'ll** probably **wait** for us.*

» *SHALL*

Shall can be used in the interrogative form with *I/ we.*

In question tags	*Let's have a snack, **shall we**?*
In suggestions	***Shall** I **close** the window?*
In requests for orders or instructions	*What **shall** I **do** with your old books?*

3.2 Future continuous

USE

- It refers to an activity that will be in progress at a specific time in the future.
  *I **will be working** between two and five this afternoon.*
- It refers to a future action that has been pre-arranged.
  *The singer **will be performing** in Rome next month.*

3.3 Future perfect

USE

- It implies that an action will have been completed by a certain time in the future.
- It is commonly used with expressions such as *by next week/ month/ year, by then, by the end of the week/ month/ year, in a week's/ month's/ year's time, within a week/ month/ year, this time next week/ month/ year.*
  *We **will have finished** the repairs to your car by tomorrow morning. It will be ready for you at 11 o'clock. (The garage will finish the repairs at some time before 11 o'clock tomorrow.)*

3.4 The future with time clauses

- A time clause begins with such words as *when, while, the moment that, as soon as, as long as, till/ until, unless, the first time, the next time, after, before, once, provided (that),* etc.
- With a time clause, even if the meaning is future, only the present tense can be used. We usually use the present simple, although we can use the present perfect when we want to stress the idea that the action contained in the time clause is completed before the other action occurs in the future.
  *We'll phone you **as soon as** we get home.*
  *We'll have a lot of fun **while** we are in Australia.*
  *Tom will stay with me **until** the train arrives.*
  ***When** you have finished your homework, we'll go out shopping.*
  ***After** I have watched this film, I'll go to bed.*

» TIME EXPRESSIONS WITH PREPOSITIONS

On time	= at the planned time; neither late nor early *Peter wants the meeting to start **on time**.*
In time	= with enough time to spare; before the last moment *Fortunately they took him to the hospital **in time**.*
At times	= occasionally ***At times**, in front of the class, I get very nervous.*
At the time	= it refers to a time or time period that has been described in some way *I saw his picture when I was young. **At the time**, I didn't realise how lovely he was.*
At that time	= at that precise moment ***At that time** the police arrived.*
At this time	= at present, now *That car model is not available **at this time**.*
At the same time	= 1) during the same moment, simultaneously *We arrived **at the same time**.* = 2) nevertheless, however *We agree with you. **At the same time**, we object strongly to your methods.*
By this time	= at some point before this moment *I would normally be in bed **by this time**.*
By that time	= 1) before or at a given period in the future *'Where will you be in fifty years' time?' '**By that time**, I will be an old man.'* = 2) before or at a given period in the past *The bus was three hours late. **By that time**, I had found a taxi to go home.*
Sometime	= at some unspecified or unknown time *Let's get together **sometime**.*
Some time	= an unspecified quantity or period of time *Choose **some time** that fits in your schedule.*

3.5 The indefinite article

USE

The indefinite articles are ***a*** and ***an***.

A/an is used:

- when a singular countable noun is introduced for the first time. → *There is a girl who lives in a house near mine.*
- to suggest that the person or thing is one of several or it is an example of a class of things. → *There was a cat outside. Have you got a motorbike?*
- in constructions with *be* + job to express profession. → *He's a teacher.*
- before the name of some illnesses. → *I've got a headache/a cold/a temperature/a cough/a sore throat.*
- in expressions of price, speed, quantity. → *2 euros a kilo, 100 kilometres an hour, a lot of, a couple of*
- in some expressions of frequency. → *four times a day, once a year*
- in exclamations before singular countable nouns. → *What a lovely day! Such an interesting book!*
- before parts of the body, if singular. → *He's got a long nose.*
- after *as*. → *She works as a nurse.*

A/an is NOT used:

- in front of a possessive adjective where other constructions must be adopted. → *a friend of mine = one of my friends*

3.6 The definite article

USE

The definite article is ***the***.

The is used:

- when a singular countable noun appears a second time. → *There is a girl who lives in a house near mine. The girl is 17 years old.*
- to show that the person or thing is the only one of its kind, it is unique. → *the Queen, the government, the sun*
- to show a special known case is being referred to. → *The house he has bought is wonderful.*
- before a noun which has become definite by the addition of a phrase or a clause. → *the man in black, the girl I saw*
- in front of a singular countable noun which represents a class of animals/things. → *The tiger is a dangerous animal.*
- Before an adjective when a class or group of people is referred to. → *the young, the poor, the Italians*
- before plural surnames to refer to a family. → *the Simpsons*
- before titles containing *of*. → *the Duke of York*
- before titles used alone. → *the Prince*
- before superlatives, *first, second, only*, etc. when they are used as adjectives. → *the best student, the second day, the only thing*
- before musical instruments after the verb *play*. → *She plays the trumpet.*
- before names of choirs, orchestras. → *the Monteverdi Choir*

The is NOT used:

- in front of a **possessive adjective** (but it is used after a noun in the possessive case = *the girl's aunt*). ➔ *my friend*
- when speaking in a **general sense** about a plural countable noun/an uncountable noun. ➔ *Tigers are dangerous. Alcohol is bad for your health.*
- before **abstract** nouns. ➔ *We all admire honesty.*
- before names of **meals**. ➔ *Dinner is ready!*
- before names of school **subjects**. ➔ *Geography is interesting.*
- when the word *man* is used to speak about the human race. ➔ *Man fears death.*
- when the word *nature* refers to the spirit underlying the world of plants and animals. ➔ *Nature can be cruel.*
- before **proper names**, also when preceded by titles or by names of family relationship. ➔ *Tom, Doctor Marvin, Captain Cook, Mr Smith, Uncle Sam*
- with some **illnesses**. ➔ *I've got measles. He has diabetes.*
- before **colours**. ➔ *I like blue.*
- before names of **sports** and **games**. ➔ *She plays tennis. I play chess.*
- before **parts of the body** preceded by a possessive adjective. ➔ *She is washing her hair. He broke his arm.*
- before **articles of clothing** which are normally preceded by a possessive adjective. ➔ *He took off his hat.*

» SIMILAR TERMS, DISSIMILAR USE

listen to **the** *radio, surf* **the** *Internet*	*watch TV*
the *Financial Times* – a newspaper	*Time* – a magazine
the *Italian language*	*I speak Italian.*
at **the** *seaside* = in the area near the sea	*at sea* = out in the sea
the *Titanic* – a boat	*Union Station*
the *Odeon* – a cinema	*Gatwick Airport*
the *Hilton* – a hotel	

» DEFINITE ARTICLES IN EXPRESSIONS OF PLACE

It is used:	It is NOT used:
before names of **rivers, canals, seas** and **oceans**. ➔ *the Thames, the Suez Canal, the Mediterranean*	before names of **lakes**. ➔ *Lake Como*
before **mountain chains** and **deserts**. ➔ *the Apennines, the Sahara*	before names of **mountains**. ➔ *Mount Rosa*
before plural names of islands and **groups of islands**. ➔ *the Azores, the Bahamas*	before **singular** names of **islands**. ➔ *Mauritius, Manhattan* (BUT it is used if the name of the island is composed of *Isle of*. ➔ *the Isle of Skye*)
before plural names of **countries**. ➔ *the Netherlands* or before names of **countries** containing the words *kingdom, republic* or *state*. ➔ *the United Kingdom, the Republic of Ireland, the United States*	before singular names of **continents, countries, regions, cities**. ➔ *Asia, Italy, Wessex, Milan* (BUT *the Riviera, the Crimea*)
in general *the* is used in names consisting of **noun** + *of* + **noun** or of **adjective** + **noun**. ➔ *the Cape of Good Hope, the high street, the West Indies, the West, the National Gallery, the Tower of London*	BUT *South Africa, West Germany, Oxford Street, Trafalgar Square, Westminster Bridge*
in front of *north, south, east* and *west* when they are used as nouns. ➔ *the north of England*	in front of *north, south, east* and *west* when they are used in expressions of direction. ➔ *They live north of Liverpool. Go south.* or when they are part of the **geographical proper noun**. *South Carolina is a State in the US.*

» PRONUNCIATION

A/An	*The*
An + letters spoken with a vowel sound. ➔ *an MP, an SOS*	It is pronounced /ðɪ/ when followed by a vowel or by a vowel sound. ➔ *the MP, the apple*
A + vowels spoken with a consonant sound. ➔ *a European country, a one-way street, a university*	It is pronounced /ðə/ when followed by a consonant or by a consonant sound. ➔ *the European Union, the boy*

4.1 Modals of ability, possibility and permission

FORM

Infinitive	Present simple	Past simple	Present perfect	Future simple
	can	*could*		*can*
to be able to	*is able to*	*was/were able to*	*have/has been able to*	*will be able to*
	may/might	*could*		*may/might*

» CONTRACTED NEGATIVE FORM

In informal speech and writing, it is common to use the contracted negative form (*can't, couldn't*, etc.) of all the modal and auxiliary verbs above except *may*. The contracted negative form of *may* is not in general use. ➔ *may not* NOT ~~*mayn't*~~.

USE

Ability	= ***can***: it suggests the possession of ability in general. *My mother **can** speak Russian fluently.* Or, in particular circumstances, the ability to perform the activity denoted by the main verb. *I **can** help him if he wants.* = ***could***: it is used to refer to the actual performance in the past. *I **could** see what you were doing.*
Ability in the past	= ***could***: in affirmative sentences it indicates that the ability existed in the past but was not necessarily performed. It is a potential ability in general. *When I was a child, I **could** sleep twelve hours without interruption.* = ***was/were able to***: in affirmative sentences they are used to talk about an ability that was performed at one particular time in the past. In this kind of sentence *could* cannot be used. *Yesterday some friends of mine **were able to** reach the top of Mt Everest.* In negative and interrogative sentences, there is no difference between the two forms. *Tom **wasn't able to/ couldn't** run 5 km yesterday.*
Possibility	= ***may/ might***: they suggest 'possibly, perhaps'. *May* suggests a stronger possibility than *might*. *He **may** be right. You **might** get the job.* *Might* is normally used when the rest of the sentence is in the past. *The plan **might** work if we tried it soon enough.* = ***can***: it expresses the idea that something is possible because certain characteristics or conditions exist. *Measles **can** be quite dangerous.* = ***could***: it is used in the past. *He **could** be very unreasonable at times.*
Permission	We use ***can/ could/ may*** to ask for permission. *Colud/ May* are more formal and polite than *can*. ***Can** I use your mobile phone?* ***Could** I ask you a personal question?* ***May** I make a suggestion?* When we give permission, we use ***can*** or ***may***, but not *could*. *You **can** borrow my bike, if you want.* (informal) *'May I open the window?' 'Of course, you **may**.'* (formal)

4.2 *Could / Manage to / Succeed in / Be able to*

- ***Could*** expresses general ability in the past.
  *I **could** run fast when I was younger.*
- ***Manage to* + base form** is used in the past simple especially when the achievement was difficult, unexpected or uncertain.
  *She **managed to** pass her exam yesterday.*
- ***Succeed in* + *-ing* form** of the verb is also used when the achievement was difficult or significant.
  *They **didn't succeed in** landing a spaceship on the Moon.*
- ***Be able to*** is used to express the achievement of something difficult or an action that has been successfully concluded.
  *I **was able to** stop my car before I hit the wall.*

4.3 Modals of deduction

Present tense affirmative: *Why is Susan eating?*	
a) *She **is** hungry.*	If we are sure that something is true in the present, we don't need to use a modal, but we can state a fact that we are sure is true by using *be*.
b) *She **must** be hungry.*	*Must* is used to express a strong degree of certainty. It is used to assert that what we infer or conclude is the most likely interpretation of a situation or event. The speaker is saying: '*Probably she is hungry. It is my logical conclusion, but I do not know it for certain.*'
c) *She **may** be hungry.*	*May, might* and *could* express a weak degree of certainty. The speaker is saying: '*Perhaps/ maybe/ possibly she is hungry. I'm only making a guess, there may be other possibilities.*'
d) *She **might** be hungry.*	
e) *She **could** be hungry.*	

Present tense negative: *Why isn't Susan eating?*	
a) *She **is not** hungry.*	100% sure. The speaker has no doubt.
b) *She **can't** be hungry.*	95% sure. The speaker believes something is impossible.
c) *She **may not** be hungry.*	Less than 50% sure. The speaker uses *may not* or *might not* to mention a possibility.
d) *She **might not** be hungry.*	

Past tense affirmative: *Why was Susan eating?*	
a) *She **was** hungry.*	100% sure
b) *She **must have been** hungry.*	95% sure
c) *She **may have been** hungry.*	less than 50% sure
d) *She **might have been** hungry.*	
e) *She **could have been** hungry.*	

Past tense negative: *Why wasn't Susan eating?*	
a) *She **was not** hungry.*	100% sure
b) *She **can't/ couldn't have been** hungry.*	95% sure
c) *She **may not have been** hungry.*	less than 50% sure
d) *She **might not have been** hungry.*	

4.4 Modals of obligation, necessity and advice

FORM

Infinitive	Present simple	Past simple	Present perfect	Future simple
	must			
to have to	*have to*	*had to*	*have had to*	*will have to*

USE

Necessity	= ***must*** is stronger than *have to*. It indicates advice and recommendations the speaker feels strongly about. *All applicants **must** take an entrance test.*
	= ***have to*** is more commonly used in everyday statements. *Where's Sue? I **have to** talk to her.*
Self-imposed obligation	= ***must/have to***: normally it is in the first person and either form is possible. *I **must/have to** stop smoking!* But when obligation is urgent or seems important to the speaker, *must* is better. *I **must** tell you something very important!*
Obligation imposed by the speaker	= ***must***: it expresses the speaker's authority. *Doctor: 'You **must** cut down on your smoking!'*
Obligation imposed from the outside	= ***have to***: it expresses an external authority, an obligation that is imposed by a circumstance. *You'**ll have to** get up early when you start to work.* Especially when habits are involved. *I **have to** take two of these pills a day.*
Strong recommendation	= ***must***: it expresses little more than pressing advice; it's a stronger form of *should*. *You **must** read this book. It's marvellous!*
Lack of necessity / absence of obligation	= ***not have to***: it expresses external authority. *Tomorrow is a holiday. We **don't have to** go to school.*
Prohibition	= ***must not***: it expresses a prohibition imposed by the speaker. *You **mustn't** tell anyone my secret!*
Advisability	= ***should/ought to***: these are conditional forms expressing a suggestion. *You **should** read this book. It's very good!* Or a statement about responsibility or duty. *Drivers **ought to** respect the speed limit.* *Ought to* is stronger than *should*.

4.5 *Need*

- ***Need*** is a modal verb and it is mainly used in questions and negatives (***needn't***) with a similar meaning to *have to*, so to express that something is necessary or not necessary.
  ***Need** he shout like that?*
  *You **needn't** worry.*
- ***Need to*** is a regular verb meaning 'avere bisogno di'. It is used to express necessity or lack of necessity.
  ***Do** we **need to** hand in the work for tomorrow?*
  *I **don't need to** change the washing machine: it still works.*
  *She **needs to** see the doctor.*

5.1 Zero, first and second conditionals

ZERO CONDITIONAL

- It is used for common states or events, universal truths, scientific facts. *If* can be replaced by *when/whenever*, even though *if* stresses the idea that it is a condition.

***If*-clause: present simple**	**Main clause: present simple**
*If the temperature **goes** below 0 °C,*	*water **freezes into ice**.*

- It is used if the main clause expresses a habitual activity or situation regarding the speaker. It is often used to speak about a real possibility.

***If*-clause: present simple**	**Main clause: present simple**
*If I **don't have** breakfast in the morning,*	*I always **get** hungry during class.*

FIRST CONDITIONAL

- It is used if the main clause concerns a particular activity or situation in the future.

***If*-clause: present simple (or any present tense)**	**Main clause: any future tense with *will* (usually future simple)**
*If the weather **is** nice tomorrow,* *If he **is working**,*	*we **will go** on a class trip.* *he **won't be listening** to the radio.*

SECOND CONDITIONAL

- The conditional clause can represent what is a) possible; b) hypothetical/imaginary; or c) contrary to present fact. This kind of *if*-clause is often used to d) persuade people to do something.

***If*-clause: past simple**	**Main clause: present conditional**
a) *If we **caught** the 10 o'clock train,* b) *If I **won** the lottery,* c) *If he **were** here right now,* d) *If you **worked** here,*	*we **could get** there for lunch.* *I **would stop** working.* *he **would help** us.* *you **would earn** more.*

» EXPRESSING HYPOTHETICAL MEANING

- The *if*-clauses in all the examples so far have begun with *if*, but other conjunctions are commonly used. In them, the verb tense used is the past subjunctive (which is the same as the simple past in all verbs except the verb *to be*, which is *were* for all persons).
- *If*-clauses can be introduced using *as if* or *as though* to indicate unreality, improbability or doubt in the present. The tense of the verb before *as though* can be present or past.
  He behaves ***as though*** *he* ***were*** *the owner!*
- They can also be introduced by *it's time* or *it's high time* to indicate that it is a little late.
  It's time *we* ***went*** *home.*
- *It's time* can also be followed by the infinitive or by *for* + object + infinitive, but these two forms merely state that the correct time has come.
  It's time to go *home.*
  It's time for us to go *home.*
- *If*-clauses may also be introduced by other expressions, such as *suppose* or *what if*.
  Suppose *you* ***told*** *him the truth, what could he do about it?*
  What if *I* ***decided*** *to go away?*

5.2 *Unless / In case / As long as / Provided that*

There are several conjunctions that use the same verb structure as conditional clauses.

- ***Unless*** **+ affirmative verb**: stresses the idea that the condition must be fulfilled.
  She never <u>answers</u> the door ***unless*** *you <u>ring</u> three times.*
- ***In case***: contains the meaning 'if the possibility arises'.
  <u>I'll come</u> tomorrow ***in case*** *Ann <u>wants</u> me.*
- ***As long as***: means 'on the condition that' or 'for the time that it takes'.
  <u>I'll stay</u> with you ***as long as*** *there <u>is</u> a room free.*
- ***Provided (that)***: can replace *if* when there is a strong idea of limitation or restriction.
  <u>I'll come</u> ***provided*** *you <u>pay</u> my fare.*

» DEPENDENT CLAUSES

I'll come tomorrow ***in case*** *Ann wants me.*	*I'll come tomorrow* ***if*** *Ann wants me.*
In this sentence the meaning of the main clause doesn't change if we drop the 'in case' clause. (→ *Perhaps Ann wants me, perhaps she doesn't, but I will come anyway. My action doesn't depend on Ann.)*	In a conditional sentence the action in the main clause depends on the action of the *if*-clause. (→ *I will only come if Ann asks me.)*

5.3 Third conditionals

USE

***If*-clause: past perfect**	**Main clause: past conditional**
a) *If you* ***had told*** *me the truth,*	*I* ***would have given*** *you my opinion.*
b) *If they* ***had studied***,	*they* ***would have passed*** *the exam.*
These sentences are completely hypothetical, and represent what is contrary to past fact. The past perfect tense is used to indicate past unreality. In reality: a) *You* ***didn't*** *tell me the truth,* ***so*** *I couldn't give you my opinion.* b) *They* ***didn't*** *study,* ***so*** *they failed the exam.*	

» INVERTED CONDITIONALS

- With *were*, *had* (past perfect) and *should*, sometimes *if* can be omitted with an inversion of subject and verb.
- This kind of sentence occurs in both written and (less commonly) spoken language, but is considered formal.
  Were I you, *I wouldn't do that. (= If I were you...)*
  Had the referee seen *the foul, our team would have won the game. (= If the referee had seen the foul...)*
  Should you need *my help again, just give me a ring. (= If you should need...)*
- Note that, in the negative, *not* follows the subject and contracted forms are not used.
  Were you not *in class, what would you be doing right now?*
  Had I not seen *it with my own eyes, I wouldn't have believed it.*

5.4 Mixed conditionals

USE

- They are used when the time in the *if*-clause and the time in the main clause are different: one may refer to the present and the other to the past. There are two possibilities:
  a) a present result of an impossible past event;
  b) or an impossible past consequence of a present action.

a) *I didn't eat breakfast this morning,*	*so I am hungry now.*
This refers to past time.	This refers to present time.
***If*-clause: past perfect**	**Main clause: present conditional**
If I ***had had*** *breakfast this morning,*	*I* ***wouldn't be*** *hungry now.*

b) *He isn't a good student.*	*He didn't study for the exam yesterday.*
This refers to present time.	This refers to past time.
***If*-clause: past simple**	**Main clause: past conditional**
If he ***were*** *a good student,*	*he* ***would have studied*** *for the exam.*

5.5 Expressing wishes and regrets: *I wish / If only*

The verb *wish* is used when the speaker wants reality to be different or when his/her wishes or regrets are expressed. It is followed by a noun clause in which *that* is usually omitted.

About the past We use the past perfect tense after *wish* to refer to something the speaker wished for in the past, or to express his/her regrets about something which happened/didn't happen in the past.	*I **wish** John **had come** to my birthday party. (But he didn't.)* *I **wish** John **could have come** to my birthday party. (But he couldn't.)*
About the present We use the past tense after *wish* to refer to present unreality.	*I **wish** I **were** rich. (But I'm not.)* *I **wish** I **could speak** French. (But I can't.)*
The same idea can also be given by *if only*.	***If only** I **were** rich.*
We can also use *would* to say that people or events frustrate our desires.	*I **wish** you **would stop** talking!*
Would can also be used to make a request.	*I **wish** you **would hurry** up.*
About the future We can also use *would* to say that the speaker wants something to happen in the future. The wish may or may not come true.	*I **wish** it **would stop** raining!*

» PREFER, WOULD RATHER, HAD BETTER

PREFER

- In the conditional, it is followed by the infinitive.
  *I **would prefer** to go to the cinema.*
- In the present or past tenses, it is followed by the gerund.
  *I **prefer/preferred** walking **to** cycling.*
- *Prefer* can also be followed by a noun.
  *He **prefers** mathematics **to** geography.*
- It is followed by object + infinitive when the two subjects are different.
  *She **prefers** us not to stay out late.*

WOULD ('D) RATHER

- This form can be used instead of *would prefer + infinitive.*
  *I would prefer to go out to eat. = I **would rather** go out to eat.*
- It is followed by the bare infinitive when the subject of *would rather* is the same as the subject of the following action.
  *Tom **would rather** read **than** talk.*
- It is followed by subject + past tense when the two subjects are different. The same idea can be rendered with *would prefer.*
  *I'd prefer my son stayed at home. = I'**d rather/would rather** my son **stayed** at home.*
- It can be used instead of *prefer* + gerund for present actions.
  *I prefer playing tennis to watching TV. = I **would rather play** tennis **than** watch TV.*
- It is followed by subject + past perfect to express what someone would have preferred someone else to do or not to do.
  *My mother **would rather** I **had studied** more.*
- *Would rather* always requires a verb and cannot be followed directly by a noun.
  *I **would rather play** tennis **than** watch TV.* NOT *I ~~would rather~~ tennis.*

HAD ('D) BETTER

- In this form *had* is an unreal past; its meaning is present or future. It is always followed by the bare infinitive.
  *You **had (you'd) better** hurry.*
- It is used to give advice. It's meaning is similar to *should*, but it is used for particular situations and not for general statements.
  *It's cold outside. You **had better** take a coat.*

NEGATIVE FORMS

Affirmative	Negative
Prefer	
I prefer to go to the cinema.	*I **prefer not to go** to the cinema.*
I prefer you to go to the cinema.	*I **prefer** you **not to go** to the cinema.*
Would rather	
I'd rather go to the cinema.	*I'**d rather not go** to the cinema.*
I'd rather my son stayed at home.	*I'**d rather** my son **didn't stay** at home.*
Had better	
You'd better hurry.	*You'**d better not** hurry.*

6.1 Comparative and superlative adjectives and adverbs

FORM

One-syllable adjectives
They form the comparative by adding ***-er*** and the superlative by using ***the*** before the adjective and adding ***-est*** to the positive form of the adjective. *cold – cold**er** – **the** cold**est*** *long – long**er** – **the** long**est***
Adjectives of three or more syllables
They form the comparative and superlative by putting ***more*** and ***the most*** before the positive form of the adjective. *interested – **more** interested – **the most** interested* *beautiful – **more** beautiful – **the most** beautiful*

Two-syllable adjectives
Most take **more** and **the most**. *doubtful – **more** doubtful – **the most** doubtful* *obscure – **more** obscure – **the most** obscure*
Those ending in *-er*, *-le*, *-ow* or *-y* usually add **-er** and **-est** to the positive form of the adjective. *clever – clever**er** – **the** clever**est*** *humble – humbl**er** – **the** humbl**est*** *narrow – narrow**er** – **the** narrow**est*** *silly – silli**er** – **the** silli**est***
BUT *eager – **more** eager – **the most** eager* *tender – **more** tender – **the most** tender*
AND The adjective *common* has got both forms. *common – common**er** – **the** common**est*** *common – **more** common – **the most** common*

USE

- Comparatives are followed by *than*.
  *The weather is warmer **than** last week.*
- Comparatives may be followed by a noun or a clause.
  *Pizza is **better than** sushi.*
  *The film was **better than** I expected.*
- If there is a pronoun after *than*, we use an object pronoun in informal English, but we use a subject pronoun in a more formal style or when the pronoun is followed by a verb.
  *She is older than **me**.* (informal)
  *She is older than **I**.* (formal)
  *She is older than **I am**.*
- After superlatives, we use *in* (or other prepositions) to show what places we are talking about.
  *It's the most expensive car **in** the world.*
  *She's the happiest girl **under** the sun.*
  *Mark is the tallest **among** the three boys.*
  *El Azizia is the hottest place **on** earth.*
- *Of* is used when there is a superlative followed by plural nouns and pronouns.
  *She is the most sensible **of** the girls.*
- *That* + clause is often found after superlatives.
  *She is the funniest person **that** I know.*
- Adverbs usually have comparative and superlative forms with *more* and *the most* respectively.
  *Boys usually run **more quickly than** girls.*
  *Tom speaks **the most quietly** of all his brothers.*
- BUT *early, fast, hard, late, long, loud, near, slow* and *soon* have comparative and superlative forms with *-er* and *-est*.
  *Elle runs **faster** than Becca.*
- If we want to say that people, things or actions are equal in some way, we can use the structure *as ... as* in the affirmative and *not so/not as ... as* in the negative.
  *He was **as** white **as** a sheet.*
  *Your coffee is **not as/so** good **as** the coffee my mother makes.*
- *Not so/as ... as* can also be expressed using *less ... than*.
  *This book was **less** interesting **than** the last one I read.*
- *Fewer ... than* is used with plural nouns.
  *There were **fewer** people at the lecture **than** we expected.*

» IRREGULAR ADJECTIVES AND ADVERBS

bad – worse – the worst
good/ well – better – the best
far – farther – the farthest / far – further – the furthest (both are used for distances)
far – further – the furthest (it is used to mean 'additional, extra')
little – less – the least
many/ much – more – the most
old – older – the oldest (it is used when there is *than* in the sentence: *He is older than I am.*)
old – elder – the eldest (it is used for comparisons within a family, but only in an attributive way, that is, in front of a noun: *my elder brother, his eldest daughter*)

6.2 Expressions using comparatives

***The* + comparative ... *the* + comparative**	
It says that two changes happen together in a sort of parallel increase.	***The older** I get, **the happier** I am.* ***The sooner** you start, **the more quickly** you'll be finished.*

Comparative + *and* + comparative	
It expresses the idea of continuing change, either gradual decrease or increase.	*I am getting **fatter and fatter**.* *We are going **more and more slowly**.*

6.3 Modifiers of comparatives

- To emphasise comparatives we use ***much, a lot*** or ***far***.
  *You are **far** more tolerant than I am.*
- To emphasise *less* we use ***a little, a bit*** or ***slightly***.
  *He looks **a bit** older than he is.*
  *This coat is **slightly** cheaper than that one.*
- Other adverbs can be used, such as ***even, rather, any/no***.
  *He is quite fat, but a few years ago he was **even** fatter.*
  *I met her **no** later than yesterday.*
- To emphasise superlatives we use ***by far***.
  *This is **by far** the best DVD I've ever seen.*

» OTHER MODIFIERS

- Modifiers like *absolutely, almost, completely, entirely, extremely, fairly, far, hardly, just, much, nearly, only, quite, rather, really,* etc. are adverbs of degree that modify adjectives or another adverb. They are placed before the adjective or adverb.
  *He is **fairly** tall.* (modifier before adjective)
  *He runs **fairly** fast.* (modifier before adverb)
- Some of them, like *a bit* or *completely*, are easy to use, but some, like *quite* or *rather*, are more complicated.

FAIRLY, QUITE, RATHER, PRETTY

These four adjectives are easily confused because, even if they can all be used to change the strength of adjectives and adverbs, they do not mean the same thing. They are, however, all used to mitigate the meaning of the following adjective/ adverb.

Fairly It is the weakest of the four. It means 'moderately' with favourable adejctives and adverbs (*good, well, nice*).	*That film is **fairly** good. = It is worth seeing but not worth going a long way to see.*
Quite It is a little stronger than *fairly*.	*That film is **quite** good. = It is not the best film ever but it is worth seeing.*
It can also mean 'completely' when it is used with a word or phrase expressing the idea of completeness: *certain, finished, full, ready, right, wrong*, etc.	*The glass was **quite** empty.*
Rather It is generally stronger than *quite*. It often means 'more than is usual', 'more than expected' or 'more than you want'.	*That film is **rather** good. = You should see it; it's better than most.*
It can also mean 'moderately' before unfavourable adjectives and adverbs (*bad, ugly, stupid*).	*Jo is fairly clever, but her sister is **rather** silly.*
It can be used with comparatives.	*It's **rather warmer** today.*
It can be used with *too*.	*She is **rather too** sure of herself.*
Pretty It is similar to *rather*, but more informal.	*That film is **pretty** good. = It is better than most.*

A BIT, SLIGHTLY

These are also used to mitigate.

A bit It is similiar to *rather*.	*The play was **a bit** boring.*
It can be used with comparatives.	*This exercise is **a bit easier**.*
It can be used with *too*.	*This soup is **a bit too** salty for me.*
Slightly It means 'a bit/a little', 'to a small degree'.	*The window was **slightly** open.*

HIGHLY, EXTREMELY, INCREDIBLY

These are used to intensify.

Highly It is used only in an abstract sense.	*He was a **highly** paid official.*
Extremely It means 'very'.	*The mountains were **extremely** high.*
Incredibly It has the same meaning as *extremely*.	*The entrance exam to that university was **incredibly** hard.*

6.4 Linkers of manner: *like / as*

***As* + noun**	
= comparison of situations or actions, to say they are similar (in these cases, *as* is a conjunction, which is followed by a clause with a subject and a verb,	*He went to live in France **as** his brother had the year before.*
or by a prepositional phrase)	*In France, **as** in Italy, the production of wine is widespread.*
= the job,	*I work **as** a nurse.*
function,	***As** a nurse, she is able to give shots.*
use	*I used my shoe **as** a hammer.*
or role of a person or thing	*She went to the party dressed **as** a witch.*
(in these cases, *as* is a preposition, which is followed by a noun or a pronoun)	

Like	
= to say that people, things, actions or situations are similar to each other	*I'm **like** my father.*
= for example	*My father is **like** me.*
(it is a preposition and is followed by a noun or a pronoun)	*I would like to visit far-off countries **like** China and Thailand.*

7.1 Passives

USE

- It is used when the active form would involve the use of an indefinite or vague pronoun or noun as subject (for ex. *someone, they, people*) or of a subject that is unknown.
  I've been robbed! (Instead of *Someone has robbed me.*)
  *The school **had to be closed**.* (Instead of *They had to close the school.*)
- It is used when the emphasis is on the agent, which is preceded by the preposition *by*.
  *The Sistine Chapel **was painted by** Michelangelo (NOT by Raphael.)*

- It is used when we are more interested in what happened than in who did the action; sometimes this is because the agent is obvious and therefore unnecessary.
The building ***was designed*** *by an American architect. (I am telling you about the building NOT the architect.)*
The burglars ***were arrested****. (It is obvious that it was the police who arrested the burglars.)*
- Here is how to change an active form into a passive form:
  1. The object of the active becomes the subject in the passive.
  2. Look at the tense of the main verb in the active form.
  3. Form the same tense of the verb *be* for the passive.
  4. Add to the verb *be* the past participle of the main verb being used in the active form.
  5. The subject of the active form may be omitted or added at the end of the passive form using *by*.
  Michelangelo painted the Sistine Chapel. → *The Sistine Chapel was painted by Michelangelo.*
- Remember that only transitive verbs (those which can take an object) can be used passively.

Tense	Active	Passive
present simple	***I eat*** *an apple.*	*An apple* ***is eaten****.*
present continuous	*I* ***am eating*** *an apple.*	*An apple* ***is being eaten****.*
present perfect	*I* ***have eaten*** *an apple.*	*An apple* ***has been eaten****.*
past simple	*I* ***ate*** *an apple.*	*An apple* ***was eaten****.*
past continuous	*I* ***was eating*** *an apple.*	*An apple* ***was being eaten****.*
past perfect	*I* ***had eaten*** *an apple.*	*An apple* ***had been eaten****.*
past perfect continuous	*I* ***had been eating*** *an apple.*	*An apple* ***had been being eaten****.*
future simple	*I* ***will eat*** *an apple.*	*An apple* ***will be eaten****.*
future perfect	*I* ***will have eaten*** *an apple.*	*An apple* ***will have been eaten****.*
present conditional	*I* ***would eat*** *an apple.*	*An apple* ***would be eaten****.*
past conditional	*I* ***would have eaten*** *an apple.*	*An apple* ***would have been eaten****.*
present infinitive	***(to) eat***	***(to) be eaten***
perfect infinitive	***(to) have eaten***	***(to) have been eaten***
gerund/present participle	***eating***	***being eaten***
past gerund/perfect participle	***having eaten***	***having been eaten***
past participle	***eaten***	***been eaten***

» THE PASSIVE WITH TWO OBJECTS

- When in an active sentence there are two objects (one direct and one indirect) and this sentence must be expressed in the passive, we generally make the indirect object the subject. This is because we tend to be more interested in people than things, and putting a person in the subject position helps us to understand the context more readily.

Active	Passive the indirect object = subject
John ***gave*** *Tom a present.*	*Tom* ***was given*** *a present by John.*

- There are occasions, though, when we want to make the direct object the focus of interest. In this case we place it in the subject position because there is a greater interest in what is done than to whom it is done.

Active	Passive the direct object = subject
John ***gave*** *Tom a present.*	*A present* ***was given*** *to Tom by John.*

7.2 *Be supposed to, be expected to, be asked to, be allowed/permitted to, be told to*

These verbs are used in the passive form to talk about what people say about something or what you have heard, been asked or told about something.
These verbs can have two different constructions:

1. ***It*** **+** ***be*** **+** ***supposed / expected / asked / allowed / permitted / told*** **+** ***(that)*** **+ subject + main active verb**
   It ***is supposed (that) he has moved*** *to another town.*
2. **Subject +** ***be*** **+** ***supposed / expected / asked / allowed / permitted / told*** **+ to + main verb**
   He ***is supposed to have moved*** *to another town.*

7.3 *Have/Get something done*

FORM

have/get **+ object + past participle**

USE

- The past participle is used after *have* and *get* to give a passive meaning in a construction which suggests that the subject is taking an active part in any arrangement made.
- The past participle shows the real action being carried out. The subject is not doing this action but is causing someone else to do it.
I ***had/got*** *my watch* ***repaired****. (I am not repairing the watch but arranging for someone else to do this for me.)*

7.4 Expressing emphasis with *so* and *such*

	So … that	***Such … that***
+ adjectives or + adverbs	*The weather was* ***so nice that*** *we went to the park.* *She speaks* ***so fast that*** *I can't understand her.*	
+ adjective + uncountable noun		*It was* ***such good coffee that*** *I had another cup.*
+ adjective + countable singular noun		*It was* ***such an expensive car that*** *we couldn't afford to buy it.*
+ adjective + plural noun		*They were* ***such ignorant people that*** *I felt ashamed of knowing them.*
+ quantifiers		
many	*She made* ***so many*** *mistakes* ***that*** *she failed the exam.*	
few	*He has* ***so few*** *friends* ***that*** *he is often lonely.*	
much	*She has* ***so much*** *money* ***that*** *she can buy whatever she wants.*	
little	*There was* ***so little*** *traffic* ***that*** *it took us only ten minutes to get home.*	

8.1 Gerunds and infinitives

USE

Gerunds	Infinitives
The gerund is the *-ing* form of a verb: ***playing.***	The infinitive is the base form of a verb preceded by *to*: ***to play.***
It can be used as the subject of a sentence. ***Climbing*** *can be dangerous.*	Sometimes an infinitive is used as the subject of a sentence. ***To drive*** *when drunk is dangerous.* An infinitive is commonly used with the construction *It …* ***It*** *is dangerous* ***to drive*** *when drunk.*
Both can function as the complement of the verbs *appear*, *be* and *seem*. *My worst vice is* ***smoking***.	
Go is followed by a gerund in certain idiomatic expressions that express recreational activities. *go* ***fishing***, *go* ***hunting***, *go* ***jogging***, *go* ***shopping***, etc.	The infinitive of purpose is expressed by *in order to* followed by the infinitive. *He came here* ***in order to study*** *English.* *In order* is often omitted. *He came here* ***to study*** *English.*
Gerunds can be used as the object of a preposition. *He insisted* ***on coming***. *I'm used* ***to sleeping***. *We talked about* ***not going***.	Certain adjectives, for example: *afraid, anxious, ashamed, glad, happy, lucky, pleased,* can be immediately followed by infinitives. In general, they describe a person, not a thing. *We were* ***sorry to hear*** *that.*
Gerunds are used after these verbs (among others): *admit, appreciate, avoid, complain, consider, deny, detest, discuss, dislike*, doubt, enjoy, fancy, finish, forgive, keep (continue), mention, mind, object, postpone, practise, prevent, recall, recollect, recommend, regret, resist, risk, stop*, suggest, tolerate,* etc. *He* ***admitted talking*** *to you.* *I* ***don't mind saying*** *I was wrong.* and after these expressions (among others): *can't help, can't stand, it's no good/use, it's (not) worth.*	Some verbs are immediately followed by an infinitive. *I* ***hope to see*** *you soon.* *He* ***promised not to be*** *late.* Verbs of this group (among others): *afford, agree, aim, appear, arrange, ask, beg, bother, care, choose, claim, consent, decide, demand, deserve, determine, expect, fail, forget*, happen, hesitate, hope, intend, learn, manage, mean, need, offer, plan, prepare, pretend, promise, propose, refuse, regret, remember*, seem, swear, tend, try*, wait, want, wish, would like.*
When verbs, nouns or adjectives are followed by a preposition, the *-ing* form must be used after them. *The students* ***complained about having*** *too much homework.* *He* ***apologised for breaking*** *the vase.*	Some verbs require this construction: verb + (pro)noun + infinitive *The police* ***ordered the boys to stop***. *He* ***told me to speak***. Verbs of this group (among others): *advise, allow, ask, beg, cause, challenge, convince, dare, encourage, expect, forbid, force, hire, instruct, invite, need, order, permit, persuade, remind, request, require, see, teach, tell, urge, want, warn, would like.* These verbs are followed immediately by an infinitive when they are used in the passive: *I* ***was told to speak***.

There are special expressions that are followed by the *-ing* form: *have fun, have a good time, have trouble, have difficulty, have a hard time, have a difficult time.*	There are special expressions that are followed by the infinitive: *cost, take* + expression of time or money.
*I **had a good time playing** tennis with Tom.*	*It would **take years to build** such a villa!*
spend, waste + expression of time or money:	verb + *how, what, when, where, which, why*:
*I **waste** a lot of **time watching** TV.*	*I didn't know **when to switch** the light off.*
lie, sit, stand + expression of place:	*I showed my brother **which** button **to press**.*
*Susan **is lying in bed reading** a newspaper.*	*the first, the second... the last, the only,* and superlatives:
find, catch + (pro)noun (= discover):	*He loves parties: he is always **the first to come** and **the last to leave**.*
*When I got home, I **found my son sleeping** on the sofa.*	*It was **the best** play **to be performed**.*
	Some nouns can be followed directly by the infinitive: *ability, ambition, attempt, decision, demand, desire, effort, offer, plan, promise, refusal, request, wish.*
	*He made an **attempt to speak** in public.*
	too + adjective/adverb:
	*You are **too young to understand**.*
	adjective/adverb + *enough*:
	*My son is **old enough to travel** by himself.*
	so + adjective + *as*:
	*He was **so foolish as to leave** his car unlocked.*
*Both the gerund and the infinitive can be used after these verbs: *advise, agree, allow, begin, cease, continue, dislike, forget, hate, intend, like, love, mean, need, permit, prefer, propose, regret, remember, start, stop, try.*	
*I **began studying/to study** English when I was three.*	

8.2 Verbs + both *-ing* and infinitives

Some verbs can take both the gerund and the infinitive, but there is a change in meaning:

stop **+ gerund**

- indicates the cessation of an activity.
  *He **stopped smoking**. (= He quit his habit.)*

stop **+ infinitive**

- indicates that the subject stops (whatever he is doing) in order to do something else.
  *He **stopped to smoke.** (= He stopped walking in order to smoke a cigarette.)*

remember/forget **+ gerund**

- indicates something that has been done. The action expressed by the gerund is the earlier action.
  *I **remember reading** this novel when I was 18. (= I read it in the past and I still remember it now.)*
  *I **remember him/his telling** me about it.*
- *forget* can only be followed by the gerund when it is negative.
  *I'll **never forget quarrelling** with him for hours.*

remember/forget **+ infinitive**

- indicates something that should be or needed to be done.
  *Did you **remember to pick up** the flowers for Lucy's party? (= You needed to pick up the flowers. Did you do it?)*
  *I'll **remember to ring** Tom.*
  *I often **forget to lock** the car.*

try **+ gerund**

- means 'carry out an experiment' or 'test something out'.
  *If you want to lose weight, why don't you **try eating** less?*
  ***Try taking** the other road. It may be faster.*

try **+ infinitive**

- means 'attempt' with reference to an effort.
  *I'll **try to study** harder.*
  *You should **try to be** nicer to your sister.*

8.3 Relative clauses

USE

There are two kinds of relative clauses: a) **defining** and b) **non-defining**:

a) *The man **who is over there** is my father.*
The clause *who is over there* describes the preceding noun (*the man*) and is essential to the understanding of the noun itself. If we omit this part of the sentence, it is not clear what man we are talking about.
Note: the noun and the defining relative clause are NOT separated by a comma.

b) *My father**, who is 45,** is sitting over there.*
Non-defining relative clauses are placed after nouns which are already definite and merely add some more information about them. The clause *who is 45* is not essential in the sentence and can be omitted without causing confusion.
Note: the non-defining relative clause is always preceded and followed by commas.

RELATIVE PRONOUNS

a) Defining relative pronouns		
for people		
SUBJECT	***who***	*The man **who** robbed you has been arrested.*
	that	*Everyone **that** knew him liked him.*
	(these pronouns cannot be omitted)	

OBJECT	***whom*** (more formal)	*The man **whom** I saw is Mr Jones.*
	that	*The man **that** I saw is Mr Jones.*
	(it is common to omit these pronouns)	*The man Ø I saw is Mr Jones.*
for animals and things		
SUBJECT	***which***	*This is the picture **which** was taken in Australia.*
	that	*The book **that** is on the table is mine.*
	(these pronouns cannot be omitted)	
OBJECT	***which***	*The film **which** we saw last night wasn't very good.*
	that	*The film **that** we saw last night wasn't very good.*
	(these pronouns can be omitted)	*The film Ø we saw last night wasn't very good.*

b) Non-defining relative pronouns		
for people		
SUBJECT	***who*** (this pronoun cannot be omitted)	*My uncle, **who** is very old, is leaving tomorrow for England.*
OBJECT	***whom*** (this pronoun cannot be omitted; in informal language it is often changed to *who*)	*She wanted Tom, **whom** she liked, as a partner.*
for animals and things		
SUBJECT	***which*** (this pronoun cannot be omitted)	*The 8:15 train, **which** is usually punctual, was late today.*
OBJECT	***which*** (this pronoun cannot be omitted)	*She gave me this jumper, **which** she had knitted herself.*
	which (this pronoun refers to the entire clause preceding it; it cannot be omitted and is always preceded by a comma)	*The explorers had been injured during the avalanche, **which** made the rescuers' work very difficult.*

» RELATIVE CLAUSES WITH PREPOSITIONS

When using **defining relative clauses** with prepositions:

- In formal English the preposition is placed before the relative pronoun, which must then be put into the form *whom/ which*.
  *The girl **to whom** I spoke is my sister.*
  *The ladder **on which** I am standing is very old.*
- In informal speech, however, it is more usual to move the preposition to the end of the clause; *whom/ which* is then replaced by *that/ who* (for people), or *that/ which* (for animals or things).
  *The girl **that/ who** I spoke **to** is my sister.*
  *The ladder **that/ which** I am standing **on** is very old.*
- But it is even more common to omit the relative pronoun altogether.
  *The girl I spoke **to** is my sister.*
  *The ladder I am standing **on** is very old.*

When using **non-defining relative clauses** with prepositions:

- The pronouns cannot be omitted, and the preposition is normally placed before *whom* or before *which*.
  *Peter, **with whom** I played tennis on Saturday, is my best friend.*
  *The town, **in which** many famous authors were born, is quite large and beautiful.*
- In more informal speech the preposition may be placed at the end of the clause.
  *His house, **which** he paid £10,000 **for**, is now worth much less.*

» *WHOSE*

Whose	**Possessive: defining** (people) *The film is about a spy **whose** wife betrays him.* (animals and things) *Mr White has a painting **whose** value is inestimable.* **Possessive: non-defining** (people) *Ann, **whose** children are at school all day, is trying to get a job.* (animals and things) *His house, **whose** windows were all broken, was a depressing sight.*

» *WHERE, WHEN* AND OTHER RELATIVE ADVERBS

Where	*The building **where** he lives is very old.* *The building **in which** he lives is very old.* *The building **which** he lives **in** is very old.* *The building **that** he lives **in** is very old.* *The building Ø he lives **in** is very old.*
When	*I'll never forget the day **when** I met you.* *I'll never forget the day **on which** I met you.* *I'll never forget the day **that** I met you.* *I'll never forget the day Ø I met you.*

9.1 Reported speech

USE

- It can be referred to as 'reported' or 'indirect' speech: it is a clause in which we 'report' what someone has said.
  *He **said** he **loved me**.*
- When we turn direct speech into indirect, some changes are usually necessary in tenses, word order, pronouns and other words relating to time, place and situation.
  *'Why weren't you here last night?' he asked. = He **asked me** why **I hadn't been there the night before**.*
- In some cases, words may disappear or be expressed in other ways. For example *yes, no, well*, question tags, etc. cannot be fitted into the reported speech construction.
  *He said, 'Can you swim?' I said, 'No.' = He asked if I could swim and I said **I couldn't**.*
  'You can come to the party, can't you?' = He asked me if I could come to the party.
- If the indirect speech is introduced by a verb in a present, present perfect or future tense, no changes are needed in the tense of the verb, but only in the person, time and place based on the changes in the situation.
  *Tom says, 'I'm trying to study!' = Tom **says** he **is trying** to study.*
- But indirect speech is often introduced by a verb in the past tense and verbs in the direct speech have to be changed into a corresponding past tense.

Direct speech	Reported speech
simple present	**simple past**
present continuous	**past continuous**
present perfect	**past perfect**
present perfect continuous	**past perfect continuous**
simple past	**past perfect/past simple**
past continuous	**past continuous/past perfect continuous***
past perfect	**past perfect**
future with *be going to*	**future in the past with *was/ were going to***
future simple *will*	**present conditional *would***
future continuous (*will be* + *-ing*)	**present conditional continuous (*would be* + *-ing*)**
imperative *He said, 'Come here!'* *He said, 'Don't come here.'*	**infinitive** ***He said to go there.*** ***He said not to go there.***
can	***could***
may	***might***
must	***had to*/NO CHANGE**
would, could, might, should, ought to, needn't	**NO CHANGE**

- *The past continuous tense in theory changes to the past perfect continuous, but in practice it usually remains unchanged except when it refers to a completed action.
  *She said, 'We **were thinking** of going to Rome, but then we decided not to.' = She said that they **had been thinking** of going to Rome, but then they decided not to.*
  VS: *She said, 'When I saw them, they **were running** home.' = She said that when she saw them they **were running** home.*
  Note: the tense in the time clause also remains unchanged.
- In some cases, even after past reporting verbs, the tenses can remain the same, when we are reporting people saying things that are still true when we report them.
  *He said, 'The earth **goes** round the sun.' = He said that the earth **goes** round the sun.*

» SPECIAL CASES

Direct speech	Reported speech
simple past after ***wish*, *would rather*, *it is time***	NO CHANGE
Ann: 'I'd rather Tom went home.'	*Ann said she**'d rather** Tom **went** home.*
He said, 'It's time we began studying.'	*He said **it was time** they **began** studying.*
had better	NO CHANGE or it can be reported using *advise*
Susan said, 'You had better phone the doctor.'	*Susan said that we **had better phone** the doctor. = Susan **advised us to phone** the doctor.*
used to	NO CHANGE
Bob said, 'I used to live here.'	*Bob said he **used to live** there.*

» OTHER CHANGES

Direct speech	Reported speech
Pronouns, possessive adjectives and others	
first/second person	third person (except when the speaker is reporting his own words); second person pronouns may change to the first person
this (used in time expressions)	*that*
this/ that (used as adjectives)	*the*
this/ these (used as pronouns)	*it, they/ them*
Time expressions	
now	*then*
today	*that day*
tonight	*that night*
yesterday	*the day before*
the day before yesterday	*two days before*

last week/ month/ year	*the previous week/ month/ year, the week/ month/ year before*
ago	*before*
tomorrow	*the next day, the following day*
the day after tomorrow	*in two days' time*
next week/ month/ year	*the following week/ month/ year*
Place expression	
here	*there* or by some phrase using prepositions of place

» PUNCTUATION

When using punctuation in reported speech:

- *She said, 'I am a girl.'*
  There is a comma after *she said* and a full stop at the end of the sentence before the quotation marks.
- *'I am a girl,' she said/said she.*
  There is a comma at the end of the sentence before the quotation marks, if the quoted sentence precedes *she said.* The inversion of *say* and the subject is possible when *say* follows the statement.
- *'My sister,' he said, 'is a university student.'*
  If the quoted sentence is divided by *he said*, there is a comma after the first part of the direct speech and *he said.* The first word of the rest of the quoted sentence is not capitalised.
- *She asked, 'Are you leaving tomorrow?'*
  There is a comma after *she asked* and a question mark at the end of the sentence before the quotation marks.
- *'Are you leaving tomorrow?' she asked.*
  If a question mark is used, there is no comma before *she asked.*

9.2 *Say* and *tell*

	Say	*Tell*
DIRECT	It introduces the direct speech, either with or without the person addressed. If this is specified, it must be introduced by *to.* *Laura **says**: 'I want to see you later.' = Laura **says to me**: 'I want to see you later.*	
INDIRECT	It introduces the indirect speech, when there is no person addressed. *Laura **said that** she wanted to see me later.*	It introduces the indirect speech when there is the person addressed. *Laura **told me** that she wanted to see me later.*

- Note: *that* can usually be omitted after *say* and *tell*, but it should be kept after *complain, explain, object, point out, protest*, etc.

9.3 Reporting verbs

USE

There are a number of verbs that can be used instead of *say* and *tell* to introduce reported speech. Some of them are used with an infinitive, while others use the gerund. (See also 8.1)

+ Infinitive	+ Gerund
advise, agree, claim, offer, promise, refuse, threaten ➔ *Susan: I'll wait, but I won't take a taxi. = Susan **agreed to wait** but she **refused to take** a taxi.*	*accuse of, admit, apologise for, complain about, deny, insist on, suggest* ➔ *He says, 'I know you took the money.' = He **accused** me **of taking** the money.* *My sister: 'Sorry I'm late!' = My sister **apologised for being** late.*

9.4 Reported questions

USE

- When we turn direct questions into indirect speech, some changes are necessary apart from the ones referred to in 9.1.
- The interrogative form of the verb changes to the affirmative form and the question mark is omitted.
  *Bob: 'How old are you? = Bob **asked** me **how old I was.***
- If there is a question word (*what, why, where, when, how*), it must be repeated.
- If no question word is used in the direct speech, the reported speech must be introduced by *if* or *whether.*
  *Mum: 'Is there any milk left? = Mum asked **if/whether there was** any milk left.*
  *Dad: 'Are you going to school or not? = Dad asked **whether or not I was going** to school.*
- If the verb introducing the direct speech question is *say*, it must be changed into a verb like *ask, want to know, wonder* or other similar verbs.
  *Jane: 'What happened to you?' = Jane **wanted to know** what **had happened** to me.*

Offers *Assistant: 'Can I help you?'*	*The assistant **offered to help** me.*
Suggestions *Mary: 'Shall we go to the theatre?'*	*Mary **suggested going** to the theatre.*
Requests *'Would you please send this postcard?' he said.*	*He **told/ asked** me **to send** the postcard.*
Invitations *A husband to his wife: 'Would you like to go to the cinema?'*	*The husband **invited** his wife **to go** to the cinema.*

10.1 Causative verbs

USE

- ***Get***, ***have*** and ***make*** can be used to express the idea that the subject 'causes' the object to do something. When they are used in this way, they are called 'causative' verbs; their meanings are similar but not identical.
- ***Let*** and ***allow*** can be used to express the idea that the subject 'permits' the object to do something.

***make* + object + bare infinitive**	
*I **made** my son **tell** me the truth. = My son had no choice: I insisted on him telling me the truth.*	***Make*** gives the idea that somebody **forces/obliges** somebody else to do something.
*The floodwaters **made** the wall **collapse**. = The floodwaters were the cause of the wall's collapse.*	***Make*** gives the idea that something **causes or leads** something else to do something.
***have* + object + bare infinitive**	
*I **had** my husband **paint** the kitchen. = My husband painted our kitchen simply because I asked him to.*	***Have*** gives the idea that somebody **requests/asks** somebody else to do something.
***get* + object + *to* infinitive**	
*I **got** my father **to take** me to school. = I managed to persuade my father to take me to school.*	***Get*** gives the idea that somebody **persuades** somebody else to do something.

***let* + object + bare infinitive**	
*I **let** my daughter **go** out with her friends. = I allowed my daughter to go out with her friends.*	***Let*** gives the idea that somebody **permits** somebody else to do something. It is not normally used in passive sentences.
***allow* + object + *to* infinitive**	
*The boss **allowed** his secretary **to leave** the office early. = He let his secretary leave the office early.*	Same meaning as *let*; ***allow*** gives the idea that somebody **permits** somebody else to do something. It is used in passive sentences instead of *let*.

» PASSIVE FORMS

Active	Passive
*I **made** my son **tell** me the truth.*	*My son **was made to tell** me the truth.*

The structure in which *have* and *get* are followed by an object + past participle is used to refer to situations where you ask somebody to do something for you. (☞ See also 7.3) It has a passive meaning.

10.2 Uses of *get*

- On its own *get* can mean:
  a) 'obtain'; ➔ *He **got** a good job.*
  b) 'receive'; ➔ *I usually **get** presents for my birthday.*
  c) or 'arrive'. ➔ *She **got** home late yesterday.*
- When *get* is used with an adjective or comparative form it means 'become'. ➔ ***get fit***, ***get older***
- When a preposition is added, a phrasal verb with a new meaning is created. ➔ ***get on/ off*** *(the bus)* = climb aboard/ disembark, ***get over*** = recover from/overcome (an illness/a difficult period)

10.3 Linkers of reason and result

Linkers of reason	
Because, Since, As ***Because of* + noun**	= introduces a reason ***Because/Since/As*** *the company is expanding, we need more employees.* ***Because of*** *bad weather, the flight was cancelled.*
Due to* + noun / *Due to the fact that	= introduces a reason *His low marks were **due to** lack of study.*
Owing to* + noun / *Owing to the fact that	= introduces a reason *The inflation rate has gone up **owing to the fact that** oil prices have risen.*

Linkers of result	
Therefore	= shows result or the consequence of an action *He missed the last train home, **therefore** he decided to stay in a hotel for the night.*
So	= shows result or the consequence of an action *I couldn't stand the job, **so** I looked for a different one.*
Consequently	= shows result or the consequence of an action *I wasn't able to save enough money, **consequently** I couldn't go on holiday.*
As a result	= shows result or the consequence of an action *He fell off the stairs **as a result** of his carelessness.*
Accordingly	= shows result or the consequence of an action *She had temperature and **accordingly** refused the invitation to the party.*
Thus (formal)	= shows result or the consequence of an action *They found an agreement and **thus** signed the contract.*

» PUNCTUATION

Therefore and ***as a result*** can either have a semi-colon or a full stop before them. They also have a comma after them.

Useful grammar revision points

Adjectives ending *-ing* and *-ed*

Present participle (*-ing*)	Past participle (*-ed*)
a) *The issue interests the students.* *It is an **interesting** issue.*	c) *The issue interests the students.* *They are **interested** students.*
b) *The story amuses the children.* *It is an **amusing** story.*	d) *The story amuses the children.* *They are **amused** children.*

USE

- The present participle describes the effect that something has on someone's feelings (in ex. a, *an interesting issue*; in ex. b, *an amusing story*).
- On the contrary, the past participle describes people's feelings (in ex. c, *the interested students*; in ex. d, *the amused children*).
- Many examples can be made, as, in theory, every transitive verb can have both a present and a past participle form.

Verb	*-ing*	*-ed*
depress	*depressing*	*depressed*
disappoint	*disappointing*	*disappointed*
embarrass	*embarrassing*	*embarrassed*
exhaust	*exhausting*	*exhausted*
frighten	*frightening*	*frightened*
frustrate	*frustrating*	*frustrated*
tire	*tiring*	*tired*

Countable and uncountable nouns

USE

- **Countable nouns** are the names of things of which there can be one (singular) or more than one (plural).
  an apple, two apples, three apples
- **Uncountable nouns** have only a singular form. They can't be preceded by indefinite articles and have no plural form.
  bread, sugar, water
- Some nouns can be countable or uncountable according to their meaning:
  a light/ lights C; *light and darkness* U
  a crime C; *crime* (in general) U
  a business (a company) C; *business* U
  a chocolate C; *chocolate* U
  and also: *cold, force, glass, ice, iron, manner, sense, tea*
- Some countable nouns end in *-s*, but they must always be used with a singular verb form.
  news, billiards, maths
- Some nouns are only uncountable and are used with a singular verb form. It is advisable to study them in groups, in order to remember them more easily:

Groups of similar things:
accommodation, baggage, clothing, damage, equipment, food, fruit, furniture, garbage, jewelry, luggage, machinery, mail, make-up, money/ cash/change, scenery, spaghetti, traffic, etc.

Fluids:
blood, coffee, milk, oil, soup, tea, water, wine, etc.

Solids:
bread, butter, cheese, cotton, glass, gold, meat, paper, wood, etc.

Gases:
air, nitrogen, oxygen, pollution, smog, smoke, steam, etc.

Particles:
corn, dirt, dust, flour, grass, hair, rice, salt, sand, sugar, wheat, etc.

Abstractions:
beauty, confidence, courage, death, education, enjoyment, experience, fear, fun, happiness, health, help, honesty, hope, intelligence, justice, knowledge, laughter, luck, magic, peace, pity, pride, progress, recreation, relief, sleep, violence, wealth, etc.
- *advice, evidence, information, news, proof*, etc.
- *energy, time, space*, etc.
- *homework, housework, work*, etc.
- *grammar, slang, vocabulary*, etc.

Languages:
Arabic, Chinese, English, Japanese, etc.

Fields of study:
chemistry, history, literature, mathematics, psychology, etc.

Recreation:
baseball, bridge, chess, poker, soccer, tennis, etc.

General activities (*-ing* forms):
shopping, studying, swimming, travelling, walking, etc.

Natural phenomena:
darkness, electricity, fire, fog, gravity, heat, humidity, light, lightning, rain, snow, sunshine, thunder, weather, wind, etc.

Quantifiers

Uncountable nouns	Plural countable nouns
much (negative and interrogative sentences) *a lot of* (affirmative sentences)	*many* (negative and interrogative sentences) *a lot of* (affirmative sentences)
too much	*too many*
so much	*so many*
little	*few*
too little	*too few*
so little	*so few*
some, a little	*some, a few*
enough	*enough*
How much?	*How many?*

	one, two, three, etc.
	each, every
	several
lots of, plenty of	*lots of, plenty of*
most	*most*
all	*all*

- Countable and uncountable nouns can be preceded by nouns of containers or by nouns that define their quantity.

Containers	Quantity
a ***cup*** *of tea*	*a* ***pair*** *of jeans*
a ***glass*** *of coke*	*a* ***bar*** *of chocolate*
a ***bottle*** *of wine*	*a* ***piece*** *of cheese*
a ***carton*** *of milk*	*a* ***slice/loaf*** *of bread*
a ***bowl*** *of soup*	*a* ***litre*** *of water*
a ***tube*** *of mayonnaise*	*a* ***kilo*** *of sugar*
a ***jar*** *of jam*	***half a kilo*** *of meat*
a ***tin*** *of tuna*	*50* ***grams*** *of butter*
a ***can*** *of soda*	*a* ***dozen*** *eggs*
a ***packet*** *of crisps*	*a* ***pint*** *of milk*
a ***box*** *of cereal*	

» NOUNS WITH ONLY A PLURAL FORM

- Some nouns only have a plural form and therefore must always be used with a plural verb form and plural quantifiers. ➔ *trousers, clothes, scissors, glasses*
- When referring to 'one' or 'more than one' of this type of noun, another noun or a quantifier must be added. ➔ *a pair of trousers/glasses/scissors, too many clothes*

Too much, not enough, so much

So much	= in such a large amount *We have got* ***so much*** *food to eat that we can avoid going shopping for at least three days.*
Too much	= more than is needed or wanted *There is* ***too much*** *salt in this soup! I can't eat it.*
Not enough	= insufficient, less than is needed or wanted *We have****n't*** *got* ***enough*** *food for the party. You should buy some more.*

Question tags

USE

- A question tag is a question added at the end of a sentence which asks for agreement or confirmation.
- The subject of the tag is always a pronoun and the verb used is always the auxiliary verb or the verb *be* when it is the main verb in the preceding clause.
  You have *got two brothers,* ***haven't you****?*
  Sally isn't *a nice girl,* ***is she****?*
- Contraction is obligatory in negative question tags.
  It's a hot day, ***isn't it****?* NOT *It's a hot day,* ~~*is not it*~~*?*

FORM

Affirmative statement	Negative tag
You are Tom,	***aren't you****?*
She has been in London,	***hasn't she****?*
I'm late,	***aren't I****?* (irregular form)

- In these cases an affirmative answer is expected:
  'You like coffee, don't you?' 'Yes, I do.'

Negative statement	Affirmative tag
You don't like skiing,	***do you****?*
The children hadn't been watching TV,	***had they****?*
She wouldn't have gone away,	***would she****?*

- In these cases a negative answer is expected.
  'You don't like beer, do you?' 'No, I don't.'

» IRREGULAR QUESTION TAGS

Let's *go to the disco,*	***shall we****?*
Let's not *go to the disco,*	***shall we****?*
Stop *talking,*	***will you****?*
Don't forget,	***will you****?*
Please sit, / Do sit,	***won't you****?*
That/This isn't your car,	*is* ***it****?*
Those/These *aren't your parents,*	*are* ***they****?*
There *is some milk,*	*isn't* ***there****?*

neither, never, no (adjective), *nothing, none, no one, nobody, hardly, hardly ever, seldom,* etc.	→	statement is negative and is followed by an affirmative tag
Nothing *is wrong,*		***is it****?*

subject: *anyone, anybody, no, no one, nobody, none, neither,* etc.	→	subject of the tag: *they*
***Neither** of them came,*		*did **they**?*

subject: *everyone, everybody, someone, somebody,* etc.	→	subject of the tag: *they*
***Someone** recognised you,*		*didn't **they?***

» INTONATION

Rising	The speaker is looking for a real answer.
Ann is Australian,	↗ *isn't she?*
Falling	The speaker is expressing an idea which doesn't need any confirmation. Only agreement is expected.
The weather is lovely today,	↘ *isn't it?*

Participles

PRESENT PARTICIPLE

- It is the *-ing* form of the verb.
- It can replace a relative pronoun + verb when the verb form is active.
- It can be used when the verb in the original clause is in the continuous tense.
  *The man **who is talking** to John is from Canada. = The man **talking** to John is from Canada.*
- It can be used when the verb in the original clause expresses a habitual action.
  *English has an alphabet **that consists** of 26 letters. = English has an alphabet **consisting** of 26 letters.*

PAST PARTICIPLE

- For regular verbs it is the *-ed* form but there are also many irregular verbs. (☞ See irregular verbs list on pages 191-193)
- It can replace a relative pronoun + verb when the verb form is passive.
  *The ideas **which are presented** in that book are interesting. = The ideas **presented** in that book are interesting.*

» STRUCTURE

- A participle belongs to the noun/pronoun preceding it.
  *Tom, **horrified** by the accident, immediately called for an ambulance.*
- Only a main verb can separate a participle from its noun/pronoun.
  *Bob and Sarah entered the hall, **followed** by their children.*
- If no noun/pronoun precedes the participle, this is considered to belong to the subject of the following main verb.
  ***Choosing** his words with care, the son told his mother the truth.*

Irregular verbs

* The verbs marked with an asterisk also have a regular form; however, it is not commonly used.

Infinitive	Past simple	Past participle	Italian
to arise	arose	arisen	*sorgere*
to awake*	awoke	awoken	*svegliare, svegliarsi*
to be	was, were	been	*essere*
to bear	bore	born / borne	*portare, sopportare, generare*
to beat	beat	beaten / beat	*colpire, sbattere, sconfiggere*
to become	became	become	*diventare*
to begin	began	begun	*iniziare*
to bend	bent	bent	*piegare, piegarsi*
to bet*	bet	bet	*scommettere*
to bind	bound	bound	*legare, rilegare*
to bite	bit	bitten	*mordere*
to bleed	bled	bled	*sanguinare*
to blow	blew	blown	*soffiare*
to break	broke	broken	*rompere, rompersi*
to breed	bred	bred	*allevare, generare*
to bring	brought	brought	*portare*
to broadcast*	broadcast	broadcast	*trasmettere (radio, TV)*
to build	built	built	*costruire*
to burn*	burnt	burnt	*bruciare*
to burst	burst	burst	*scoppiare*
to buy	bought	bought	*comprare*
to cast	cast	cast	*gettare, fondere*
to catch	caught	caught	*prendere, acchiappare*
to choose	chose	chosen	*scegliere*
to come	came	come	*venire*
to cost	cost	cost	*costare*
to creep	crept	crept	*strisciare*
to cut	cut	cut	*tagliare*
to deal	dealt	dealt	*trattare*
to dig	dug	dug	*scavare*
to do	did	done	*fare*
to draw	drew	drawn	*disegnare, tirare*
to dream*	dreamt	dreamt	*sognare*
to drink	drank	drunk	*bere*
to drive	drove	driven	*guidare*
to dwell	dwelt	dwelt	*abitare*
to eat	ate	eaten	*mangiare*

Infinitive	Past simple	Past participle	Italian
to fall	fell	fallen	*cadere*
to feed	fed	fed	*nutrire*
to feel	felt	felt	*sentire, sentirsi*
to fight	fought	fought	*combattere*
to find	found	found	*trovare*
to flee	fled	fled	*fuggire*
to fling	flung	flung	*scagliare*
to fly	flew	flown	*volare*
to forbid	forbade	forbidden	*proibire*
to forecast	forecast	forecast	*prevedere, predire*
to foresee	foresaw	foreseen	*prevedere*
to forget	forgot	forgotten	*dimenticare*
to forgive	forgave	forgiven	*perdonare*
to freeze	froze	frozen	*gelare, congelare*
to get	got	got	*ottenere, diventare*
to give	gave	given	*dare*
to go	went	gone	*andare*
to grind	ground	ground	*macinare, tritare*
to grow	grew	grown	*crescere*
to hang	hung	hung	*appendere*
to have	had	had	*avere*
to hear	heard	heard	*udire*
to hide	hid	hidden	*nascondere*
to hit	hit	hit	*picchiare, colpire*
to hold	held	held	*tenere, trattenere*
to hurt	hurt	hurt	*ferire, fare del male*
to keep	kept	kept	*tenere, conservare*
to kneel*	knelt	knelt	*inginocchiarsi*
to knit*	knit	knit	*lavorare a maglia*
to know	knew	known	*conoscere, sapere*
to lay	laid	laid	*deporre, posare*
to lead	led	led	*condurre, guidare*
to lean*	leant	leant	*appoggiare, appoggiarsi*
to leap*	leapt	leapt	*saltare*
to learn*	learnt	learnt	*imparare*
to leave	left	left	*partire, lasciare*
to lend	lent	lent	*prestare*
to let	let	let	*lasciare, permettersi*
to lie	lay	lain	*trovarsi, giacere*
to light*	lit	lit	*illuminare, accendere*
to lose	lost	lost	*perdere*

Infinitive	Past simple	Past participle	Italian
to make	made	made	*fare*
to mean	meant	meant	*significare, intendere*
to meet	met	met	*incontrare, conoscere per la prima volta*
to mislay	mislaid	mislaid	*mettere fuori posto*
to mislead	misled	misled	*fuorviare, traviare*
to misread	misread	misread	*leggere erroneamente*
to misspell*	misspelt	misspelt	*sbagliare l'ortografia*
to mistake	mistook	mistaken	*sbagliare, confondere*
to misunderstand	misunderstood	misunderstood	*fraintendere*
to miswrite	miswrote	miswritten	*scrivere scorrettamente*
to overcome	overcame	overcome	*superare, sopraffare*
to overeat	overate	overeaten	*mangiare troppo*
to overhang	overhung	overhung	*sovrastare*
to overhear	overheard	overheard	*udire per caso*
to oversleep	overslept	overslept	*dormire troppo*
to overtake	overtook	overtaken	*sorpassare*
to overwrite	overwrote	overwritten	*sovrascrivere*
to partake	partook	partaken	*prendere parte*
to pay	paid	paid	*pagare*
to plead*	pled	pled	*perorare, patrocinare*
to prepay	prepaid	prepaid	*prepagare*
to prove*	proved	proven	*provare, dimostrare*
to put	put	put	*mettere*
to read	read	read	*leggere*
to remake	remade	remade	*rifare*
to reread	reread	reread	*rileggere*
to reset	reset	reset	*regolare, aggiustare*
to retell	retold	retold	*ridire*
to rid	rid	rid	*liberare, sbarazzare*
to ride	rode	ridden	*cavalcare*
to ring	rang	rung	*suonare, squillare*
to rise	rose	risen	*sorgere, alzarsi*
to run	ran	run	*correre*
to saw*	sawed	sawn	*segare*
to say	said	said	*dire*
to see	saw	seen	*vedere*
to seek	sought	sought	*cercare*
to sell	sold	sold	*vendere*
to send	sent	sent	*spedire*
to set	set	set	*porre, tramontare*

Infinitive	Past simple	Past participle	Italian
to sew*	sewed	sewn	*cucire*
to shake	shook	shaken	*tremare, scuotere*
to shave*	shaved	shaven	*radere*
to shed	shed	shed	*versare, spargere*
to shine	shone	shone	*splendere, brillare*
to shoot	shot	shot	*sparare, germogliare*
to show	showed	shown	*mostrare*
to shrink	shrank	shrunk	*restringersi*
to shut	shut	shut	*chiudere*
to sing	sang	sung	*cantare*
to sink	sank	sunk	*affondare, sprofondare*
to sit	sat	sat	*sedersi*
to sleep	slept	slept	*dormire*
to slide	slid	slid	*scorrere, scivolare*
to smell*	smelt	smelt	*odorare, avere odore*
to sow	sowed	sown	*seminare*
to speak	spoke	spoken	*parlare*
to speed	sped	sped	*affrettare*
to spell*	spelt	spelt	*compitare*
to spend	spent	spent	*spendere, trascorrere*
to spill*	spilt	spilt	*versare, spandere*
to spit	spit / spat	spit / spat	*sputare*
to split	split	split	*spaccare, dividersi*
to spoil*	spoilt	spoilt	*rovinare, viziare*
to spread	spread	spread	*diffondere, diffondersi*
to spring	sprang	sprung	*scaturire, saltare*
to stand	stood	stood	*stare in piedi*
to steal	stole	stolen	*rubare*
to stick	stuck	stuck	*attaccare, attaccarsi*
to sting	stung	stung	*pungere (di insetti)*
to stink	stank	stunk	*puzzare*
to stride	strode	stridden	*camminare a lunghi passi*
to strike	struck	struck	*battere, colpire*
to strive*	strove	striven	*sforzarsi, lottare*
to swear	swore	sworn	*giurare, imprecare*
to sweat*	sweat	sweat	*sudare*
to sweep	swept	swept	*spazzare, scopare*
to swell	swelled	swollen	*gonfiare*
to swim	swam	swum	*nuotare*
to swing	swung	swung	*dondolare, oscillare*

Infinitive	Past simple	Past participle	Italian
to take	took	taken	*prendere, portare*
to teach	taught	taught	*insegnare*
to tear	tore	torn	*lacerare, strappare*
to tell	told	told	*dire, raccontare*
to think	thought	thought	*pensare*
to throw	threw	thrown	*gettare, buttare*
to thrust	thrust	thrust	*spingere, ficcare*
to tread	trod	trodden	*calpestare*
to undergo	underwent	undergone	*subire, sopportare*
to understand	understood	understood	*capire*
to undertake	undertook	undertaken	*intraprendere*
to underwrite	underwrote	underwritten	*sottoscrivere, assicurare*
to upset	upset	upset	*ribaltare, turbare*
to wake*	woke	woken	*svegliare, svegliarsi*
to wear	wore	worn	*indossare, logorare*
to weave	wove	woven	*tessere*
to wed*	wed	wed	*unire in matrimonio*
to weep	wept	wept	*piangere*
to wet	wet	wet	*bagnare, inzuppare*
to win	won	won	*vincere*
to wind	wound	wound	*avvolgere, serpeggiare*
to withdraw	withdrew	withdrawn	*ritirare, prelevare*
to wring	wrung	wrung	*torcere*
to write	wrote	written	*scrivere*

Speaking reference

Part 1

Greetings and salutations

Hello.
Good morning/afternoon.
How do you do?
Nice to meet you.
Pleased to have met you.
Thank you.
Goodbye.

Giving personal information

I come from ...
I live ... / I've always lived ...
There are (three) of us in my family. There is me, ...
My father/mother is a ...
What I like about my house is ...
I'm in the (third) year of High School ...
I like doing ... , but I don't like ...
In the future, I think I will ... but I haven't decided yet.
My ambitions are ...

Talking about personal tastes

I really/quite like ...
I much/personally prefer ...
I don't particularly like ...
I (really) can't stand ...
My favourite (things/activities) are ...
I think ... is the best because ...
That's what I like/prefer because ...
If I could choose, ...

Asking about personal tastes

Do you like ... ?
What do you think about ... ?
What do you like/dislike about ... ?

Giving a physical description

tall, short, attractive, beautiful, blonde/blond, dark-haired, with glasses, with a beard, pale, tanned, slim, plump, thin, young-looking, serious, sunny, smart, well-dressed, casual, athletic

Describing personality

stubborn, generous, tense, childish, impulsive, helpful, honest, gentle, fun, funny, polite, rude, unbearable, arrogant, friendly, sociable, sensible, miserable, mean, fussy, serious, sincere, nasty, tough, shy

Part 2

Describing the pictures

To begin with ...
First of all, ...
Firstly, ...
In this photo, I can see ...
There are several ...
In the first/second photo I can see ...
On the right/left of the picture ...
In the centre of the picture ...
In the background there are ...
I can't quite make out ... , but I think ...

Comparing the pictures

In this picture ... whereas in that one ...
A key difference is that ...
There are more ... in this one than ...
On the one hand, ... on the other hand, ...
Another difference might be ...
While in this picture ... , in that picture ...

Talking about emotion in pictures

In this picture, from the expressions on the people's faces, I can tell they are feeling (happy/sad/excited/frightened) ...
If it were me in that particular situation, I would be feeling ...
We can't see the people's faces, but I am sure they must be feeling ...
In the picture the (boy/girl) is (smiling/grinning/laughing), so (he/she) must be feeling (happy).
In this picture the (man/woman) is looking (serious/sad/upset), so I think (he/she) is feeling (apprehensive/tense/nervous).

Giving your opinion

I think ...
I prefer ... because ...
The ... is better/worse because ...
Most people would agree that ...
Although I can see the benefits of ... , I still consider ... to be more ...
Life would probably be (more difficult/easier) with/if ...
I can't imagine what it must be/have been like to live without ...
There are so many advantages, like/for example ...
I would go for ...
I'm not 100% sure but ...
I would definitely rather ...

Looking at the pictures

1 the background: where you think it is – the country, town, inside, outside, forest, mountains, type of room or office or internal space, time of year, weather, time of day.

2 atmosphere of the picture: dominant colours, dominant expressions, type of activity, number of people or lack of people, how you think the people in the picture look.

3 detail: description of people – clothes, age, expression, possible feelings, attitude to the rest of the picture.

4 personal reaction to picture: I think ... / I consider ... / I would.... / I wouldn't ...

5 conclusion: response to specific task with motivations.

Part 3 & Part 4

Describing and Comparing the options

The first option is interesting because it ...

I like the idea of the second option because ...

The third option can be done in ...

Everyone would enjoy the forth option because ...

What do you think about option five? Don't you think that ... ?

The idea of option ... is certainly more interesting/challenging/ difficult than that of option ...

Things to think about

Read the question carefully before you begin to look at the different options.

Try to find something to say about all the different options before you compare them.

Encourage your partner to participate.

Relate the options to the target of the central question.

Use personal experience where relevant.

Giving your opinions

If you ask me, ...

It seems to me that ...

In my opinion ...

I think that ...

I would also like to say ...

I'd like to make a further point ...

I think the possible problems with this idea are ...

The advantages of this type of solution are ... , but there are also disadvantages, like ...

All things considered, perhaps the best/worst ...

Agreeing

Of course.

I absolutely agree.

Exactly!

That's an excellent point!

Disagreeing

I'm afraid I disagree/don't agree ...

You're right/That's a good point, but ...

That's not how I see it ...

Giving reasons or examples

because ... / as ... / due to ...

such as ... / for example ... / like ...

Giving examples from your own experience

I have seen this type of solution ...

I remember once (seeing/reading) about ... (in a newspaper/on the Internet).

Once I was near/tried ...

Taking the discussion forward

On the other hand, ...

Don't you think ... ?

What's more ...

Positive comments

This kind of (activity/event) is (interesting/appealing). It encourages people to ...

The people doing (the event/game/sport) always look as if they are (enjoying themselves/happy/having fun).

The (people/children) usually find this ... (interesting/ stimulating).

Negative comments

This kind of (activity/event) may be too (difficult to organise/ expensive/complicated).

The people don't normally enjoy it.

People doing this usually get (rather bored/quite fed up).

I think it might be an activity that is more suitable for (younger/older) people.

I think most people find it (difficult/tiring/boring).

Concluding

So, which should we choose?

To sum up ...

We have thought about all the various options, I therefore think we should choose ...

For me, considering all we've said, the choice would be these options ...

Writing reference

Essay

Example question

In your English class you have been talking about part-time jobs for teenagers. Now your teacher has asked you to write an essay for homework.

Write your essay in **140–190** words using all the notes and giving reasons for your point of view.

Should teenagers have a part-time job?

Notes

Write about:

1 gaining experience in the working world
2 concentrating on their studies
3 .... (your own idea)

Essay

How to do it	Layout tips	Language tips

Refer to the question or task in the first paragraph.

Introduce the subject and outline the main arguments related to it.

Essays are formal pieces of writing and need to be expressed in a formal style.

Nowadays more and more people agree that teenagers should have part-time jobs, which could give teenagers a sense of responsibility and increase their self-esteem. However, some people think that teenagers should not work, so they can just concentrate on their schoolwork.

Use discourse markers to make clear how your different points are related.

Devote a paragraph each to the arguments for and against. The second paragraph should provide details in support of one side of the argument.

Briefly introduce both sides of the argument.

There is no doubt that teenagers have quite a few interests and hobbies, but the question is whether – besides relaxing and enjoying themselves – they could devote a few spare hours to a part-time job. It could help them understand about life in the real world. They could also learn new skills and earn a little money for their extra needs.

Use discursive words to connect ideas and sentences.

The third paragraph should present the other side of the argument.

A good essay includes clearly stated opinions supported by examples and convincing reasons.

Of course, studying is important: they need time to concentrate on their studies, and to get good marks and therefore improve their chances of going to university and finding a well-paid job in the future. Teenagers also need time to spend with friends, doing sports or recreational activities in order to grow in a healthy and balanced way.

In the concluding paragraph express your own opinion without repeating concepts already expressed.

In conclusion, I think that time is precious and should be used well. That is why I am always eager to learn and experience new things, even if this may take some effort.

The conclusion should begin with a clear indication like *in conclusion, finally, for all these reasons.*

Useful language
Today ... / These days ...
Many people believe ... / It is often said ... / Some people think ...
On the one hand, ... on the other hand ...
but, so, although, even so, however, nevertheless, in spite of this ...
One good example ... / For instance ...
I think ... / I feel ... / It seems to me ... / It is my opinion that ...

Article

Example question

You have seen this announcement in your school magazine.

> Do you agree that people need places to meet and have fun? Write and tell us what an ideal recreational centre should include.
> The most interesting article will be published in our next issue.

How to do it	Layout tips	Language tips
Think of a title that will get the reader's attention.	**A place for everyone**	
	The first paragraph should involve the readers in some way. Address them directly.	
Start your article in an attention-grabbing way. A question or a strong statement can be appropriate.	**Have you ever thought about a place where young people can spend time together, having fun and sharing experiences? In our town a new recreational centre is going to be built, and it will offer free-time opportunities for all.**	Use an informal, lively style.
	Build on the interest you have raised in the first paragraph.	
	There have been lots of requests from families with young children. Moreover, a safe place for teenagers is really needed if we want to prevent social issues such as drugs, violence and vandalism.	Use suitable linking words like *moreover*, *furthermore*, etc.
	Put each topic in a separate paragraph.	
	Ideally, it will be divided into different areas. The first will be dedicated to children, where they can play, take part in different labs and listen to stories. On the second floor, there will be a café with books and magazines, so adults and young people can have an espresso while reading their favourite books! Furthermore, there will be a Wi-Fi area where both teenagers and adults can use the Internet. Lastly, an American bar will offer 'happy hours' and themed dinners.	Use expressions like *first*, *second* and *lastly* to introduce different ideas.
Finish the article in an interesting way. It could be thought-provoking, ironic or humorous.	**Whatever you are looking for in our small town, I am sure our new recreational centre will make a difference and improve our lifestyle.**	Use the first-person singular or plural to make the article personal and involve the reader.
	I think you'll agree it is high time we got a safe and pleasant place where people of all ages can spend time, meet up with friends and have new, interesting experiences.	

Useful language

Have you ever … ? / Have you heard about … ? / … , don't you think?
First of all, … / To start off … / For starters …
However, … / Although … / Even though …
Apart from that … / Still, …
One more thing …
On the one hand … , on the other hand …
Thus … / Therefore … / So …
I think … / If you ask me, … / Personally, …

Informal email/letter

Example question
You have received a letter from an English pen friend. Write your letter in 140–190 words.

Hi Cinzia, I'm coming to visit you! How are you? How's school? Do you remember that I decided to come to your town for the film festival? Do you know what's on? Can you show me round your town? Can you suggest a cheap place to stay and will I be able to meet your friends? Looking forward to seeing your soon. Joanne

How to do it	Layout tips	Language tips
OPENING PARAGRAPH Begin by saying something about the letter you have received.	Hi Joanne,	Use the name of the person who sent you the letter.
React to the sender's news or questions.	Thanks so much for your letter. It's great to know you are coming! I'm fine, but always busy with school and extra activities like my drama course.	Use colloquial expressions and contractions.
	Divide what you want to say into different topics in separate paragraphs.	
BODY OF THE EMAIL Follow the order of the questions in the letter. In this case: first, say how you are; then, say you are happy she is coming; and finally, give information about the festival.	Of course I remember you decided to come to my town for the festival. I'm thrilled that we are going to spend time together! As for the festival, it seems that there will be an extended version of the last Harry Potter movie. The actors will be welcoming their fans from all over Europe. That means you'll be given a chance to meet your hero!	Use exclamation marks when you want to emphasise your statements. Keep the language informal. Invent details if/when necessary.
	Leave a space between paragraphs. This will help make the layout clearer.	
Make sure you've included all the information required.	I'll show you my beautiful town. Every Saturday there's a street market where you can buy souvenirs. And, if you need a place to stay, there's a good, comfortable youth hostel in the centre. Also, if you need a little time to relax, I'll be happy to take you to our school swimming pool, where you can meet my friends. They can't wait!	Use linking words appropriately.
CLOSING PARAGRAPH Make an excuse to stop writing. Express your hope to receive an answer.	It's time to go now! I'm late for my drama course. I hope to hear from you soon. All the best, Cinzia	Finish with an informal salutation.

Useful language

Dear (name), / Hi!
How are you? / How's it going?
Glad to hear from you.
Thanks for writing!

That's good news about ... / It's nice to hear ....
What do you think about ...? / How about ...?

Got to go. / Have to run.
Let me know! / Can't wait to hear from you! / Write soon.
Cheers! / Lots of love, (name)

Formal letter/email

Example question

Recently you have been to a lecture about multi-tasking activities. Unfortunately, there were a number of problems with the organisation of the event. Write to the office responsible for the services explaining the situation and asking them for a refund of the enrolment fee.

How to do it	Layout tips	Language tips
Begin a formal letter with: • *Dear Sir or Madam* if you don't know the person's name or whether the person is a man or a woman; • otherwise use *Dear Mr/Mrs/Miss/Ms*. Use the person's title and surname. Say why you are writing and state the subject clearly.	Dear Sir or Madam, I am writing to complain about the lecture on multi-tasking activities I attended last month. I regret to inform you that the services and facilities offered were totally unsatisfactory. State the main complaint briefly in your first paragraph then organise the information in a clear and logical way in the main paragraphs of your letter.	Keep the language formal. Don't use contractions, colloquial expressions or phrasal verbs. Instead of direct questions, use conditionals.
Expand on your main complaint, giving further details.	First of all, at the bus station none of the promised buses were available. They were all late (more than one hour later than the scheduled time!) and then there was not enough room. Although this transportation service was included in the enrolment fee, I had to pay extra for a taxi in order to get to the lecture on time. In addition to this, just as the lecture was due to begin, we were informed that the main lecturer would be absent due to illness. Owing to this inconvenience, the lunch break lasted three hours instead of one. Furthermore, no extra reading material was distributed because the photocopying machines were out of order due to some electrical problems.	Use linking expressions like: *firstly, furthermore, in addition to this.*
	Naturally, I was extremely disappointed with this experience and with your company, although I would still be interested in taking part in future lectures about multi-tasking activities.	Be polite. Avoid being too familiar. Use conditionals to make your requests.
Say clearly how you expect the reader to respond to your complaint.	I would be grateful if you could take into consideration the possibility of a full refund for the cost of the enrolment fee.	
Finish your letter with: • *Yours faithfully*, if you started with *Dear Sir or Madam*; • *Yours sincerely*, if you started with the person's name.	I look forward to hearing from you. Yours faithfully, *Michael Richardson* Michael Richardson	

Useful language

Dear Sirs, / Dear Sir or Madame, / Dear (title + surname),
I'm writing to / with regard to / in order to ...
First, ... / To begin with ... / I would like to start by ...
Another point ... , / Secondly, / Furthermore ...
As you can imagine ... / I'm sure you will agree ...
Could you please ... ? / Would you kindly ... ? / If you don't mind ...
Thank you for your time / consideration.
Please let me know as soon as possible. / I look forward to your reply.
Yours faithfully, / Yours sincerely,

Report

Example question

You have been asked to find out if low-fat foods are as healthy as they claim to be. Write a report with your recommendations.

How to do it	Layout tips	Language tips
	Use clear headings to help the reader see how the report is organised. Give the report a title. Begin with a clear introduction.	
State the purpose of the report and say where you got the information from.		Use formal vocabulary and don't use contractions.

ARE LOW-FAT FOODS HEALTHY?

Introduction

This report is intended to analyse whether low-fat foods can be considered a healthy alternative in our diet. First of all, I took a look at what really makes people overweight. These first conclusions were reached by interviewing people at the supermarket.

Give each section in the report its own paragraph. Use numbers or bullets to make them stand out.

The main body of the report clearly states the points you want to raise.

Use impersonal language, like the passive form.

Findings

After analysing the answers from numerous interviews, it was found that:

1. For most people who are not fit or are gaining a lot of weight, there are usually some reasons like: they are not active enough; they are eating more calories than they burn.
2. People generally think that low-fat foods are healthier than other foods and so they consume more of them. Yet, often this leads to overeating and being overweight.
3. In some low-fat products fat is taken out, but the amount of sugar can be raised or the amounts of vitamins and minerals can be changed. Thus, these products can be more rather than less fattening.

In your conclusion refer to the points made and to the title of the report. Conclude with a personal recommendation.

Conclusion

Nowadays there are a lot of different kinds of diet plans which include low-fat foods, but these are not necessarily what they claim to be. To be healthy, all we need to have is an active lifestyle and a well-balanced diet.

Useful language

The aim/purpose of this report ...
Having looked at the information, ...
The information shows that ...
In the first place, ... secondly,/thirdly, ...
It seems clear that ...
In conclusion, it is clear that ...
I would therefore recommend ...

Review

Example question

Do you like technology? If so, write us a review of a technology exhibition you have been to recently. Include information about the place, people and products. Give both positive and negative aspects of your experience and say whether you would recommend it to others.

How to do it	Layout tips	Language tips
	State the name of the event or the name of the product with some key information at the start of the review.	
The review gives information to the reader in order to help him decide whether to try something or not.		Use a light-hearted style to capture the reader's attention.
Introduce the topic of the review in the first paragraph.	Put each topic in a separate paragraph.	Be careful about punctuation. Remember to use commas in lists.
You can give positive and negative opinions.		Use linking words and phrases to connect ideas and sentences.
Finish with a final recommendation and a personal opinion.		

Last week we went to the New Millennium Exhibition in Milan. It was crowded and most of the people were teenagers between the ages of fifteen and seventeen with their new smartphones. The exhibition was dedicated to the new generation of smartphones and there were some experts in the field who showed us the new services included in the smartphone software.

The very first impression I got there was that all those teens were addicted to their phones; in fact, they had their devices switched on all the time. They used the phone during meal times, in the toilets, at the bar, just everywhere! Their main activities were phone calls and texts. They kept on sending messages, listening to music, taking photos, playing games and visiting social networks.

Apart from this, I found the new smartphones extremely attractive, elegant and colourful. Their touchscreens were wide and bright and easy to use. Commands could also be given vocally and not only by touching the screens!

The fair was a pleasant experience overall, but it also confirmed my opinion of smartphones. Although I enjoy them for the services they offer, I find them really easy to get addicted to. For this reason, I would suggest using this technology only where it improves the quality of our lifestyles, and I wouldn't encourage anyone to have an unlimited dose of it.

Useful language

I was impressed by …
I found the … (disappointing/attractive).
… would appeal to …
Unfortunately …
I would highly recommend …
I think … is (overvalued/overrated).
Don't buy/read/go to see … it isn't worth it!

Story

Example question

An international magazine you subscribe to is running a short story competition. You have decided to enter it. The rules say that the story must begin with the following sentence:

It was the last week of July, and it was really hot in Los Angeles.

How to do it	Layout tips	Language tips
	Give your story a title.	
	The girl of my dreams	
	The first paragraph should involve the readers in some way. Create an atmosphere of suspense or expectation.	
Start with the given sentence without changing it.	*It was the last week of July, and it was really hot in Los Angeles. After a difficult year in his computer course, Josh was looking forward to relaxing.*	Use PAST tenses: past continuous for the background and simple past for actions or events. Introduce the characters.
Describe the situation with some details to help the reader imagine it. Create a mysterious atmosphere by referring to events without explaining immediately what they are.	*He decided to go for a walk on the beach surrounded by kids playing football. He knew he shouldn't think about it. It had happened two weeks earlier and he could not get it out of his mind. The sun was shining and the temperature was incredibly high. Nevertheless, Josh was cold. He could not stop thinking about it.*	Use time expressions to make the story clear and linear. Use adverbs to enrich your language. Remember linking words, too.
	Divide the story into clear paragraphs: one for the background and introduction, two for the development and one for the conclusion.	
Give shape to the interest you have raised in the first paragraph and think of a surprising ending.	*His last dance with that girl had been a dream. She was so beautiful and sweet, and she was surprisingly funny. They had danced and laughed for two hours and then she had disappeared giving neither a name nor a telephone number. Josh couldn't stop thinking about her. What could he do now? Suddenly a sweet voice behind him called his name...*	Use questions to lighten up your story and involve the reader.
	In the last paragraph bring your story to an end.	
Refer back to the title sentence to give a feeling of completeness.	*There she was! How did she know his name? Josh couldn't believe his eyes! He was so happy and excited that his heart felt as if it were going to explode! The girl asked Josh to follow her, but as soon as he started getting closer, she turned back and disappeared. Josh woke up and realised he was just dreaming. He looked out at the steaming heat of the city and wondered if he would ever see that lovely girl again.*	Use a neutral style.

Useful language

At first ... / It all began ... / In the beginning ...
After that ... / Then ... / Some time later ... / Next ...
It was totally (unexpected/sudden/dramatic) ...
What finally happened ... / In the end ... / Eventually ...

Break

Phrasal verbs are verbs which change their meaning in some way by adding a **preposition**, or an **adverb**, or **both**.

- The meaning of a phrasal verb can be a combination of the meanings of its separate parts:
  Sit down! ***Come in!***
- In other cases, it has a completely different meaning:
  *He's **given up** smoking.* ➔ *He's stopped smoking.*
- With **transitive phrasal verbs**, the object usually comes after the preposition or between the verb and the preposition:
  *Can you **look up** this word in the dictionary?*
  *Can you **look** this word **up** in the dictionary?*
- If the object is a pronoun (*it/ them/ me/ him*, etc.), it can only go before the preposition:
  *Can you **look** it **up** in the dictionary?*
- With **intransitive phrasal verbs**, the verb cannot be separated from the preposition:
  *I'm **looking for** a new job.*
  *I'm **looking for** it.*
- When the phrasal verb is made up of a preposition and an adverb, the three parts cannot be separated:
  *I'm **looking forward to** my holidays.*

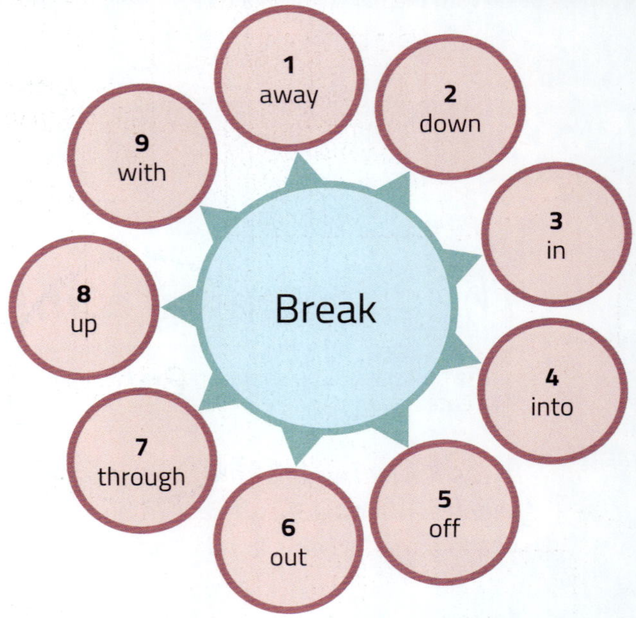

1 **MATCH** the phrasal verbs with *break* in the diagram to their definitions.

A ☐ force entry (into a building)
B ☐ start abruptly, appear suddenly, escape from prison
C ☐ stop suddenly
D ☐ end, disperse
E ☐ overcome obstacles
F ☐ quarrel, separate
G ☐ run away, escape
H ☐ interrupt, enter forcibly
I ☐ fail, collapse, cry

2 **CHOOSE** the correct preposition/adverb to complete the sentences.

1 They got home late because their car broke ... on their way back.
A off B down C in

2 Jean decided to break ... with Tom because he had lied to her.
A up B into C away

3 The student broke ... when he heard he had failed the test.
A up B off C down

4 An epidemic of cholera broke ... after the earthquake.
A through B off C out

5 A dangerous criminal broke ... of the high-security jail last night.
A out B in C with

6 The thieves broke ... through the back door.
A out B in C away

7 He was able to break ... all the obstacles.
A through B up C away

8 The Prime Minister broke ... during her speech.
A away B out C down

3 **FILL** the gaps using phrasal verbs with *break* in the correct form.

1 The USA .... all commercial transactions with North Korea.
2 Someone .... our school last night and burnt all the tests.
3 My granny .... with her husband when she was 80!
4 The lift .... so he had to walk up the stairs.
5 Sean and Viola .... last Saturday. We all were so shocked!
6 The European Union is threatening .... trade links with the UK.
7 The robbers who were trying .... the shop were stopped by the police.
8 The police .... the crowd after the riots.
9 He was driving so fast that he .... the barrier of the car park.
10 They .... of prison by digging a tunnel out of their cell.

2 Bring

Bring

- **back** return, restore, revive
- **down** lower in position of power, demolish
- **forth** give birth to sth
- **forward** anticipate the time or date of an event, state an argument or proposal
- **around/round** persuade, make sb recover consciousness
- **in** introduce sth new, invite sb to do a job, earn money
- **along** take sth or sb with you
- **about** cause, make sth happen
- **up** look after a child until he is an adult, introduce a particular subject into conversation
- **out** produce and put on sale, cause to show a feeling or behaviour

1 **CHOOSE** the correct preposition/adverb to complete the sentences.

1 Our favourite band is bringing ... a new album next month.
A about **B** down **C** out **D** in

2 I think the new government will bring ... new taxes.
A in **B** forward **C** up **D** down

3 In his speech, he brought ... new challenging arguments.
A out **B** back **C** around **D** forward

4 She was brought ... on a farm, so she doesn't like living in town.
A along **B** up **C** down **D** around

5 The doctor has just brought ... his patient by heart massage.
A out **B** around **C** in **D** up

6 The World Wide Web has brought ... big changes in people's lives.
A down **B** along **C** about **D** forward

7 Listening to this song brings ... many happy memories.
A up **B** forward **C** in **D** back

8 Come to dinner and bring ... a friend!
A along **B** around **C** forth **D** in

9 She fell asleep wondering what the following day would bring ... .
A forth **B** out **C** around **D** up

10 The Prime Minister was brought ... by a serious scandal.
A up **B** forth **C** down **D** in

2 **REWRITE** the underlined parts of the sentences using phrasal verbs with *bring*.

1 I would like the new government to introduce new laws to guarantee civil rights.

2 My parents educated me to be tolerant and respect the weak.

3 Looking at these photographs has made me remember my childhood.

4 They had planned the meeting for the following week but they had to reschedule it for tomorrow.

5 Fiona takes her dog with her whenever she comes to see us.

6 I easily persuaded my daughter to talk about her school problems.

7 I wish they would reduce the price of petrol.

8 The painter's imagination gave birth to the image of the beach at dawn.

9 The new project will produce a considerable amount of money for the business.

10 Her new job is revealing her inner strengths.

Come

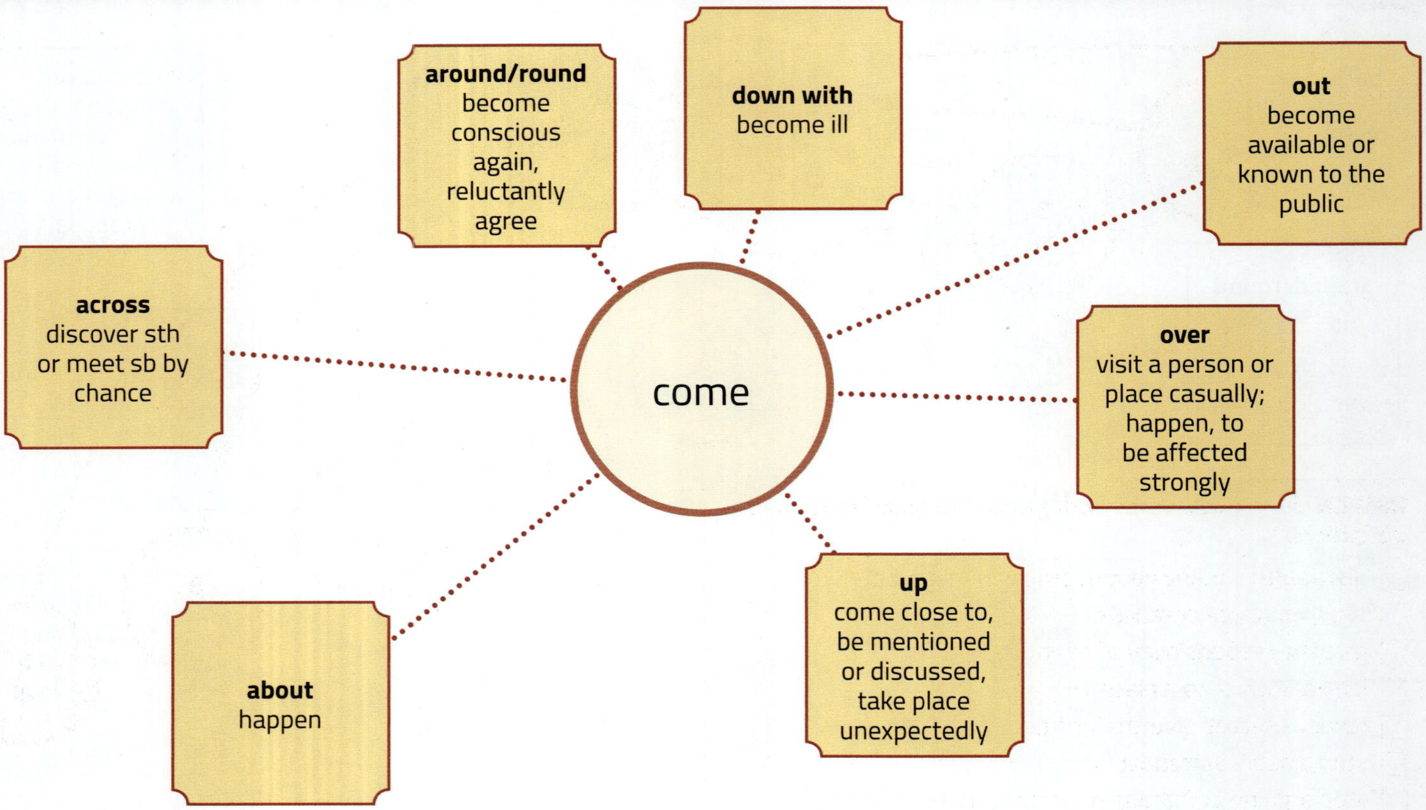

1 **CHOOSE** the correct preposition/adverb to complete the sentences.

1 'We lost everybody's email address!' 'How did that come ...?'
A out B across C up D about

2 I hope I come ... my new neighbours soon. I'd like to get to know them.
A across B around C out D over

3 Sean and his wife came ... a terrible cold.
A up B down with C around D out

4 Most magazines come ... every month.
A round B over C out D across

5 My daughter doesn't want to spend a month in New York, but I think she will come ... to this idea eventually.
A about B round C over D down with

6 Several interesting topics came ... at yesterday's meeting.
A over B around C across D up

7 Why doesn't Tom come ... for dinner?
A over B about C up D round

2 **FILL** the gaps using phrasal verbs with *come* in the correct form.

1 She .... this jumper in a street market yesterday.

2 Would you like .... to my place for my birthday party on Saturday?

3 'When .... the exam results .... ?' 'I think it's tomorrow.'

4 He will pass his history test if nothing about the Puritans ....

5 John .... flu every winter.

6 She fainted because of the heat during the ceremony but .... soon after.

7 The discovery of penicillin .... by chance.

3 **MATCH** the phrasal verbs with *come* (1-7) to a suitable ending (A-G) to form phrases.

1 ☐ come out	A an interesting event
2 ☐ come down with	B whenever you like
3 ☐ come across	C in a conversation
4 ☐ come round	D hay fever
5 ☐ come about	E an old friend
6 ☐ come over	F in the hospital
7 ☐ come up	G a new book

4 **USE** the phrases from exercise 3 to write down sentences.

4 Give

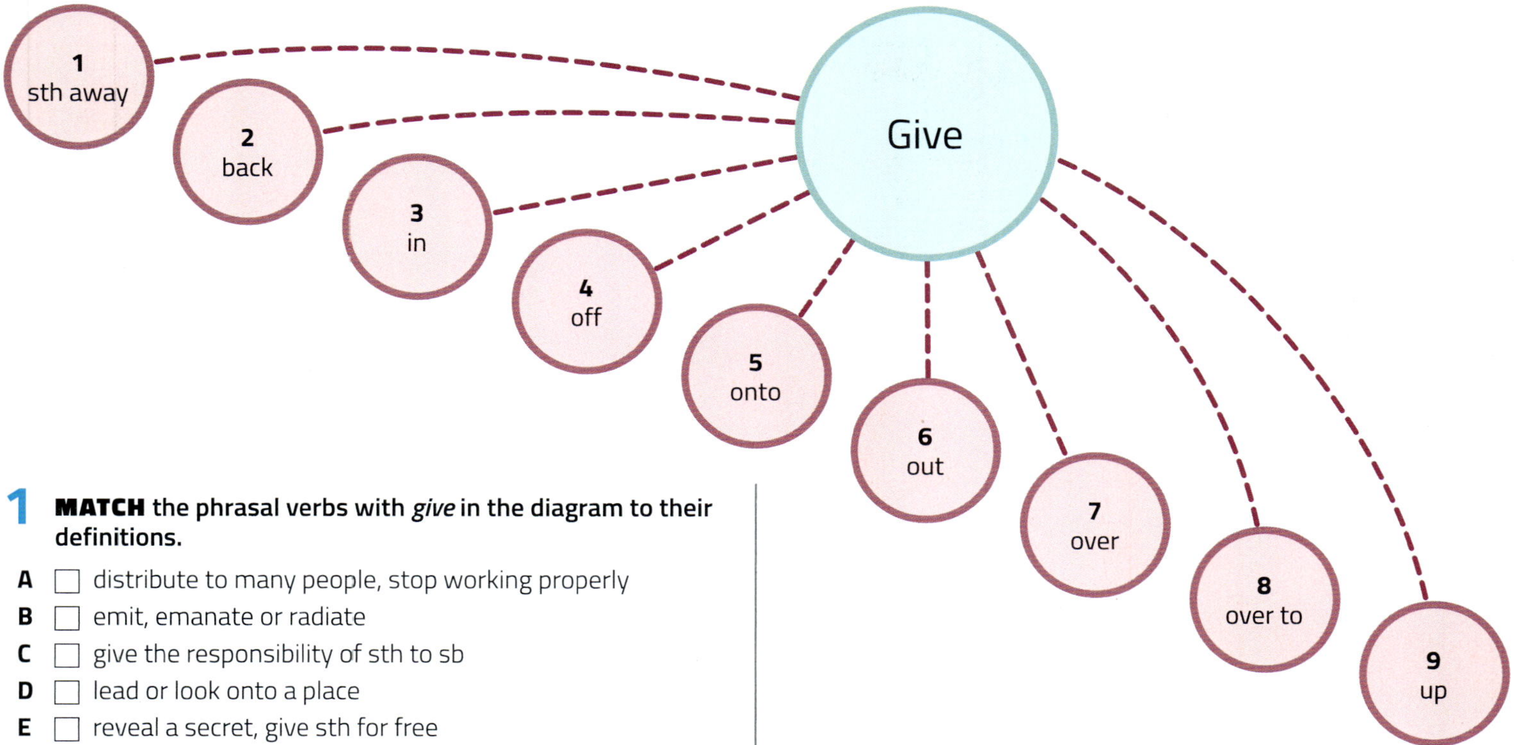

1 **MATCH** the phrasal verbs with *give* in the diagram to their definitions.

- **A** ☐ distribute to many people, stop working properly
- **B** ☐ emit, emanate or radiate
- **C** ☐ give the responsibility of sth to sb
- **D** ☐ lead or look onto a place
- **E** ☐ reveal a secret, give sth for free
- **F** ☐ stop a habit, surrender
- **G** ☐ stop arguing or fighting reluctantly; hand in (work)
- **H** ☐ dedicate to sth
- **I** ☐ return a borrowed or lost item

2 **CHOOSE** the correct preposition/adverb to complete the sentences.

1 I don't think the meat is fresh: it gives ... a bad smell.
A off **B** onto **C** over **D** back

2 Could you give ... your essay as soon as possible, please?
A away **B** up **C** off **D** in

3 David insisted so much on buying a new scooter that his father finally gave ... .
A out **B** back **C** in **D** over

4 She gave herself ... the care of the doctor when she was ill.
A away **B** over to **C** in **D** out

5 At Christmas, they are going to give ... candles if you spend at least £50.
A up **B** over **C** in **D** away

6 The assistant gave .... the new product brochures to the customers.
A out **B** away **C** up **D** in

7 My friend has just given ... the bike he borrowed two days ago.
A in **B** back **C** over **D** off

8 The rescue workers gave ... the search when they realised nobody had survived the avalanche.
A away **B** off **C** up **D** out

3 **FILL** the gaps using phrasal verbs with *give* in the correct form.

1 I have .... trying to change what I can't.

2 Can you .... me .... the hoodie I lent you last week?

3 The window of our classroom .... the park.

4 When she retired, she .... the keys to the new secretary.

5 They are launching that new café so they are .... free hot chocolate.

6 I wish my husband would .... smoking.

7 At the Buddhist monastery, most of the day was .... meditation.

8 The fire is .... a lot of smoke. Can you check it, please?

9 We wanted to organise a surprise party for Jake but Muriel .... it .... by telling him about it.

10 The students must .... their homework tomorrow morning.

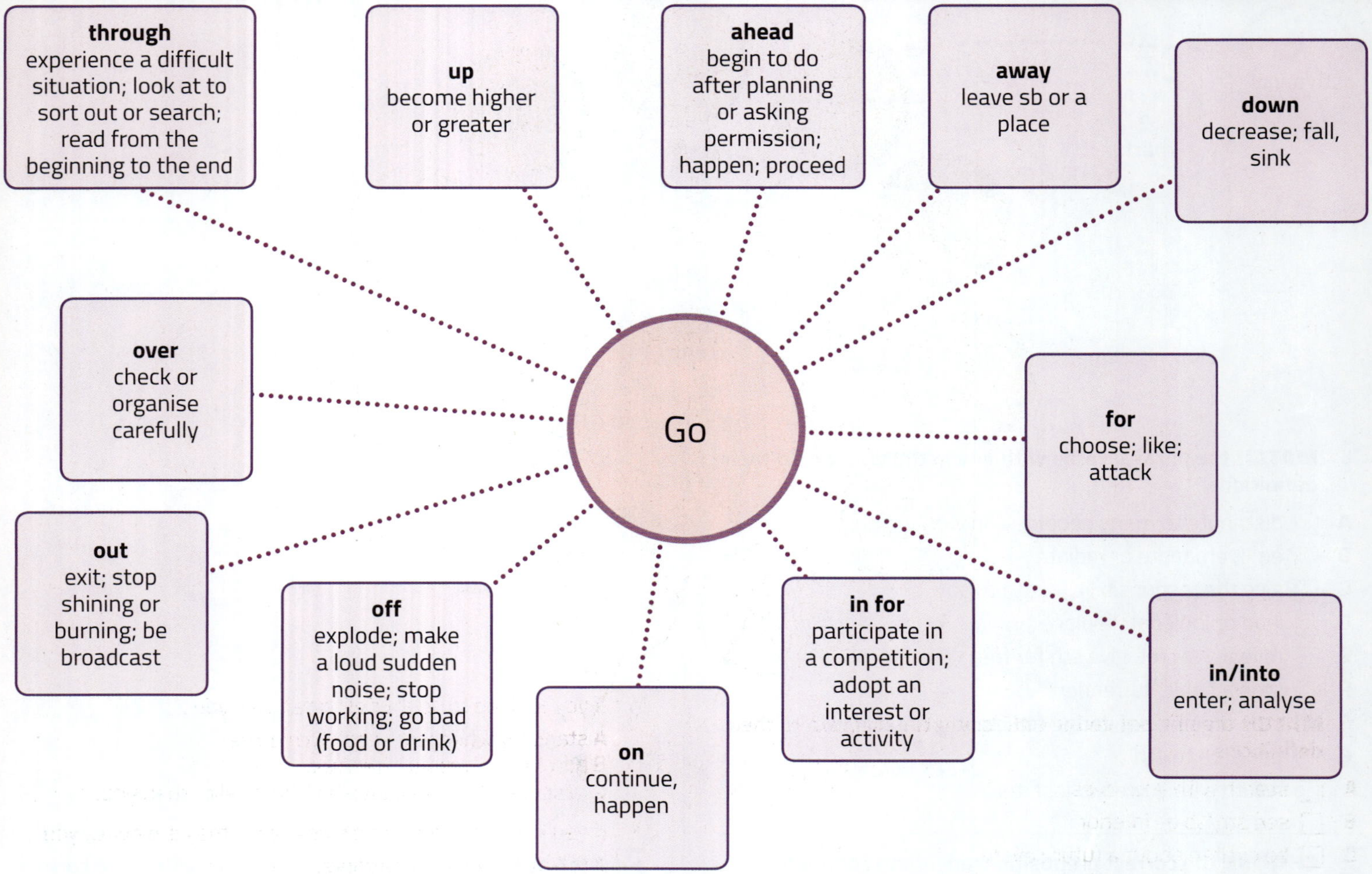

1 REWRITE the underlined parts of the sentences using phrasal verbs with *go*.

1 My family and I have had some hard times recently.
2 After the alarm had made a loud sudden sound, I fell asleep again.
3 Let me check the documents before the meeting!
4 Did they say goodbye before they left?
5 The light stopped shining while I was reading my favourite novel.
6 The council will proceed with the plan after the board has voted in favour of it.
7 What is happening in the children's room? We can hear someone crying.
8 The global temperature is increasing; it's getting hotter and hotter.
9 He fell onto his knees and proposed to her.
10 She had to finish that essay for the following day and continued to work until late.
11 The teacher entered the room and began the lesson.
12 My brother competed in the Milan marathon last year.

2 FILL the gaps using phrasal verbs with *go* in the correct form.

1 The meat …………, so I had to throw it away.
2 The average life expectancy at birth ………… to about 71.4 years in 2015.
3 Megan is ………… for a few days because she needs a break.
4 'Can I use your laptop?' 'Please, ………….'
5 I am ………… the drawers because I can't find my necklace.
6 She ………… the events of the day wondering why everything had gone wrong.
7 Did the dog really attack the stranger and ………… his neck?
8 That famous TV series ………… next week.
9 I want ………… deeper ………… this matter, there is something that is not clear.
10 We must ………… if we want to reach a shelter before it gets dark.
11 The students should study harder if they want ………… the First Certificate examination this year.
12 The ship hit an iceberg and ………… into the sea.

6 Look

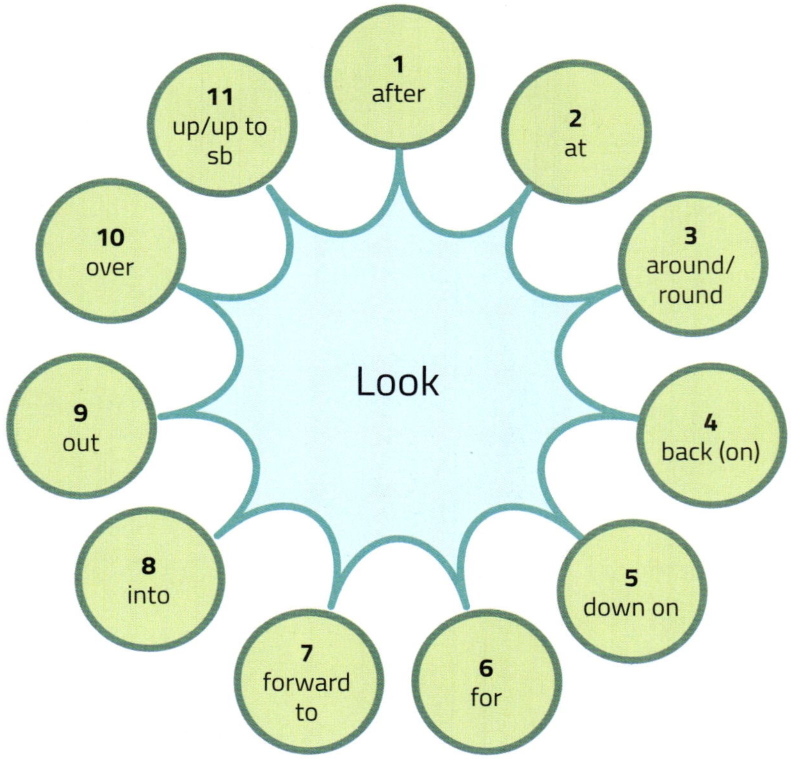

1 **MATCH** the phrasal verbs with *look* in the diagram to their definitions.

A ☐ search with your eyes
B ☐ see sth/sb as inferior
C ☐ be excited about a future event
D ☐ pay attention, be careful
E ☐ investigate
F ☐ turn eyes towards
G ☐ find in a dictionary; find and visit sb; admire
H ☐ try to find
I ☐ remember, usually with nostalgia
J ☐ examine, review
K ☐ take care of sb or sth

2 **CHOOSE** the correct answer.

1 When you are looking arounc for a new job, you are ...
A worried about your job.
B applying for a new job.
C trying to find a new job.

2 If you look for someone in the crowd, you ...
A are searching for someone.
B carefully avoid hitting other people in front of you.
C warn other people of an imminent danger.

3 If you look down on cheap hotels, you ...
A consider them not good enough for you.
B see them from the top windows of your house.
C always consider them befcre going to a more expensive one.

4 If you look up to your English teacher, you ...
A stand up when you speak to him/her.
B admire and respect him/her.
C raise your head because he/she is taller than you.

5 If you look after someone's dog while they are away, you ...
A follow the dog everywhere.
B search for it.
C care for it.

3 **FILL** the gaps using phrasal verbs with *look* in the correct form.

1 I'm really .... seeing my niece next week.
2 Harry is a terrible snob. He .... most other people.
3 You must .... new words in your dictionary.
4 .... ! A bus is coming.
5 When I .... my time at Secondary School, I smile.
6 She is .... a new course because she is not satisfied with the one she is attending at the moment.
7 We need to .... the conclusions and make some decisions.
8 My teacher told me to .... the classwork before the end of the lesson.
9 Detectives are .... the murder.
10 He .... to his grandfather, he admires him a lot.

7 Make and do

Make

- **off** run away
- **out** discover the meaning of, understand
- **up** form sth as a whole
- **up (a quarrel)** end it
- **for** travel towards
- **up (a story/an excuse...)** invent it
- **with** manage with what is available, compromise
- **up with sb** become friends again after a quarrel
- **up one's mind** come to a decision
- **up for** compensate

1 **FIND the mistakes with the phrasal verbs with *make* in the sentences and correct them.**

1. As soon as we had collected our luggage at the airport, we made up the hotel.
2. She made out some stories about the bus being late, but she just overslept.
3. Can you make off what that white thing in the distance is?
4. Your report is made of three sections.
5. He has made out to leave his job by the end of the month.
6. They finally made off after months of quarrelling.
7. Perhaps €50 will make with your trouble.
8. The thieves made up before the police arrived.
9. There is no coffee, so we'll have to make up with tea.
10. I think it is never too late to make off with an old friend.

Do is used when the general meaning of 'perform' is implied. Otherwise in the phrasal verbs and collocations below, it implies the carrying out of some action.

Do

- **away with** — put an end with, get rid of, abolish
- **for** — be dying for, cause sb's downfall/defeat (in a game, competition)
- **over** — redecorate; steal, rob (usually passive)
- **up** — wrap, fasten, close
- **with** — benefit from
- **without** — manage without

2 **CHOOSE** the correct preposition/adverb to complete the sentences.

1 I could do ... a holiday, I'm getting very tired.
A without B for C with

2 There are some things I cannot do ... .
A up B without C away with

3 They did ... the house before moving into it.
A up B over C for

4 The Government did ... that old law a few months ago.
A for B away with C without

5 They did ... the box and sent it to me.
A for B away with C up

6 You must be really hungry. I'm sure you could do ... something to eat!
A with B up C for

3 **FILL** the gaps using phrasal verbs with *do* in the correct form.

1 As soon as my parents opened the door, they understood their place ....
2 When you go camping in the woods, you must .... electricity.
3 My school .... a lot of paper when they realised it was not helpful for them.
4 You don't need to .... the top button of your coat.
5 I'm very thirsty! I could really .... a cup of tea.
6 You must .... your seatbelt. It is the law.
7 It was her being tired that .... her in that tennis match.

4 **USE** phrasal verbs with *make* and *do* to replace the words in italics. Make sure you use the correct tense.

1 Don't believe him, he *invents it* as he goes along.
2 It's so hot I *really need* an iced drink.
3 It's a difficult friendship, we have quarrelled and *become friends again* too many times.
4 It's too late to arrive in the mountains this evening, let's *go in the direction of* a good campsite.
5 When we arrived, we hardly recognised my aunt's house: it had been *renovated* so beautifully.
6 We left Milan at five and *travelled towards* the mountains.
7 Don't believe him! He is always *inventing* stories.
8 He makes money by buying old houses and *rapairing* them.

Collocations with *make* and *do*

Make	Do
Make implies the creation of something new.	*Do* is used when the general meaning of 'perform' is implied.
Food, drink, meals make coffee / a cake / breakfast **Plans, decisions, promises** make a bargain / a choice / an agreement / an appointment / an arrangement / a promise / a request / a reservation / an effort / an exception / change / arrangements / improvements / plans / preparations **Speaking and sounds** make a speech / a will / a noise / a phone call **Create** make an enemy of / an offer / a copy / a difference / a discovery / a dress / a fool of sb / a fortune / a fuss (of sth) / a mess / fun of / haste / money (become rich) / peace / progress / sense / sure **Activities** make a journey / a living / a mistake / the beds / the most of / time (find time) / trouble / war / friends with	**Jobs, tasks** do a job / a translation / an exercise / a test / an examination / lessons / homework / a good turn do the cleaning / the cooking / the housework / the ironing / the washing / the washing up / the shopping do one's best / one's duty / one's hair do good / harm / evil

5 **COMPLETE** the sentences using the collocations with *make* and *do*.

1 Ron is not a good student but he always .... his best.
2 I generally .... the housework at weekends when I'm alone at home.
3 My father always says: 'If you .... a job, you should .... it well'.
4 Hobbies can also be a good way to .... money.
5 My sister can't cook. The last time she .... supper it was awful.
6 You can't have everything: you have to .... a choice.
7 The students love .... fun of their teachers.
8 It's your turn to .... the dishes.
9 We'll have to .... a decision quickly.
10 I'll have to .... three exams by the end of January.
11 She had toothache so she .... an appointment with the dentist for the following day.
12 They'll .... the shopping tomorrow morning. We need milk, bread and cereals.
13 Because of the snow, try not to .... any journeys which are not essential.
14 After being stuck in a traffic jam for an hour, now we're .... some progress.
15 My students .... a great job with that business plan.

Put

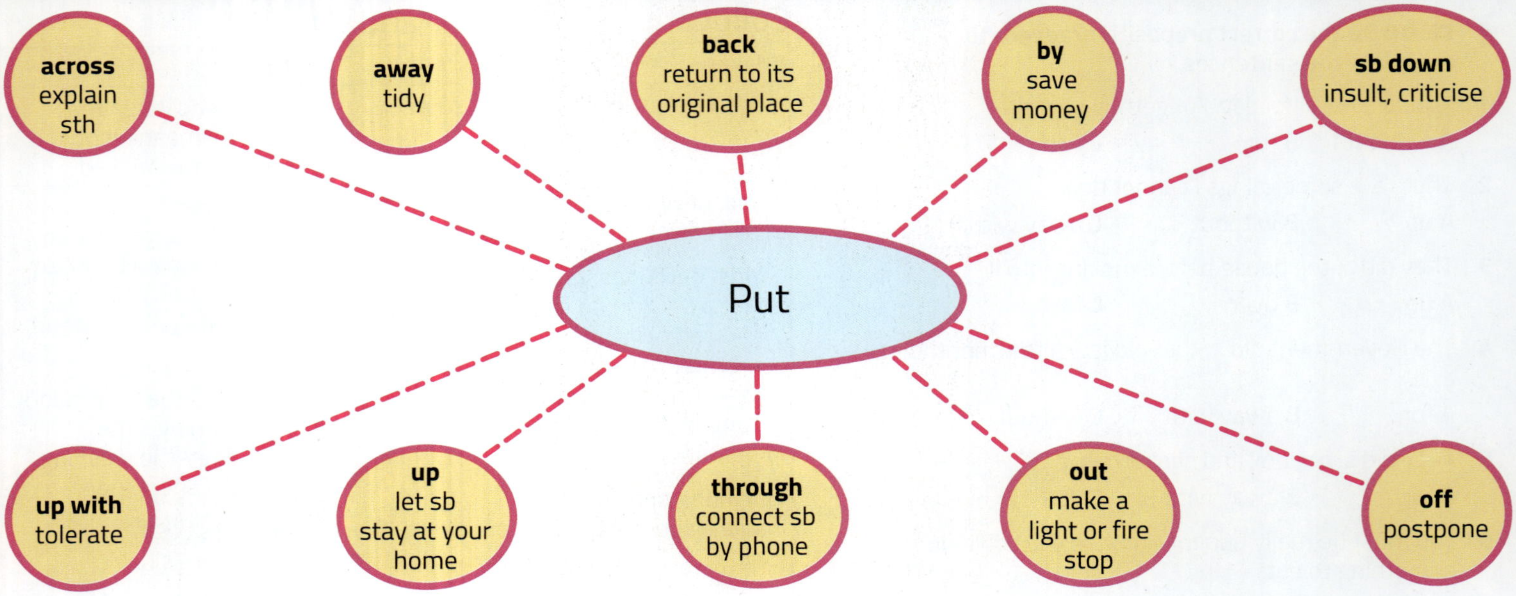

1 DECIDE which situation is described in the following sentences.

1 We've had to put off the meeting until Friday.
A We've had to cancel the meeting.
B We've had to postpone the meeting.

2 He is always putting me down.
A He's always trying to make me feel stupid.
B He's always knocking me down when we fight.

3 It's so cold! I'll put on a jumper.
A I'll wear something warmer.
B I'll look for something warmer.

4 If you come and visit Rome, we'll put you up.
A We'll find you somewhere to stay near our home.
B We'll let you stay at our home.

5 I'm not going to put up with that man's rudeness.
A I'm very surprised about that man's behaviour.
B I have no intention of tolerating that man's behaviour.

6 Children, put away your toys when you have finished playing.
A Put your toys in their place after using them.
B Leave the toys where they are when you have finished.

7 My brother puts by £100 a week to buy a new bike.
A My brother regularly saves money to buy a bike.
B My brother hides some money to buy a bike.

8 Could you put me through to the manager, please?
A I would like an appointment with the manager.
B I would like to speak to the manager on the phone.

9 Put out the light when you leave the classroom.
A Turn on the light.
B Turn off the light.

10 She tried to put across her ideas to him but he wouldn't listen.
A She explained her ideas.
B She refused to explain her ideas.

2 FILL the gaps using phrasal verbs with *put* in the correct form.

1 The firefighters at last succeeded in .... the fire in the building.

2 I cannot .... this heat, will you open the window, please?

3 My father is .... a small amount of money every month to go on a cruise.

4 If I were you, I would .... your raincoat because it's starting to rain.

5 The football match was .... till next Sunday because of the fog.

6 The children were eating too many biscuits, so I .... them ....

7 She .... the book .... onto the shelf after reading it.

8 Miss Gavan, can you .... me .... to the sales office, please?

9 I'm sure you'll be able to .... your message, you are a good communicator.

10 Stop .... everyone .... , you're getting on my nerves!

3 CHOOSE the correct alternative to complete the phrasal verbs with *put*.

1 Are you making a shopping list? Have you put *up* / *off* / *down* some chocolate biscuits?

2 You needn't find a hotel, we can put you *down* / *up* / *up with* for the night.

3 The teacher has put *on* / *off* / *out* this assignment till next week.

4 Here are your ironed shirts. Please put them *across* / *away* / *by*.

Take

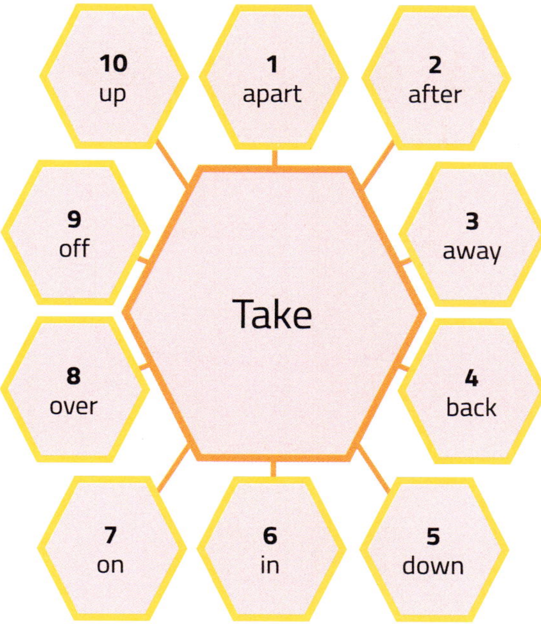

1 MATCH the phrasal verbs with *take* in the diagram to their definitions.

A ☐ return sth to where it was bought; admit that sth you said was wrong
B ☐ understand, deceive
C ☐ start doing a job, an activity or hobby; occupy time or space; resume after an interruption
D ☐ write down
E ☐ disassemble sth; analyse and criticise; defeat easily
F ☐ begin a flight; not work for a period of time; remove clothing
G ☐ remove; subtract
H ☐ get control of sth
I ☐ accept additional responsibility or work
J ☐ be like, resemble in character or appearance

2 FIND the mistakes in the phrasal verbs with *take* in the sentences and correct them.

1 The customer took up his shoes to try a new pair on.
2 She bought a new blouse but it had a hole in it so she took it over.
3 He took us completely away with the sad story of his childhood.
4 When the kettle stopped working, my husband took it after to see what was wrong.
5 Brian is taking off as general manager next week.
6 Do you take down your father or mother?
7 He gave up his job as an accountant to take in farming.
8 Don't you think you are taking out too many responsibilities?
9 Who has taken on the clock from the wall?
10 Are you sure you took the number plate after correctly?

3 FILL the gaps using phrasal verbs with *take* in the correct form.

1 He .... his hat when he went into the church.
2 She .... her grandmother, they have the same nose.
3 This wardrobe is too big! It .... most of the room.
4 A bigger company is going to .... the small firm.
5 My best friend Fiona .... yoga recently as a way to relax and meditate.
6 There's someone with a message for Mr Gallagher. Can you .... it .... ?
7 It was hard to .... all that the teacher said.
8 Why .... (you) all that extra work, haven't you got enough?
9 What time is the plane due to .... ?
10 He .... the engine .... but wasn't able to reassemble it.
11 I've thought about it and I'm ready to .... what I said.
12 The shop assistant .... 15% .... the price because it was the last item.

10 Turn

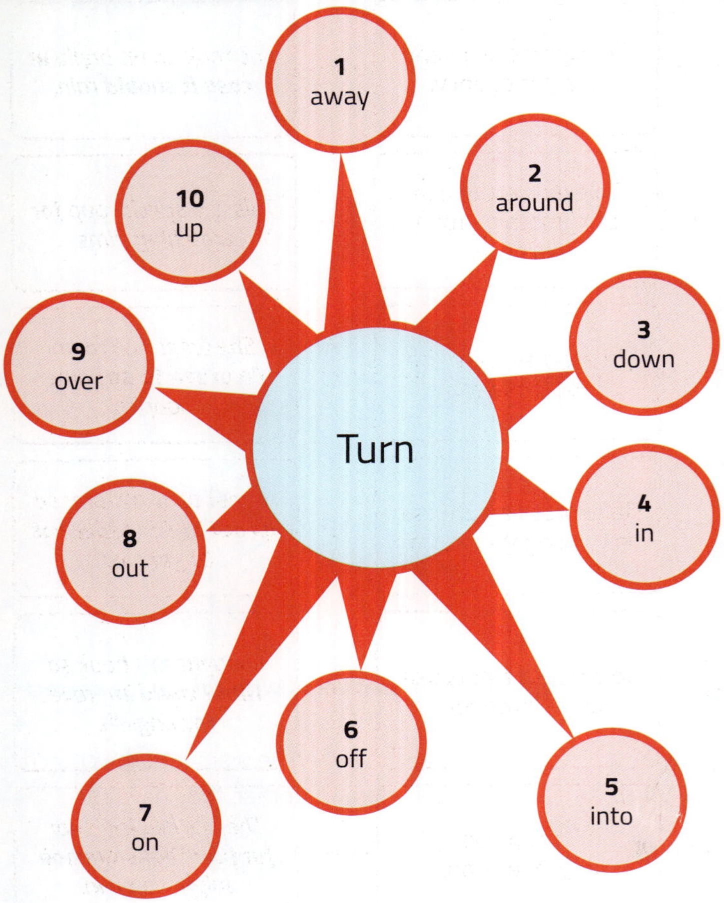

1 **MATCH** the phrasal verbs with *turn* in the diagram to their definitions.

A ☐ submit; go to bed
B ☐ deliberately stop sth working
C ☐ transform
D ☐ produce; switch off a light; end up being
E ☐ change/reverse direction
F ☐ start to use TV, radio, car
G ☐ move into a different position; give to authorities or rightful owners
H ☐ refuse entrance or service
I ☐ increase the volume; arrive or find unexpectedly
J ☐ reduce the volume, refuse an offer/application

2 **CHOOSE** the correct preposition/adverb to complete the sentences.

1 I think we are going the wrong way. Let's turn ... .
A up **B** in **C** out **D** around

2 Could you turn the volume of your radio ...?
A down **B** off **C** in **D** out

3 In the end, everything turned ... all right.
A up **B** around **C** out **D** on

4 It was a good offer but she turned it ... .
A around **B** on **C** up **D** down

5 Turn ... the page. The information you are looking for is on the other side.
A out **B** over **C** up **D** around

6 Turn ... the oven. I want to bake a cake.
A up **B** on **C** up **D** over

7 At one time, the workers could turn ... 20 cars a day.
A into **B** over **C** out **D** on

8 Paul was a difficult child but he has turned ... a charming young man.
A over **B** on **C** in **D** into

9 You need to turn ... your essay by the end of the week.
A in **B** over **C** up **D** down

10 They turned us ... at the temple because we had our shoes on.
A up **B** over **C** away **D** around

3 **FILL** the gaps using phrasal verbs with *turn* in the correct form.

1 I don't know how many people .... at the concert, but the stadium was really crowded.
2 .... the radio. Chris Martin is singing my favourite song.
3 Our neighbour .... to be a Russian spy during World War II.
4 I had to .... the invitation as I had the flu.
5 The centre of my town has .... a place full of tourists.
6 Don't forget to .... the light before going out.
7 My plane .... and came back to the airport because of technical problems.
8 I was sure I had lost my keys but they .... near my car in the garage.
9 'Did you see CSI last night?' 'No, I didn't. I .... very early.'
10 The new management could not .... the company.
11 .... the TV. It's time for the news.
12 Melanie had a restless night and .... in her bed several times.

1 Purpose

Linkers of purpose

Linker	Use	Example
in case + subject + should	To express an event or a contigency.	*She took an umbrella **in case it should** rain.*
for + *-ing* form	To express the use of something for a purpose.	*This is a special app **for watching** films.*
to / so as to / in order to + base form	To express 'with the purpose of'.	*She went into town **(in order) to do** some shopping.*
so as not to / in order not to + base form	To express a purpose in the negative form.	*He put on a sweater **so as not to / in order not to get** cold.*
so that + subject + will/can (present/future context) **so that** + subject + would/could (past context)	To express a purpose or an intention.	*I bought this book **so that I could** improve my English.*
for fear that / for fear + noun/*-ing* form	To express apprehension.	*They locked the door **for fear that someone** might come in.*

1 CHOOSE the correct alternative to complete the sentences.

1 They are studying very hard *to / for* pass their final exam next week.

2 Sean went to bed early *so that / for fear that* he wouldn't be tired in the morning.

3 I have to be at school early in the morning. I usually set the alarm *so as to / in order not to* oversleep.

4 They waited for Malcolm for an hour *for / so that* they could meet him.

5 My sister gave English lessons last year *in order not to / in order to* earn some extra money.

6 Make sure your bags are tagged *so as not to / so that* you can identify them.

7 We left early *for / so as to* avoid the traffic jam.

8 Film directors use special effects *in case / in order to* make their films more impressive.

2 JOIN these pairs of sentences using the linkers of purpose. You may need to make some changes.

1 She changed the subject. She didn't want us to know about her mistake.

2 Lindy took a taxi yesterday. She didn't want to be late.

3 The teacher worked on her lesson plans. She wanted to be well prepared.

4 I will go to university. I want to continue my studies.

5 He exercises regularly. He wants to be fit.

6 They bought some knives. They wanted to cut steaks.

7 Concentrate on your exercises. Avoid making mistakes.

8 You have to register. You want to participate in the forum.

3 COMPLETE the sentences with the correct linker of purpose.

1 The teacher spoke slowly .... every student could understand her.

2 I talked to the new classmate .... she wouldn't feel left out.

3 We stopped at a pub .... have a drink.

4 You need to be over 16 .... watch that film.

5 Lorenzo was angry with me .... waking him up.

6 Recycling is good .... avoid pollution.

7 They had a map with them .... getting lost.

8 I'm planning to move house .... be closer to my place of work.

9 Mum tiptoed into the room .... wake the baby.

10 I've just locked the door of my study .... no one can disturb me.

2 Addition

Linkers of addition

Linker	Use	Example
also	Between subject and main verb. After *be* and auxiliary verbs.	*They ordered a soup. They **also** wanted a dessert.* *This boy is very tall and he is **also** slim.*
as well as	At the beginning or in the middle of a sentence.	*We like rugby **as well as** tennis.*
besides	Often used when we list different reasons.	***Besides** being too small, the flat was too expensive.*
furthermore	Used to add extra information to the point you are making.	*The acting of the film was superb. **Furthermore**, the location is very famous.*
moreover	Used to show two equally important facts.	*Bob made his bed. **Moreover**, he hoovered the floor.*
in addition (to)	Often used in a list of actions; it is rather factual in tone.	*The school trip was a success. **In addition**, the students were well-behaved.*

1 **COMPLETE** the text with linkers of addition.

1. The surfer was steady and .... strong.
2. He could stand on the board .... ride the waves.
3. .... standing, the surfer lay on his belly on the board.
4. The surfer was suntanned and athletic. .... , he was brave.
5. He was able to balance on the board. .... , he could ride on the top of a high wave.
6. He was not afraid of the waves. .... , he had an aggressive attitude in the water.

2 **CHOOSE** the correct alternative to complete the sentences.

1. I can't tell you all that you want to know. *Moreover / In addition to,* it's a secret.
2. Not only can he swim, but *besides / also* ski.
3. Susan has got a bike *also / as well as* a scooter.
4. The migrants are poor. *Furthermore / As well as,* they need a job.
5. The student did badly in the test. *In addition / In addition to,* he was very rude to his teacher.
6. They not only speak English; they *moreover / also* speak Chinese.
7. He's too proud to apologise. *Moreover / As well as,* he thinks he is right.
8. I am too busy to come to the cinema. *Besides / As well as,* I don't like historical films.

3 **JOIN** the sentences with linkers of addition.

1. Smoking is bad for your health. Many people are annoyed by it.
2. I think Mrs Smith is rather old for this job. She has little experience in this field.
3. The food in this restaurant is delicious. The waiters are very kind.
4. Josh is very good at acting. He is good at dancing, too.
5. They visited a lot of castles. They visited a lot of museums.
6. My father is a careful driver. He has never got a fine.
7. He won the gold medal in the race. His was the fastest time.
8. We have two dogs. We have a little rabbit.

3 Contrast

Linkers of contrast

although / though / even though	+ sentence	***Even though*** *the town is crowded, it is very green.*
despite / in spite of	+ noun / gerund / the fact that	***In spite of*** *the rain, we went for a walk.*
however / yet / nevertheless	after a comma	*The house was very old,* ***however*** *he managed to sell it.*
on the other hand	Used to introduce a contrasting point of view.	*It is an interesting picture.* ***On the other hand****, it might be disturbing.*
whereas	Used to link two contrasting ideas.	*The north of the country is mountainous* ***whereas*** *the south is desert.*

1 **CHOOSE the correct alternative to complete the sentences.**

1 She is very shy. *However / In spite*, she accepted his invitation to dinner.
2 *Despite / Although* I am fond of dogs, I've never had one.
3 We enjoy walking in the mountains *whereas / nevertheless* we hate sailing.
4 The student did very well in the maths test. *On the other hand / In spite*, he failed the English exam.
5 *Yet / In spite of* the rainy weather, I love Ireland.
6 That restaurant is very famous. *Yet / Though* I found the food tasteless.

2 **COMPLETE the sentences using linkers of contrast.**

1 .... that student is clever, his results are not good.
2 I slept deeply .... the noise in the street.
3 The runner joined the race .... he had sprained his leg.
4 He had to accept the job .... it was paid less.
5 .... I didn't feel very well, I went to work as usual.
6 Mary was wearing an elegant dress .... her sister was dressed casually.
7 The Health Service costs a lot of money. .... , it saves lives.
8 That sports car was expensive. .... , Eddie bought it.

3 **COMPLETE the second sentence so as to have a similar meaning to the first sentence.**

1 The young boy did not have much money, but he bought a birthday present for his mother.
Although ....
2 I don't agree with his choice, but I can understand his motivations.
Even ....
3 While most students in the class agreed that the lecture could be interesting, none of them attended it.
Despite ....
4 It is not easy to get on well with Brian, but no one doubts his working ability.
No one .... , however ....
5 Though it seems unlikely, we will go jogging even if it is snowing.
In spite ....
6 This is a fascinating journey but it may hide some dangers.
The journey .... On the other ....
7 Joel had always been self-confident, while Kate had always struggled to find her way.
Whereas ....

Acknowledgements

Illustrations

BUILD UP
6 gopixa/123RF. Ghenadii Boiko/123RF. (2) Cathy Yeulet/123RF; **8** Nick Pavlakis/Shutterstock. Krishna.Wu/Shutterstock. Natalia Dobryanskaya/Shutterstock. LiudmylaSupynska/Istock. Joerg Steber/Shutterstock. Kotenko Oleksandr/Shutterstock. EpicStockMedia/Shutterstock. **10** Medusa/Webphoto. Pictorial Press Ltd/Alamy Stock Photo. **11** xalanx/Istock. **12** Peeradach R/Shutterstock. Ditty_about_summer/Shutterstock. Syda Productions/Shutterstock. rawpixel.com/Shutterstock. altanaka/Shutterstock. **14** Albina Glisic/Shutterstock. Brasil Creativo/Shutterstock. **15** martin-dm/Istock.

UNIT 1
17 Jean-Marie Guyon/123RF. Marcel De Grijs/123RF. xalanx/123RF. Fabiana Ponzi/123RF. Katarzyna Białasiewicz/123RF. **18** Syda Productions/Shutterstock. **20** dolgachov/123RF. **23** Gajus/Shutterstock. **24** MilsiArt/Shutterstock. Olhastock/Shutterstock. **24** Katarzyna Białasiewicz/123RF. **26** Tyler Olson/123RF. Cathy Yeulet/123RF. Petinov Sergey Mihilovich/Shutterstock. Dmitriy Shironosov/123RF. Blend Images/Thinkstock.

UNIT 2
29 VogelSP/Alamy Stock Photo. Cosmo Condina North America/Alamy Stock Photo. Universal Images Group North America LLC / DeAgostini/Alamy Stock Photo. mihtiander/Istock. Keith Dannemiller/Alamy Stock Photo. **30** Skouatroulio/Istock. Onfokus/Istock. **31** nonimatge/Istock. **32** pius99/Istock. **34** Stocktrek Images Inc./Alamy Stock Photo. **35** RTimages/Alamy Stock Photo. **37** Martin Harvey/Alamy Stock Photo. anouchka/Istock.

UNIT 3
43 Konstantin Chagin/Shutterstock. Dmytro Zinkevych/Shutterstock. Solis Images/Shutterstock. pan_kung/Shutterstock. Natasa Adzic/Shutterstock. REDPIXEL.PL/Shutterstock. Bojan Milinkov/Shutterstock. rawpixel.com/Shutterstock. Pressmaster/Shutterstock. Roman Kosolapov/Shutterstock. 2p2play/Shutterstock. Dmitry Kalinovsky/Shuttertsock. **44** EtiAmmos/Istock. **47** alexsl/Istock. Cookie Studio/Shutterstock. rawpixel.com/Shutterstock. **50** tinatin maglakelidze/Shutterstock. **51** vectorfusionart/Shutterstock. **52** mubus7/Shutterstock. Julia Velychko/Shutterstock. mtreasure/Istock. skynesher/Istock. **54** extravagantni/Istock. romul014/Shutterstock. piovesempre/Istock.

UNIT 4
55 Opachevsky Irina/Shutterstock. JMiks/Shutterstock. plantic/Shutterstock. Fer Gregory/Shutterstock. Fotosenmeer/Shutterstock. Ryan DeBerardinis/Shutterstock. **56** rawpixel.com/Shutterstock. AlexLMX/Shutterstock. Martin Shields/Alamy Stock Photo. **63** atarzynaBialasiewicz/Istock. kokkai/Istock. **64** REDPIXEL.PL/Shutterstock. **66** DeiMosz/Shutterstock.

UNIT 5
69 Bartosz Hadyniak/Istock. Avatar_023/Shutterstock. sakhorn/Shutterstock. Vardhan/Istock. Bartosz Hadyniak/Istock. **71** Sasiistock/Istock. **73** Lonely Guineapig/Shutterstock. DiversityStudio/Shutterstock. **74** Janossy Gergely/Shutterstock. ajr_images/Istock. Filipe Frazao/Shutterstock. **77** jaimaa85/Istock. Vardhan/Istock. Poznyakov/Shutterstock. **78** CatLane/Istock.

UNIT 6
81 Philip Lange/Shutterstock. PHOTOCREO Michal Bednarek/Shutterstock. Nejron Photo/Shutterstock. David Lichtneker/Alamy Stock Photo. Odyssey-Images/Alamy Stock Photo. Patricia Spinelli/Alamy Stock Photo. HBO/Webphoto. **82** Ashley Scott/Alamy Stock Photo. **83** Guillem Lopez/Alamy Stock Photo. **85** HBO/Webphoto. Peter Horree/Alamy Stock Photo. **86** Paolo Trovò/Alamy Stock Photo. Wolfandg Volf. **87** jonathan tennant/Alamy Stock Photo. quietbits/Shutterstock. **89** Anna Yakimova/123RF. **90** emka74/Shutterstock. vitmore/Shutterstock. Twin Design/Shutterstock. monotui/Shutterstock. dnd_project/Shutterstock. underworld/Shutterstock. Asvolas/Shutterstock. **92** adam eastland/Alamy Stock Photo. Ian Dagnall/Alamy Stock Photo.

UNIT 7
95 Krivosheev Vitaly/Shutterstock. Gerain0812/Shutterstock. Pung/Shutterstock. Andrey_Popov/Shutterstock. Sergey Peterman/Shutterstock. oriontrail/Shutterstock. **96** Ociacia/Shutterstock. **99** Maxiphoto/Istock. **100** Rocky89/Istock. **101** cybrain/Istock. **102** Mayuree Moonhirun/Shutterstock. **103** Ollyy/Shutterstock. **104** Mixmike/Istock. hocus-focus/Istock. milindri/Istock. Ian Dagnall/Alamy Stock Photo. **105** a Sk/Shutterstock. mrwebhoney/Shutterstock. Mr Aesthetics/Shutterstock.

UNIT 8
107 Galyna Andrushko/Shutterstock. Samo Trebizan/Shutterstock. Sezeryadigar/Istock. joshschutz/Istock. apomares/Istock. KoKi/Alamy Stock Photo. **108** JulNichols/Istock. **109** Al Seib, 2009/Los Angeles Times via Getty Images. **111** gldburger/Istock. Leonard Zhukovsky/Shutterstock. **112** Dizzo/Istock. filo/Istock. bokan76/Istock. **113** Richinpit/Istock. gregepperson/Istock. FatCamera/Istock. **116** avid_creative/Istock. simonkr/Istock. simonkr/Istock. mayo5/Istock. **118** gilaxia/Istock. Halfpoint/Istock. kali9/Istock.

UNIT 9
121 Kletr/Shutterstock. Golf Photographer/Shutterstock. Juergen Faelchle/Shutterstock. LALS STOCK/Shutterstock. Harold Stiver/Shutterstock. Aleksandra Suzi/Shutterstock. vchal/Shutterstock. pum_eva/Shutterstock. austinding/Shutterstock. imagedepotpro/Istock. Valentino Nobile/Istock. Ig0rZh/Istock. **122** apomares/Istock. kojihirano/Istock. **126** ASEAN. Photo Courtesy Alex Linn. Give Running. Byou Magazine. **129** Florin Patrunjel/Shutterstock. ESB Professional/Shutterstock. **130** matthieu Gallet/Shutterstock. tomic Roderick/Shutterstock. Paulphin Photography/Shutterstock. Ondrej Prosicky/Shutterstock. tristan tan/Shutterstock. Wang LiQiang/Shutterstock. Andrey Armyagov/Shutterstock. Vaclav Sebek/Shutterstock. **132** Jim West/Alamy Stock Photo.

UNIT 10
133 ridvan_celik/Istock. PeopleImages/Istock. Corepics VOF/Shutterstock. Bullstar/Shutterstock. sanjeri/Istock. vgajic/Istock. FERNANDO BLANCO CALZADA/Shutterstock. PeopleImages/Istock. **134** g-stockstudio/Istock. **137** Todor Tsvetkov/Istock. **138** kan_chana/Shutterstock. **139** alicja neumiler/Shutterstock. **140** sebra/Shutterstock. **141** Paul Bradbury/Istock. becon/Istock. **142** kenary820/Shutterstock. rawpixel.com/Shutterstock. **144** BrianAJackson/Istock. Bacho/Shutterstock.

DOSSIER 1
148 pixelfusion3d/Istock. Businesswire/WFP. IvorPrickett/UNHCR. freshnessmag.com. Zed Nelson/Oxfam. AFP. **149** R_Tee/Shutterstock. **150** Guy Corbishley/Alamy Stock Photo. **151** track5/Istock. rawpixel.com/Shutterstock.

DOSSIER 2
152 DianaHirsch/Istock. serts/Istock. monkeybusinessimages/Istock. michael melia/Alamy Stock Photo. **153** Scanrail1/Shutterstock. GN ILLUSTRATOR/Shutterstock. **154** Steve Debenport/Istock. **155** FatCamera/istock. Panda Vector/Shutterstock. Anna Tochennikova/Shutterstock.

DOSSIER 3
156 mapodile/Istock. PeopleImages/Istock. anouchka/Istock. skynesher/Istock. Choreograph/Istock. Todor Tsvetkov/Istock. **157** Peopleimages/Istock. **158** petrenkod/Istock. **159** kemalbas/Istock. skynesher/istock.

DOSSIER 4
160 Sportactive/Istock. Tonkovic/Istock. choice76/Istock. **161** Hung Chung Chih/Shutterstock. **162** Cristian Zamfir/Shutterstock. 400tmax/Istock. **163** ALotOfPeople/Istock. UberImages/Istock. 07_av/istock.

DOSSIER 5
164 lionvision/Istock. **165** studiocasper/istock. **166** skynesher/Istock. fizkes/Istock. **167** EdwardSamuelCornwall/Istock.